R. Stigwater
1975

The Ecclesiology
of
Vatican II

The Ecclesiology

of

Vatican II

by

Bonaventure Kloppenburg O.F.M.

Translated by

Matthew J. O'Connell

FRANCISCAN HERALD PRESS
CHICAGO, ILLINOIS 60609

The Ecclesiology of Vatican II, by Bonaventure Kloppenburg O.F.M., translated by Matthew J. O'Connell — from the original Portuguese *A Eclesiologia do Vaticano II,* published 1971 by Editora Vozes Limitada, Petropolis, Rio de Janeiro, Brazil. Copyright © 1974 by Franciscan Herald Press, 1434 West 51st Street, Chicago, Illinois 60609. Made in the United States of America.

Library of Congress Cataloging in Publication Data:

Kloppenburg, Boaventura, 1919-
  The ecclesiology of Vatican II.

    Translation of A eclesiologia do Vaticano II.
    1. Church—History of doctrines—20th century. 2. Vatican Council. 2d, 1962-1965. I. Title.
BX8301962.K54313   1974   262'.02   74-8035
ISBN 0-8199-0484-8

Nihil Obstat:
    Mark Hegener O.F.M.
      Censor

Imprimatur:
    Msgr. Richard A. Rosemeyer, J. D.
      Vicar General, Archdiocese of Chicago

February 22, 1974

Table of Contents

Abbreviations

Abbott: *The Documents of Vatican II*, edited by Walter M. Abbott, S.J. (New York: Herder and Herder, Association Press, 1966). The sixteen documents:

AA: *Apostolicam Actuositatem:* Decree on the Apostolate of the Laity

AG: *Ad Gentes:* Decree on the Church's Missionary Activity

CD: *Christus Dominus:* Decree on the Bishops' Pastoral Office in the Church

DV: *Dei Verbum:* Dogmatic Constitution on Divine Revelation

DH: *Dignitatis Humanae:* Declaration on Religious Freedom

GE: *Gravissimam Educationis:* Declaration on Christian Education

GS: *Gaudium et Spes:* Pastoral Constitution on the Church in the Modern World

IM: *Inter Mirifica:* Decree on the Instruments of Social Communication

LG: *Lumen Gentium:* Dogmatic Constitution on the Church

NA: *Nostra Aetate:* Declaration on the Relationship of the Church to the Non-Christian Religions

OE: *Orientalium Ecclesiarum:* Decree on the Eastern Catholic Churches

OT: *Optatam Totius:* Decree on Priestly Formation

PC: *Perfectae Caritatis:* Decree on the Appropriate Renewal of the Religious Life

PO: *Presbyterorum Ordinis:* Decree on the Ministry and Life of Priests

SC: *Sacrosanctum Concilium:* Constitution on the Sacred Liturgy

UR: *Unitatis Redintegratio:* Decree on Ecumenism

AAS: *Acta Apostolicae Sedis,* Rome, 1909—

Acta Synodalia   *Acta Synodalia Sacrosancti Concilii Oecumenici Vaticani Secundi.*
Rome, 1970—. Part I, volumes 1-4 (the first session) and Part II, volumes 1-4 (about two thirds of the second session) have thus far appeared. The source for addresses at the Council that have not yet been printed in the *Acta Synodalia* is Fr. Kloppenburg's private files.

Coll. Lac.   *Collectio Lacensis: Acta et decreta sacrorum conciliorum recentiorum,* edited by the Jesuits of Maria Laach. 7 volumes. Freiburg im Breisgau, 1870-1890.

DS (D)   Henry Denzinger, *Enchiridion symbolorum, definitionum, et declarationum de rebus fidei et morum.* 32nd edition by Adolf Schönmetzer, S.J. Freiburg im Breisgau: Herder, 1963. Number of entry in older editions is given in parentheses.

Mansi   Giovanni Domenico Mansi, *Sacrorum conciliorum nova et amplissima collectio.* 31

volumes. Florence-Venice, 1757-98. Reprint
and continuation by L. Petit and J.-B.
Martin, 60 volumes; Paris, 1899-1927.

PG   *Patrologia Graeca*, edited by Jacques-Paul
Migne. 161 volumes. Paris, 1857-1866.

PL   *Patrologia Latina*, edited by Jacques-Paul
Migne. 217 volumes and 4 volumes of In-
dexes. Paris, 1878-1890.

TCT   *The Church Teaches: Documents of the
Church in English Translation*, selected and
translated by John F. Clarkson, S.J., *et al.*
St. Louis: B. Herder, 1955. (Partial translation of Denzinger, *Enchiridion*.)

TPS   *The Pope Speaks*. Washington, D.C., 1954—

Note: Scripture is quoted from the *New American Bible*,
except where otherwise indicated. Technical terms pertaining
to Vatican II have been translated as follows: *congregatio
generalis*= general meeting; *schema* = position paper or draft;
sessio = session (of the Council); *relatio* = official explanation; *relator* = official expositor.

Introduction

The present crisis of faith within the Church, especially among priests and religious men and women is, in the main, a crisis of ecclesiology. In the Medellin document on priests the Latin American episcopate drew attention to this point when it said that "there is an evident questioning in this age of transition, an ever-growing questioning which in some cases amounts to a scorn for everything institutional, and threatens even the divine institution of the Church. It appears to us that this danger to faith is beyond doubt the most dangerous element to the priest of our day."[1]

The same observation holds for Brazil. A great deal of light is thrown on our present-day situation by the dossier *Documents on the Priesthood*, which was approved by the National Conference of Brazilian Bishops and published for the use of every priest by the National Secretariat for Priestly Ministry in 1969. It contains statements by official representatives of every region. After reflection on the crisis of faith through which the Brazilian priest of today is passing, these authorities conclude: (1) that there is no crisis of faith as such, that is, of intellectual acceptance of dogmatic truths (North I, p. 10); (2) that strictly theological doubt concerning the content of faith is not very widespread (North-East, p. 40); (3) that there is no crisis of faith in the historical

Christ or in the existence of God (Central, p. 52); (4) that there is no lack of faith in the revealed dogmas proclaimed by the infallible magisterium of the Church (East II, p. 83); (5) that doubts in the strict sense are not a problem (South I, p. 110); (6) that the crisis is not one of acceptance of revealed truth (South II, p. 121).

All this amounts to something positive and quite consoling: the crisis of faith is not as deep as might be expected amid the present confusion. Nonetheless, these authorities maintain that "there is a crisis of faith among priests." They see it as (1) a crisis that concerns persons and structures rather than faith (North I, p. 10); (2) a crisis of acceptance of the numerous structures which the visible Church contains (North-East, p. 40); (3) a crisis of faith in Christ in so far as he lives in the Church and directs it as a hierarchical body (Central, p. 52); (4) a crisis of acceptance of the authoritative way in which the hierarchy exercises its function as guide of the Church (North I, p. 10; Central, p. 52); (5) a crisis caused by the present structures of the Church (Central, p. 52); (6) a crisis of acceptance of the Church's way of life and a crisis of acceptance of persons in the Church (South II, p. 121).

Such "disillusionment with ecclesiastical personalities and manners," as the priests of South III put it, "leads to disbelief in the Church" (p. 132). If, then, there is indeed a crisis of faith among our priests, it revolves, in practice, around ecclesiological questions. "The greater part of the clergy of Amazonia is in rebellion against authoritarianism, and a smaller group is looking for a new image of the Church," observe the priests of North I (p. 10). The observation seems applicable to Brazil as a whole. The priests of East II claim that "our ecclesiology was a study of the hierarchy" (p. 84) and those of South I object to the concept of the Church as "laying disproportionate stress on its hierarchical character" (p. 94). The priests of the North-East provide a more detailed description of this juridical, "pyramidal, monarchic, regalist"

Church: "At the top of the pyramid is the pope, chief inter-mediary between the Lord who rules the Church, and the Church itself. The Church is regarded as being a perfect juridical society, that is, completely independent and self-sufficient in its own field. The chief characteristic of the pope is his universal jurisdictional power. He delegates some of his authority to the bishops who, each in his own diocese, com-plement the pope, as it were, and represent him. The bishops in turn delegate some of their authority to the parish priests within their parishes and to other priests and laymen who have received a canonical mission. The laity form the base of the pyramid; their role in the Church is a passive one. The local or base communities lack vitality; they have no share in the life and destiny of the Church or in its pastoral deci-sions. The laity are minors and all powers, functions, and ministries are correspondingly in the hands of the priest. In the light of such a vision of the Church it is easy to under-stand the prominence given to the Roman curia, the juridical orientation of canon law, the spontaneous reaction of many bishops to Rome and the pope, the attitude of the faithful to the priest and vice versa" (p. 27).

Such is, more or less, the concept of the Church which priests received in the seminary and which is now under fire; it is the concept which, through its applications, is also the main cause of the crisis through which many of our best priests are passing. The bishops at the Council were aware of all this, and it was precisely this turbulent state of affairs that gave rise to the Dogmatic Constitution on the Church, *Lumen Gentium*. The latter offers us a new image of the Church, its nature, its powers, and the place of the hierarchy in it. For this reason we will find important help for resolving the present crisis in the attentive study of the conciliar documents and in meditation on the doctrine of Vatican II concerning the nature and mission of the Church. It is with this intention that the following chapters on the Church are presented to the public; they are to help us reach a more accurate and loving grasp of the mystery of the Church, to which we priests have dedicated our lives and energies.

Agere sequitur esse (being determines action). The action of the Church must correspond to its nature. All are agreed that at Vatican Council II the Church reached a clearer and more accurate self-understanding. But that understanding must influence the human structures of the Church and the behavior of the persons who make it up, especially those persons who provide the services most needful for the well-being of the Catholic Communion. Yet precisely here it seems that the expected changes have not taken place; everything has gone on as before, as though Vatican II had never happened.

If then the present crisis is primarily a "crisis of acceptance of the Church's way of life and a crisis of acceptance of persons in the Church," it is precisely there that correctives must be brought if the crisis is to be resolved. The crisis is not one of faith as such or of the Church as such or even of the hierarchy as such. It is a crisis of ways or manners. Such "modes" are, according to Aristotle, accidental, not substantial or essential. It is within the Church's power to change, adapt, or suppress them. We published earlier a long analysis of "contestation" or the process of questioning that is going on in the Church,[2] and in it we reached the same conclusion. What is being questioned is certain exercises of authority, not authority as such: arbitrary power in the use of authority, the seeking of personal gain through such exercise, the pompous illusions which accompany authority, the attitude that authority makes one somehow superior. What is being questioned is juridicism, not jurisprudence; authoritarianism, not authority; legalism, not law; sclerosis, not order; uniformity, not unity.

Such a crisis will not be resolved by another encyclical on authority in the Church. The need is for churchmen to meditate in the Lord on the nature and mission of the Church and to be consistent in accepting the Church as mystery, sacrament, communion, brotherhood, and people of God. Since the

Church is a mystery or the visible instrument which the Lord uses, it may not be or represent itself as a mere society, however well structured and minutely organized (a society of a "pyramidal, monarchic, regalist" kind), that has difficulty in thinking of itself as also a sign and instrument of the glorified Lord and his Spirit. Since the Church is a communion in which all are brothers and truly equal in dignity, it may not be or represent itself as a monarchy, however well established, that never realizes how in fact all the baptized play a part in perserving the faith we have received. Since the universal Church really exists in the form of particular churches and on the basis of these, it may not organize itself primarily as a "universal" Church which demands subjection and uniformity of all members. Since the Church is both immanent and transcendent, it must always be open, ready, and disposed to recommence its incarnation in new forms and in new historical and cultural contexts, and not link itself exclusively or indissolubly to any race or nation, to any one set of customs, to any particular way or life, old or new. Since the unity of the Church must be compatible with communion, brotherhood, and collegiality, it may not present itself in such a way that it seems to have no room for a real application of the principles of subsidiarity, immanence, and co-responsibility.

Notes for Introduction

[1] *The Church in the Present-Day Transformation of Latin America in the Light of the Council* (Second General Conference of Latin American Bishops, Bogotá and Medellin, 1968), edited by Louis Michael Colonnese (Bogotá: General Secretariat of CELAM, 1970), volume 2: *Conclusions*, p. 175.

[2] Boaventura Kloppenburg, O.F.M., "A contestaçao na Igreja de hoje," *Revista Eclesiástica Brasileira*, 29 (1969), 650-79. [On the idea of "contestation"—questioning, protest, challenge, rebellion, etc.—cf. *Contestation in the Church* (*Concilium* 68), edited by Theodoro Jiménez Urresti (New York: Herder and Herder, 1971). — Tr.]

Chapter 1

The Present Situation of the Church in its Historical Context

Not even the boldest dreamers could have imagined ten years ago what would happen at Vatican II and, above all, what is now happening in the life of the Church after the Council. Many people are really frightened today and ask themselves fearfully whether we are still truly Catholics and in what direction we are moving. Not a few are convinced that the Church, or at least many of its most prominent representatives, took a dangerous turn towards the Protestantism that was condemned in the sixteenth century or the Modernism that was rejected at the beginning of the twentieth. The leaders in the present movement of renewal and purification, which was expressly desired and clearly initiated by Vatican II, are suspect, in some sectors of the Church, of being opposed to tradition and of rejecting the valuable lessons of history.

In order to understand and interpret correctly the present situation of the Church and its characteristic movements we must put it into its historical context, that is, the context of what is happening today. *The Church is a pilgrim, set down in the midst of history and therefore inevitably and deeply marked and conditioned by events.* The historical situation and circumstances of the sixteenth century forced the Church, at the Council of Trent, to take a clear and strong position against Protestant doctrinal innovations. The doctrine formulated by the Council of Trent (the same holds for earlier Councils) was therefore characteristically anti-heretical and anti-Protestant. This is to say that it was the heretic who determined both the subject treated by the Council and the point of view from which they were treated. Certain dogmas which were to be solemnly defined had to receive the importance they did in the theological awareness of the Church, not precisely and formally because they were important or central from the viewpoint of the intrinsic requirements of revelation or Christian life, but simply because they were challenged or said to be doubtful. Certain religious practices (for example, indulgences, prayers for the dead, devotion to the saints) were officially protected or defended by the highest teaching authority in the Church, not because they were in themselves essential or vital to Christian life, but because they were mocked or downgraded by one or other influential innovator. These doctrines and practices, once they had been authoritatively confirmed in this way, came to receive a value and emphasis which they had perhaps not had in earlier times and which, from a purely theological point of view, they may not have deserved. Nonetheless it was on such declarations of dogma and such defences of practices, as gathered together in Denzinger's famous *Handbook of Creeds, Definitions, and Declarations concerning Faith and Morals*,[1] that theology came to be based. Other truths and practices, which may have had as much or more Biblical and patristic foundation but had never been challenged, were not taken into the *Handbook* and therefore found no place in the manuals of theology and spirituality. More than that: certain revealed truths and Christian practices, completely Biblical and patristic in character, were maintained and emphasized by the Reformers; for this very reason they were not given the importance and value which they objectively deserved and even should have been given. We must even say that at times they were not only not stressed but were ignored or passed over in silence.

A few examples may be given. In regard to the related pair, Scripture and Tradition, the sharply anti-Protestant position of Catholics led to pretty much the following state of affairs: the Protestant was regarded as a man of the Bible and the Catholic as a man of Tradition (generally identified with the Magisterium of the Church or, more concretely, with the cathechism). Over against Protestant emphasis on Scripture, the Tridentine and post-Tridentine Church laid heavy stress on "Tradition" and "traditions." In further reaction against Catholic traditionalism Protestants developed a typical spirituality based on the power of God's word. It is fully clear that the Church never denied the value and power of God's word as spiritual food, but it is equally clear that post-Tridentine Catholics never learned to draw due profit from this spiritual food. The Protestant attitude thus led the Church to disturb the balance between Scripture and Tradition, with more weight being given to "Tradition."

A similar imbalance came to characterize the solutions given to the tensions between the visible and the invisible Church. The Protestants denied the visible, external, juridical, institutional, and hierarchic Church and retained only an invisible, internal, and charismatic Church. In reaction, post-Tridentine, anti-Protestant Catholics decided to put the primary stress on the Church as a hierarchically organized society, directed from above by the bishop of Rome. Once again, it is fully clear that the Church never denied its own properly invisible elements (especially the constant, life-giving presence of the glorified Lord and his Spirit), but it is equally certain that these elements, although more central and important than the visible elements, received little attention in Catholic manuals of ecclesiology.

Analogous statements could be made in relation to many other pairs of concepts, such as hierarchy-charisms, ministerial priesthood—universal priesthood, sacraments—faith, universal Church—local Church, Saints—Christ as sole mediator, etc.

In a few instances certain doctrines which were heavily emphasized simply because some people had denied them, led the Church in the post-Tridentine period to liturgically dubious and pastorally problematic practices. In the minds of many, for example, the supreme liturgical celebration was Mass in the presence of the exposed Blessed Sacrament (the combination being intended to profess the abiding Real Presence and the necessity of adoring the Blessed Sacrament). Such Masses, which were universally prescribed at an earlier time, are today forbidden (since the Instruction on the Eucharist of 1967[2]). This example shows that even the highest authorities in the Church were capable of imposing on the universal Church practices which, liturgically speaking, were absurd. Likewise questionable is the pastoral value, whatever be the historical and geographical situation or circumstances, of the strict requirement of Latin for all liturgical acts without exception and of total liturgical uniformity for each and every community: large or small, educated or uneducated people, adults, young people, or children, white, black, or yellow. Yet the uniform use of Latin was one of the preferred arguments in proving to Protestants the value of ecclesial unity and the beauty of the Church's catholicity. The end-result of these and similar moves was a Church that was unbalanced in its doctrinal and practical stresses. In that anti-heretical and anti-Protestant Church, which lasted officially until November 21, 1962,[3] all of us were born, formed, and educated. We identified ourselves with it.

Then there came—"by divine inspiration," said John

XXIII (August 9, 1959), "like an unexpected Spring flower"
—the idea and reality of the Twenty-First Ecumenical Council, Vatican II.[4] But by the express wish of him who conceived the idea, this would be a Council quite different from
those which had preceded it: "Nowaday . . . the Spouse of
Christ prefers to make use of the medicine of mercy rather
than that of severity; she considers that she meets the needs
of the present day by demonstrating the validity of her teaching rather than by condemnations. . . . The Catholic Church,
raising the torch of religious truth by means of this Ecumenical Council, desires to show herself the loving mother of all,
benign, patient, full of mercy and goodness toward the
brethren who are separated from her" (Abbott, 716). Thus
John XXIII in his opening speech to the Council. It was indeed a different mode of procedure, stripped of the terrifying
anathemas that marked other ages. The bishops of the whole
world had been called together to be teachers and shepherds,
not judges; they did not convene in order to condemn, and
the Council would not be directed against heresy. In their
opening Message to Humanity, issued October 20, 1962, at
the very beginning of the great assembly, the Council Fathers
declared: "In this assembly, under the guidance of the Holy
Spirit, we wish to inquire how we ought to renew ourselves,
so that we may be found increasingly faithful to the gospel of
Christ. We shall take pains so to present to the men of this
age God's truth in its integrity and purity that they may understand it and gladly assent to it. Since we are shepherds we
desire that all those may have their longing satisfied who
seek God. . . . Hence . . . we are pastors devote all our
energies and thoughts to the renewal of ourselves and the
flocks committed to us, so that there may radiate before all
men the lovable features of Jesus Christ" (Abbott, 3-4).

Thus it would be a positive, optimistic Council, bent on
construction, not condemnation; blessings, not anathemas;
love, not fear, dialogue, not monologue; union, not separation;
self-renewal, not correction of others; drawing men through

kindness, not repelling them through severity; vital intelligible communication of revealed truth, not the mere complicated preservation of a rigidly maintained deposit; openness to the world, not isolation in a ghetto. It would be a sign, an example, a witness, the salt of the earth, the leaven penetrating the dough, a standard raised among the nations, a city built on a hilltop, a light shining among the peoples and able to enlighten all men with the radiant light of Christ that shines on the face of the Church, a sacrament and instrument of intimate union with God and unity among all men. The Council would be an event "that ought to move heaven and earth," said John XXIII (May 17, 1959);[5] it would be "the starting point for a general renewal and a new and mighty flowering of the Holy Spirit throughout the world" (July 27, 1960);[6] it would be an "extraordinary Epiphany," a "new Pentecost" (September 12, 1960).[7]

Vatican II, therefore, would not be an anti-heretical Council. The Protestants and the Orthodox (the "heretics" and the "schismatics") would be officially present as guests and observers. In its first official document the Council stated: "It is the goal of this most sacred Council . . . to nurture whatever can contribute to the unity of all who believe in Christ" (SC 1/137). And in another document it declares that "promoting the restoration of unity among all Christians is one of the chief concerns of the Second Sacred Ecumenical Synod of the Vatican" (UR 1a/341).

Given this outlook and purpose Vatican II would be able, and obliged, to adopt an attitude basically different from that of the Council of Trent. In this new atmosphere the goal would be to explain and formulate Catholic doctrine "in ways and in terminology which our separated brethren too can readily understand" (UR 11b/354). Minds were already favorably disposed to recognizing that outside the visible structure of the Church ecclesial elements of sanctification and truth are to be found (cf. LG 8b/23 and 15/33) and even numerous and very significant elements (cf. UR 3b/345) that can engender an authentic life of grace and open the door to the community of salvation (UR 3c/346). "Catholics must joyfully acknowledge and esteem the truly Christian endowments from our common heritage which are to be found among our separated brethren" (UR 4h/349). Although they are not in full or perfect ecclesial communion with us, we proclaim that "justified by faith through baptism [they] are incorporated into Christ. They therefore have a right to be honored by the title of Christian, and are properly regarded as brothers in the Lord" (UR 3a/345).

In this new and salutary atmosphere, which has certainly been willed and brought about by the Holy Spirit (cf. UR 1b/341; 4a/347), a Protestant affirmation of something does not stimulate us to deny it or pass it over in silence. For "whatever is wrought by the grace of the Holy Spirit in the hearts of our separated brethren can contribute to our own edification" (UR 4i/349). A new spirit has thus arisen which makes it possible to correct the imbalance that occurred in the Tridentine and Post-Tridentine Church in its attempts to resolve the tensions latent in such pairs of concepts as tradition—Scripture, hierarchy—charisms, authority—free, superior—subject, magisterium—private inspiration, universal Church—local Church, Christ—Saints, etc.

To bring home more clearly the point we are making, we can say that Vatican II as a Council is distinguished much more by a new spirit than by any new explicitations of Christian doctrine. Such new explicitations are indeed not lacking (for example, concerning the Church, the episcopate, the presbyterate, tradition, religious freedom, etc.), but the *specifically new and important* thing about the Twenty-First Ecumenical Council is its pastoral, ecumenical, and missionary attitude in the face of today's world; its spirit of openness to new values; its willingness to enter into dialogue and even cooperation with non-Catholics, non-Christians, and non-believers; its spirit of understanding towards others; its conviction of being only the sign, instrument, or sacrament ("mystery")

of the glorified Lord; its recognition that it must prepare itself to be in fact the universal sacrament of salvation; its
declaration that there are ways of supernatural salvation
which God alone knows; its great confidence in the presence
and action of the Holy Spirit; its splendid Christocentrism;
its rediscovery of the liturgy as the principal means of sanctification; the emphasis it puts on a Christian life that is more
personalist but also more communal and centered on charity;
its recognition of the signs of the times as a manifestation of
God's will; its resultant stress on the existential and on concrete situations; its new concept of unity (not synonymous
with uniformity) and catholicity (admitting and even valuing
a theological, liturgical, disciplinary, and spiritual pluralism);
its surprising humility in acknowledging its limitations and
weaknesses; its determination to renew and purify the face of
the Church; its intention of identifying itself with Christ and
his Gospel; its greater understanding of the power of God's
word; its determination to be a servant, especially of the poor
and lowly; its abandonment of juridicism and extrinsecism;
its less triumphalist attitude; its greater respect for the freedom and universal, inalienable rights of man and his upright
conscience; its acceptance of autonomies; its confidence in
man, his dignity, and his sense of responsibility; its optimism
about earthly realities; its desire to help in the building of
the temporal city and the development of peoples; its disposition to avoid human compromises; its renunciation of fixism
and legalism; its awareness of being a pilgrim, essentially
oriented to the final goal, always on the move, incomplete,
dynamic, alive, set amid present-day history and a passing
world, among creatures that groan and suffer, until He returns. . . .

Vatican II is primarily a Council of new emphases and rediscovered words. To highlight a word or phrase is undoubtedly a subjective act, one that is conditioned by particular
situations and circumstances, which may be passing or occur
only from time to time. If a dozen people were asked to read

the preceding paragraph with pen in hand to note what struck them, the result would probably be a dozen different readings of the same text. Each one would underline what seemed to him more useful, important, noteworthy, or interesting, depending on his point of view at this moment or in this situation; tomorrow, in other circumstances, each would underline other words. The same is true of the Church: if it is to carry out its task it must at each moment scrutinize the signs of the times (GS (4a/201) and act, speak, and pray according as events and the requirements and aspirations of varying times and places demand (GS 11a/209; 44b/246). In this sense (and, be it noted, only in this sense) it is possible and even necessary to say that the Church is inevitably relative and mutable in its truths and practices. Otherwise it would never be in a position to carry out its most important mission: the pastoral. The circumstances of the Protestant uprising of the sixteenth century obliged the Church of that time to stress words like tradition, hierarchy, obedience, submission, sacraments, saints, indulgences, purgatory, etc. Since such stresses color everything, the theology and spirituality of the post-Tridentine period were strongly marked by them. The stresses were certainly not the same in the scholastic, patristic, or apostolic periods. There are many ways of being authentically Christian while maintaining a complete and loving fidelity to what is strictly necessary (cf. Acts 15:28; UR 18/360). The contemporary way, since Vatican II, has obviously been changing rapidly from the way of the anti-Protestant, post-Tridentine age. This is, in my opinion, the main point on which those who style themselves "traditionalists" (in a certain sense we all want to be, and must be, traditionalists!) must reflect calmly, attentively, and sympathetically. *An important shift in emphases took place at the Council and has continued to take place ever since.* But a shift in emphasis does not mean or even imply a change of doctrine. The emphasis is an accidental, not a substantial, thing, but, to repeat, it is precisely the emphasis that colors everything else and creates a style. In the atmosphere created by the forceful Protestant negation it was suitable, perhaps even necessary, to stress such words as tradition, magisterium, obedience, the objective effect of the sacraments, etc. Now, in the healthy climate of a divinely blessed ecumenism and the search for unity, it will be useful and even indispensable to put the stress on the Biblical and patristic values which are contained in the word of God, the invisible Church, charisms, universal priesthood, the worship value of the act of preaching the Gospel, personal faith and conscience, etc. This is not, of course, to call in question the values on the other side of the scale. In this way we are, in fact, recovering a sense of proportion. In this sense, Vatican II is, I believe, the great Council of balance or proportion. People whose education and formation were marked by the pre-conciliar outlook and who closely identified themselves with the post-Tridentine Church have the impression that since Vatican II the Church has become Protestant in outlook and tendency. In fact, however, it is not so. The values now being stressed are authentically Biblical, evangelical, and patristic. In becoming less inhibited and formalistic the Church of Vatican II is becoming enriched: more spontaneous, more human, more Christian. It is also of great importance that in becoming less legalistic and juridical (which obviously does not mean doing away with necessary structures and laws) and especially in becoming less highly organized and less antecedently determined in every detail of its life, the Church is better able to be the sign and instrument of the Holy Spirit. Excessive organization and determination of details always run the risk of not giving sufficient scope to the Holy Spirit. Man, even the Christian, even the pope, can stifle the Spirit. But all will be well "as long as they [priests] are docile to Christ's Spirit, who vivifies and leads them" (PO 12d/559).

Notes for Chapter 1

¹ [Henry Denzinger, *Enchiridion symbolorum, definitionum, et declarationum de rebus fidei et morum,* first edition, 1864. The thirty-second edition (1963), under the sixth editor, Adolf Schonmetzer S.J., contains many new texts, ancient and modern, and a numbering. References throughout this book will be to DS (Denzinger-Schönmetzer), with the numbering of the older editions in parentheses (D . . .). — Tr.]

² Instruction of the Sacred Congregation of Rites, *Eucharisticum Mysterium: On* the Worship of the Eucharistic Mystery, May 25, 1967, in *TPS,* 12 (1967), 211-36; cf. no. 61, p. 234.

³ On November 21, 1962, during the twenty-fourth general meeting of Vatican II, Pope John XXIII, in agreement with the vote of 1368 Council Fathers (as against 822), rejected the typically post-Tridentine position paper, *The Sources of Revelation* and, with it, all the other theological position papers prepared by the preconciliar Theological Commission. Cf. *Acta Synodalia* I/3, p. 259.

⁴ John XXIII, *Il mondo intero: Address to Diocesan Directors of Catholic Action in Italy,* August 9, 1959, in *Osservatore Romano,* August 10-11, 1969; reprinted in *Acta et Documenta Concilio Oecumenico Vaticano II Apparando,* Series I (*Ante-praeparatoria*), vol. 1: *Acta Summi Pontificis Ioannis XXIII* (Rome: Vatican City Press, 1960), p. 45. (Henceforth cited as *Acta Ante-praeparatoria.*)

⁵ John XXIII, *Volge il settimo: Address to the Faithful after Vespers on Pentecost Sunday,* May 17, 1959, in *TPS,* 5 (1958-59), 404.

⁶ John XXIII, *Espressa la sua gratitudine: Allocution at a General Audience,* July 27, 1960, in *Osservatore Romano,* July 29, 1960; reprinted in *Acta et Documenta Concilio Oecumenico Vaticano II Apparando,* Series II (*Praeparatoria*), vol. 2: *Acta Summi Pontificis Ioannis XXIII* (Rome: Vatican City Press, 1964), p. 14.

⁷ John XXIII, *E grande la gioia: Address to the Roman Seminarians,* September 12, 1960, in *TPS,* (1959-60), 322.

Chapter 2

The Nature of the Church

Introduction

It is difficult for the human mind to understand why God cannot save and sanctify men individually, each by himself, directly and without intermediaries: without social institutions, without organized religion, without visible means, without attachment to a people or a community. On the other hand, it was not easy, even after Pentecost, for St. Peter, as a Jew accustomed to see salvation linked with membership in a people, to reach the conclusion he did: "I begin to see how true it is that God shows no partiality. Rather, the man of any nation who fears God and acts uprightly is acceptable to him" (Acts 10:34).

Yet despite these words of St. Peter, and even, in fact, after citing them, Vatican Council II, in its Dogmatic Constitution *Lumen Gentium*, teaches: "It has pleased God, however, to make men holy and save them not merely as individuals without any mutual bonds, but by making them into a single people, a people which acknowledges Him in truth and serves Him in holiness" (9a/25). The Council repeats the same principle, in identical form,[1] in another context: "God did not create man for life in isolation, but for the formation of social unity. So also 'it has pleased God to make men holy and save them not merely as individuals, without any mutual bonds, but by making them into a single people . . .'" (GS 32a/230). Again, in the Decree *Ad Gentes*, we read: "It has not pleased God to call men to share His life merely as individuals without any mutual bonds. Rather, He wills to mold them into a people in which His sons, once scattered abroad, can be gathered together again" (AG 2c/586). And again, in the Decree on the lay apostolate: "Man is naturally social and . . . it has pleased God to unite those who believe in Christ in the People of God . . . and into one body" (AA 18a/508).

As these texts indicate, the Council bases its statements on two arguments: the social or communal nature of the human being ("By his innermost nature man is a social being": GS 12e/211; "This social life is not something added on to man": GS 25a/224) and the positive will of God or the divine plan ("It has pleased God"). The first argument is made quite explicit in the Declaration on religious freedom: "The social nature of man itself requires that he should give external expression to his internal acts of religion; that she should participate with others in matters religious; that he should profess his religion in community" (DH 3e/681); more than this, "Religious bodies are a requirement of the social nature both of man and of religion itself" (DH 4a/682).

Consequently, "from the beginning of salvation history He has chosen men not just as individuals but as members of a certain religious community. . . . This communitarian character is developed and consummated in the work of Jesus Christ. . . . As the first-born of many brethren and through the gift of the Spirit, He founded after His death and resurrection a new brotherly community composed of all those who receive Him in faith and in love. This He did through His Body, which is the Church" (GS 32/230-31). This is the Church which we are now going to study.

The Church as "Mystery"

The title "The Mystery of the Church" appears in the scheme that was sent to the bishops in 1963 for use in the Second Session; earlier, the title had been "The Nature of the Church Militant." The purpose of the new title was to direct attention, right from the beginning, to the Church "as object of faith," and not simply to the Church in its external manifestation. The term "mystery" as applied to the Church occurs only in the title of Chapter 1 of the Dogmatic Constitution on the Church and in numbers 5a, 39a, 44c, and 63a of the same document; in other documents it occurs in UR 2f, 20a; OT 9a, 16d; AG 16c; GS 2a, 40a; NA 4a. But nowhere is the term defined. In the official explanation given to the bishops in 1964 the word is explained as follows: "The word 'mystery' in this context does not indicate simply that a thing is unknowable or hidden. Rather, as many authorities recognize today, it points to a transcendent, divine reality that has to do with salvation and that is in some sensible way revealed and manifested. The term, therefore, which is found in the Bible, is very suitable as a designation for the Church." The explanation then referred the bishops back to the speech of Bishop Emilio Guano, of Livorno, at the 39th General Meeting (October 2, 1963), in which he had said: "This word [mystery] is taken from Sacred Scripture; it seems suitable for expressing the fact that the external visibility of Church, like the holy human nature of Christ, both conceals and reveals the inner divine reality of the Church, a reality which surpasses all knowledge."[2]

According to the mind of the Council, then, the expression, "the Church is a mystery," means that *the Church is a divine, transcendent, and salvific reality which is visibly present among men.* Or, as Pope Paul VI put it in his address at the

opening of the Second Session (September 29, 1963), "The
Church is a mystery, a mystic reality, steeped in the presence
of God."[3] Or, as we read in the Constitution on the liturgy,
"It is of the essence of the Church that she be both human
and divine, visible yet invisibly endowed, eager to act and yet
devoted to contemplation, present in this world and yet not
at home in it. She is all these things in such a way that in
her the human is directed and subordinated to the divine, the
visible likewise to the invisible, action to contemplation, and
this present world to that city yet to come, which we seek"
(SC 2/137-38). Or again, as the Constitution on the Church
will say, the Church is a complex reality, made up of human
and divine elements, and comparable therefore to the mystery
of the Incarnate Word; the human, earthly, visible, juridical,
hierarchic, and social part is the organ (or instrument; cf.
SC 5a/139) which the Spirit of Christ uses in order to sanctify
and save men (LG 8a/22). This Spirit, who is one and the
same in Head (Christ) and members, "vivifies, unifies, and
moves the whole body. This He does in such a way that His
work could be compared by the holy Fathers with the function which the soul fulfills in the human body, whose principle of life the soul is" (LG 7h/22).

"To accomplish so great a work, Christ is always present in
His Church" (SC 7a/140); *Christ will,* in fact, *always be the
principal subject of ecclesial actions.* "For only the Lord can
give fruitfulness and increase to the works in which they
[priests] are engaged. 'Without me,' He said, 'you can do
nothing' (Jn 15:5)" (SC 86/164).

The Church acts as Church only when it acts as the instrument of the glorified Lord. The whole Church can and ought
to say with the Apostle: "The life I live now is not my own;
Christ is living in me" (Gal 2:20). The Church is "a sign
of God's presence in the world" (AG 15b/602), "a sign which
points out Christ to others" (AG 20a/609), "a perfect sign of
Christ among men" (AG 21a/610), and "it is the function of
the Church . . . to make God the Father and His Incarnate

Son present and in a sense visible" (GS 21e/219). If it does not do so, it ceases to exist as the Church. Thus the Church is, primarily and wholly, the living and glorified Christ, present and acting in all his members. "Without me you can do nothing" (Jn 15:5). The Church is the fulness (*pleroma*) of Christ (cf. Eph 1:18-23): Christ fills her with the treasures of his glory and with divine life (cf. LG 7e). "Sitting at the right hand of the Father, He [Christ] is continually active in the world, leading men to the Church, and through her joining them more closely to Himself and making them partakers of His glorious life by nourishing them with His own body and blood" (LG 48b/79). "The mystery of Christ . . . is ever made present and active within us" (SC 35c/150), says the Council, reminding us of the vivid way in which Odo Casel O.S.B. spoke of the liturgy. The same document does not hesitate to say that the very redemptive actions of Christ, or "mysteries of redemption," which we recall in the course of the liturgical year, "are in some way made present at all times, and the faithful are enabled to lay hold of them and become filled with saving grace" (SC 102c/168). According to the Decree on priestly formation, these mysteries of salvation have a "presence and activity in liturgical actions and in the whole life of the Church" (OT 16c/452). "This mystery of Christ and of man's salvation they [students of theology] should discover and live in the liturgy" (AG 16c/604). Elsewhere we are told that it is precisely the liturgy which helps us come to a better knowledge of "the mystery of Christ and the real nature of the true Church" (SC 2/137). For the liturgy is simply "an exercise of the priestly office of Jesus Christ" (SC 7c/141), inasmuch as the ministers of the liturgy "share by a special title in the priesthood of Christ" (PO 5a/541), or, more clearly, are "living instruments of Christ the eternal priest" (PO 12b/558). The liturgy has this great value and efficacy because Christ is always the principal subject of liturgical acts, "so that when a man baptizes it is really Christ Himself who baptizes" (SC 7a/141). But in all this "Christ

. . . always associates the Church with Himself" (SC 7b/141); she is his visible instrument or organ, "an instrument for the redemption of all" (LG 9e/26).

The Church is the instrument or organ of the glorified Lord and his Spirit for continuing through the centuries the mission of the Incarnate Word. This is the principal reason why we love and should love the Church. Pius XII, in his encyclical on the Mystical Body says therefore: "To ensure that this genuine and whole-hearted love will reign in our hearts and grow every day, we must accustom ourselves in the Church to see Christ Himself. For it is indeed Christ who lives in the Church, and through her teaches, governs, and sanctifies; and it is also Christ who manifests Himself in manifold guise in the various members of his society."[4]

The Church has saving power not because she possesses good institutions or laws, nor because she is well organized and up-to-date, but because Christ acts in and through her. This is a primary and fundamentally important fact which ought to shape our consciousness concerning the Church. Without in any way depreciating the great usefulness of the instrument and indeed even while affirming the necessity of it, we can nonetheless not attribute to it a function, value, or causality which, as an instrument, it cannot claim.

In this context we must emphasize another surprising principle of God's action among men and on men: *He uses insignificant means (or instruments) for carrying out his plans* (cf. GS 76d/288). St. Paul waxes unusually eloquent in describing this principle: "God chose those whom the world considers absurd to shame the wise; he singled out the weak of this world to shame the strong. He chose the world's lowborn and despised, those who count for nothing, to reduce to nothing those who were something; so that mankind can do no boasting before God" (1 Cor 1:27-29). Or, just previously: "God's folly is wiser than men, and his weakness more powerful than men" (v. 25). And: "Since in God's wisdom the world did not come to know him through 'wisdom,' it pleased God to save those who believe through the absurdity of the preaching of the gospel" (v. 21). The principal reason for this odd and surprising manner of acting is given in the words: "so that mankind can do no boasting before God." God wants to show his power in the midst of weakness. In the second letter to the Corinthians the Apostle repeats the same principle and motivation: "As to the extraordinary revelation, *in order that I might not become conceited* I was given a thorn in the flesh, an angel of Satan to beat me and *keep me from getting proud.* Three times I begged the Lord that this might leave me. He said to me, 'My grace is enough for you, *for in weakness power reaches perfection.*' And so I willingly boast of my weaknesses instead, that the power of Christ may rest upon me. Therefore I am content with weakness, with mistreatment, with distress, with persecutions and difficulties for the sake of Christ; for *when I am powerless, it is then that I am strong*" (2 Cor 12:7-10, italics added). Speaking of the power of his ministry, the Apostle says: "This treasure we possess in earthen vessels to make it clear that its surpassing power comes from God and not from us" (2 Cor 4:7). We will always be weak sheep sent among wolves (cf. Mt 10:16).

This is, then, from the outset an important matter for our reflection and meditation, as we dispose ourselves to enter more fully into the "mystery of the Church." We are faced here with something really essential, something that ought always be a part of our consciousness and conception of the Church and its mission, that is, its action in sanctifying and saving mankind and the world. If we do not grasp this point, we shall fail to understand. The matter is especially important today when, with the Council, we are undertaking the "renewal of the whole Church" (OT Preface/437), and "renewal within the Church" in particular (PO 12f/559), and when, as John XXIII, said we are trying to bring it up to date or, as the Council will explain, "to make more responsive to the requirements of our times those Church observances which are open to adaptation" (SC 1/137). No one will deny the urgency of such adaptation. When the new means and new methods have been adopted, the principle of divine action which God has revealed to us through St. Paul will continue to be no less valid than before. In the renewed Church, "so that mankind can do no boasting before God," God will choose what is absurd and lowborn and weak and counts for nothing. And "that we might not become conceited," in the updated Church, too, "power will reach perfection in weakness." The impression is given that many churchmen today are scandalized at these "weakness" and pray and cry out with the Apostle, begging God to take them away. And, along with the Apostle, our prayer will probably not be granted; perhaps we shall receive the same answer he received: "My grace is enough for you." Then, still with St. Paul, we will have to go along with the methods and ways of the Lord and rejoice in our bewilderment. For it is precisely when we are weak that we will be strong; it is when we are aware of being only instruments in the hands of the glorified Lord, that his Spirit will be able to act in us and by means of us. If the visible Church were strong and triumphant, well structured, highly organized, and determined down to the last detail, there would be no room for the Church as "mystery." It would get along perfectly without the Lord, and it would cease to be a sacrament.

The Church as "mystery of the moon"

The Council begins its Dogmatic Constitution on the Church with the words, *Lumen gentium*. But this "light of the nations" is not the Church: "Christ is the light of all nations"! (LG 1/14). From its very opening words, therefore, Vatican II seeks to give a completely Christocentric and thus relativized idea of the Church. We can understand the Church only if we relate it to Christ, the glorified Lord. *The Church lives by Christ*. If the Church is absolutized, separated from Christ, consider only in its structures, viewed only in its

history, and studied only under its visible, human, and phe-
nomenological aspects, it ceases to be a "mystery" and becomes simply one of countless other religious societies or organizations. It does not then deserve our special attention
and total dedication. Only because it is a "mystery" can it
arouse our love. "May this Ecumenical Council have a clear
realization of that bond which binds us to Jesus Christ—a
bond that is one yet manifold, stringent yet compelling,
mysterious yet manifest, tightly drawn yet most welcome. It
binds us, the living, holy Church, to Christ from whom we
come, through whom we live, toward whom we tend. May
this our present assembly shine with no other light than
Christ, the light of the world. May our minds seek no other
truth than that proclaimed by the words of the Lord, our
only teacher."[5]

John XXIII, in his famous radio message of September 11,
1962, had referred to the symbolism of the Paschal candle and
the singing of the *Lumen Christi!* and had exclaimed: "Yes!
Light of Christ! Light of the Church! Light of the nations"[6]
It was these words that inspired the Fathers of Vatican II
to begin their most important document with the words:
Lumen gentium, and to end the third section of Chapter 1
with the words of Pope Paul: "Christ, who is the light of
the world, from whom we go forth, through whom we live, and
toward whom our journey leads us" (LG 3b/16).

Christ came "to shine on those who sit in darkness and in
the shadow of death" (Lk 1:79). He came to be "a revealing
light to the Gentiles" (Lk 2:32). He is "the light of men"
and "the light shines on in darkness" (Jn 1:5). He is "the
real light which gives light to every man" (Jn 1:9). With
him "the light came into the world" (Jn 3:19). He himself in these terms: "I am the light of the world. No follower
of mine shall ever walk in darkness; no, he shall possess the
light of life" (Jn 8:12); "I have come to the world as its light,
to keep anyone who believes in me from remaining in the
dark" (Jn 12:46). "A people living in darkness has seen a

great light" (Mt 4:16).

Only Christ is the light of the world. He is the Sun, sole source of light. At the side of this Sun, which is Christ, stands the Church like the moon which receives all its light, brilliance, and warmth from the Sun. This expressive symbolism was extensively explored in the early Church.[7] Didymus the Blind even speaks of the "lunar constitution of the Church." Like a light amid darkness, the Church shines forth in the darkness of this world, shedding light in the night of our ignorance in order to show us the path of salvation. Its borrowed light is, however, no more than a pale shimmer, a "dark radiance," as St. Bonaventure puts it; it symbolizes a truth that cannot be directly seen by our mortal eyes. While the sun remains always glorious, the moon constantly passes through its various phases, now waxing, now waning, both in its external measurable size and in its inner lightsomeness, for it experiences without ceasing the interplay of human vicissitudes. But it never grows small to the point of disappearing and its integrity is constantly renewed. Its witness can at times be obscured: the salt of the earth can become tasteless, the "excessively human" prevail, and faith may grow weak in our hearts, but the saints shine with undiminished brilliance. These darker phases of the moon show us that the Church is in continuous distress in this world and that it renews itself when it draws close to Christ. Then it can become so united with the Sun that it disappears, as it were, within the latter's brilliance.

Thus the Church is able to be a "light of the world" (cf. Mt 5:14) only in the measure that it reflects the light of Christ. It will always be "light in the Lord" (Eph 5:8); that must be its basic preoccupation. Therefore "she exhorts her sons to purify and renew themselves so that the sign of Christ may shine more brightly over the face of the Church" (LG 15/34; cf. GS 43h/244). Then it will be a "sign of Christ among men" (AG 21a/610), "a sign of God's presence in the world" (AG 15b/602), "a shining beacon of . . . salvation"

(AG 21g/612), and will "make God the Father and His In-carnate Son present and in a sense visible" (GS 21e/219). In its Constitution on the Church in the modern world the Coun-cil shows a clear awareness of the Church's dependent, "lunar" role, when it sets itself to shedding light on the mystery of man "in the light of Christ" (GS 10h/209). The Church knows that its teaching office "is not above the word of God, but serves it, teaching only what has been handed on" (DV 10b/118; cf. LG 25f/49).

In this way the Church can indeed "shed on all men that radiance of His which brightens the countenance of the Church" (LG 1a/15) and carry out its mission which is "to shed on the whole world the radiance of the gospel message" (GS 92a/305-6).

The Church as "Sacrament in Christ"

After what has been said thus far, we are not surprised to find Vatican II teaching that "by her relationship with Christ, the Church is a kind of sacrament or sign of intimate union with God, and of the unity of all mankind" (LG 1b/15). We have here a kind of definition of the Church.[8]

The word "sacrament" as applied to the Church occurs in the following conciliar texts:

LG 9f/26: The Church was convoked and established so that "for each and all she may be the visible sacrament of this saving unity"; in note 29, the Council quotes St. Cyprian, Ep. 69:6: "the unbreakable sacrament of unity."

LG 48b/79: Christ established his Church as "the universal sacrament of salvation." The expression is repeated in GS 45a/247 and AG 1a/584.

SC 5b/140: "From the side of Christ as He slept the sleep of death upon the cross . . . there came forth the wondrous sacrament which is the whole Church"; in note 10, the Coun-cil refers to St. Augustine and to a prayer in the Roman Missal.

SC 26a/147: Liturgical services are celebrations of the Church, which is "the sacrament of unity"; in note 27, the

Council indicates that it is citing St. Cyprian, *De catholicae ecclesiae unitate* 7.

AG 5b/589: Christ "founded His Church as the sacrament of salvation."

In none of these passages is the word "sacrament" defined. But in ecclesiastical language it means "a symbol of a sacred thing and a visible form of invisible grace" (Council of Trent[9]). In the 39th General Session of Vatican II (October 2, 1963), Bishop Guano of Livorno gives the following definition (and the general Explanation or *Relatio* refers explicitly to this address): "With Christ and through Christ, in itself and by its very presence in the world and by the whole of its life, the Church is a sacrament (the 'primordial sacrament,' in the words of Cardinal Frings), that is, it is the effective sign both of the redemption and sanctification which Christ brings to men through her and of the glory which Christ gives to the Father through her."[10]

However, the text of *Lumen Gentium*, inspired at this point by Bishop Guano's speech, does give us a very brief description of what is meant. After saying that the Church is a sacrament, the Council goes on to say: "or sign . . . [and] also the instrument." Through the sign which serves as instrument or organ, God's action is exercised. What was said of the Church as "mystery" applies here as well. The concepts are the same. Thus we recover the knowledge that the "mystery" of the Greeks and the "sacrament" of the Latins are synonymous. But the Church is a sacrament "in Christ." Christ himself is the fundamental, fontal, or primary sacrament. The Church is a sacrament by derivation; it is the sign and instrument of Christ; it is the sacrament of the glorified Lord and his Spirit.

Lumen Gentium attributes two effects to the Church considered as a sacrament: "sign of intimate union with God, and of the unity of all mankind. She is also an instrument for the achievement of such union and unity." The first effect, communion with God, is succinctly described in classical terms in the Constitution on revelation: "In His goodness and wisdom, God choose to reveal Himself and to make known to us the hidden purpose of His will (cf. Eph. 1:9) by which through Christ, the Word made flesh, man has access to the Father in the Holy Spirit and comes to share in the divine nature (cf. Eph. 2:18; 2 Pet. 1:4). Through this revelation, therefore, the invisible God (cf. Col. 1:15; 1 Tim. 1:17) out of the abundance of His love speaks to men as friends (cf. Ex. 33:11; Jn. 15:14-15) and lives among them (cf. Bar. 3:38), so that He may invite and take them into fellowship with Himself" (DV 2/122). Man is called by God "to communicate in life and glory with Himself" (AG 2b/585), to "a personal relationship with Him in Christ" (AG 13b/600), to an "intimate and vital link with God" (GS 19b/216), "to commune with God and to share in His happiness" (GS 21c/218), "so that with his entire being he might be joined to Him in an endless sharing of a divine life beyond all corruption" (GS 18d/215). The Church is therefore the sign and instrument given to men by God so that they can unite themselves to His life, glory, and blessedness.

In regard to the second effect, communion with men or the unity of the whole human race, the Council explains: "The union of the human family is greatly fortified and fulfilled by the unity, founded on Christ, of the family of God's sons" (GS 42a/241; cf. 43c/243).

Since the Church's mission is to unite in one Spirit all men of all nations, races, and cultures, she "stands forth as a sign of that brotherliness which allows honest dialogue and invigorates it" (GS 92a/306). In this way she will be "a lasting and sure seed of unity, hope, and salvation for the whole human race" (LG 9e/26).

The Church "from the Trinity"

The Church "[comes] forth from the Father's eternal love [*philanthropia:* love for men; cf. Tit 3:4], [is] founded in time by Christ the Redeemer, and made one in the Holy

Spirit" (GS 40b/238). "It is from the mission of the Son
and the mission of the Holy Spirit that she takes her origin,
in accordance with the decree of God the Father" (AG 2a/
585). To express this same idea, *Lumen Gentium* uses a text
from St. Cyprian: the Church is "a people made one with
the unity of the Father, the Son, and the Holy Spirit" (LG
4c/17). Msgr. Philips, who suggested the use of this text, observes that the concatenation of words is almost untranslat-
able: "de unitate . . . plebs adunata."[11] The Latin preposition *de* expresses the ideas of imitation and participation:
the unification of the people of God is a prolongation of the
unity between the three divine Persons; by its own unity the
people shares in that other Unity, so that, for St. Cyprian,
the unity of the Church cannot be understood apart from the
Trinity. In the Decree on ecumenism, Vatican II teaches that
the "highest exemplar and source of this mystery [of Church
unity] is the unity, in the Trinity of Persons, of one God, the
Father and the Son in the Holy Spirit" (UR 2f/344). When
comments were made on this passage with its statement that
the unity within the Trinity is accomplished "in the Holy
Spirit," modifying proposals were made which claimed that
such a formulation "smacked of heresy," on the grounds that
the principle of unity in God is the divine nature, not one of
the Persons. But the Commission kept the formula, claiming
that it agreed with the doctrine of the holy Fathers and the
theologians who call the Holy Spirit "the bond of love between
Father and Son." Shortly before this, the World Council of
Churches (Protestant and Orthodox) had presented the following formulation in a New Delhi report: "The love of the
Father and the Son in the unity of the Holy Spirit is the
source and goal of the unity which the Triune God wills for
all men and creation. We believe that we share in this unity
in the Church of Jesus Christ, who is before all things and
in whom all things hold together. In Him alone, given by the
Father to be Head of the Body, the Church has its true unity.
The reality of this unity was manifest at Pentecost in the

gift of the Holy Spirit."[12]

Marked as it is with the seal of the Trinity, the Church has its origin, model, and end in God One and Three. "That all may be one as you, Father, are in me, and I in you; I pray that they may be [one] in us . . . that they may be one, as we are one—I living in them, you living in me—that their unity may be complete" (Jn 17:21-23).

1. The Church "[comes] from the eternal Father's love" (GS 40b/238). This love of the Father is an *amor fontalis*, a love which is a fountain from which life flows forth (AG 2b/585). Time and again Vatican II speaks to us of the plan or purpose of the Father and, on two occasions, describes it explicitly (LG 2; AG 2). According to *Lumen Gentium* (2/15-16) this plan, which is eternal, free, mysterious, wise, and good, involves dignifying men with a participation in the divine life; bringing all men into conformity with the image of God's Son; gatherng all believers in Christ into a community (the Church) so that they may be finally gathered together with the Father "in the universal Church"; making Christ the Head of the universe so that the latter may have meaning, a reason for existence, unity, and coherence. This is the great revelation of "the mysterious design which for ages was hidden in God" (Eph 3:9), of which St. Paul speaks at length in Eph 1:3-14 and 3:1-12. Therefore, the Council insists, God never abandoned men but "ceaselessly offered them helps to salvation, in anticipation of Christ the Redeemer" (LG 2a/15). It is in this context, in which the ecclesiological horizons of Vatican II open out to infinity, that the Council speaks unhesitatingly of an all-embracing "universal Church," which already exists, of which all just men from Abel to the last of the elect will be part, and which will be gathered together "with the Father." Everything began with the Father, the "fountain of love"; everything will end with Him. To use a formula of Johann Adam Moehler, which Paul VI quotes in a discourse of May 18, 1966: "The Father sent the Son, and the Son sent the Spirit. This is how God came to us.

And it is in the inverse way that we shall reach the Father: the Holy Spirit leads us to the Son, and the Son to the Father."[13] Therefore: from the Father—through Christ—in the Holy Spirit—to the Father.

The Council does not here enter into the difficult question of how all the just men since Abel enter into the "universal Church," even when they did not (and could not) have any contact with the Church-as-visible-institution, inasmuch as the latter has existed only since Pentecost and therefore could not, and cannot now, welcome into its visible community the just who lived, live, and shall live "outside of her visible structure" (LG 8b/23), or "outside the visible boundaries of the Catholic Church" (UR 3b/345). It does not ask how the basic principle is and always will be valid for all men without exception, ever since Adam, that those who in fact are saved receive salvation through Christ (cf. AG 8/594-95) and therefore are part of the "universal Church." This doctrine is an ancient one. In note 6 to *Lumen Gentium* 2, the Council refers to St. Gregory the Great, St. Augustine, and St. John Damascene.

It is worthwhile obtaining and reading these patristic texts, especially the last two. For St. Gregory the Great, *Sermons on the Gospels* 19:1 (PL 76:1154b), Abel (the first just man to die) is the first branch of a vine which will continue to exist until the last branch springs from it. St. Augustine, *Sermon* 341:9,11 (PL 39:1499) writes: "All of us together are the members and body of Christ: not only we who live here, but all of us throughout the world; not only we who live now, but—how shall I put it?—every just man who journeys through this life, from Abel the just down to the end of time, as long as men beget and are begotten. . . . All of them form the one body of Christ. . . . The Church which is now on pilgrimage is the same reality as the heavenly Church where we have the angels for our fellow-citizens. . . . Thus there is one Church, one city of the great king." St. John Damascene, *Against the Iconoclasts* 11 (PG 96:1358), summing up the doctrine of the Eastern Fathers, says: "The Catholic Church, then, is holy; it is the assembly of the holy Fathers of every era: patriarchs, prophets, apostles, evangelists, and martyrs, and to them are united, with one heart, all who believe." These are the three texts to which the Council refers. But there are others. For example, Origen, *Commentary on the Song of Songs* II (PG 13:134): "Do not think that the Church can be called spouse of Christ only once the Savior has come in the flesh; she is his spouse from the creation of the world or even, if we follow Paul on the origin of this great mystery, from before the creation of the world." Again, in his *Commentary on Matthew*, n. 51 (PG 13:1679): "The elect of Christ are not only those who have lived holy lives since his coming . . . but all who since the beginning of the world, like Abraham, saw Christ's day and rejoiced in it with a joy that was from God." St. Leo the Great, *Sermon* 30:7 (PL 54:234): "All the saints who lived before our Savior came were justified by this faith and became his Body thanks to this mystery [of the Incarnation]."

Some of the Church Fathers (cited in AG 3a/586, note 7) spoke of the *continuous presence of the Word among men, even before the Incarnation.* "Before he became flesh in order to save all things and to sum them up in Himself, 'He was in the world' already as 'the true light that enlightens every man' (Jn 1:9-10)" (GS 3d/263). This is the patristic doctrine of the "seed of the Word," wwhich is endorsed by the Council in other passages (AG 3a/586; 9c/595-96; 11d/598). "He ceaselessly kept the human race in His care, in order to give eternal life to those who perseveringly do good in search of salvation" (DV 3/112). Therefore, "those also can attain to everlasting salvation who through no fault of their own do not know the gospel of Christ or His Church, yet sincerely seek God and, moved by grace, strive by their deeds to do His will as it is known to them through the dictates of conscience" (LG 16c/35); they belong to the "universal Church," they are the "anonymous Christians." As Augustine wrote in his *Revisions* I:13,8: "The reality which today we call the Christian religion existed among the ancients; it existed from the beginnings of the human race until Christ came in the flesh. At that point the true religion, which already existed, began to be called 'Christian.' " The same holds for non-Christian peoples today. Therefore the Decrees on the missions urges missionaries to "be familiar with their national and religious traditions, gladly and reverently laying bare the seeds of the Word which lie hidden in them" (AG 11b/597-98).

In this doctrinal context we must at least mention the precious teaching of the Council on *the ways of supernatural salvation which God alone knows*. In *Gaudium et Spes*, after saying that all should look for the glorious resurrection, the Council adds: "All this holds true not only for Christians, but for all men of good will in whose hearts grace works in an unseen way. For, since Christ died for all men, and since the ultimate vocation of man is in fact one, and divine, we ought to believe that the Holy Spirit in a manner known only to God offers to every man the possibility of being associated with this paschal mystery" (GS 22f/221-22). In like fashion the Decree on the missions says that "God in ways known to Himself can lead those inculpably ignorant of the gospel to that faith without which it is impossible to please Him" (AG 7c/593). We may note, too, that the Motu Proprio, *Ecclesiae Sanctae*, which regulates the application of the conciliar decree on the missions, orders that a theology of the missions should henceforth be part of theological teaching and that in it "the Lord's ways of preparing for the Gospel and the possibility of salvation for those who have not had the Gospel preached to them should be meditated upon."[14]

2. The Church was "founded in time by Christ the Redeemer" (GS 40b/238). With conviction and simplicity the Council uses and repeats the word "founded": "The Church established by Christ the Lord is, indeed, one and unique" (UR 1a/341); "He founded His Church as the sacrament of

salvation" (AG 5b/589); Christ is, simply, the Founder (LG 5d/18; 8d/24; GS 3b/201; 78a/290; AG 1a/584). The Council also twice speaks explicitly of the Son's mission (LG 3; AG 3) and refers to it with great frequency in terms of admiring wonder: "God's Word, through whom all things were made, was Himself made flesh and dwelt on the earth of men. Thus He entered into the world's history as a perfect man, taking that history up into Himself and summarizing it" (GS 38a/235-36). "The Lord is the goal of human history, the focal point of the longings of history and civilization, the center of the human race, the joy of every heart, and the answer to all its yearnings" (GS 45b/247). He is "the key, the focal point, and the goal of all human history" (GS 10g/208). "God determined to intervene in human history in a manner both new and definitive" (AG 3b/586), and made Christ "head of a renewed humanity" (AG 3c/586). "By His incarnation the Son of God has united Himself in some fashion with every man" (GS 22b/220-21); "Taking on human nature, He bound the whole human race to Himself as a family through a certain supernatural solidarity" (AA 8b/498). In him men and all creation receive meaning and purpose; the "eager expectation of creation" is answered.

3. The Church is "made one in the Holy Spirit" (GS 40b/238). The mission of the Holy Spirit, too, receives special mention on two occasions (LG 4; AG 4), and there are countless allusions to it in all the documents. It would be interesting, useful, instructive, and even moving to make an exhaustive list of these passages and to meditate on the words applied to the Holy Spirit in them. Thus in *Lumen Gentium* 4/16-17 alone we are taught that the Holy Spirit
—perpetually sanctifies the Church;
—gives life to men who are dead from sin;
—dwells in the hearts of the faithful as in a temple;
—prays in them;
—bears witness to the fact that they are adopted sons;
—guides the Church to the knowledge of the truth;

—unites the Church in fellowship and service;

—directs her through various hierarchical and charismatic gifts;

—adorns her with the fruits of his grace;

—perpetually renews her;

—leads her to perfect union with her spouse.

This rich vocabulary for the Spirit is found in all the documents of Vatican II. Here are some further examples from *Lumen Gentium*: the Holy Spirit

—distributes his gifts according to his own richness and the needs of the ministries (7d/21);

—produces and urges love among the believers (*ibid.*);

—vivifies, unifies, and moves the whole body so that his role can be compared to that of the soul in the human body (7h/22);

—"assumes" the Church and makes it the instrument of redemption, just as the Word assumes the humanity of Jesus (8a/22);

—arouses and sustains the sense of faith by which the faithful receive the word of God, cling to it without fail, penetrate it more deeply, and apply it more thoroughly to life (12b/ 29-30);

—sanctifies and guides the people of God not only through sacraments and ministries but also through gifts and charisms, when, as, and to whom he decides, for the renewal and spread of the Church (12c/30);

—brings together the whole Church and each and every believer, and is the principle of unity in doctrine and fellowship (13a/31);

—arouses the desire for unity and, with his gifts, graces, and sanctifying power is at work in non-Catholic Christians (15b/34);

—impels the Church to missionary action (17b/36);

—influences those who hear the word of God to receive the gospel (19b/39);

—sees to the necessary harmony between bishops and pope

(22d/44);

—guarantees the infallibility of the Church (25e/49);

—urges many Christians to the practice of the evangelical counsels (39b/66);

—moves souls interiorly to love God with their whole heart (40a/66).

According to the Constitution, *Dei Verbum*, on revelation, the Holy Spirit

—helps the faithful in their act of faith;

—by moving the heart;

—by directing the heart to God;

—by opening the eyes of the mind;

—by giving joy in assenting to and believing the truth (DV 5/113-14);

—helps the Church to grasp the realities and words received from apostolic tradition (8b/116);

—makes the living voice of the gospel resound in the Church;

—guides believers into the fulness of truth;

—makes the word of Christ dwell abundantly in them (8c/117).

Such an already impressive list could be enriched from the other documents of Vatican II. And it is to be noted that the Council sees the presence and action of the Holy Spirit outside the Church as well. According to the He "established the kingdom of God on earth" (DV 17/123). Since that time, the kingdom of God "is now present in mystery" (LG 3a/16); "On this earth that kingdom is already present in mystery" (GS 39e/237-38). The promised final restoration which we await "has already begun" (LG 48c/79); "The renovation of the world has been irrevocably decreed and in this age is already anticipated in some real way" (LG 4d/79).

Of this kingdom of God, already begun and present but not yet perfected, the Church is the germ and beginning and, at the same time, the instrument of its fulfillment, the sacrament of it. "The Church . . . receives the mission to proclaim and to establish among all peoples the kingdom of Christ and of God" (LG 5d/18). "Its goal is the kingdom of God" in its perfect form at the end of time (LG 9d/26). Here we have the nature, the greatness, and the essential mission of the Church as visible sacrament.

We must insist on this point: *The Church is not the kingdom of God and is not identifiable with the kingdom of God, but is rather its germ and beginning.* Or, as the Council puts it, "the Church [is] the kingdom of Christ now present in mystery" (LG 3a/16). The Church thus belongs to the time of growth and maturation, and does not possess the glory of fulfillment. It is the pilgrim Church, not the Church of glory; it "strains towards the consummation of the kingdom and, with all her strength, hopes and desires to be united in glory with her King" (LG 5d/18). "The Church has a saving and an eschatological purpose which can be fully attained only in the future world" (GS 40b/238); she "will attain her full perfection only in the glory of heaven" (LG 48a/78). The Church fulfilled or the Church of glory does not exist as yet and therefore we must not attribute to the pilgrim Church the perfections proper to the Church fulfilled to which St. Paul is referring in Eph 5:27. The Church is also, therefore, the "Church of the cross" or the "Church under the cross" "moving forward through trial and tribulation" (LG 9g/26), "undertaking the narrow way of the cross" (AG 1c/585); "taking on the appearance of this passing world, She herself dwells among creatures who groan and travail in pain" (LG 48d/79). As a pilgrim, she continues to experience the passion of Christ amid "the afflictions and hardships which assail her from within and without" (LG 9e/24), in order to attain glory with Christ. Yet in that glory she already shares in some way (2 Cor 13:4)! The "weakness" and the "power" of Christ go with his apostles and his Church. It is salutary for us to meditate now and then on the words of Jesus to his disciples when he sends them on mission. He promises no triumphs or laurels. "What I am doing is sending you out like sheep among wolves. . . . Be on your guard with respect to others. They will hale you into court. . . . You will be hated by all on account of me. . . No pupil outranks his teachers, no slave his master" (Mt 10:16,17,22,24). "Hence, prompted by the Holy Spirit, the Church must walk the same road which Christ walked: a road of poverty and obedience, of service and self-sacrifice to the death, from which death He came forth a victor by His resurrection. For thus did all the apostles walk in hope. On behalf of Christ's body, which is the Church, they supplied what was wanting of the sufferings of Christ by their own many trials and sufferings (cf. Col 1:24). Often, too, the blood of Christians was like a seed" (AG 5e/590).

"Still in pilgrimage upon the earth, we trace in trial and under oppression the paths He trod. Made one with His sufferings as the body is one with the head, we endure with Him, that with Him we may be glorified" (LG 7f/21). In this way, we "follow the poor Christ, the humble and cross-bearing Christ, in order to be made worthy of being partakers in His glory" (LG 41a/67-68). We can never reflect enough on all this, especially now when we are endeavoring to reformulate our relationships with mankind and the world. When we have the feeling of being quite identified with the world and cheered on by men, as if there were no differences between us Christians and them, then we are evidently on the wrong path and are failing to be leaven, salt, and light for the world. Then we will have to open the gospels once again and read Mt 10:16-24 and especially Jn 15:18-25.

Much was said during (and since) the Council on the *Church of the poor.* To satisfy desires expressed on this score, LG 8c-d/23-24 were written, with the three parallels there given between Christ and the Church. As Christ carried out the work of redemption in poverty and persecution, so the Church must, in poverty and persecution, communicate the fruits of redemption to men; as Christ became a servant and poor, so the Church ought to walk the paths of humility and self-sacrifice ("she is not set up to seek earthly glory"); as

Christ was sent to bring the good news to the poor, so the Church ought to seek out all who are afflicted with human weakness.

A word, finally, on *the relations between the kingdom of God and the world* (creation, the cosmos, non-human creation). For, as we have already seen, "the entire world," too, "which is intimately related to man and achieves its purpose through him, will be perfectly re-established in Christ" (LG 48a/78-79). We do not know when and how it will happen, but we do know that there will be a "consummation of the earth and humanity," a transformation of the world (GS 39a/ 237). "Christ's redemptive work, while of itself directed toward the salvation of men, involves also the renewal of the whole temporal order. Hence the mission of the Church is not only to bring to men the message and grace of Christ, but also to penetrate and perfect the temporal sphere with the spirit of the gospel. ... God ... Himself intends in Christ to appropriate the whole universe into a new creation, initially here on earth, fully on the last day" (AA 5a/495). "It has pleased God to unite all things, both natural and supernatural, in Christ Jesus 'that in all things he may have the first place' (Col 1:18)" (AA 7b/497). If it is clear that "earthly progress must be carefully distinguished from the growth of Christ's kingdom" (GS 39d/237), it is equally clear that the world (the "temporal order" and, therefore "earthly progress") is part of God's kingdom; it is, as it were, the material for it. The Council even says that dedication to the earthly service of men Decree on ecumenism, the Holy Spirit rouses the desire of unity in our separated brothers (UR 1c/ 342) and through his inspiring grace gives rise to efforts at unity among Christians (UR 4a/347); he uses as a means of salvation the Churches and Communities separated from Rome (UR 3d/346), gives the interior gifts of salvation to non-Catholic Christians (3b/345), and works in them for our edification (4i/349). His grace is even at work in non-Christians who are inculpably ignorant of the gospel (LG 16c/

35). We also find rich conciliar texts which speak to us of ways of sanctification which God alone knows (cf. GS 22f/221 and AG 7c/593). Nor must we forget that "doubtless, the Holy Spirit was already at work in the World before Christ was glorified" (AG 4a/587).

The Church as Germ and Sacrament of the Kingdom of God

Light must also be thrown on the mystery of the Church from the viewpoint of its relationship to the kingdom of God. To understand what this kingdom is, we may turn to what the Council says of the eternal Father's plan. The kingdom of God is the final goal of this plan, the "consummation" that will be effected when all things are made new (cf. Acts 3:21); when the human race and the whole created world, which is so closely bound up with man and reaches its goal through him, will be perfectly renewed in Christ (cf. LG 48a/78); when Christ will be in full reality the Head of the universe (cf. Eph 1:10); when the "new earth and new heavens" take shape (cf. GS 39/237) and God will be all in all things (1 Cor 15:28).

Christ began his preaching with a categorical statement that expressed the essential Good News: "This is the time of fulfillment. The reign of God is at hand" (Mk 1:15; Mt 4:17; cf. LG 5a/17). With Christ a new phase of history began, "the final age of the world" (LG 48d/79; cf. 1 Cor 10:11); and in Christ—in his person, words, and actions—the kingdom of God began to take concrete shape (LG 5). Christ "inaugurated the kingdom of heaven on earth" (LG 3a/16); is a way "to make ready the material of the celestial realm" (GS 38d/236). Consequently, "all the good fruits of our nature and enterprise, we will find . . . again, but freed of stain, burnished and transfigured. This will be so when Christ hands over to the Father a kingdom eternal and universal; 'a kingdom of truth and life, of holiness and grace, of justice, love, and peace'" (GS 39e/237). The Church, therefore, as germ of the kingdom of God and as its earthly sacrament, "experiences the same earthly lot which the world does. She serves as a leaven and as a kind of soul for human society as it is to be renewed in Christ and transformed into God's family" (GS 40c/239).

Mystical Body of Christ

Here we have the great doctrine of the Church's internal, invisible, sacramental, and supernatural unity. Without such unity all the external, visible, social, ritual, juridical, or canonical unity is worthless. This internal unity means, in the first place, union with Christ, conformity with or configuration to Christ. Vatican II presents the doctrine in *Lumen Gentium* 7/20-22.

By his death and resurrection Christ redeemed man and transformed him into a "new creature"; and when he gave men the Holy Spirit, he made of his brothers, "mystically," his own body. (The Council does not here use the non-Biblical expression, "mystical body."[15] In this body, by means of the sacraments, men are so united to the dead and risen Christ that the very life of Christ himself is poured into or communicated to believers. Such a vital union (or "communion") with Christ takes place really but in a way beyond our grasp (this is the sense of "mystically" in 7a). Thus we are incorporated into Christ, made his body, members of his body. The incorporation takes place at the time of baptism: "In this sacred rite, a union with Christ's death and resurrection is both symbolized and brought about" (7b).

Through baptism we are made like to Christ. We must stop here and reflect. For this statement is an astounding one, and basic to our Christian faith. "We who" through baptism "have been made like unto Him, who have died with Him and been raised up with Him, are taken up into the mysteries of His life, until we reign together with Him" (LG 7f/21). By baptism "men are plunged into the paschal mystery of Christ" (SC 6/140). By baptism "man becomes truly incorporated into the crucified and glorified Christ and is reborn to a sharing of the divine life" (UR 22a/363). We are as it were identified with Christ. "Christ is in us and we in Christ," St. Paul says 160 times. "I have been crucified with Christ, and the life I live now is not my own; Christ is living in me" (Gal 2:19-20). All the members must become like Christ so that Christ may be formed in them: "You are my children, and you put me back in labor pains until Christ is formed in you" (Gal 4:19; cf. LG 7f/21). "All [of you] are one in Christ Jesus" (Gal 3:28). The Church, therefore, is "Christ" (1 Cor 12:12). This vital union with Christ is given to us in baptism, which "constitutes" the sacramental bond of unity linking all who have been reborn by means of it" (UR 22b/364). Besides the fact that all the baptized live in intimate vital union with Christ and that the one life of Christ flows in all, all are also united to one another. All are one in Christ (Gal 3:28). In the Decree on ecumenism the Council draws an important conclusion from all this when it speaks of "separated brothers": "All those justified by faith through baptism are incorporated into Christ. They therefore have a right to be honored by the title of Christian, and are properly regarded as brothers in the Lord by the sons of the Catholic Church" (UR 3a/345). Baptized non-Catholics, too, are members of the mystical body of Christ!

Lumen Gentium, 7c, goes on to indicate that the supernatural interior unity, which baptism has effected, is maintained, nourished, increased, and marvelously brought to perfection by the Eucharist: "Truly partaking of the body of the Lord in the breaking of the Eucharistic Bread, we are taken up into communion with Him and with one another." The Eucharist means communion, fellowship, Church. We can never overemphasize the function of the Eucharist: it makes the Church. Here again we must pause and reflect, and the Council offers us many rich texts for the purpose. The Eucharist is "a sign of unity" (SC 47/154). In it "the unity of all believers . . . is both expressed and brought about" (LG

3b/16; cf. UR 2a/343). It is "the fount and apex of the whole Christian life" (LG 11b/28). Through it "the Church constantly lives and grows" (LG 26a/50). "No Christian community . . . can be built up unless it has its basis and center in the celebration of the Most Holy Eucharist. Here, therefore, all education in the spirit of community must originate" (PO 6h/545). "The other sacraments, as well as every ministry of the Church and every work of the apostolate, are linked with the holy Eucharist and are directed toward it. For the most blessed Eucharist contains the Church's entire spiritual wealth, that is, Christ Himself, our Passover and living bread. Through His very flesh, made vital and vitalizing through the Holy Spirit, He offers life to men. They are thereby invited and led to offer themselves, their labors, and all created things together with Him. Hence the Eucharist shows itself to be the source and apex of the whole work of preaching the gospel. . . . The faithful . . . are through the reception of the Eucharist fully joined to the Body of Christ" (PO 5c-d/ 541-42).

This vital supernatural union with Christ and, in and through Christ, with all the baptized (so that we are all "one in Christ") is the real heart of "the mystery of the Church," for the Church is a "communion."

The Images of the Church

The Council points out that the inner nature of the Church can be known through images drawn from pastoral life or agriculture, from building, or even from family and marriage (LG 6a/18). It presents these images for our meditation:

Sheepfold: a single door; flock: many sheep but only one shepherd.

Farming: the field of God is sown (parable of the sower). Rom 11:16-22: we, branches from the wild olive tree, have been grafted on to the true Olive Tree and partake of its root and sap; that is, the life of the incarnate Word passes into us and produces fruit in us. Jn 15:1-15: we are branches and will bear fruit only as long as we are vitally linked to the vine. Vital union with Christ is a fundamental concept for the Church.

Building: cf. Paul VI, discourse of November 16, 1966.[16] 1 Cor 6:19: temple, its individual character: each Christian is a temple of the Holy Spirit (also theme of sanctity). 1 Pet 2:5: spiritual house, as collective designation for Christian communities. Rev 21:10: holy city, with all forming the one city of God.

Foundation: strength, stability, unity; building on the foundation: unity in multiplicity (of stones). 1 Pet 2:4-5: "Come to him, a living stone, rejected by men but approved, nonetheless, and precious in God's eyes. You too are living stones, built as an edifice of spirit, into a holy priesthood, offering spiritual sacrifices acceptable to God through Jesus Christ." Eph 2:20: "You form a building which rises on the foundation of the apostles and prophets, with Christ Jesus himself as the capstone. Through him the whole structure is fitted together and takes shape as a holy temple in the Lord; in him you are being built into this temple, to become a dwelling place for God in the Spirit." Heb 3:6: "It is we who are that house [of God] if we hold fast to our confidence and the hope of which we boast." Mt 16:18: "I will build my church."

Mother-Virgin. Jn 1:13: "who were begotten not by blood, nor by carnal desire, nor by man's willing it, but by God." cf. LG 63a/92.

Spouse: In the Old Testament the marriage bonds between God and his people signified that this people was called to live the life of its divine spouse. Christ compares his mission to a wedding (cf. Mt 25:1-13; 22:2-14); the preaching is represented by John the Baptist (cf. Jn 3:29) and by Christ himself (Mt 9:15) as a wedding feast; in his death Christ surrenders himself for his bride and sanctifies her (Eph 5:25-28), and wins her by his blood (Acts 20:28); Christ nourishes his spouse, protects her, and is one with her (Eph 5:29-31). The

Church is born from Christ's open side as Eve (spouse and mother) from Adam's. The figure of the spouse expresses the ideas of unbreakable covenant, commuity of life, spotlessness; the duty of keeping always without wrinkle or stain; care of the husband for the spouse; mutual love; fidelity; fruitfulness.

The Church as People of God

All that happened to the Jewish people in the Old Testament (election, covenant, gradual revelation, sanctification) was "by way of preparation and as a figure of that new and perfect covenant which was to be ratified in Christ" (LG 9a/ 25); "The principal purpose to which the plan of the Old Covenant was directed was to prepare for the coming both of Christ, the universal Redeemer, and of the Messianic kingdom" (DV 15/122; cf. LG 55a/87).

Lumen Gentium does not hesitate to use the expression "new people of God," which does not occur in the Bible (cf. 9c/25; 10a/27; 13a/30). But this "new" must be understood according to the formula of St. Augustine which Vatican II makes its own: "God . . . arranged that the New Testament be hidden in the Old and the Old be made manifest in the New" (DV 16/122). In the Declaration on non-Christian religions the Council is more cautious and measured; the whole of NA 4/663-67 should be read with care. The accent is put primarily on the fact that there is a link between the people of the new covenant and the stock of Abraham; that the new covenant receives from the old a precious heritage which we cannot and ought not neglect; that by his cross Christ reconciled Jews and gentiles and made them one in himself. It is clear that "Jerusalem did not recognize the time of her visitation"; that many Jews did not accept the good news brought by Christ; and that not a few even opposed its spread. But the Council is vividly aware that, according to the Apostles, the Jews are still loved by God (Rom 11: 282-9); and that a day will come, known to God alone, on which the Jews too will turn to Christ. Then the Council makes this solemn declaration: "Although the Church is the new people of God, the Jews should not be presented as repudiated or cursed by God" (4g/666).

Instead of "new people of God" it would perhaps be more exact to say, with the Council, "people of the New Covenant" (UR 2b/343), for the expression "new covenant" is a Biblical one (cf. Lk 22:20; 1 Cor 11:25; 2 Cor 3:6; Heb 8:13, and cf. Heb. 6:12; 9:15; 12:24). This alternative designation has the merit of making clearer the uninterrupted relationship with the people of the Old Covenant. Israel became the people of God in virtue of the choice by Jahweh who wanted them for "his own people" (cf. Ex 19:5; 23:22; Deut 7:6; 14:2; 26:18). The further idea of covenant was added on: "I will look with favor upon you, and make you fruitful and numerous, as I carry out my covenant with you. . . . I will set my Dwelling among you, and will not disdain you. Ever present in your midst, I will be your God, and you will be my people" (Lev 26:9-12). In Deuteronomy this theology of the people of God will receive its systematic development. The choice of this people as God's own represents a preference in relation to other peoples and is motivated by love alone: "He [the Lord your God] has chosen you from all nations on the face of the earth to be a people peculiarly his own. It was not because you are the largest of nations that the Lord set his heart on you and choose you, for you are really the smallest of all nations. It was because the Lord loved you and because of his fidelity to the oath he had sworn to your fathers" (Deut 7:6-8). Even after all of Israel's infidelities, God in his graciousness and goodness wants to re-establish his former relationship in a new and definitive, unalterable and indissoluble fashion: "They shall be my people, and I will be their God. . . . I will make with them an eternal covenant, never to cease doing good to them" (Jer 32:38,40). This text expresses the essential content of the repeated prophetic promises concerning an eschatological people of God (cf. Jer 24:7; 30:22; 31:1,33; Ezek 11:20; 14:11; 36:28; 37:23,27 Hos 2:3,25;

Zech 8:8; 13:9). It is evident from many passages of the New Testament that the apostolic Church regards itself as this eschatological people of God which the prophets foretold. Cf. Acts 15:14; Tit 2:14; and especially 1 Pet 2:9-10 where various Old Testament texts are combined and referred to the nascent Christian community. Peter uses four predicates with rich overtones in order to describe the glorious vocation and unique status of the Church: "a chosen race, a royal priesthood, a holy nation, a people he claims for his own to proclaim the glorious works of the One who called you from darkness into his marvelous light." Inspired by Hosea, Peter continues his enthusiastic description: "Once you were no people, but now you are God's people; once there was no mercy for you, but now you have found mercy." The basic formula of the old covenant ("I will be their God and they shall be my people") is quoted on various occasions in the New Testament and related to the new situation created by Christ. Cf. 2 Cor 6:16; Heb 8:10; Rev 21:3. The Letter to the Hebrews even cites the complete text of Jer 31:31-34 for the purpose of showing that the great prophecy is fulfilled in the "new covenant."

The Church is, then, God's people of the new covenant. This is its great title. It is a motive for pride in the Apostles. They know, of course, that it results from no merit of theirs, but only from the initiative, choice, solicitude, preference, grace, mercy, and love of God.

With Christ there comes something "new," a new election, a new divine call, a new covenant, a "new testament," a new Israel, a new people of God, a Messianic people (LG 9d/25), to which all men are called. This people has Christ for its head; its proper condition and dignity is the freedom of the children of God; its law is love; its goal is the kingdom of God, that it may be one great community of life, love, and truth (LG 9d). The Church is "a community composed of men . . . led by the Holy Spirit in their journey to the kingdom of their Father" (GS 1/200). It is the family of God (cf. GS

32e/231; 40b/238), one family in Christ (LG 51c/84).

Let us pause for a moment to consider this image of the *family*, an image so dear to the early Christians. According to repeated statements in the New Testament God's plan is that men should be offered, in Christ, the possibility of becoming, by God's completely free gift, the adopted sons of the heavenly Father: God "predestined" them "to share the image of his Son, that the Son might be the first-born of many brothers" (Rom 8:29). When Christ came into the world, "any who did accept him he empowered to become children of God. These are they who believe in his name—who were begotten not by blood, nor by carnal desire, nor by man's willing it, but by God" (Jn 1:12-13). St. John therefore speaks of Christians as sons, "men born" (*tekna*) of God (Jn 11:52; 1 Jn 3:1-2; Rom 8:16-17; Eph 5:1; Phil 2:15). The divine gift does not confer on us a mere juridical and affective relationship, but brings with it a genuine interior transformation of man, whereby the latter acquires a likeness to God that transcends his human nature and is therefore *super*natural. It brings with it the gift of the Spirit of God (cf. Gal 4:7; Rom 8:15-16), the right of inheritance, and the right effectively to share, in and with Christ, in the eternal divine glory to which God calls us (cf. 1 Thess 2:12; 1 Pet 5:10). We become "sharers of the divine nature" (2 Pet 1:4). Although this beginning of divine glory in baptized man is not an objective of human experience for us now, it is nonetheless guaranteed by faith: "We are God's children now; what we shall later be has not yet come to light. We know that when it comes to light we shall be like him, for we shall see him as he is" (1 Jn 3:2).

The Church as Visible Sign

It is essential to a sacrament that it be sign as well, and it is essential to a sign that it be sensible. St. Augustine's definition of a sign is well known: "A sign is a thing which apart from the impression that it presents to the senses, causes of itself some other thing to enter our thoughts."[17]

And since the Church is a "sacrament in Christ," it must necessarily be a sensible, visible, verifiable sign. "Sign . . . and instrument" (LG 1b/15); "a shining beacon of salvation" (AG 21g/612).

St. Robert Bellarmine, in an anti-Protestant age, defined the Church as "the community of men who are united in the confession of the one Christian faith and the participation of the same sacraments and are governed by their lawful shepherds, especially by the one vicar of Christ on earth, the pope of Rome."[18] The definition described only the external, visible, social, hierarchic, and juridical reality, the *sacramentum tantum* [the symbol, not the reality symbolized], or sign. It gave no indication of the interior reality, the *res* [reality symbolized], or most important thing of all. On December 3, 1962, at the Council, Bishop Blásio Musto, of Aquino, surprisingly gave the same kind of definition: the Church is "a perfect society, possessing a three-fold power, juridically organized, and with the duty of keeping the deposit of faith free from error and guarding it, by its unshakeable authority, from all hostile attacks."[19]

But Vatican II, though characterized by its vigorous affirmation of the interior and invisible as the primary reality of the Church, did not fail to point out the external, visible, juridical reality as well. Christ established his holy Church "as a visible structure" (LG 8a/22). The Church was "constituted and organized in the world as a society" (LG 8b/23); it was "provided . . . with those means which befit it as a visible and social unity . . . that for each and all she may be the visible sacrament of this saving unity" (LG 9f/26; cf. GS 40c/239). This visible Church, too, must be fully accepted, for in it the community of grace, uniting man to God, becomes visible and corporeal. It is, in the Tridentine formula applied to the sacraments, "a visible form of invisible grace."[20] In her the grace of God, like the soul in the body, is located in time and space and becomes accessible to man.

Consequently, "the society furnished with hierarchical

aspects and the Mystical Body of Christ are not to be considered as two realities, nor are the visible assembly and the spiritual community, nor the earthly Church and the Church enriched with heavenly things. Rather they form one interlocked reality, which is comprised of a divine and a human element" (LG 8a/22). Non-Catholics take the same view: "And yet, almost everyone, though in different ways, longs that there may be one visible Church of God" (UR 1c/342). Such visible unity is also a requirement of the social nature of man and religion: "The social nature of man itself requires that he should give external expression to his internal acts of religion; that he should participate with others in matters religious; that he should profess his religion in community" (DH 3e/681).

The Council even teaches that the Church, "one interlocked reality, which is comprised of a divine and a human element," is, "by an excellent analogy . . . compared to the mystery of the incarnate Word. Just as the assumed nature inseparably united to the divine Word serves Him as a living instrument of salvation, so, in a similar way, does the communal structure of the Church serve Christ's Spirit, who vivifies it by way of building up the body" (LG 8a/22). The point of comparison in "this excellent analogy" is the close and inseparable union between the natural and supernatural elements in the service of God's saving action. As the Word manifests himself in the human figure of Jesus, so the Spirit of Christ makes himself visible in the social structure of the Church. The Spirit "vivifies, unifies, and moves the whole body. This He does in such a way that His work could be compared by the Holy Fathers with the function which the soul fulfills in the human body, whose principle of life the soul is" (LG 7h/22).

The theandric or Christomorphic nature of the Church, along with the bold comparison to the Hypostatic Union, allows us to say that what is taught in Christology concerning the duality of natures (without any commingling or change or division or separation) and their unity (without dualism or dichotomy) in Christ holds analogously for the Church. Therefore, too, we find the classical Christological errors being repeated in ecclesiology. There is an ecclesiological docetism, Nestorianism, and monophysitism.[21]

Docetism, with its spiritualist tendency, was scandalized and denied the reality of Christ's material body and, therefore, of the Incarnation of the Word, the hard earthly life, passion, and death of Christ. In a similar way, the ecclesiological docetist, no less scandalized, refuses to accept the human, earthly, visible, social, and juridical part of the Church and its institutions. In his eyes the Church must be purely spiritual, divine, or "pneumatic."[22] He is scandalized at the idea that God's salvation could be bound up with a human organization or that material means (water, oil, bread, wine) could play a part in the reception of God's grace. He looks for a wholly spiritual Church, apart from all human organizational forms, all rites and external elements, a Church which serves God solely "in spirit and in truth." He does not take seriously the Incarnation of God in a visible, corporeal form, in the lowliness and weakness of human nature and human community. He is scandalized at the "self-emptying" of the Word (cf. Phil. 2:7-8).

Dualistic Nestorianism divided or separated the two natures of Christ by attributing them to two subjects, without their being united in the one Person. Ecclesiological Nestorianism introduces a similar dualism into the Church, dissociating the divine element from the human, and separating the visible Church from the spiritual community, the earthly Church from the Church enriched with heavenly blessings. It was especially the Protestant Reformers who took up this position. A visible, organized community was indeed accepted as important and even necessary, but it was not acknowledged to be the bearer and transmitter of the invisible divine reality of the Spirit and his grace. These men did not see that the invisible element becomes palpable precisely in the human element of the Church and that God makes use of the human to communicate his truth and his grace to us. Men speak, from this viewpoint, of the "juridical Church" as opposed to the "Church of love."[23] In reality there are not two distinct Churches, one visible, the other invisible, one a Church of law, the other a Church of love; rather the two elements join to form a single interlocked reality. We must distinguish, but not separate or divide.

Supernaturalist monophysitism claimed that in Christ the human nature is absorbed by the divine nature. In a similar fashion, ecclesiological monophysitism imagines a confusion of the human and divine elements in the Church or an absorption of the human by the divine so that the human seems to disappear into the divine. Pious people, especially, who are sincerely devoted to the Church and identify themselves with her in selfless love, have the monophysitic tendency to give the Church a divine halo; they glorify everything that happens in the Church as though the latter were divinely perfect; they hide what is humanly imperfect in the Church and, in a rather insincere and dishonest apologetics, put all the stress on what is sublime, indefectible, and holy in the Church and in its splendid works and influence, as though only heavenly agencies were at work in all this. Such people are scandalized at the movement to reform, renew, and purify the Church. In their eyes the Church, its liturgy, its canon law, its pontifical documents, even its Latin, are holy and sacrosanct and not to be touched. This monophysitic faith is now in the process of breaking down. In any event, we must realize that the Church involves the action not only to God but of men with their weaknesses and limitations.

The Christological dogma defined at the Ecumenical Council of Chalcedon (in 451) throws light, then, on our concept of the Church. "We declare that the one selfsame Christ, only-begotten Son and Lord, must be acknowledged in two natures without any commingling or change or division or separation; that the distinction between the natures is in no way removed by their union but rather that the specific character of each nature is preserved."[24] Analogously in the Church: the human element is an important reality that is not transformed or absorbed by the divine element or confused with it, but is also not separated or divided from it or left to its own resources: "they form one interlocked reality which is comprised of a divine and a human element" (LG 8a/22).

"In a faithful though shadowed way"

We are especially conscious today of the Church's faults and defects. We feel, as though they were our own, the spots and wrinkles on the Bride of Christ. We no longer share the outlook of the apologetes who tried so charitably to hide or excuse all imperfections and infidelities. Now it is not the Church's enemies but her own children who publicly criticize her for her faults. In their anxiety to discover defects and wrong-doing they seem at times to outdo in eloquence the anti-clericals of another day. This attitude became widespread after the Council and undoubtedly drew its inspiration from the example of the Council Fathers and from the declarations, confessions, and proposals to be found in the documents of Vatican II. Today the Church as a whole is conscious of being at once a holy Church and a Church always in need of purification (LG 8d/24). She declares that she wants a "renewal of the whole Church" (OT Preface/437), a "renewal within the Church" (PO 12f/559). She proclaims the need to "purify and renew" herself (LG 15b/34), admits that "the Holy Spirit . . . renews and purifies her ceaselessly" (GS 21e/219), and acknowledges that continual reformation of which she always has need" (UR 6b/350), as does any institution of men on earth. We live at a time when the Council itself invites us to examine, sincerely and attentively, what needs to be renewed and brought to perfection within the Catholic household (UR 4e/348); when the Church, with surprising and exemplary humility, is ready to admit that she too is at fault in the separation between Christians (UR 3a/345) and therefore asks pardon of God and her separated brothers (UR 7b/351); when the Church admits that her children do not always clearly acknowledge the legitimate autonomy of the sciences (GS 36d/234: allusion to the Galilei case; cf. note 99); when she proclaims that she has not always duly honored the principle of diversity in unity (UR 16/359), religious freedom (DH 12a/692), and the requirements of genuine Christianity in her dealings with Moslems (NA 3b/663) and with Jews (NA 4g-h/666-67). We are far indeed from the time when Gregory XVI could say (1822): "It is quite absurd and sovereignly harmful to her [the Church] to claim a certain 'restoration and regeneration' as necessary to provide for her conservation and increase; as if it could be claimed that she is exposed to failure, to ignorance, or to other misfortunes of this nature."[25] Using already the language of Vatican II, Paul VI said to the Council Fathers at the opening of the Second Session: "We spoke just now of the Church looking upon Christ to discern in Him her true likeness. If in so doing she discovers some shadow, some defect, some stain on her wedding garment, what should be her instinctive, vigorous reaction? Clearly no other course is open to her than to renew herself, to put herself to rights, and bring herself back into conformity with her divine model; for that is her primary duty. . . . Only then, when the Church has completed this great work of her own interior sanctification, will she be able to show her face to the world and say: 'Whoever has seen me, has seen the Father' (Jn 14:9)."[26]

In a public audience of August 10, 1966, Paul VI said: "We want to tell you now that there is another aspect of the Church in this world: the humble Church; the Church that knows its own human limitations, its own faults, its own need of God's mercy and of pardon from men. Yes, there is also a repentant Church that preaches and practices penance; that doesn't hide its own failings but deplores them; that is glad to be identified with sinful mankind and to use the consciousness of a common misery as the source of a stronger sorrow for sin, a more touching plea for God's mercy, and a more humble trust in the salvation that is hoped for. The Church is humble, not just in the ranks of the faithful, but also and above all in the highest levels of the hierarchy who, with all their consciousness and exercise of their power to generate and to guide the people of God, know that they have to work for the edification and service of souls. This holds true right up to the highest level, that of Peter, who describes himself as 'Servant of the servants of God,' who feels more than anyone else the disproportion between the mission he has received from Christ and his own weakness and unworthiness, and who always recalls the exclamation of the Apostle who was a fisherman: 'Depart from me, O Lord, for I am a sinful man' (Lk 5:8)."[27]

However, precisely because we are in a period of sincere ecclesial examination of conscience and of courageous reformation of ecclesial life, we ought to be all the more careful not to lose sight of the fact that, for all the faults we can point out and ought to denounce, the Church, as spouse of Christ (cf. Eph. 5:25-28; LG 7i/22) and our Mother (cf. Gal 4:26; Rev 12:17; LG 6e/19), *has always remained substantially faithful to Christ and his Gospel.* We must abide by and be convinced of this principle of faith: that the Church of Christ, such as the Lord acquired and established her, with all those "elements or endowments which together go to build up and give life to the Church" (UR 3b/345), is to be found in a full and perfect way only "in the Catholic Church, which is governed by the successor of Peter and by the bishops in union with that successor" (LG 8b/23). We cannot denounce her as "the Church betrayed."[28]

In the opening discourse for the Second Session of the Council, cited above, Pope Paul continued: "The question of the Church's renewal is most certainly of great concern to this Council. But the expression of this desire must not be interpreted as an admission of guilt on the part of the

Catholic Church of our day for having falsified the mind of her
founder in a matter of grave moment. It is her feeling of real
joy and gratitude at having proved loyal to Christ in matters
of the highest importance which makes her all the more ready
and anxious to correct those faults which derive from human
fraility. Hence the renewal with which the Church is concerned must not be thought of as a repudiation of the present
life of the Church or a break with essential and time-honored
traditions. She shows her reverence for tradition by rejecting
form which are spurious or moribund, and by wishing to make
them genuine and fruitful."[29]

The documents of Vatican II speak on at least four occasions of this perfect fidelity of the Church, despite the shadows
and dark spots to be found in her:

LG 8e/24: To overcome the difficulties and hardships, internal and external, which she faces the Church is strengthened by the Risen Lord so that she may always continue her
mission: to reveal to the world the Mystery of Christ. She
does it "in a faithful though shadowed way." Thus, the
Church, "like a pilgrim in a foreign land, presses forward amid
the persecutions of the world and the consolations of God"
towards the consummation. If at the end of time we wanted
to erect a monument to the pilgrim Church—and she would
indeed deserve one—we could engrave on its pedestal, for
perpetual remembrance, the splendid words: "in a faithful
though shadowed way," for they give felicitous expression to
one aspect of the nature of the pilgrim Church.

LG 9g/26: "Moving forward through trial and tribulation,
the Church is strengthened by the power of God's grace
promised to her by the Lord, so that in the weakness of the
flesh she may not waver from perfect fidelity, but remain a
bride worthy of her Lord." The Church, too, is under the law
of the Cross: "through the Cross to the light" that does not
dim.

GS 43j/245: "By the power of the Holy Spirit the Church
has remained the faithful spouse of her Lord and has never

ceased to be the sign of salvation on earth" even though "she is very well aware that among her members, both clerical and lay, some have been unfaithful to the Spirit of God during the course of many centuries."

DH 12a/692: The Church is "faithful to the truth of the gospel," despite the fact that "in the life of the People of God . . . there have at times appeared ways of acting which were less in accord with the spirit of the gospel and even opposed to it."

The kingdom of God is like a field in which weeds and wheat grow up together (Mt 13:24-30). The surprising decision of the Father is that his servants should not separate the good from the evil now: "Let them grow together until harvest." To try to order everything before then would be an undue intervention in the plans of God. The reason is that the weeds and grain are closely interwoven and the grain might be pulled up along with the weeds. The Lord therefore reserves entirely to himself all judgment and separation.

The kingdom of God is also like a dragnet that collects good fish and bad (Mt 13:47-50). Here again, the separation will occur only at the end. Before the end, good and bad live together in the same net, and it is not for us to judge or separate.

The kingdom of God is like a banquet attended by good men and bad (Mt 22:1-14). After the first guests invited have been rejected, the servants are sent to invite new guests and, without refusing any, to bring into the banquet hall whomever they meet.

This presence of the human and even of the extremely human in the Church makes possible and easy the shadows and defects that irritate us so much now, after the Council, where we were invited to help in the adaptation, renewal, and purification of the Church. *We are witnessing today a universal movement of protest*, and it is a genuine "sign of the times." Above all, it is the upcoming generation that protests. Protest in the Church is not something strange today nor is it confined to the Catholic Church; it is only a

particular form of something that is world-wide and comprehensive. As found today, especially after the events in France
of May, 1968, protest or contestation, in the narrower sense of
the term, is directed primarily against modern, highly developed society and against technology and the forms of human
oppression to be found in contemporary society. It is a total
rejection of the social system and the social structures that
oppress men. Technology becomes an instrument of domination and manipulation; it builds social systems and structures
which humiliate and enslave, tending to turn the human being
into a thing or object and to lessen his dignity. Thus protest
takes the form of a radical challenge to systems and structures
and is inspired by an acute sense of the value of the human
person. The system being attacked is not the capitalist society denounced by Marx but the one-dimensional, industrial,
technocratic society denounced by Marcuse. The Church is
the object of protest in this narrow sense to the extent that
it seems to tolerate or favor such structures or even to allow
this kind of debasing technology or bureaucracy to dominate
its own apostolic and missionary institutions or structures.
In such circumstances the Church seems to be but a spiritual
branch of the one-dimensional society, exercising a psycho-
therapy that makes the system a little more bearable and
furnishing compensation for the frustrations engendered by
public life and by work. Thus it seems to approve and
strengthen the social system that is under attack, despite
doctrinal statements to the contrary (as in GS 68 and 75, or
John XXIII's encyclical letters *Populorum Progressio*, no.
30, and *Pacem in Terris*, nos. 73-74). Then the same vigorous
protest, to the same end, is leveled at the Church as at the
whole society with which she seems to work hand in glove.

The phenomenon of protest is universal and disquiets many
of the faithful; it also seems to imply doctrinal positions. For
both reasons we must try to formulate some principles and
norms that can guide us dring the present critical period of
Church life.

1. An attitude of protest within the Church is possible in principle and can be legitimate and necessary. It is quite possible to love the Church, to identify with her, to live in and for her, and, at the same time, to want her to become more self-consistent, more holy, and more spotless, without wrinkle or stain. For, as the Council points out, the Church is, in fact, "at the same time holy and always in need of being purified" (LG 8d/24); like any human institution "she always has need" of "continual reformation" (UR 6b/350). Therefore, like a mother, "she exhorts her sons to purify and renew themselves so that the sign of Christ may shine more brightly over the face of the Church" (LG 15/34). Two words, "renewal" and "purification," appear frequently in the documents of the Council and invite us to adopt an attitude of critical protest. *Renewal* supposes that there is some useless ballast which makes life unnecessarily difficult; attachment to forms or formulas that are outdated and obsolete; a lack of updating and adaptation to concrete existential situations and what they require; at times, even a momentary inability to see and hear the signs of the times or to interpret them in the light of faith; excessive immobility and fixity in prayer formulas or in the norms for apostolic or pastoral action; undue repression of the spontaneous manifestations of a life that is naturally exuberant or even of the gifts of the Holy Spirit who inspires men where, as, and when he wishes. *Purification* supposes spots and wrinkles, stains and disfiguring marks, shadows and dark places, defects and flaws, imperfections and infidelities in her who, though substantially faithful to the Lord, is a pilgrim in the shadows, amid trials and afflictions within and without. Therefore the Council itself invites the faithful "to make an honest and careful appraisal of whatever needs to be renewed and achieved in the Catholic household itself, in order that its life may bear witness more loyally and luminously to the teachings and ordinances which have been handed down from Christ through the apostles" (UR 4e/348). The Council even says: "Let it be recognized that

all the faithful, clerical and lay, possess a lawful freedom of
inquiry and of thought, and the freedom to express their
minds humbly and courageously about those matters in which
they enjoy competence" (GS 62j/270). One of the early
canonical collections spoke of the "sin of silence," the sin
committed by those who did not boldly reprove prelates when
the latter were beginning to compromise the Church. The
good protester exercises a prophetic function. The prophet,
howeyer, is. not always a pleasing fellow! Mighty protesters
have arisen in the history of the Church and some of them
were even canonized, but first they were burned to death.

2. The contemporary movement of protest within the
Church derived its main impulse from Vatican II itself. The
wholesale rejection of the schemas elaborated by the pre-
conciliar commissions was undoubtedly a courageous and radical act of protest. An analysis of the new perspectives and
positions, the suggestions, declarations, requirements, or determinations of Vatican II would give us the key to, or the
reasons behind, a large number of the protests that have
arisen or which can and will have to arise if the conciliar documents are not to remain a dead letter. It is not difficult to
discern the seeds of positive protest in the declarations of
Vatican II on the rights of conscience; the universal and inalienable freedoms; religious freedom; the necessity of assuming personal responsibility for one's actions; free, active,
responsible obedience; the charisms of the Holy Spirit which
are independent of the sacraments and ministries; the ways
of supernatural salvation of which the Church is ignorant and
which God alone knows; the positive religious values to be
found outside the Church, even in non-Christian religions;
ecumenism; the need to dialogue and cooperate with the world
and even with atheists; the urgency of working in the temporal order so as to make the world more human; the autonomy of the temporal order; the obligation for the Church to
leave its ghetto and make itself understood and loved by the
men of today; respect for the greatness and dignity of man,

even when it is corrupted by false religions; the obligation to heed the signs of the times as a manifestation of God's will; the necessity of a deep-going change of mentality; the human person as source, subject, and end of social institutions, even within the Church; the Church as people of God; collegiality at the episcopal level, the altter including the Bishop of Rome; co-responsibility in the Church; the principle of subsidiarity; the theological possibility of a ministerial priesthood wthout celibacy; the word of God as the soul of theology and norm of Christian life and prayer; the need of a more mature, adult, personal, and conscious faith; the exercise of authority as a service and not a domination; the purely religious finality of the Church; the invitation to theologians to revise their theology in the light of new problems; the necessary distinction between the content of faith and its formulation; the hierarchy of truths within Catholic doctrine; the splendors of diversity and pluralism within the unity of the Church; the liturgy as principal means of sanctification; the suitability of adapting the liturgy to the varying situations and conditions of peoples; active participation of the laity in the Church's mission; the possibility of a freely chosen lay apostolate; the value and importance of conjugal love and responsible parenthood; etc., etc. It would not be difficult to extend the list: "Quite an impressive list could be made of theological positions taught in Rome in the recent or more distant past as the only true ones, which were simply done away with by the Council Fathers," said Cardinal Suenens, one of the conciliar Moderators, not too long ago.[30] Our generation watched the Council at its work; newspapers and magazines provided plenty of information on it all. These were examples which could not fail to have an important influence on the attitude and behavior of priests and laity alike. Protest was entering the Church and taking an increasingly collective, organized form.

3. A state of tension between the forces of conservation and the forces of renewal is a quite normal and healthy phe-

nomenon, for it is a basic law of life itself. Without the active, watchful presence of the forces of renewal we would have fixism, immobility, sclerosis, and death; without the active, watchful presence of the forces of conservation we would have instability, insecurity, confusion, and anarchy. As a body that is alive and constantly growing, the Church must see to it that both forces are always active. But we must honestly recognize that among our older people (who are also the administrators of the established order) the conservative tendency is usually predominant and, with it, the desire (sometimes unconscious) of suppressing the forces of renewal which are ordinarily to be found in the upcoming generations. The desire may, of course, be held within bounds by a conscious effort at genuine asceticism. In any event, it is clear that we are now living in one of the most decisive transitional moments of human history. In such a time of transition it would be the fatal if the conservative forces were to dominate to the extent of suffocating the forces of renewal. More than in any past period, we need today the help, inventive power, imagination, spontaneity, and vitality of the young and of the forces of renewal. Here we have the indispensable role of protest. The protector does not accept as final and exclusive the values by which we now live, he discovers a world of new values, as yet unexplored. This is an important factor in growth. For that reason he should not be rejected out of hand as though he were a backward child. But protest is especially fruitful when it rejects one order of values in the name of another that is higher or more Christian, more human, more effective. The good Christian protester will be most careful always to be uncompromisingly faithful to the will of the Lord, attentive to the requirements of the fellowship, open to the impulses of the Holy Spirit. The protesters "battle against juridicism, but not against justice; against authoritarianism, but not against authority; against legalism, but not against law; against rigidity, but not against order; against uniformity, but not against unity," said Cardinal Suenens.[31]

They do not challenge the Gospel message as such, but the garb in which it is decked out, the way it is lived in a Church which is heir to twenty centuries but which wants to and must continue to be alive, accepted, and loved in a new and radically changed cultural situation. Protesters must, however, have a clear awareness of their mission and responsibility. Therefore, says the Council, "they should subject all their undertakings to the test of God's will, which requires that projects should conform to the laws of the Church's evangelical mission. For loyalty toward Christ can never be divorced from loyalty toward His Church" (PO 14e/563).

4. It is also necessary to recognize that the will to preserve and the will to renew can easily become one-sided and change into sectarism. That is when conservatives turn into reactionaries and renovators into revolutionaries. Each group seeks to eliminate the other. This state of affairs is neither normal nor healthy, and ought to be avoided at any cost. Christian charity demands it. All, young and old, conservatives and renovators, all without exception ought to reflect calmly on this point before the Lord, and at the present time the avoidance of these extremes ought to be a constant intention in our prayers and plans. May the Spirit of the Lord keep up from all sectarism, be it reactionary or revolutionary! All of us must cultivate the dispositions which charity requires. We must take every step, make every sacrifice, to make it possible to have encounter and dialogue, mutual esteem, respect, and harmony "through the full recognition of lawful diversity" (GS 92b/306). Without love or apart from love even the most careful orthodoxy, even total fidelity, "would be nothing" (1 Cor 13:2). We lose everything when we lose love. It is the basic and most necessary gift of all, and must direct, vitalize, and lead to their goal all the other means of sanctification (cf. LG 42b/71). Faith without love is a body without a soul. Love ought to be the intention behind every initiative, the preoccupation guiding every action, the life in every word. It is patient and kind, not jealous; it is not prone to anger

nor does it brood over injuries; it excuses everything, believes everything, hopes for everything, puts up with everything (cf. 1 Cor 13:4-7).

5. Unfortunately the present wave of protest has given rise to some excesses that must be condemned. Paul VI is tireless in pointing them out. Some people give the impression of challenging the Church in its entirety as a visible, social institution. Such protest is synonymous with apostasy. Then men are criticizing the Church from outside it. That is the stance of the "third man," described some years back.[32] These people want to be Christians without a Church. The Church as an institution has disillusioned them. They are scandalized at the inadequate human instruments which the glorified Lord and his Spirit use. They do not understand that God habitually makes use of insignificant means in carrying out his plans (cf. 1 Cor 1:27-29). In this sense, too, the Church is a mystery. One is deluded, then, if one claims to be a Christian but denies the Church, for without the Church there is no Christianity. That is obviously the way the Lord wanted it. "Whosoever, therefore, knowing that the Catholic Church was made necessary by God through Jesus Christ, would refuse to enter her or to remain in her could not be saved" (LG 14a/32-33). That Church was "constituted and organized in the world as a society" by the Lord (LG 8b/23) and "provided . . . with those means which befit it as a visible and social unity" (LG 9f/26).

6. Even so, especially in our present situation, it is quite possible, and human, to err. Many of the doubts and questions felt today in Catholic circles are questions and uncertainties which were raised by the Protestant Reformers of the sixteenth century and by the Modernist intellectuals at the beginning of our own century. Instead of receiving a reply, they they found appeal being made against them to the authority of the pope. It may be that such a reaction was, in itself, legitimate, but it was not a reaction which necessarily resolved the objective difficulties. The principle of unconditional

obedience to the Magisterium does not automatically shed light on religious, theological, or cultural problems. It is usually the case that, far from settling crises, inquisitorial, repressive, and juridical methods only heighten and intensify them. As Newman observed, error deserves an answer, not a punishment. The counsellors whose advice is pleasing are not always the most objective and loyal ones. In our present cultural context, however, numerous new questions are being asked for which tradition and the hierarchy have no ready-made answers. Vatican II itself recognizes that "recent studies and findings of science, history, and philosophy raise new questions which influence life and demand new theological investigations" (GS 62b/268). Therefore the Council asks theologians, "through a sharing of resources and points of view . . . , to collaborate with men well versed in the other sciences" (GS 62i/270) and urges them to seek a deeper understanding of the faith "without neglecting close contact with [their] own times" (*ibid.*). By their position in the evolving world, laymen are more aware of these questions and feel more deeply the inadequacies of answers they regard as artificial. In such a situation a better answer can often be reached only through challenge, hesitation, and experience, all of which requires an atmosphere of freedom. It is highly important, indeed indispensable, that those in authority honestly look and listen and recognize, with the Council, that although the Church is guardian of the treasure of God's word, she fulfills her role "without always having at hand the solution to particular problems" and therefore "desires . . . to add the light of revealed truth to mankind's store of experience, so that the path which humanity has taken in recent times will not be a dark one" (GS 33c/232). There is no reason to panic, since truth is of its nature stronger than error. But "the truth cannot impose itself except by virtue of its own truth, as it makes its entrance into the mind at once quietly and with power" (DH 1e/677). It is not we, with our methods and institutions, but the Holy Spirit who

"move[s] the heart and turn[s] it to God, opening the eyes
of the mind and giving 'joy and ease to everyone in assenting
to the truth and believing it' " (DV 5/114).

7. We must trust the theologians and their work. Problems
are not solved by hiding them but by serious and deep study
of them. Faith itself seeks clear-minded theological investigation, and in this latter we must trust. If the magisterium is
to fulfill its role, it needs the work of theologians, who, in
turn, require freedom to study, think, speak, write, and communicate. Suspicion is being dissipated and friendly relations are being developed between bishops and theologians,
so that neither group will be left to its own resources. A law
can be promulgated by authority but a truth must be investi-
gated, and there will never be any scientific research that is
not open to the possibility of error. The theologians need freedom, stimulus, and understanding, rather than supervision,
suspicion, and warnings. As other sciences are possible and
make progress without the constant watchful presence of a
magisterial authority but rather with the help of mutual criticism among scientists themselves, so theological science must
be possible under the same system of mutual criticism by
theologians themselves. The first and specific duty of theologians as such is to investigate the truth; only secondarily do
they furnish help to the ecclesiastical magisterium. To expound the truth in terms which present-day man can understand is the basic and essential duty of the magisterium. There
was a time when the most effective remedy for lessening and
overcoming doctrinal crises was thought to be the simple condemnation of errors and, as far as possible, the silencing of
theologians and the prohibition of their books. This approach
was based on the simplistic supposition that the cause of such
evils was the bad will of thinkers. But thunder-bolts never
solve problems.

8. There is no reason for such negative attitudes as pessimism, despair, insecurity, and anxiety. There would be, indeed, if the Church were a purely human institution and if

everything depended on our watchfulness and initiative. But it is not men, but the Holy Spirit dwelling in the Church and in the hearts of the faithful, that leads the Church to the knowledge of the full truth, unifying her in fellowship and ministry, vitalizing and activating, rejuvenating and renewing her (cf. LG 4/16-17; 7h/21-22). "Although guided by human shepherds, her sheep are nevertheless ceaselessly led and nourished by Christ Himself, the Good Shepherd and the Prince of Shepherds" (LG 6b/18). In all truth, Christ continues, unchanging, to rule the visible structure of the Church "*through* the Supreme Pontiff and the bishops" (LG 14b/33). The latter are and must be only means, instruments, signs of Christ, the Shepherd and High Priest (LG 21d/41-42; PO 12b/558). This is why we have confidence in the Church. On this account, too, we remain calm and joyful, even when the Lord allows the ship of Peter to be tossed by storms. In his own good time the Lord will calm the tempest. We are not ourselves the saviors of the Church!

The Church and the Separated Churches or Ecclesial Communities

The encyclical *Mystici Corporis Christi* of Pius XII (1943) made an unqualified identification of the Catholic Church with the Mystical Body of Christ. In the encyclical *Humani generis* of 1950 Pius XII repeated the teaching that "the Mystical Body of Christ and the Roman Catholic Church are one and the same thing."[33] The position paper on the Church, which was presented to the Council Fathers in 1962 and discussed in the final days of the first session, affirmed solemnly in its first chapter ('The sacred synod therefore teaches and solemnly proclaims . . .") : "The Roman Catholic Church is the Mystical Body of Christ" (title of no. 7).[34] The official explanation of the text, as given by Bishop Franic on December 1, 1962, stressed this point: "The purpose of Chapter 1 is to show clearly . . . that there is no real distinction between the Mystical Body of Christ and the visible Church, but that the two names only point to different aspects of one and the same reality."[35] Another explanation (given by R. Gagnebet O.P. in the name of Cardinal Ottaviani) ran along similar lines: "The main purpose is to emphasize the real identity of the Mystical Body of Christ, as this is found on earth, and the catholic, apostolic, Roman Church." Gagnebet went on to insist: "If, then, the Council rejects this doctrine, it will be casting doubt on the doctrinal value of encyclicals and thus of the ordinary teaching authority of the Church. For almost all the bishops of the world now teach this doctrine."[36]

Against this view, which was in practice the official position of the Church, there was strong opposition at the Council. On that same day, December 1, 1962, Cardinal Liénart, the first to speak on the subject of the Church, had this to say:

"We must be very careful not to let formulas or ways of talking about the Church do an injustice to the mystery; for example, not to state the relationship and identity of the Roman Church with the Mystical Body as though the Mystical Body were to be found wholly within the confines of the Roman Church. For the Roman Church is the true Body of Christ but not coextensive with it. For to the Mystical Body belong all men who have been justified, inasmuch as no grace is given to men that is not the grace of Christ and no one is justified without being incorporated into Christ. To the Roman Church on the other hand only they belong who have received the sacrament of baptism and become its members and who have not renounced the bonds of faith and communion. The Mystical Body is thus much more inclusive than the Roman Church on earth. . . . And what of the separated Christians who through valid baptism have been buried in Christ in order to rise to supernatural life in him and to abide in him? I grieve that those outside the Roman Church do not share with us all the supernatural gifts which she dispenses; but I would not dare to say that they in no way belong to the Mystical Body of Christ, despite their not being incorporated into the Catholic Church. It is clear, then, that our Church, though it is the visible manifestation of the Mystical Body of Jesus Christ, cannot be absolutely and unqualifiedly identified with it."[37]

A few days later, on December 5, 1962, the then Cardinal Montini spoke: "I agree with those Fathers who find difficulty with the advisability of expressing the Mystical Body of Christ simply in the words 'Roman Church.' "[38] On October 3, 1963, Cardinal Lercaro said:

"The Church as a society and the Mystical Body express two distinct aspects which are fully and perfectly co-extensive as far as the essential order of things and the constitutive norm set by the divine Founder are concerned, but they cannot be similarly identified in the existential, historical order. In the latter order the two aspects do not always have the same extension; there is now a tension between them, and that tension will last until the end of history, when the identity and equivalence of Church and Mystical Body are finally effected and manifested. I am very much in agreement, then, with what the Bishop of Haarlem [van Dodewaard] has said in the name of the Conference of Dutch Bishops. If that view is not acceptable, I wish to propose that we affirm the real identity of Church and Mystical Body but qualify the statement by adding 'but from different points of view.' For if we affirm the identity without qualification, unwarranted conclusions can be drawn as we already know from some of the theological doctrines proposed in the wake of the encyclical *Humani Generis*."[39]

The documents of Vatican II did not, in fact, endorse the doctrine so firmly and insistently taught by Pius XII. *Lumen Gentium* states that "the society furnished with hierarchical agencies and the Mystical Body of Christ are not to be considered as two realities, nor are the visible assembly and the spiritual community, nor the earthly Church and the Church enriched with heavenly things. Rather they form one interlocked reality which is comprised of a divine and a human element" (LG 8a/22). The Council goes on to say that this Church is the one Church of Christ which the Creed proclaims to be one, holy, and catholic, and which our risen Savior entrusted to Peter as its shepherd and to him and the other Apostles that it might be spread abroad and governed, being intended, as it is, to be a pillar and mainstay of truth. The text continues: "This Church, constituted and organized in the world as a society, subsists in the Catholic Church, which is governed by the successor of Peter and by the bishops in union with that successor" (LG 8b/23). At an earlier stage the text had read: "This Church . . . *is* the Catholic Church." But, as the official explanation provided by the Theological Commission tells us, after long debate the *is* was replaced by *subsists in* "so as to be more consonant with the teaching about ecclesial elements to be found elsewhere than in the Roman Church." This important correction was preserved even after the vote on modifying the text, in which thirteen Fathers asked that the simple *is* be restored.

We have, then, the firm teaching that *the one Church, as Christ has intended, exists in historical form and is knowable as such, and that its concrete, existential form is the Church as this has been directed by the successor of Peter.* However, as the official explanation indicates, in the non-Catholic churches and ecclesial communities many "elements of sanctification and truth can be found" (LG 8b/23; these elements are listed in detail in LG 15/33-34 and in UR 3b/345-46). "Churchness," therefore cannot be simply identified with the Catholic Church, since elements of ecclesiality, and these "very many" and "most significant" (UR 3b/345), along with a genuine power to sanctify ('these actions can truly engender a life of grace": UR 3c/346), exist in fact and are active outside the visible limits of the Catholic Church. In other words, it can be said that the Church of Christ exists in its full form (with all the essential elements or ecclesial goods) in the Catholic Church and that it is to be found more or less incompletely and imperfectly (according to the number of essential ecclesial elements possessed) in the separated churches or ecclesial communities, which consequently have significance and importance in the mystery of salvation (cf. UR 3d/346).[40] In the vote on modifications, nineteen Fathers suggested that the text read: "subsists in an integral way in . . .": that is, the Church of Christ is to be found in a full and complete or integral way in the Catholic Church, the implication being that it is also to be found in the other churches, but in a less complete or imperfect way. The commission commented that this doctrine is presented further on: "They are fully incorporated into the society of the Church who . . ." (LG 14b/33). The same doctrine is clearly stated elsewhere: "It is through Christ's Catholic Church alone, which is the all-embracing means of salvation, that the fullness of the means of salvation can be obtained. It was to the apostolic college alone, of which Peter is the head, that we believe our Lord entrusted all the blessings of the New Covenant, in order to establish on earth the one Body of Christ into which all those should be fully incorporated who already belong in any way to God's People" (UR 3e/346).

Since, then, many highly significant eccesial elements of sanctification and truth exist outside the visible boundaries of the Catholic Church, even if they be less perfect and complete there, it follows that the true Church of Christ (or the Mystical Body of Christ) takes various concrete forms and in them works to save and sanctify. Consequently it is inaccurate to say with Pius XII, in his encyclical letters *Mystici Corporis Christi* and *Humani Generis*, that the Roman Catholic Church and the Mystical Body of Christ are one and the same reality. The Decree on Ecumenism is explicit: "Men who believe in Christ and have been properly baptized are brought into a certain, though imperfect, communion with the Catholic Church. . . . All those justified by faith through baptism are incorporated into Christ. They therefore have a right to be honored by the title of Christian, and are properly regarded as brothers in the Lord by the sons of the Catholic

Church" (UR 3a/345).

"Outside the Church there is no salvation"

The conciliar documents, said Paul VI in his letter of September 21, 1966, on the Theological Congress, "should be thought of as an impulse to a new journey, not as a goal achieved."[41] Vatican II, as we have seen, initiated an extraordinary openness to the values of truth, goodness, love, beauty, justice, and holiness that exist outside the visible structure of the Church, whether among non-Catholics or in the non-Christian world. We find now the open admission that "some, even very many, of the most significant elements or endowments which together go to build up and give life to the Church herself can exist outside the visible boundaries of the Catholic Church" (UR 3b/345); that not a few sacred actions of the separated brothers "can truly engender a life of grace, and can be rightly described as capable of providing access to the community of salvation" (UR 3c/346); and that, consequently, these separated churches and communities, though defective in some ways, "have by no means been deprived of significance and importance in the mystery of salvation. For the Spirit of Christ has not refrained from using them as means of salvation" (UR 3d/346). Therefore, "Catholics must joyfully acknowledge and esteem the truly Christian endowments from our common heritage which are to be found among our separated brethren" (UR 4h/349). "They [neophytes in the missions] should rightly consider that the [non-Catholic] brethren who believe in Christ are Christ's disciples, reborn in baptism, sharers with the People of God in many riches" (AG 15e/602).

This new way of speaking which the Twenty-First Ecumenical Council has adopted is difficult to harmonize with the text of the Seventeenth Ecumenical Council (the Council of Florence in its Decree for the Jacobites, 1442), where we read that "the holy Roman Church believes, professes, and preaches that 'no one remaining outside the Catholic Church, not just pagans,' but also Jews of heretics or schismatics, can become partakers of eternal life; but they will go to the 'everlasting fire which was prepared for the devil and his angels' (Matt. 25:41), unless before the end of life they are joined to the Church. For union with the body of the Church is of such importance that the sacraments of the Church are helpful to salvation only for those remaining in it; and fasts, almsgiving, other works of piety, and the exercise of Christian warfare bear eternal rewards for them alone. 'And no one can be saved, no matter how much alms he has given, even if he sheds his blood for the name of Christ, unless he remains in the bosom and unity of the Catholic Church' "[42] In contrast, Vatican II states that "in some real way they [non-Catholic Christians] are joined with us in the Holy Spirit, for to them also He gives His gifts and graces, and is thereby operative among them with His sanctifying power. Some indeed He has strengthened to the extent of the shedding of their blood" (LG 15b/34; cf. UR 4h/349).

The difference in language and especially in mentality and attitude is evident. The text of the Seventeenth Ecumenical Council can be justified only if it be understood and maintained on a purely ideal, abstract, non-existent, and non-real level where, by supposition (and the very supposition indicates the profound differences in mentalities!), all schismatics, heretics, Jews, and pagans are what they are by ill will and formal lack of proper dispositions towards the Catholic Church. That is to say, such men are supposed to be in a formal and subjectively sinful state of heresy, schism, and infidelity. Vatican II, of course, likewise teaches that "whosoever . . . , knowing that the Catholic Church was made necessary by God through Jesus Christ, would refuse to enter her or remain in her could not be saved" (LG 14a/32-33). But the basic restriction here expressed, a restriction required by justice, is not voiced in the Decree for the Jacobites (which rather seems even to suppose that some one could "shed his blood for the name of Christ" in a state of subjective bad

faith). We receive the impression that in former times bad
faith seems to have been presupposed, while good faith needed
to be proved in each instance. Today we would maintain
exactly the opposite: in every instance good faith is presupposed as long as bad faith is not proved. Vatican II says that
"one cannot impute the sin of separation to those who at
present are born into these Communities and are instilled
therein with Christ's faith. The Catholic Church accepts
them with respect and affection as brothers" (UR 32/345).
Vatican II therefore is situating its doctrine (or its manner
of formulating doctrine) on the real, concrete, or, as people
like to say today, existential level, which is quite different
from the abstract and ideal world in which the Council of
Florence moves. For this reason there is a profound difference
in the two Councils, a difference which resides not in their
doctrine as such but in their way of expressing the doctrine.
The example we have been adducing is one of the most typical.
If we do not pay close attention to these differences of mentality, which are always historically conditioned, we will find
it impossible to reconcile the doctrine of today with the doctrine of another age. It is not enough to read the texts in
isolation, apart from their historical circumstances and from
the necessary qualifications which these circumstances require (the famous *Sitz im Leben*, or vital context, of the Scriptural exegetes, holds for the exegesis of dogma as well), and
simply to restate the dogma as immutable. For then, as in
the example we have given, we could easily play the doctrine
of one Council off against the doctrine of another. New situations (or new signs of the times) require new formulations,
even in the field of dogma. It is for this reason that, in order
to carry out its mission, the Church "has always had the duty
of scrutinizing the signs of the times" (GS 4a/201); that
pastors and theologians must "hear, distinguish, and interpret
the many voices of our age" (GS 44d/246); and that theologians "are invited to seek continually for more suitable ways of
communicating doctrine to the men of their times" (GS 62c/

268). Simply to condemn these efforts as "dogmatic relativism" and to cling comfortably and intransigently to ready-made, received formulas (tradition with a small *t*) may be easy but it means a retreat to the ghetto and a refusal to let the Church be "the universal sacrament of salvation" which she claims she seeks to be and must be (LG 48b/79; GS 45a/247; AG 1a/584; 5b/589).

The documents of Vatican II provide us with the following principles on *the real possibility of supernatural salvation even for non-Christians*:

1. Even after sin God never abandons mankind but always offers to each individual the helps he needs for salvation. In the Dogmatic Constitution on Revelation we read that after the fall of the first parents God "ceaselessly kept the human race in His care, in order to give eternal life to those who perseveringly do good in search of salvation" (DV 33/112). And in the Dogmatic Constitution on the Church the Council teaches that God's "plan was to dignify men with a participation in His own divine life. He did not abandon men after they had fallen in Adam, but ceaselessly offered them helps to salvation, in anticipation of Christ the Redeemer" (LG 2a/15).

2. God has his ways, known to him alone, of saving even non-Christians. The Constitution on the Church in the Modern World is particularly strong on this point. After pointing out that all ought to advance towards the glorious resurrection, the Council teaches: "All this holds true not only for Christians, but for all men of good will in whose hearts grace works in an unseen way. For, since Christ died for all men, and since the ultimate vocation of man is in fact one, and divine, we ought to believe that the Holy Spirit in a manner known only to God offers to every man the possibility of being associated with this paschal mystery" (22f/221-22). In the Decree on the Missions the Council again proclaims that "God in ways known to Himself can lead those inculpably ignorant of the gospel to that faith without which it is impossible to

please Him" (AG 7c/593). A little earlier the same document says that the universal design of God for the salvation of mankind can be accomplished "in the soul of a man, with a kind of secrecy" or "through those multiple endeavors, including religious ones, by which men search for God, groping for Him that they may by chance find Him (though He is not far from any one of us)" (AG 3a/586).

3. In saving and sanctifying men God is not limited to the sacraments and ministries of the Church. The Constitution on the Church teaches that "it is not only through the sacraments and Church ministries that the . . . Holy Spirit sanctifies and leads the People of God and enriches it with virtues" (LG 12c/30). The Council is aware that "doubtless, the Holy Spirit was already at work in the world before Christ was glorified" (AG 4a/587) and that even now the Holy Spirit continues to open the hearts of non-Christians (AG 13a/600).

4. "Those also can attain to everlasting salvation who through no fault of their own do not know the gospel of Christ or His Church, yet sincerely seek God and, moved by grace, strive by their deeds to do His will as it is known to them through the dictates of conscience" (LG 16c/35). For, when he enters into his own heart, "God, who probes the heart, awaits him there. There he discerns his proper destiny beneath the eyes of God" (GS 14c/212). For "conscience is the most secret core and sanctuary of a man. There he is alone with God, whose voice echoes in his depths" (GS 16b/213). Even if conscience should err through invincible ignorance—and the Council allows that this may happen frequently—it does so "without losing its dignity" (GS 16c/214): "The person in error . . . never loses the dignity of being a person, even when he is flawed by false or inadequate religious notions. God alone is the judge and searcher of hearts; for that reason he forbids us to make judgments about the internal guilt of anyone" (GS 28b/227). We have the example of the Apostles who "showed respect for weaker souls even though these persons were in error. Thus they made it plain

that 'every one of us will render an account of himself to God' (Rom. 14:12)" (DH 11g/691). Consequently, the Council proclaims as universal and inviolable each person's "right . . . to activity in accord with the unright norm of one's own conscience" (GS 26b/225). Although the ideal is to follow "right and true judgments of conscience" (DH 3a/680), Vatican II knows that in practice it is enough for these judgments to be "right" (without necessarily being "true"), as the texts we have been quoting indicate.

5. The reason for this is that "divine Providence [does not] deny the help necessary for salvation to those who, without blame on their part, have not yet arrived at an explicit knowledge of God, but who strive to live a good life thanks to His grace" (LG 16c/35). For "God Himself [is not] far distant from those who in shadows and images seek the unknown God" (LG 16b/35). "The plan of salvation also includes" all of them (*ibid.*)

6. In the light of these principles Vatican II, in various documents, assigns a positive value to non-Christian or pagan religious: all of them possess elements that are good, true, beautiful, just, and holy, even if these elements be mingled with others that are unacceptable, evil, or erroneous. The Constitution on the Church declares: "Whatever goodness or truth is found among them is looked upon by the Church as a preparation for the gospel. She regards such qualities as given by Him who enlightens all men so that they may finally have life" (LG 16c/35). For the "ways of conduct and of life" and the "rules and teachings" of non-Christians "often reflect a ray of that Truth which enlightens all men" (NA 2e/662). In the Decree on the Missions the Council bids missionaries to become "familiar with the national and religious traditions [of the people being evangelized], gladly and reverently laying bare the seeds of the Word which lie hidden in them" (AG 11b/597-98), inasmuch as "whatever truth and grace are to be found among the nations . . . [are] a sort of secret presence of God" (AG 9c/595-96). The many efforts

by which men search for God, groping for him, may "through the kindly workings of divine Providence . . . sometimes serve as a guidance course toward the true God, or as a preparation for the gospel" (AG 3a/586). Note 7 on this last passage gives a number of patristic texts on the ceaseless presence of the Word among men.

It is clear that, for all the surprising and unusual wealth of texts on this point, Vatican II is not simply guaranteeing the salvation of all men. In the Constitution on the Church, which we have several times cited here, the Council notes that "rather often men, deceived by the Evil One, have become caught up in a futile reasoning and have exchanged the truth of God for a lie, serving the creature rather than the Creator (cf. Rom. 1:21,25). Or some there are who, living and dying in a world without God, are subject to utter hopelessness" (LG 16d/35). In addition, the texts we have quoted make it clear that the Council always requires loyal cooperation with grace, a sincere search, and good will on man's part. Nonetheless it cannot be denied that the perspective in which the Councily situates itself is certainly positive and optimistic. If we apply the principles proposed by the Council to the countless children who die unbaptized, we must surely think that the concept of "Limbo" which in the last analysis is always a form of "hell" and final condemnation) will be difficult to maintain in the future. God has his ways, known only to himself (GS 22f/222; AG 7c/593), for saving men who through no fault of their own do not, and cannot, walk the known path that has been revealed by God to mankind (cf. DH 1d/677). — In addition to reaffirming the possibility of eternal damnation, the Council says in unqualified terms that "whosoever . . . knowing that the Catholic Church was made necessary by God through Jesus Christ, would refuse to enter her or remain in her could not be saved" (LG 14a/32-33), and that "he is not saved, . . . who, though he is part of the body of the Church, does not persevere in charity. He remains indeed in the bosom of the Church, but, as it were, only in a 'bodily' manner and not 'in his heart' " (LG 14b/33).

All these previous doctrinal elements from Vatican II lead us, however, to an obvious conclusion: Outside the Church (that is: outside the visible structure of the Catholic Church as it has taken concrete shape in history) there is salvation! Today we are even forbidden to understand the ancient axiom, "Outside the Church there is no salvation," in the sense intended by St. Cyprian, its author,[43] or St. Augustine[44] or the Creed prescribed by Innocent III for the Waldensians[45] or the Fourth Lateran Council[46] or Boniface VIII[47] or the Decree for the Jacobites of the Council of Florence, which we have already quoted. We are here confronted with one of those cases (there are others) of defective formulation of doctrine, to which the Decree on Ecumenism refers (UR 6b/350). It is in such cases that the theologian is invited by the Constitution on the Church in the Modern World to search for a formulation that is more suited for communicating the doctrine to contemporary man and more intelligible and acceptable (GS 62c/268-69). Father Congar therefore suggests that instead of "Outside the Church, no salvation," we adopt the expression "the Church, universal sacrament of salvation," an expression which, as we have seen, occurs several times in the documents of Vatican II.

What Cyprian's formula really aims at bringing home to us is two undoubtedly Biblical truths: The Church is the only created institution which God has commissioned to bring to all men the salvation given in and through Christ (cf. DH 1d/677; and especially DH 14b-c/694-95); and the Church received from its Founder and Lord all that is required for bringing salvation to the whole of mankind. It remains true, for Vatican II, that "the Church, now sojourning in earth as an exile, is necessary for salvation" (LG 14a/32), in the sense that "it is through Christ's Catholic Church alone, which is the all-embracing means of salvation, that the fullness of the means of salvation can be obtained" (UR 3e/346). But today, after the geographical and anthropological discoveries which the modern era has brought with it, and now that the Constantinian era is over and done with, the Church is painfully aware of being only a little flock set amid a vast world and an enormous multitude of men, many of whom are men of good and honest will. But at the same time it finds in itself a new missionary urge and discovers itself to be, by God's will, the universal sacrament of salvation. Consequently the two Biblical and traditional truths contained in the axiom: "Outside the Church there is no salvation," are much better expressed in the formula: "The Church, universal sacrament of salvation." For, this Messianic people, although it does not actually include all men, and may more than once look like a small flock, is nonetheless a sure and lasting seed of unity, hope, and salvation for the whole human race" (LG 9e/26).

This last statement of the Council invites us to penetrate more deeply into the meaning of the Church as a "little flock" in the vast world of men. In the light of the law of representation as it works in the divine plan, we shall better understand an important aspect of the true nature of the Church.

Notes for Chapter 2

¹ In an address on the priestly people of God, February 9, 1966, Paul VI formulated the principle as follows: "God does not save us apart from this purpose for the collectivity, but within a plan in which each individual is part of a community which God chooses and helps" (*Osservatore Romano,* February 10, 1966). In an earlier discourse, *Quando noi abbiamo: On the People of God,* September 29, 1965, he had said: "God saves man by carrying out a historical plan for a community" (*Osservatore Romano,* October 1, 1965). — In view of what will be said further on of the possibility of supernatural salvation for non-Christians (that is, for those who do not consciously take part in such a historical plan for a community), this principle must be understood as expressing the ordinary norm for those who in fact seek to know and put into effect the plan of God. As we shall see, the same Council which teaches that "God himself has made known to mankind the

way in which men are to serve him, and thus be saved in Christ and come to blessedness" (DH 1d/676-77) also speaks without reservation of positive ways of supernatural salvation that are known to God alone (cf. GS 22f/22i; AG 7c/595).

[2] *Acta Synodalia,* II/1, p. 455.

[3] Paul VI, *Salvete Fratres: Address to the Council Fathers at the Opening of the Second Session,* September 29, 1963, in *TPS,* 9 (1963-64), 131. In a speech to the Council, December 5, 1962 (thirty-fourth general meeting), Cardinal Montini had already spoken in the same vein: "I was glad to hear the Council praising St. Joseph, patron of the Church; still more gladly do I hear that the Council will honor the Blessed Virgin Mary as Mother of the Church. Most of all, however, would I be gladdened, as I think all the Fathers would be, if this gathering would undertake to celebrate our Lord Jesus Christ in a solemn way. For the Church is the continuation of Jesus Christ; from him her life comes; to him her life is directed. . . . Great emphasis, then, is to put on the doctrine of the relations between the Church and Christ. It should be said, in a way that will be clear to all, that the Church is fully aware that she can do nothing of herself but receives all from Jesus Christ, and that she acts effectively because Jesus Christ lives and acts in her. The Church is not only a society or community established by Christ the Lord; she is also an instrument in which he is secretly present, acting to accomplish the salvation of men by teaching, sacramental sanctification, and a pastoral care that is filled with the spirit of the Good Shepherd" (*Acta Synodalia,* I/4, p. 292)

[5] Pius XII, Mystici Corporis, no. 92, in *Selected Letters and Addresses of Pius XII* (London: Catholic Truth Society, 1949), p. 82. (Henceforth cited as *Selected Letters.*)

[6] John XXIII, *La grande aspettazione,* September 11, 1962, in *AAS,* 54 (1962), 685.

[7] Cf. Hugo Rahner, S.J., *"Mysterium Lunae," Zeitschrift fur katholische Theologie,* 63 (1939), 311-49 and 428-42; 64 (1940), 61-80 and 121-31. There is a shorter treatment in Rahner's *Greek Myths and Christian Mystery,* tr. by Brian Batthershaw (New York: Harper & Row, 1963). Cf. also Henri de Lubac, S.J., *The Church: Paradox and Mystery,* tr. by James R. Duane (Staten Island, N.Y.: Alba House, 1969), pp. 16-18, for a brief summation of what Rahner has to say. The words of Didymus are from his *In Psalmos,* 71:5 (PG 39:1465).

[8] On the concept of "sacrament" as applied to the Church, cf., e.g., Edward Schillebeeckx, O.P., *Christ the Sacrament of the Encounter with God,* tr. by Paul Barrett O.P. et al. (New York: Sheed & Ward, 1963), pp. 47-54.

[9] Council of Trent, Decree on the Eucharist, DS, 1639 (D, 876); *TCT,* no. 721, p. 282.

[10] *Acta Synodalia,* II/1, pp. 455-56.

[11] Cf. Gérard Philips, *L'Eglise et son mystère au deuxième Concile du Vatican: Histoire, texte, et commentaire de la Constitution "Lumen*

Gentium" (Paris: Desclee, 1967-68), vol. 1, p. 91.

[12] Report of the Section on Unity, Third Assembly of the World Council of Churches, 1961, in *The New Delhi Report,* ed. by W. A. Visser 't Hooft (New York: Association Press, 1962), p. 116. Also in *A Documentary History of the Faith and Order Movement, 1927-1963,* ed. by Lukas Vischer (St. Louis: Bethany Press, 1963), pp. 144-45.

[13] Paul VI, *In questi incontri settimanali: An Allocution on the Holy Spirit in the Church,* May 18, 1966, in *Osservatore Romano,* May 19, 1966.

[14] Motu Proprio, *Ecclesiae Sanctae: On Implementing Four Decrees of the Council,* August 6, 1966, in *TPS,* 11 (1966), 397.

[15] On the origin of the expression "Mystical Body of Christ," cf. Estêvao Bettencourt, "A doutrina do Corpo Mistico no pensamento patristico e medieval," *Revista Eclesiástica Brasileira,* 19 (1959), 289-309. Here we learn that as late as the Berengarian debate (eleventh century) the "mystical body" of Christ meant the Eucharist; only later did it come to mean the Church. Even when it did, the addition of "mystical" to the Scriptural "body of Christ which is the Church" initially simply emphasized the traditional doctrine that the Eucharist signifies the Church and the ecclesial body is symbolized by the Eucharistic body; "mystical" was, as it were, a contraction of "mystically signified." In the thirteenth and fourteenth centuries "mystical body of Christ" became a common designation for the Church and was opposed to "true body of Christ," that is, the Eucharist. From the fourteenth century on, the phrase began to be applied to the Church independently of any reference to the Eucharist.

[16] Paul VI, *Noi invitiamo: Address to a General Audience,* November 16, 1966, in *TPS,* 12 (1967), 56-58.

[17] St. Augustine, *Christian Instruction,* tr. by John J. Gavigan O.S.A. (*The Fathers of the Church,* 4; New York, CIMA, 1947), p. 61.

[18] St. Robert Bellarmine, *Controversiae,* vol. II, book 3, chapter 2.

[19] *Acta Synodalia,* I/4, p. 107.

[20] DS, 1639 (D, 876); *TCT,* no. 721, p. 282.

[21] Cf. Ferdinand Holböck, "Das Mysterium der Kirche in dogmatischer Sicht," in Ferdinand Holböck and Thomas Sartory (eds.), *Mysterium der Kirche in der Sicht der theologischen Disziplinen* (Salzburg: Otto Müller, 1962), I, pp. 234-39.

[22] Cf. Pius XII, *Mystici Corporis,* no. 14, in *Selected Letters,* p. 58.

[23] This dualism, too, is criticized in *Mystici Corporis,* no. 63 (*Selected Letters,* p. 84).

[24] DS, 301 (D, 148); *TCT,* no. 414, p. 172.

[25] Gregory XVI, *Mirari vos,* in *Papal Teachings on the Church,* tr. by E. O'Gorman, R.S.C.J. (Boston, St. Paul Editions, 1962), p. 126.

[26] Paul VI, *Salvete Fratres,* September 29, 1963, in *TPS,* 9 (1963-64), 133.

[27] Paul VI, *Quando Noi Ci vediamo: Address to a General Audience,* August 10, 1966, in *TPS,* 11 (1966), 227.

[28] This was the title of an unfortunate book by Sérgio Zanella (*A Igreja Traida* [Sao Paulo, 1968]).

[29] Paul VI, *Salvete Fratres*, in TPS, 9 (1963-64), 134.

[30] Cardinal Suenens, interview of May 15, 1969, in José de Broucker (ed.), *The Suenens Dossier* (Notre Dame: Fides, 1970), p. 24.

[31] *Op. cit.*, p. 42.

[32] François Roustang S.J., "Le troisième homme," *Christus* (Paris), 13 (1966), 561-67.

[33] Pius XII, *Humani generis*, in *Catholic Mind*, 48 (1950), 695.

[34] *Acta Synodalia* I/4, p. 15.

[35] *Acta Synodalia* I/4, p. 122.

[36] Note that Pius XI, in the strong encyclical *Mortalium animos* of January 6, 1928, had taught that non-Catholic Christians are not members of the Mystical Body or linked to Christ: "Whoever therefore is not united with it [Christ's Mystical Body, the Church] is not a member of it nor does he communicate with the Head who is Christ" (Pius XI, *Encyclical Letter Mortalium Animos: The Promotion of True Religious Unity* [Washington, D.C.: National Catholic Welfare Conference, 1928], p. 15).

[37] *Acta Synodalia*, I/4, p. 126-27.

[38] *Acta Synodalia*, /I4, p. 294, note 4.

[39] *Acta Synodalia*, II/2, p. 10.

[40] But we should not forget that this situation "openly contradicts the will of Christ" (UR 1a/341) and is "the sin of separation," for which, at times, men of both sides were to blame," that is, even on the Catholic side (UR 3a/345).

[41] Paul VI, *Cum iam appropinquat: Letter to Cardinal Pizzardo on the Opening of the International Congress on the Theology of Vatican II*, September 21, 1966, in *AAS*, 58 (1966), 878.

[42] DS, 1351 (D, 714); *TCT*, no. 165, p. 78. The first and last quotations in the text are from Fulgentius of Ruspe, *De fide liber ad Petrum*, ch. 39, nos. 79 and 80 (PL, 65:704A and 704B).

[43] St. Cyprian, *De catholicae ecclesiae unitate*, ch. 6 (PL, 4:518-20); cf. *Ep. 73 ad Jubaianum*, 21 (PL, 3:1123).

[44] St. Augustine, *Sermo ad Caesariensis ecclesiae plebem* (PL, 43:659): "Outside the Catholic Church you can find everything except salvation. You can have the honor of the episcopacy and you may have the sacraments; you may sing Alleluja and answer Amen; you may have the gospel; you may have faith in the name of the Father and the Son and the Holy Spirit and preach that faith. But only in the Catholic Church can you have salvation."

[45] Innocent III, *Ep. ad Archiepiscopum Terraconensem*, December 18, 1208, enclosing profession of faith to be made by the Waldensians: "We believe in our heart and profess with our lips the one Church, not a church of heretics, but the holy, Roman, Catholic, apostolic Church. We believe that outside this Church no one is saved" (DS, 792 [D, 423]; *TCT*, no. 150, p. 72).

[46] Fourth Lateran Council: "Indeed there is but one universal Church of the faithful outside which no one at all is saved" (DS, 802 [D, 430]; *TCT*, no. 151, p. 72).

[47] Boniface VIII, Bull *Unam sanctam* (A.D. 1302): "We are compelled in virtue of our faith to believe and maintain that there is only one Catholic Church, and that one apostolic. This we firmly believe and profess without qualification. Outside this Church there is no salvation and no remission of sins" (DS, 870 [D, 468]; *TCT,* no. 153, p. 73.

[48] Yves M. J. Congar O.P., in the collection of essays by various writers, *L'Eglise aujourd'hui* (Paris: Desclée, 1967), pp. 28-29.

Chapter 3

The Church and the
Law of Representation

The concept of "representation" is here to be studied from
the theological viewpoint of its functioning in the relationship of man with God or in the encounter of God with man.
The experience of religious men is at one with the data of
divine revelation in affirming that there is normally no immediate, direct, and purely individual relationship of man
with God. Rather, man reaches God through others who are
mediators, priests, or representatives. God, correspondingly,
is accustomed to use mediators or representatives in revealing himself to men, in inviting them to communion with himself, and in receiving them into that communion. *Mediation
seems to be a basic factor in God's action and in our relationship with God.* Such is the clearest and most important
conclusion reached by Josef Scharbert in his long study of
mediators of salvation in the Old Testament and the ancient
Near East.[1] Although the Old Testament knows special cases

of immediate encounter of men with God, the general rule seems to be that God gives men his grace through other men who act as instruments of his saving action; he chooses some, shows his kindness to them, and heaps his graces upon them so that through them he may offer salvation to others. Thus, in their relations with God, men depend upon each other. Those who are specially chosen and graced would be nothing without their brothers, for they are chosen and enriched in order to open to others the way to God and to salvation. Correspondingly, the great mass of the others would be unable to enter into contact with God and his blessings, if God had not manifested his saving will to some at least of their brothers. There would have been no choosing of the patriarchs if God had not intended to make Israel a convenanted people with a view to bestowing his blessings on the gentiles. There would have been no calling of Moses or Joshua or the Judges or the prophets, there would have been no choosing of the house of David or of the generations of priests, if God had not intended the salvation of the people and of mankind. There would have been no covenant with Israel, if God had not intended to reveal to the pagans, through this people, his redemptive power and his merciful will to save. That is how the author of the Letter to the Hebrews understands the function of a mediator: "taken from among men and made their representative before God, . . . He is able to deal patiently with erring sinners, for he himself is beset by weakness" (Heb 5:1-2). God effects his salvation in the many through the few, in order to show forth his power to bless and redeem.

Oscar Cullmann, who has dedicated so much of his attention to the history of salvation, insists on the "notably theological" principle at work in the divine economy of salvation: "the election of a minority for the redemption of the whole."[2] The principle is the principle of representation. Cullmann reminds us that at the level of creation man is shown to be a kind of representative of the Creator, when he receives a commission to master the earth and all that is in it and

especially when by his sin he affects all creation, the latter
now being cursed because of man's actions. The principle of
representation will, at a next stage, clearly determine the un-
folding of salvation. As the destiny of all creation depended
on the attitude of man, so the history of *one* people will now
be determinative for the salvation of *all* men. In order to
save mankind God will choose out of sinful mankind a single
community, the Israelite people which originates in Abraham.
Abraham received a promise: "All the communities of the
earth shall find blessing in you" (Gen 12:3; 18:18; 22:18).
The history of salvation then unfolds in accordance with the
same principle of divine choice and human representation,
with the numbers of representatives being steadily lessened.
Since the people of Israel did not as a whole understand its
mission, it will be replaced by the "remnant of Jacob" (cf.
Is 1:9; 10:21). This remnant in turn will continue to decrease
in size until finally it is concentrated in a *single* person who,
all by himself, will carry out the salvific mission of Israel: the
"servant of Jahweh" (Is 53, 1-12), the "Son of Man" (Dan
7:13-14), Jesus Christ, who will, simultaneously, fulfill the
mission of the suffering servant of God and the Son of man,
and, through his death and resurrection, accomplish fully the
purpose for which God chose the people of Israel.

Cullman thus shows how the history of salvation develops
initially through a progressive reduction: mankind—people of
God—remnant of Jacob—Christ. Multiplicity was still ordered to unity, for Jesus, as Christ of Israel, became redeemer
of mankind and even of creation itself. In Christ the history
of salvation reaches its central point and will henceforth develop in a contrary movement of progressive growth from one
to many, in such a way that the "many" always stand in the
place of the one, who is Christ. Now the way goes from Christ
to those who believe in him and recognize themselves to be
redeemed through faith in his vicarious death for them. It
leads to the Apostles and to the Church which is the Body of
Christ and now must fulfill, in regard to all mankind, the

mission of the "remnant," of the "holy people." Thereby it
leads to a human race that is redeemed in the kingdom of
God and to the redeemed creation of the new heavens and the
new earth. The whole of this all-embracing movement with
its successively opposite directions is admirably expressed in
a symbolic way by the Christian chronology, which takes the
year of Jesus' birth as the year 1, making the whole previous
period move towards him by counting backwards and referring
the whole following period to the same initial year. Christ
is the center of time.

The Servant of Jahweh

The fullest expression of the law of representation is to be
found in the *Ebed Jahweh*, the suffering servant of God, who
is represented by Second Isaiah in the so-called "songs of the
servant of Jahweh" (Is 42:1-4; 50:4-11; 52:13-53:12) as being an extraordinary minister of God, sent as teacher and
lawgiver; in the fulfillment of his mission he is greatly burdened, meets intense opposition, suffers, and even dies as a
victim of expiation for the sins of others. The servant of
Jahweh shatters all nationalistic limitations and becomes a
light to enlighten the nations; his salvific, redemptive action
touches all, even at the ends of the earth. "Upon [him] I
have put my spirit; he shall bring forth justice to the nations"
(42:1); "I will make you a light to the nations, that my salvation may reach to the ends of the earth" (49:6). It is above
all in chapter 53:3-12 that the servant of Jahweh appears as
the great Representative:

He was spurned and avoided by men,
    a man of suffering, accustomed to infirmity,
One of those from whom men hide their faces,
    spurned, and we held him in no esteem.
Yet it was our infirmities that he bore,
    our sufferings that he endured,
While we thought of him as stricken,

as one smitten by God and afflicted.
But he was pierced for our offenses,
   crushed for our sins;
Upon him was the chastisement that makes us whole,
   by his stripes we were healed.
We had all gone astray like sheep,
   each following his own way;
But the Lord laid upon him
   the guilt of us all.
Though he was harshly treated, he submitted
   and opened not his mouth;
Like a lamb led to the slaughter
   or a sheep before the shearers,
   he was silent and opened not his mouth. . . .
If he gives his life as an offering for sin,
   he shall see his descendants in a long life,
   and the will of the Lord shall be accomplished through him.
Because of his afflictions
   he shall see the light in fulness of days;
Through his suffering, my servant shall justify many,
   and their guilt he shall bear.
Therefore I will give him his portion among the great,
   and he shall divide the spoils with the mighty,
Because he surrendered himself to death
   and was counted with the wicked;
And he shall take away the sins of many,
   and win pardon for their offenses.

The whole Christian tradition, and even the older Jahweh
tradition, sees in the servant of Jahweh a prefiguring of the
Messiah. The New Testament is before all else a theology
of representation. Today it seems clear that the oldest
Christology of the Church at Jerusalem is a theology centered on the servant of Jahweh.[3] That Christ is our representative was the basic conviction of the early Christians: "For
our sakes God made him who did not know sin, to be sin, so

that in him we might become the very holiness of God" (2 Cor 5:21). "Christ has delivered us from the power of the law's curse by himself becoming a curse for us" (Gal 3:13). On this account, "he became the source of eternal salvation for all who obey him" (Heb 5:9). For "the Son of Man has not come to be served but to serve—to give his life in ransom for the many" (Mk 10:45).

Human Conditions for Representations

The human being is not born a complete and finished product. He needs a long time to grow and become adult and fully responsible. Only gradually, with effort, and with the constant help of others does he succeed in activating his own potentialities, faculties, abilities, and aptitudes. While thus "growing" (in the many senses of this term) he is naturally dependent on others. "To grow" means to fulfill oneself, to actuate one's virtualities, broaden one's potentialities, develop one's faculties, increase one's capacities, and effectively apply one's aptitudes. "To grow" means to achieve an ever fuller self-identity, to become independent, to become oneself, to become "adult." But even when the human being is fully adult and developed, he always continues to be related in many ways to others from whom he receives for his own sake and to whom he gives of himself. He is by nature a social being, that is, from others and for others. To be social means both dependence and fulfillment, contingency and greatness. He grows in the measure that he receives from others and in the measure that he goes out of himself and gives of himself to others. In this dialectical interplay of receiving and giving, being filled and being emptied, the human being encounters himself and achieves self-identity. For, as we read in the prayer of St. Francis of Assisi, "it is in giving that we receive, it is in pardoning that we are pardoned, and it is in dying that we are born to eternal life." Vatican II draws a daring comparison with the Holy Trinity: as each Person in God so lives in the others that his very being is constituted by this relationship, so man, who is made in the image of the one and triune God, "cannot fully find himself except through a sincere gift of himself" (GS 24c/223). Or, as Christ puts it, "Whoever tries to preserve his life will lose it; whoever loses it will keep it" (Lk 17:33).

In this variable inter-human relationship we are to see the ultimate basis of the law of representation. Because man is a contingent, dependent being, he needs representatives if he is to find his own true identity. When he is a minor or ill or absent in some fashion, he needs some one to take his place or act for him. To this phenomenon we give the name "representation." But representation is not simply a synonym for "substitution." Dorothee Sölle rightly calls attention to the great difference there is between "representation" and "substitution."[4] Representation is a provisional standing-in-the-place of one person by another; substitution is a definitive exchange made for a being that has been turned into an object, as though it (he) were already non-existent or dead. The representative's role is provisional, temporary, interim, passing; the substitute's role is final and permanent. The representative's role is conditional, limited, partial, and supplemental; the substitute's is unlimited and total. The representative is aware that he stands in the place of a living being, a person with a name and rights, who must find himself or rediscover himself and take or regain his place or function; the substitute simply replaces another whom he judges as henceforth useless, without name or rights, a dead thing. Representation is possible only in a context of temporality and the provisional, or, in ontological terms, of minority, weakness, absence, illness, or some other form of dependence. Only a being that lives in time can be represented; for something outside of time there can only be substitution. Only a being that is a person and does not seek to abandon himself and his identity can be represented. To be a person is an essential presupposition of being represented. Whatever is turned into a thing, an object, can be substituted for, but not represented.

Any representation can, however, turn into a substitution when it pre-empts the place of the other and makes it no longer available. Consequently, the desire of finding a representative is accompanied by the fear of finding only a substitute. He who is represented runs the risk of being substituted for.

Today we are very sensitive to the difference between person and thing, and we react strongly against any effort or tendency to reduce us to simple objects. As a person, the human being is always irreplaceable but he is representable. Dorothee Sölle lays great stress on this principle: "Man is irreplaceable yet representable."[5] Each human person therefore receives from his Creator a place and a mission in the world; in taking this place or exercising this mission he is irreplaceable, but, since he can temporarily fail or be deficient, he is representable as long as he lives.

To be a person and to exist in time are, then, the essential conditions required for being represented. Since he is irreplaceable yet can be represented, man gains time and can hope. His irreplaceability in time is the basis for his capacity to be represented. Only what is irreplaceable is representable. Representation is thus a guarantee of identity. Representation is salvation and restores the person to himself, to his place and mission. The dependent human person who does not want to lose his identity has an unqualified need of representation and can acquire it as long as he exists in time. On the other hand, the absolute dependence of the person represented brings a lessening of the person, and the exclusive responsibility of the representative brings with it an evident dominion over the one represented. Representation can thus stifle the one represented and can evolve into a simple substitution. The dependent person who is not disposed to accept his eventual responsibilities seeks to cling to hs position as a minor; minority then ceases to be a temporary stage and turns into infantilism and total dependence. The person who seeks only to be "redeemed" without accepting responsibility, who

seeks only to be represented without himself in turn becoming
a representative, will eventually be willing to pay too high a
price: he will renounce responsible action and leave the world
to its fate. Being represented is, then, correlative with accepting responsibility. Anyone who receives must be disposed to
give. As long as we live in time we can and ought, in normal
circumstances, be both represented (in order to receive from
others) and representative (in order to give to others). A
man wins self-identity in the measure that he goes out of
himself and takes an interest in the identity of others.

The Magical Concept of Representation

In the religious sphere the principle of representation is almost always vitiated and deformed by magic. Representation
is then turned into an objective process and becomes pure substitution. In magical thought man finds his representative in
an image (a "representation"), and everything that happens
to the image is transferred by magic to the man. In Brazil we
have examples of such "imitative, symbolic socery," especially
in Umbandism. This kind of imitative magic is based on the
occultists' law of "correspondence": what exists above is like
what exists below, and vice versa. It is also based on the law
that the effect is like the cause: by imitating the result desired, you bring the originating cause of that result into play.
People therefore try to imitate the desired effect by making
images or dolls which represent the person in mind and by
doing to the image what they would like to do to the person.
People even go so far as to take the doll to the cemetery and
bury it.[6]

The Old Testament "scapegoat" is evidence of a view of
representation that is based upon imitative magic. We are
told that Aaron is to lay both hands on the head of the live
goat and "confess over it all the sinful faults and transgres-
sions of the Israelites, and so put them on the goat's head.
He shall then have it led into the desert by an attendant.
Since the goat is to carry off their iniquities to an isolated

region, it must be sent away into the desert" (Lev 16:21-22).

In such magical conceptions the "representative" is always a thing or is at least objectified (sin, for example, is objectified, being treated as if it were a thing, as we can see from the case of the scapegoat). Magic really deals only with substitutions, for it is has no place for the personal, for the provisional, conditional, and supplemental, which are constitutive elements in authentic representation.

Not all representation in the Old Testament is magical, however.[7] In fact the scapegoat must be regarded as an exception, an alien intrusion. It is from the Old Testament, after all, that we derive the imposing figure of the suffering servant of God and the idea of a vicarious action that is not substitutional but temporary, suppletory, and genuinely representational.

Application of the Concept of Representation to Christ

We have seen that if man is to be able to achieve fullfillment and find his own identity, he has need of representation and that such representation is not simply a need felt by reason as a conclusion from human contingency but ought to be the decisive event of human life as such. The search for an authentic representative who makes no claim to become instead a substitute seems to be at the heart of anthropology, and the answer to the need felt, the question asked, is in Christology. Christ is the answer to the basic question which man raises because he is man. Christ is our representative: temporary, conditional, suppletory. For even in the presence of Christ we continue to be persons: irreplaceable, irreducible. Christ therefore cannot be our substitute (final and total) but only our representative (temporary, conditional, suppletory, incomplete). Exaggeration in Christology would make Christ a substitute and do away with the necessary respect for our personality and irreplaceability; our persons would be turned into things and what is irreplaceable in us would be done away with or reduced to insignificance. Our irreplaceable dignity requires a representative, not a substitute; a representative who provisionally acts in our place to help us to grow or to be healed and fulfilled. Christ believes, hopes, loves, prays, and suffers in our stead, but in such a way that he brings us gradually to believe, hope, love, pray, and suffer in our own name and even, when we achieve greater self-identity, in the name of our brothers. Christ supplements our love but does not substitute his own for ours as though we were superfluous and there were no hope for us and for any dedication and self-surrender from us. Despite all the abundant and more than abundant atonement made by our Representative, God still expects to receive something from us. He does not let us off because of Jesus. Christ prays and intercedes for us, but we too must learn to pray and intercede. We cannot and may not live permanently in a state of minority, incapacity, and unfulfillment. God takes no pleasure in his creatures when unfulfilled. He wants us to be his fellow-workers (1 Cor 3:9), heirs according to the promise (Gal 3:29), fulfilled and in full possession of the "glorious freedom of the children of God" (Rom 8:21). The Spirit who represents us and prays in us and for us "with groanings which cannot be expressed in speech" (Rom 8:26) does not want to substitute his prayer for ours but to bring us to pray with him. We have an unqualified need of Christ as Representative if God is not to look on us with anger; because of our native incapacity God would send us away from him, were it not for Christ. Precisely because Christ is our representative and not a substitute for us, he does not ask for us to be sent away, nor does God send us away because he has Christ.

The Church Too Must Be a Representative

"The way we came to understand love was that he laid down his life for us; we too must lay down our lives for our brothers" (1 Jn 3:16). Receiving is to be matched by giving. Having been redeemed by the vicarious action of Christ and having acquired our identity as men and Christians, we must in turn become the representatives of others: "I find my joy in the suffering I endure for you. In my own flesh I fill up what is lacking in the sufferings of Christ for the sake of his body, the church" (Col 1:24). The representation of Christ is not something over and done with, but must continue in the life of the apostle: something "is lacking" to the passion of Christ and the apostle must "fill it up." Paul is vividly aware that Christ is sole Mediator, yet he sees in his own action and suffering "for" his communities (cf. 2 Cor 12:15; Eph 3:1-13; Col 2:1; 4:12). He is ever ready and disposed to be a representative for all, even to the point of shedding his blood for others (cf. Phil 2:17; 2 Tim 4:6). To the Colossians he speaks of Epaphras as one "who is always pleading earnestly in prayer that you stand firm" (Col 4:12).

We are faced here with the rich traditional doctrine and practice of the "communion of saints": the saints "intercede" for us. We must take the word "intercede" in its etymological sense of stepping between God and us: the saints are our representatives, advocates, and mediators. The vicarious action of Christ continues in the saints; in them Christ continues to be our representative across the centuries. But "saints" is here meant in the Biblical sense of the word: all the baptized who live by the Spirit of Christ. After insisting, with Paul, that there is only one Mediator (1 Tim 2:5-6), Vatican II teaches that "the maternal duty of Mary toward men in no way obscures or diminishes this unique mediation of Christ, but rather shows its power. For all the saving influences of the Blessed Virgin on men originate, not from some inner necessity, but from the divine pleasure. They flow forth from the superabundance of the merits of Christ, rest on His mediation, depend entirely on it, and draw all their power from it. In no way do they impede the immediate union of the faithful with Christ. Rather, they foster this union" (LG 60/90-91). "The unique mediation of the Redeemer does not exclude but rather gives rise among creatures to a manifold cooperation which is but a sharing in this unique source" (LG 62c/92).

Here we have a central element in Christian life, that which provides basis and meaning for the Christian calling. "This is truly a tremendous mystery, upon which we can never meditate enough; that the salvation of many souls depends upon the prayers and voluntary mortifications offered for that intention by the members of the mystical Body of Jesus Christ, and upon the co-operation which pastors and faithful, especially parents, must afford to our divine Savior." Thus Pius XII in the encyclical letter on the Mystical Body.[8] Further on in the same encyclical he says: "For though the treasure of graces which our Savior merited for His Church by His bitter passion and painful death is quite unlimited, yet God's providence has so disposed that these gifts of grace shall be bestowed upon us only little by little; and their greater or less abundance depends in no small measure upon our good works by which this rain of heavenly gifts, God's free bounty, is drawn down upon the souls of men. This gracious rain will be brought down from heaven in abundance if we pray earnestly to God, especially by taking part devoutly, and daily if possible, in the Eucharistic Sacrifices; and if we strive to relieve the sufferings of the needy by the duties of Christian charity. But it will descend in greater abundance still if, in addition to all this, we prefer imperishable goods to the transitory things of this life; if we tame this mortal flesh by voluntary mortification, denying it what is unlawful and even imposing upon it what is unpleasant and difficult; and, finally, if we submissively accept the trials and sufferings of this present life as coming from the hand of God. For in this way, the Apostle tells us, 'we shall fill up in our flesh those things that are wanting of the sufferings of Christ, for his Body, which is the Church' (cf. Col 1:24)."[9]

In a certain sense what the Apostle says of himself holds for all the baptized: "Preaching the gospel is not the subject of a boast; I am under compulsion and have no choice. I am ruined if I do not preach it" (1 Cor 9:16). Therefore the Council remarks that "the member who fails to make his proper contribution to the development of the Church must be said to be useful neither to the Church nor to himself" (AA 2a/491).

We would like to end with a splendid thought that is developed as follows by Joseph Ratzinger. In the light of the law of representation we can better understand the unqualified necessity which Christianity claims for itself when it comes to the salvation of mankind, as well as the doctrine of the Church as sole means of salvation. We now see that within mankind *there are essential services which are not required of all yet which are indispensable for all, inasmuch as all depend upon them and live by reason of them before God.* We see more clearly that the unique and wholly central service on which all mankind depends is the service given by Christ; that this ministry must be carried on by the community of those who accept the Lord in a spirit of faith; and that without this ongoing service or ministry mankind cannot persevere in its divine calling. Here we have a new perspective which enables us to discern in what sense the Church is absolutely necessary for salvation. Anyone who seeks to understand along these lines the content of Christianity will never again make the mistake of comparing his Christian existence with the existence of others in order to find out what advantages he has in being a Christian, either for living a moral life or for cultivating a greater assurance of eternal happiness. The Christian will now rather realize that his life is not made easier by his Christian and ecclesial vocation but, if anything, rendered more difficult, since through it he has agreed to exercise an important function *in favor of others.* He now sees that being a Christian means being-for-others. He cannot deny that often enough this means a further burden, but it is a holy burden, that of being at the service of mankind. To be a Christian is to be called to great-hearted generosity. To be a Christian means to be ready, as Simon of Cyrene was, to serve under the weight of Christ's Cross for the good of the world and for man's true life. The Christian will accept his task with a glad heart and not look enviously at others as he compares the heavy burden of his own duties with the perhaps lighter burdens borne by others who, as he believes, will also reach heaven. The Christian feels humbly proud and sincerely satisfied and happy to have been chosen and called by God for such an important and holy task. His function is not important because he will be saved while others will be condemned; it is important because *through* it others will be able to be saved. Vatican II teaches that "this Messianic people, although it does not actually include all men, and may more than once look like a small flock, is nonetheless a lasting and sure seed of unity, hope, and salvation for the whole human race. Established by Christ as a fellowship of life, charity, and truth, it is also used by Him as an instrument for the redemption of all, and is sent forth into the whole world as the light of the world and the salt of the earth" (LG 9e/26). Thus the role of the servant of Jahweh will be continued in the Church. In very truth, "by her relationship with Christ, the Church is a kind of sacrament or sign of intimate union with God, and of the unity of all mankind. She is also an instrument for the achievement of such union and unity" (LG 1b/15). In order to be the salvation of all, the Church need not be outwardly identified with all. What is essential is that, following Christ, the "one," she should be the "few" through whom God seeks to save the "many." Her mission is carried out not *by* all but *for* all.

A proper understanding of the vicarious or representative task proper to the Church must not lead us to the false doctrine of the easy salvation of all. As we have seen, the law of representation does not deny the principle of individual responsibility or do away with the possibility of real personal sin and consequently of rejection and damnation. It is clear that the gift of saving grace which flows from the power of representation is not a magical or mechanical gift but requires of each individual an openness and a ready good will to receive the influence of grace. Christ, in short, represents other men but is not a substitute for them; he helps them to be able to reach fuller self-realization and find their identity, that which in each is irreplaceable, unique, proper, and personal.

Notes for Chapter 3

[1] Josef Scharbert, *Heilsmittler im Alten Testament und im Alten Orient* (Quaestiones Disputatae 23-24; Freiburg: Herder, 1964). Cf. especially the general conclusion, pp. 308-20.

[2] Oscar Cullmann, *Christ and Time: The Primitive Christian Conception of Time and History*, tr. by Floyd V. Filson (Phila.: Westminster Press, 1950), p. 115.

[3] Cf. Joseph Ratzinger, "Stellvertretung," in Heinrich Fries (ed.), *Handbuch theologischer Grundbegriffe*, 2 (Munich: Kosel, 1963), pp. 569-70.

[4] Dorothee Sölle, *Christ the Representative: An Essay in Theology after the "Death of God"*, tr. by David Lewis (Phila.: Fortress, 1967). Chapter 1 (pp. 17-56) analyzes the difference between representation (*Stellvertretung*) and substitution (*Ersatz*); chapter 2 (pp. 57-97) studies the magical and juridical conceptions of representation; chapter 3 (pp. 99-149) speaks of Christ's function as vicar or representative. Sölle's analyses, especially the linguistic analyses, seem to me excellent. The final section (pp. 130-49), however, raises serious doubts. Here Christ is presented as being simply the representative of God. It seems to me that the author, a Protestant, has let herself be carried away by her brilliant presentation of "representative."

[5] Sölle, *op. cit.*, p. 43.

[6] [On Umbandism, cf. Bonaventure Kloppenburg, "Brazil: Spiritism," in *New Catholic Encyclopedia*, 2:771-72. For a more concrete description of Brazilian spirit religion with its four varieties—Candomblé, spiritism or Kardecism, Umbanda, and Quimbanda, cf. David St. Clair, *Drum and Candle* (Garden City: Doubleday, 1971), especially chapter 7, pp. 127-57. — Tr.]

[7] Cf. Ratzinger, *art. cit.*, pp. 566-69; Scharbert, *op. cit.*, pp. 313-14.

[8] Pius XII, *Mystici Corporis*, no. 42, in *Selected Letters*, pp. 72-73.

[9] *Mystici Corporis*, no. 106, in *Selected Letter*, pp. 106-7.

[10] Ratzinger, *art. cit.*, pp. 573-75.

Chapter 4

The Mission of the Church

The Specific Mission of the Church

The main purpose of the Dogmatic Constitution on the Church, as enunciated at the very beginning of the document, is to set forth more precisely the nature and *the mission of the Church* (LG 1b/15). Yet the text in fact gives us only a few indications of this mission. There is no chapter on subdivision or special number that speaks in any systematic way about the specific mission of the Church. Consequently, if we are to have the doctrine of the Council in this matter, we must pull together the indications scattered throughout the various documents of the Council. In this period of secularization and "horizontalism" it is important to have a clear grasp of the Church's specific mission and of Vatican II's teaching on it.

The Church is the sacrament of Christ, that is, the sign and instrument he uses in continuing his mission in the world until the rule of God becomes perfect. Consequently *the mission of the Church must be sought in the mission of Christ*

97

himself. In its Constitution on the Church in the Modern World the Council states: "Inspired by no earthly ambition, the Church seeks but a solitary goal: to carry forward the work of Christ Himself under the lead of the befriending Spirit" (GS 3c/201). Now, according to the Council, Christ was sent by the Father and came

—to inaugurate the kingdom of God on earth (LG 3a/16; 5a/17);

—to enter in a new and definitive way into human history, to be the head of a new mankind, and to make men sharers in the divine nature (AG 3c/586-87);

—to make the whole human race the one People of God, uniting it into the one Body of Christ and building it up into a single temple of the Holy Spirit (AG 7e/594);

—to take the history of the world up into himself and to summarize all things in himself (GS 38a/236) or to re-establish all things (LG 3a/16);

—to be the light of the nations (LG 1a/14; 3b/16);

—to reveal the Father's will to men (LG 2/15-16);

—to effect a new and perfect covenant between God and men (LG 9a/25);

—to preach the good news to the poor, heal the contrite of heart, save what was lost (LG 8d/24; SC 5a/139);

—to achieve redemption through obedience (LG 3a/16), in poverty and amid persecution (LG 8c/23);

—to be the source of salvation for the whole world (LG 17b/36);

—to rescue men from the power of darkness and of Satan (AG 3b/586);

—to reconcile the world to himself (AG 3b/586);

—to bear witness to the truth, to save and not to condemn, to serve and not to be served (GS 3c/201);

—essentially to save men, but also to restore the temporal order (AA 5/495).

Such is the mission of Christ. Into it the Church is inserted. "Just as Christ was sent by the Father, so also He sent the apostles, filled with the Holy Spirit. This He did so that, by preaching the gospel to every creature (cf. Mk. 16:15), they might proclaim that the Son of God, by His death and resurrection, had freed us from the power of Satan (cf. Acts 26:18) and from death, and had brought us into the kingdom of His Father. His purpose was also that they might exercise the work of salvation which they were proclaiming, by means of sacrifice and sacraments" (SC 6/140; cf. AG 5d/590). On the mission of the Church, taken generally, we find the following formulations in the documents of Vatican II:

—to be in Christ as the sacrament or sign and instrument of intimate union with God and of the unity of all mankind (LG 1b/15);

—to be for the whole race a sure seed of unity, hope, and salvation (LG 9e/26);

—to be an instrument of redemption for all (LG 9e/26);

—to be for each and all the visible sacrament of saving unity (LG 9f/26);

—to be the universal sacrament of salvation (LG 48b/79; GS 45a/247);

—to proclaim the kingdom of Christ and God, to establish it among all the nations, and to be the germ, beginning, and instrument of this kingdom (LG 5d/18);

—to spread abroad the faith and salvation of Christ (AG 5c/589);

—all the actions of the Church are for one purpose: to sanctify men in Christ and to glorify God (SC 10b/142);

—the Church's mission is to save men through faith in Christ and through his grace (AA 6c/496);

—its goal is the kingdom of God which was begun by God himself on earth and is to be extended ever further until it reach its perfection at the end of time (LG 9d/26);

—to reveal to the world the mystery of Christ (LG 8e/24);

—to manifest the mystery of God (GS 41a/240);

—to bring light to the whole world through the gospel message and to bring together in the one Spirit all men of all nations, races, and cultures (GS 92a/305-6);

—to extend the kingdom of God throughout the world, for the glory of God the Father, making all men sharers in redemption and salvation and, through them, directing the whole world to Christ (AA 2a/491).

In the Decree on the Laity, after teaching that the redemptive work of Christ consists essentially in the saving of men, while also including the restoration of the temporal order, the Council declares: "Hence the mission of the Church is not only to bring to men the message and grace of Christ, but also to penetrate and perfect the temporal sphere with the spirit of the gospel" (AA 5/495). For, on the one hand, it is certain that the kingdom of Christ is not of this world (cf. Jn 18:36); that it is "a kingdom which is of a heavenly and not an earthly nature" (LG 13b/31); that "earthly progress must be carefully distinguished from the growth of Christ's kingdom" (GS 39d/237); that Christians "are not seeking a mere material progress and prosperity for men" (LG 12f/599); that the Church "is not set up to seek earthly glory" (LG 8c/23). On the other hand, we may not forget that "the entire world, which is intimately related to man and achieves its purpose through him, will be perfectly restored in Christ" (LG 48a/78-79); that therefore the kingdom of God also includes a "perfected earth" and a "transformed universe" (cf. GS 39a/237); that man's earthly service makes ready the material of the heavenly kingdom (cf. GS 38d/236); that charity and its fruits endure (GS 39b/237); that we shall find the "good fruits of our nature and enterprise . . . freed of stain, burnished and transfigured" when Christ hands over the kingdom to his Father (GS 39e/237).

It is extremely important to see clearly this *essential ordination of temporal things to the kingdom of God*. Since the Church is the germ and beginning of the kingdom of God and the instrument of its spreading (LG 5d/18), she must be concerned with what the Council calls the "material" of the

kingdom (GS 38d/236). It is clear beyond all doubt that man
has a divine or "Christian" ("supernatural") vocation: "God
has called man and still calls him so that with his entire being
he might be joined to Him in an endless sharing of a divine
life beyond all corruption" (GS 18d/215). That is man's ultimate vocation and the one of greatest importance for the
kingdom of God. To be faithful to this calling ought to be his
main preoccupation, as it is the source of his greatness, dignity,
and honor. But it is equally certain that the same man also
receives from God a "human" vocation: to be lord and master
of all earthly things in order to dominate them, use them,
rule them in a just and holy way, and refer them to God so
that through man they may praise God and reach their perfection in the kingdom of God (cf. 12d/210; LG 48a/78-79;
GS 34a/232). The world is thus *humanized*, for "all things
on earth should be related to man as their center and crown"
(GS 12a/210). To humanize the world is, chronologically,
the first commandment God gave to man (cf. Gn 1:26; Wis
2:23; Ps 8:5-7; Eccles 3:11; Sir 17:3-10). The Christian who
does not take up the task of building the temporal order so as
to make the world more human and just "jeopardizes his
eternal salvation" (GS 43c/243), that is, he cannot enter the
kingdom of God. The Christian ("supernatural") vocation
does not eliminate the human ("natural") vocation, and the
search for the kingdom of God does not dispense us from
earthly tasks. It is clear, of course, that to humanize (that is,
so to act that man fulfills his natural vocation) is not the
same as to evangelize (that is, so to act that man fulfills his
supernatural vocation); yet evangelization cannot simply forget humanization.

Evangelization, in the proper sense of the word, will always
mean proclaiming the good news of Christ concerning the
kingdom of God (man's "supernatural" vocation) or "to promote God's glory through the spread of His kingdom and to
obtain for all men that eternal life which consists in knowing
the only true God and Him whom He sent, Jesus Christ"

(AA 3b/492); or to "announce the good tidings of salvation
to those who do not believe, so that all men may know the
true God and Jesus Christ whom He has sent, and may re-
pent and mend their ways. To believers also the Church must
ever preach faith and repentance. She must prepare them for
the sacraments, teach them to observe all that Christ commanded, and win them to all the works of charity, piety, and
the apostolate" (SC 9b/142). Humanization is simply a
"preparation for the acceptance of the message of the gospel"
(GS 57g/264; cf. 40d/239). But we should note that the
Council asks bishops to show "that earthly goods and human
institutions, structured according to the plan of God the
Creator, are also related to man's salvation, and therefore
can contribute much to the upbuilding of Christ's Body" (CD
12b/404). It remains true, however, that "the deepest vocation of the Church" is fulfilled when we are in communion
with one another through love and when we praise the Blessed
Trinity (LG 51c/84).

In his message for World Mission Sunday, October 18,
1970, in a carefully elaborated text, Pope Paul VI speaks as
follows of the difference between evangelization and development or humanization: "In this re-thinking of the Church's
missionary vocation, one question stands out in particular,
bringing about a confrontation between two different concepts that bear on the general direction of missionary activity—concepts which may be summed up in the two words,
evangelization and development. By evangelization is meant
strictly religious activity, aimed at the preaching of God's
kingdom, of the Gospel as a revelation of the plan of salvation in Christ, through the action of the Holy Spirit—activity
that has the ministry of the Church as its instrument, the
building up of the Church itself as its aim, and God's glory
as its final end. This is the traditional doctrine, to which the
Council has given its authoritative support. By development
is meant the human, civil, temporal advancement of those
peoples who, by contact with modern civilization and with the

help that it can provide, are becoming more aware of themselves and are setting out on the road to higher levels of culture and prosperity. The missionary cannot excuse himself from taking an interest in this advancement. The confrontation between these two concepts is a serious one and entails two dangers: that we may consider them as mutually exclusive, and that we may fail to establish a correct relationship between them. We hope that the confrontation will not be looked upon as a dilemma that excludes a synthesis between evangelization and development, in which the one complements the other. It would be unthinkable for us believers that missionary activity should make of earthly reality its only or principal end, and lose sight of its essential goal: namely, to bring to all men the light of faith, to give them new life in baptism, to incorporate them into the Mystical Body of Christ, the Church, to teach them to live like Christians, and to hold out the expectation of an existence beyond this earthly one. It would likewise be inadmissible for the Church's missionary activity to neglect the needs and aspirations of developing peoples and, because of its religious orientation, to omit the basic duties of human charity. We cannot forget the Gospel's solemn teaching on the love of our needy and suffering neighbor, reiterated by the Apostles, and confirmed by the Church's whole missionary tradition. We Ourself, in Our encyclical *Populorum Progressio*, have stressed the duty of resolutely and intelligently fostering the growth of economic, cultural, social, and spiritual well-being among peoples, and especially among those of the so-called Third World, where missionary activity finds its main scope. There should be no dilemma. It is a question of priority of ends, of intentions, of duties. There is no doubt that missionary activity is concerned primarily with evangelization, and that it must maintain this priority both in the concept that inspires it and the way in which it is organized and exercised. Missionary activity would be failing in its reason for being if it turned aside from its religious axis: the kingdom of God understood in its vertical,

theological, religious sense, freeing man from sin and presenting him with the love of God as the supreme commandment
and eternal life as his ultimate destiny—that is to say, the
kerygma, the word of Christ, the Gospel, faith, prayer, the
Cross, Christian living. We must realize that fidelity to this
primary program of missionary activity may create great difficulties, which at times may prevent it from developing and
expanding. Our mission is 'folly and scandal.' But that is
precisely its strength and its wisdom, today no less than in
the beginning. Even today, in fact, what by earthly standards
would seem an obstacle to evangelization—namely, its spiritual character—can help it by freeing it from the material
fetters of economics, from suspicion of colonialism, from the
ineffectiveness of naturalism when faced with differing cultures."[1]

Thus the growth of the kingdom of Christ and the progress
of the temporal order are not to be identified or confused, but
neither are they to be separated or opposed. They are part
of a single divine plan and are ordered to a single goal which
is the perfected kingdom of God. In a similar way, we must
distinguish—without identification and confusion; without
separation, dualism, dichotomy, antinomy, and opposition;
but requiring harmony, collaboration, co-existence, and even
interpenetration—between evangelization and humanization.
Both of these are part of a single plan and both must lead
to the same final kingdom of God. But the two are distinct
realms (cf. AA 5/495); "distinction and . . . harmony"
must be the rule (LG 36f/63). Some find it difficult to
admit a duality of realms, for they fear that duality
must lead to dualism or dichotomy. There are good
historical reasons for such fears, since relations between
Church and world are marked by a good deal of dualism and
by excessive separation. We have a classical example of such
separation, with all its disastrous consequences, in St. Augustine's "two cities." Dualism must indeed be avoided. Yet we
cannot afford not to affirm a duality. Christ implies the

duality when he says: "My kingdom does not belong to this world" (Jn 18:36); when he bids us: "Give to Caesar what is Caesar's, but give to God what is God's" (Mt 22:21); when he answers "someone in the crowd": "Friend, who has set me up as your judge or arbiter?" (Lk 12:14). We must distinguish between the order of creation and the order of redemption: the divine act of creating and conserving is not formally identical with the divine act of redeeming and saving; the intervention of God in creation is not identical with his intervention in redempton. "In order to establish peace or communion between sinful human beings and Himself, as well as to fashion them into a fraternal community, God determined to intervene in human history in a way both new and definitive" (AG 3b/586). *The divine act from which the Church results is not identical with the act of creation.* It was with the former act, or in view of it, that the history of salvation began, and the latter is, consequently and as such, distinct from the history of mankind. But the same Word who entered human history in a new and definitive way to inaugurate the order of redemption is also author of the created order (GS 38a/235-36; 45b/247); the same God is Lord of human history and of the history of salvation (GS 41c/240). This is why there can be no opposition between the two realms.

We must insist on this point: the two realms or two planes are both ordered to the same goal: the perfected kingdom of God, when God will be all in all. Then, and only then, Church and world will become identical in the kingdom of God. *Until then the two advance along distinct paths*, each retaining its autonomy, its internal coherence, its own laws. They are like two elements in tension (law of life), but also harmonizing with each other and even penetrating each other (cf. GS 40d/ 239); the two cities serve each other in many ways (cf. GS 11c/210). "This [Christian] community realizes that it is truly and intimately linked with mankind and its history" (GS 1/200): the joys and the hopes, the griefs and the anxieties of men are also the joys and hopes, the griefs and anxieties of Christ's disciples, and nothing human fails to find an echo in their hearts. For the Church, "at once a visible assembly and a spiritual community, goes forward together with humanity" (GS 40c/239); "she exists in the world, living and acting with it" (GS 40a/238); and "the lay faithful fully belong at one and the same time both to the People of God and to civil society" (AG 21b/611; cf. GS 40c/239; 76c/288; AA 5/495-96; and cf. LG 36b-d/62-63, an important text). We must be very careful, then, to avoid thinking of the Church as a society separated from the world; that only leads to a separation between God and his world. The Church does not exist for its own sake; it is not an end in itself, but exists for the sake of the world.

Humanization or progress in the temporal order or the fulfillment of man's natural vocation is the proper goal of the human community with its political, economic, social, and cultural organization. It is the specific task of statesmen, economists, sociologists, scientists, and technologists; all these, if they are to be able to carry out their task, must in their own field enjoy autonomy and follow their own principles (cf. LG 36f/63; GS 36b/233; AA 7b/497). All this makes up the temporal order in which the work of humanization is undertaken. To humanize, then, is the specific task of politics, economics, cultures, civilization. But Christians must be present in all these spheres as a leaven in the mass.

Evangelization or the growth of the kingdom of God or the fulfillment of man's supernatural vocation is the proper mission of the Church. The Council speaks incisively in saying that "Christ . . . gave His Church no proper mission in the political, economic, or social order. The purpose which He set before her is a religious one" (GS 42b/241). (In note 132, on this passage, the Council cites a well-known text of Pius XII, March 9, 1956, in which the pope speaks even more incisively: Christ has not given the Church "any end of the cultural order," and she has a "strictly religious, supernatural goal.")

But the Council is quite aware that the Church's religious mission has repercussions in the cultural sphere and in the building of the temporal order. The text we have just quoted goes on to say: "But out of this religious mission itself comes a function, a light, and an energy which can serve to structure and consolidate the human community according to the divine law" (GS 42b/241). Once again, distinction and harmony. The Council knows that "the good news of Christ constantly renews the life and culture of fallen man. It combats and removes the errors and evils resulting from sinful allurements which are a perpetual threat. It never ceases to purify and elevate the morality of peoples. By riches coming from above, it makes fruitful, as it were from within, the spiritual qualities and gifts of every people and every age. It strengthens, perfects, and restores them in Christ" (GS 58d/264). Consequently, "by the very fulfillment of her own mission the Church stimulates and advances human and civic culture" (*ibid.*). In note 192, the Council adds the words of Pius XI: "It is necessary never to lose sight of the fact that the objective of the Church is to evangelize, not to civilize. If it civilizes, it is for the sake of evangelization." *To civilize by evangelizing.* "Thus the mission of the Church will show its religious, and by that very fact, its supremely human character" (GS 11c/210). For, "by preaching the truth of the gospel and shedding light on all the areas of human activity through her teaching and the example of the faithful, she shows respect for the political freedom and responsibility of citizens and fosters these values" (GS 76d/288). "Whoever follows after Christ, the perfect man, becomes himself more of a man" (GS 41c/240).

It is thus not the mission of the Church to create a culture or "Christian civilization," that would be set apart, parallel to, at the side of, or in the midst of other cultures and civilizations. Her mission is rather to evangelize all cultures: "In virtue of her mission and nature, she is bound to no particular form of human culture, nor to any political, economic, or social system" (GS 42e/242). Or, as the Council says in the words of the Letter to Diognetus (written 190-200 A.D.), "what the soul is to the body, let Christians be to the world" (LG 38/65). We must insist, then, that "the Christian faithful, gathered together in the Church out of all nations, 'are not marked off from the rest of men by their government, nor by their language, nor by their political institutions.' So they should live for God and Christ by following the honorable customs of their own nation" (AG 15g/603). *Here we have the definitive condemnation of "Christendom" and of the recurring temptation to form a ghetto.* It is not the Church's mission to build within the world of men a world apart, with a Christian form of government, with its own political party, with its own magistrates and its own schools. Instead, the Church "experiences the same earthly lot which the world does" and "serves as a leaven and as a kind of soul for human society" (GS 40c/239; cf. 44a/245-46; AA 2b-c/491-92). Her mission is to form Christians who live according to the Sermon on the Mount in the midst of men and in the states, parties, schools, undertakings, and institutions of human society, whatever the latter's type, style, culture, and civilization. Her mission is to form Christians who "seek the kingdom of God by engaging in temporal affairs and by ordering them according to the plan of God. They live in the world, that is, in each and in all of the secular professions and occupations. They live in the ordinary circumstances of family and social life, from which the very web of their existence is woven. They are called there by God so that by exercising their proper function and being led by the spirit of the gospel they can work for the sanctification of the world from within. In this way they can make Christ known to others, especially by the testimony of a life respondent in faith, hope, and charity" (LG 31c-d/57-58).

The Church: Immanent and Transcendent

In order to fulfill its mission and to spread to all parts of the world, "while she transcends all limits of time and of race, the Church is destined . . . to enter into the history of mankind" (LG 9g/26). The Church is thus both immanent and transcendent.

She is *immanent*. That is, as Christ enters into human history (cf. AG 3b/586), so the Church must enter into human history and identify herself with men. "In order to be able to offer all of them the mystery of salvation and the life brought by God, the Church must become part of all these groups for same motive which led Christ to bind Himself, in virtue of His Incarnation, to the definite social and cultural conditions of those human beings among whom He dwelt" (AG 10b/597). The Church too must become incarnate, become part of mankind; it must "realize that it is truly and intimately linked with mankind and its history" (GS 1/200). It must go forward with humanity and experience the same earthly lot (GS 40c/239); it must help men in their effort to make "the family of man and its history more human" (GS 40e/239). Consequently, being itself conditions by history, the Church must undergo change and must adapt itself to each generation, constantly scrutinizing the signs of the times and knowing and understanding the world in which it lives here and now, with that world's hopes and aspirations and often dramatic characteristics (cf. GS 4a/201-2; 11/209-10). Because of its nature as immanent the Church must take flesh among every people. Therefore, "from the beginning of her history, she has learned to express the message of Christ with the help of the ideas and terminology of various peoples, and has tried to clarify it with the wisdom of philosophers, too. Her purpose has been to adapt the gospel to the grasp of all as well as to the needs of the learned, insofar as such was appropriate. Indeed, this accommodated preaching of the revealed Word ought to remain the law of all evangelization. For thus each nation develops the ability to express Christ's message in its own way" (GS 44b-c/246). As immanent, incarnate, present, inserted into the life of peoples, the Church "takes nothing away from the temporal welfare of any people by establishing that kingdom. Rather does she foster and take to herself, insofar as they are good, the ability, resources, and customs of each people. Taking them to herself, she purifies, strengthens, and ennobles them" (LG 13b/31). She works in such a way that "whatever good is in the minds and hearts of men, whatever good lies latent in the religious practices and cultures of diverse peoples, is not only saved from destruction but is also healed, ennobled, and perfected" (LG 17c/36); she "respects and fosters the spiritual adornments and gifts of the various races and peoples" (SC 37/151; cf. AG 9c/595-96; 18b/606; 22a/612; NA 2e/662). Because this law of immanence is at work, the local churches come into existence.

But the immanent Church is also *transcendent*. That is, "she transcends all limits of time and of race" (LG 9c/26). In order to be immanent, the Church must take flesh in the various human cultures and give rise to the local churches. But, because she is transcendent, she "is not bound exclusively and indissolubly to any race or nation, nor to any particular way of life or any customary pattern of living, ancient or modern. Faithful to her own tradition and at the same time conscious of her universal mission, she can enter into communion with various cultural modes, to her own enrichment and theirs too" (GS 58c/264). We must note carefully the mature and apt formulation of this doctrine by the Council: the Church not only can but must be closely linked to particular cultures (her immanence or duty to take concrete historical form in local churches requires this); yet this cultural incarnation may not be exclusive and indissoluble. That is, it may not be *exclusive* so that a plurality of forms is rendered impossible; nor *indissoluble*, so as to prevent the abandonment of obsolete and outdated cultural forms. The Church must be always open and ready to undertake its incarnation in new forms or, as the Council puts it, to enter into communion with various cultural forms, even entirely new ones such as the "secularized culture" which is now coming into existence, or with others that will surely arise in the future. The incarnation of the Church in Greco-Roman culture, for example, was certainly providential and successful, giving rise to a specific Church called the Latin Church. But because this Latin Church was in fact also the visible center of unity for the universal Church, it could give (and does give) the impression that it is, in an unqualified way, *the* expression of the Church. In fact it is not and may not be such. Even for the Latin Church, since it is a specific Church, the principle of transcendence holds: the Church is not bound exclusively and indissolubly to Greco-Roman culture. In other words: the Latin Church as such can disappear without affecting the permanence and survival of the Church as established by Christ (who certainly did not establish it as "Latin"). We ought to be ready to die in defense of the Church, even in defense of her right and duty to be "Latin" in the regions where that culture is predominant; but we need not shed our blood to maintain the permanence of the Latin Church in a world whose culture is non-Latin.

The Tension between Tradition and Progress in the Church

In carrying out her mission the Church is aware, especially today, of a tension between tradition and progress. Organized movements arise which call themselves "traditionalist" and aim at safeguarding the heritage of the past and at doing open battle with what they call "progressivism." Spirits are roused and we are increasingly aware of an atmosphere of struggle and crusade, of party and fanaticism, that blinds and deafens men to the point where they are no longer calm enough to see, hear, and discern what is good and true, just and holy, in the opposing camp. We see the unfortunate generalizations made by professional cullers of the isolated deplorable fact. The diabolical work of spying, delation, and accusation has been started, and "documents" multiply on the desks of intimidated authorities. The trials of the Inquisition seem to be starting again. Unfortunately not all the authorities who receive the disquieting documentation have the confidence, faith, and good sense which mark the words of John XXIII in his address at the opening of the Council: "In the daily exercise of our pastoral office, we sometimes have to listen, much to our regret, to voices of persons who, though burning with zeal, are not endowed with too much sense of discretion or measure. In these modern times they can see nothing but prevarication and ruin. They say that our era, in comparison with past eras, is getting worse, and they behave as though they had learned nothing from history, which is, none the less, the teacher of life. They behave as though at the time of former Councils everything was a full triumph for the Christian idea and life and for proper religious liberty. We feel we must disagree with those prophets of gloom, who are always forecasting disaster, as though the end of the world were at hand" (Abbott 712).

Those who style themselves "traditionalists" must admit that the authentic Christian tradition, which they and all of us want and defend, is a living thing, a life, and thus, of its nature, demands progress. There is then a tension, but not an opposition, between tradition and progress. Vatican II provides us with a sufficiently explicit concept of tradition in its Dogmatic Constitution on Revelation, when, in Chapter 2, it speaks of the transmission of divine relevation. For, "in His gracious goodness, God has seen to it that *what He had revealed for the salvation of all nations* would abide perpetually in its full integrity and be handed on to all generations" (DV 7a/114-5; italics added). To help us understand how the Church understands this tradition, the Council adopts as a principle: *the gospel is the source of all saving truth and moral teaching* (cf. 7a/115). Strictly speaking, there is no other source: "the gospel . . . is for all time the source of all life for the Church" (LG 20a/39). For, after the promulgation of the gospel, those who teach in the Church "do not

allow that there could be any new public revelation pertaining
to the divine deposit of faith" (LG 25g/50), and declare that
"we now await no further new public revelation before the
glorious manifestation of our Lord Jesus Christ" (DV 4b/
113).

The gospel, then, is the necessary, sufficient, definitive, and
sole source from which we must derive all the truths required
for our salvation (the "saving truth") and all the moral and
disciplinary norms required for living our Christian lives. This
gospel was handed on to us, first by the Apostles and apostolic
men (through oral preaching, living example, institutions, and
books written under the inspiration of the Holy Spirit), then
by their successors, the bishops, who are helped by the Holy
Spirit to preserve it in its vital integrity until the end of time
(cf. DV 7b/115). This faithful handing of the gospel in its
vital integrity is called *paradosis* or *tradition*, and "includes
everything which contributes to the holiness of life, and the increase of faith of the People of God" (DV 8a/116). It is to be
found, as a living and life-giving presence, in the life and practice of the believing and praying Church (DV 8c/116). Tradition thus understood necessarily originates with the Apostles
(DV 8b/116) and, in order to remain alive and life-giving,
"*develops* in the Church with the help of the Holy Spirit"
(*ibid.*). It develops, not in the sense that new truths are
added on, but in the sense that there is a growth in understanding both the realities and the words handed on.

The Council lists four factors in development, which, always
with the help of the Holy Spirit, aid in this growth in understanding: contemplation, study, the intimate understanding
which the faithful receive of spiritual things, and the preaching of the successors of the Apostles. Consequently, "the development of tradition" is the work of the entire Church, of
all the holy and prophetic people of God and not of the bishops
alone (cf. also LG 12a/29). "In holding to, practicing, and
professing the heritage of the faith, there results on the part
of the bishops and faithful a remarkable common effort" (DV

10a/117). The teaching office of the bishops has a specific and exclusive function in relation to tradition: that of authentically interpreting the word of God (cf. DV 10b/117). The bishops are "authentic teachers, that is, teachers endowed with the authority of Christ" (LG 25a/47). However, "this teaching office is not above the word of God, but serves it, teaching only what has been handed on" (DV 10b/118; cf. LG 25f/49). Thus we are dealing here always and only with "tradition from the Apostles." For, apart from the gospel handed on by the Apostles, there is no other source. We must stress this point: the gospel is the source of all saving truth and of all discipline and customs; it is for the Church of every age the fountainhead of all its life (cf. DV 7a/115; LG 20a/ 39).

But the gospel that is to be faithfully preserved and to be handed on in a life-giving way is intended to be a leaven in the mass, the light of the world, the salt that makes food edible; it is to take flesh in the reality of the human mass with all its diversity and particularity of peoples, civilizations, cultures, religions, and circumstances of time and place.

In all this diversity the gospel is always and only to be the leaven, the light, the salt; it is not to be the leavened mass, the enlightened world, the salted food. What the Church is to preserve and hand on is the leaven, not the mass, the light and not a particular illumined world, the salt and not a particular food. When the gospel is incarnated in a concrete way in a specific cultural, historical, or geographical situation, it will be able to bring forth splendid fruits of salvation and sanctification and to give rise to a flourishing and highly Christian individual church (in the sense in which "individual church" is used in OE 2/374, or LG 31c-d/31-32). Such a concrete incarnation of the gospel will have its particular usages, its special ways of praying, thinking, and expressing the content of faith, its characteristic customs and institutions. It will have, in a word, its own "traditions" within the encompassing, permanent, single Tradition of the gospel.

There is a necessary and inevitable pluralism within the one Church of Christ.

Unfortunately there always exists for churchmen the temptation to fix the Church in a particular, successful form of incarnation; to render a particular style permanent, even when the earlier situation has ceased to exist; or to try to repeat a form exactly in other circumstances. Then we have the fixism that leads to legalism and juridicism, to a dangerous kind of pharisaism, to the ghetto. If ever the Church considered itself fully made and finished, forever henceforth the same, immutable, permanent, having found its definitive structure, institutions, and laws, it would cease to be leaven, light, and salt, to be the sacrament of universal salvation, to fulfill its essential mission ("go and teach"), and would fall prey to substantial infidelity. For the Church is always unfinished, always on the way, always moving toward its perfection, always thrown into new situations, and must therefore always be in continuous development. "Christ summons the Church, as she goes her pilgrim way, to that continual reformation of which she always has need, insofar as she is an institution of men here on earth" (UR 6b/350).[2]

Such is the concrete situation of the Church: she was convoked and established by God in order "that for each and all she may be the visible sacrament of this saving unity. While she transcends all limits of time and of race, the Church is destined to extend to all regions of the earth and so to enter into the history of mankind. Moving forward through trial and tribulation, the Church is strengthened by the power of God's grace promised to her by the Lord, so that in the weakness of the flesh she may not waver from perfect fidelity, but remain a bride worthy of her Lord; that moved by the Holy Spirit she may never cease to renew herself, until through the cross she arrives at the light which knows no setting" (LG 9f-g/26).

Because the Holy Spirit helps her in a special way, the Church is substantially indefectible in the faithful conservation and transmission of the gospel. She carries out her task faithfully, but amid shadows, and is therefore quite human and subject to defects when it comes to incarnating the gospel in new concrete situations or to the task of adaptation in the light of the signs of the times (many defects here are by omission) or to the correct interpretation of these signs.

Because she is essentially a pilgrim and an eschatological reality, and advances through trials and tribulations, the Church cannot stand still: the Holy Spirit impels "the Church to open new avenues of approach to the world of today" (PO 22c/575). That is what development means. Because she is essentially missionary and is sent to men who always live and must live in concrete historical situations which undergo continual and often rapid and radical change, the Church will always find itself in new situations and in new quests which bring uncertainty, perplexity, and confusion. She knows it is neither possible nor necessary always to give immediate, clear, concrete answers to the new problems, even serious ones, that can arise at any moment (GS 33c/232; cf. 43e/244). Today we live at an extremely important historical turning: "The living conditions of modern man have been so profoundly changed in their social and cultural dimensions, that we can speak of a new age in human history" (GS 54a/260). Contemporary culture "has passed from a rather static concept of reality to a more dynamic, evolutionary one. In consequence, there has arisen a new series of problems, a series as important as can be, calling for new efforts of analysis and synthesis" (GS 5d/204). The outstanding, responsible men of the present-day Church who gathered at Vatican II had a clear grasp of these new and complex situations. "Recent studies and the findings of science, history, and philosophy raise new questions which influence life and *demand new theological investigations*. Furthermore, while adhering to the methods and requirements proper to theology, theologians are invited to seek continually for more suitable ways of communicating doctrine to the men of their time" (GS 62b-c/268). For the

Church has the duty of expressing "the message of Christ with the help of the ideas and terminology of various peoples" and of adapting "the gospel to the grasp of all as well as to the needs of the learned. . . . This accommodated preaching of the revealed word ought to remain the law of all evangelization" (GS 44b-c/246).

New problems, new investigations, new ways of expressing the ancient deposit. That is our contemporary situation. We cannot simply close our eyes and ears so as not to see and hear the signs of the times, nor enclose a "little flock" in a kind of ghetto where men go on affirming sincerely the formulas of other times and insisting piously on practices which came into being in response to now non-existent circumstances. If we did, we would betray our mission; we would not do our duty. Yet men of the Church, even the most powerful and pious of them, can be subject to that temptation. They can even succumb to it for a time; we need only read the history of the Church for examples. There always exists the fearful possibility of putting obstacles on the paths of Providence and of prejudging the impulses given by the Holy Spirit (cf. UR 24b/365).

In a striking document of March, 1968, the bishops of Holland noted: "Change is impossible without disturbance and confusion. The comparison which we have drawn with rebuilding a house falls short in two ways. First, the architect and the builders who undertake the job know exactly what they have to do. But the ecclesial community can only surmise what the new building will look like. Uncertainty reigns over all sorts of questions, and at best we see the broad outlines of renewal. Secondly, the re-building of the Church will never come to an end. The new building will never be complete. There is nothing, indeed, in this life on earth about which we can pronounce a finnal and conclusive word. The fellowship of the Church, like individual men, is always evolving. When our present problems are solved, there will be others which will call us to renewal. Hence it would be better to compare the Church to a nomads' tent than to a house in which men have settled down to a fixed dwelling-place. The tent has to be taken down again and again, and pitched once more when we have gone a little further on. It never offers more than a temporary shelter. But it is precisely here, in the provisional character of all human certainty, that the true nature of faith can be clearly revealed. We shall only be able to bear the confusion and uncertainty if we believe. . . . Hence faith means adhering firmly to God in spite of all confusion, trusting that he is with us."[3]

It is, then, the nature and mission of the Church to be true at the same time to God and to men (GS 21a/218). Fidelity to God and tradition; fidelity to man and development.

Tradition is thus the gospel becoming real in the life of the Church; it is the faithful, integral, living, and vigorous handing on of the gospel. Development springs from the Church's native capacity to carry out its mission among the peoples of the world, to adapt and renew itself, to purify itself. Tradition is fidelity to the gospel (grace and truth) which must reach men in order to save them; development is fidelity to man who is to receive the gospel. By its nature the Church is tradition; by its mission the Church is development. If the Church abandoned tradition it would be unfaithful; if it abandoned development it would play the traitor. It would sin against tradition if it denied development; it would sin against development if it let tradition harden. Tradition is viable only when it develops; development is possible only in tradition, in fidelity to gospel, Christ, and Church, in an identification with gospel, Christ, and Church. Like the teaching office which the bishops exercise), development (which, like tradition, is the work of the whole people of God, bishops and laity alike) must always be at the service of the word of God, never above it or separated from it. Development proceeds along two lines: one is the line of better understanding of and penetration into the revealed truths; the other is the line of constant adaptation of these truths and their practical implications to the varied historical, geographical, cultural, and religious situations of mankind. To help development along we need more than imagination, courage, and boldness; he alone is able to effect development who lives the gospel, tries to identify himself with it, and seeks to understand it in its richness, its divine life, its loving consecration to the Father, its faith in the active presence of the Lord, its confident self-surrender to the Holy Spirit. We are easily tempted to depart from the gospel, especially in its more demanding and difficult passages when the gospel is the Cross, when it is a stumbling block to the Jews and folly to the Gentiles, when it demands a life of ceaseless prayer and virtues that seem more than human. "Every renewal of the Church essentially consists in an increase of fidelity to her own calling" (UR 6a/350). Therefore, "let all Christ's faithful remember that the more purely they strive to live according to the gospel, the more they are fostering and even practicing Christian unity. For they can achieve depth and ease in strengthening mutual brotherhood to the degree that they enjoy profound communion with the Father, the Word, and the Spirit" (UR 7c/351). The Council must deplore the fact that we Catholics, though we have such a wealth of means of sanctification at our disposal, unfortunately do not live with the required fervor, and that as a result we scandalize others. Hence there is the need of tending towards Christian perfection and of each person, according to his station, playing his part "so that the Church, which bears in her own body the humility and dying of Jesus, may daily be more purified and renewed" (UR 4f/348).

All this should be a subject for profound reflection by those who are called, or call themselves, "progressives" in the Church or who have been chosen by the Holy Spirit to be instruments of progress. For development, too, is and must be the work primarily of the Spirit. Only he who lives Tradition and is penetrated by it through study, meditation, and prayer will be able to work fruitfully for development. Otherwise he would be taking giant strides away from the right path. The development would be development outside the tradition; it would be betrayal and infidelity; it would be lost effort and wasted dedication. And it could be the cause of harm to others. There are disquieting signs and real reasons for trepidation when we see the boldness with which some people push novel and inadequate ways of formulating doctrine and living the life of grace. Ignorance of sacred tradition makes them arrogant about their supposed progress. They are not holy people nor do they lead others to sanctity; they do not pray nor do they induce others to pray. They give the impression of having lost their sense of the divine (the supernatural) and the authentically sacred, and of reducing a transcendent Christianity to a purely immanent humanism. They tend to identify the kingdom of God with the development of peoples. I fear reformers who do not pray and do not study theology (tradition). "Only by the light of faith and by meditation on the word of God can one always and everywhere recognize God . . . , seek His will in every event, see Christ in all men . . . , and make correct judgments about the true meaning and value of temporal things. . . ." (AA 4c/493).

It is beyond doubt—and this must be said to those who with pharisaic pride claim to be "traditionalists"—that the Church must adapt, renew, and purify itself. The Council says as much on countless occasions. But the whole process must take place within fidelity to the gospel which was entrusted to us and passed on in its integrity by the Apostles and their successors. Pope Paul VI never tires of insisting on this. On the first anniversary of the ending of the Council, he said that it would be an error "to suppose that the Ecumenical Council, Vatican II, broke with earlier doctrinal and disciplinary tradition, as if it were itself something new, a kind of revolutionary discovery, an emancipation of subjectivity that would justify jutting aside in a process of psuedo-liberation, what the Church had until yesterday authoritatively taught and professed, and as if it had decided to offer new and arbitrary interpretations of Catholic dogma, often derived from outside of inescapable orthodoxy, and to provide Catholic life with new and extreme expressions, often borrowed from the spirit of the world. Such a view of the Council's work would be alien to the historical reality and authentic spirit of the Council, as anticipated by Pope John XXIII."[4] On another occasion, at the opening of the second session of the Council, Pope Paul VI had explained to the assembled Fathers that "the renewal with which the Church is concerned must not be thought of as a repudiation of the present life of the Church or a break with essential and time-honored traditions. She shows her reverence for tradition by rejecting forms which are spurious or moribund, and by wishing to make them genuine and fruitful."[5]

It may seem superfluous to do so, but we must remind ourselves, before ending this chapter, that the definitive statements of earlier Councils continue to be valid even after Vatican II. At the very beginning of its first document, the Dogmatic Constitution on the Church, the Council declares that it intends to propose a more precise doctrine on the nature and mission of the Church, "following in the path laid out by its predecessors" (LG 1b/15). At the beginning of Chapter 3, in which the most important doctrinal contribution of Vatican II is to be found, the Council says that it "again proposes to be firmly believed by all the faithful" the doctrine of Vatican I on the institution, permanence, powers, and nature of the sacred primacy of the Roman Pontiff and on his infallible teaching office (LG 18c/38). In the Preface to the Dogmatic Constitution on Divine Revelation, the Council expresses its intention of setting forth authentic teaching about divine revelation and its transmission, "following in the footsteps of the Councils of Trent and of First Vatican" (DV 1/ 110). It would be easy to multiply similar quotations. When, in his address at the opening of the Council, John XXIII was sketching the broad lines of a new outlook for our time, he said: "From the renewed, serene, and tranquil adherence to all the teaching of the Church in its entirety and precise-ness, as it still shines forth in the Acts of the Council of Trent and First Vatican Council, the Christian, Catholic, and apostolic spirit of the whole world expects a step forward . . ." (Abbott 715).

There exists a tension, then, between dynamic development and constant tradition. Balance is not easy: it is not even clear just where it lies. But it is urgent that we reach a balance. The achievement of it takes time, serenity, maturity, love, study, dialogue, and a great deal of prayer. It will be possible only if we are disposed to make a serious effort at re-education and a sincere change of mentality and attitudes, in the spirit of Vatican II. To act hastily, foster suspicion, generalize from isolated instances, make accusations, alarm and disquiet those in authority, create an atmosphere of party or schism: all this will settle nothing at this historical moment which is ours, and can only serve to waste time and (once again) postpone the necessary change. In the homily we have already cited, on the first anniversary of the closing of the Council, Pope Paul VI went on to say: "The other error which is opposed to the fidelity we owe the Council would be to fail to recognize the immensely rich teaching and providen-tial power of renewal which comes from the Council itself. We ought to be ready to grant the Council this initiatory power and not think of it as the ending of something. For, while it is true that historically and in its subject matter Vatican II is a complement and logical conclusion to Vatican I, it is also a new and original act of vital awareness on the part of God's Church; it is an act which opens new and won-derful paths for the Church, by reason of its internal develop-ment as well as the relationships it fosters with our separated brothers, with the adherents of other religions, and with the modern world in all its magnificent complexity, its fears, and its anxieties."[6]

Notes for Chapter 4

[1] Paul VI, *Message for World Mission Sunday,* dated June 5, 1970, in *TPS,* 15 (1970-71), 105-6.

[2] In an essay "What Still Separates Us from the Catholic Church? A Protestant Reply," in *Post-Ecumenical Christianity* (Concilium 54; New York: Herder and Herder, 1970), Kristen Skydsgaard quotes a text published in 1931 by Josef Dillersberger, then a young scholar, in the *Osterreichisches Klerusblatt* for May 21, and entitled "Pentecostal Prayer at a Critical Time." It is a prayer for the renewal of the Catholic Church. Dillersberger addresses the Holy Spirit, "tempestuous breath of God" that renews all things. "But where are you on this earth? They say that your Church is full of the Spirit, yet everything there is so quiet, so motionless—even partly dead. 'Two-thirds corpse-meat!' was the judgment of a Soviet Communist. . . . *Lord, everything in your Church is so old!* The old counts—much more than the new. For us, an innovator is virtually a heretic. If anything new threatens our Church there's an immediate outcry: 'Take care! Old ways are best. We've never done anything different. Why change all of a sudden?' In your Church that asks you to make all things new, ever and again that which is new meets with the greatest mistrust and rejection. . . . Spirit of the Lord, you love the new. When will you renew the face of your Church? When will you show us how much that is old in your Church should and must disappear so that its countenance may once again be new and beautiful and young? If you will it, the old will vanish in the power of your descent upon us and all will be made new. If you will it . . . already I can hear from afar the many thousands of those who do not believe, calling out with strong emotion and impressive faith: 'The old is gone—but see, the new has come to pass!' But now it is often difficult to have faith in you, Holy Spirit; and it is painful now to add a hallelujah! to the prayer that asks you to renew the earth. . . . Let your Church be *stirred up* once more! Make *new* its countenance, and let the banner of *freedom* wave once again over the children of God" (p. 37). Skysgaard then notes that the author of this prayer was immediately suspended from his academic post by the Pontifical Congregation of Studies and was only recently fully rehabilitated.

[3] *Herder Correspondence,* 5 (1968), 147.

[4] Paul VI, *Quanti pensieri: Homily on the Anniversary of the Closing of Vatican II,* December 8, 1966, in *AAS,* 59 (1967), 40.

[5] Paul VI, *Salvete Fratres,* September 29, 1963, in *TPS,* 9 (1963-64), 134.

[6] Paul VI, *Quanti pensieri,* in *AAS,* 59 (1967), 40-41.

Chapter 5

The Unity of the Church

"The Church established by Christ the Lord is, indeed, one and unique. . . . This discord openly contradicts the will of Christ, provides a stumbling block to the world, and inflicts damge on the most holy cause of proclaiming the good news to every creature" (UR 1a/341). Vatican II teaches, then, that the Church of Christ is "unique" (LG 8b/22), "one and unique" (UR 1a/341; cf. LG 23a/44; UR 3a/345; 24b/366); that the people of God is "one and unique" (LG 13a/30; 32b/58; AG 1c/342; 7c/351); that there is but one flock of Christ (LG 15b/34; UR 2e/344; AG 6j/592), a single body of Christ (LG 7/20-22; UR 3e/346; AG 7d/593).

In the Decree on Ecumenism the Council speaks of "that unity of the one and only Church which Christ bestowed on His Church from the beginning," and states: "This unity, we believe, dwells in the Catholic Church as something she can never lose, and we hope that it will continue to increase until the end of time" (UR 4c/348). But, in tones of great satisfaction, the Council also affirms that an intense desire of

unity exists today among all Christians, and that almost all,
even among non-Catholics, long "that there may be one visible
Church of God, a Church truly universal and sent forth to
the whole world that the world may be converted to the gospel
and so be saved, to the glory of God" (UR 1c/342).

The current Protestant concept of the Church's unity is, in
fact, quite close to the doctrine of Vatican II. The declaration of the World Council of Churches at Toronto (1950)
recognizes that the "divisions between existing churches . . .
ought not to be, because they contradict the very nature of the
Church."[1] The Lund declaration (1952) by the Conference
on Faith and Order states that the division between the
churches is irreconcilable with unity in Christ and adds that
"the Church is called to continue the mission of Jesus Christ
to the world, so that the way of Christ is the way of the
Church. . . . We are agreed that there are not two Churches,
one visible and the other invisible, but one Church which
must find visible expression on earth."[2] At Evanston (1954)
the Lund declaration was accepted by the General Assembly
of the World Council of Churches. A negative answer was
given to the question whether churches divided among themselves could be said to be united in Christ; there was a unanimous admission that the existing divisions represent a great
sin on the part of the churches, and all were urged to face up
to their obligation of trying to discern and implement the
unity which Christ desires. At New Delhi (1961), the General Assembly approved a description of unity, in which we
read: "The love of the Father and the Son in the unity of the
Holy Spirit is the source and goal of the unity which the
Triune God wills for all men and creation. We believe that
we share in this unity in the Church of Jesus Christ. . . . We
believe that the unity which is both God's will and his gift
to his Church is being made visible as all in each place who are
baptized into Jesus Christ and confess him as Lord and
Savior are brought by the Holy Spirit into one fully committed
fellowship, holding the one apostolic faith, preaching the one

Gospel, breaking the one bread, joining in common prayer, and having a corporate life reaching out in witness and service to all and who at the same time are united with the whole Christian fellowship in all places and all ages in such wise that ministry and members are accepted by all, and that all can act and speak together as occasion requires for the tasks to which God calls his people. It is for such unity that we believe we must pray and work."[3] At the Fourth Assembly of the World Council of Churches, at Uppsala (1968), there was renewed insistence on unity: "To the emphasis [at New Delhi] on 'all in each place' we would now add a fresh understanding of the unity of all Christians in all places. This calls the churches in all places to realize that they belong together and are called to act together. In a time when human interdependence is so evident, it is the more imperative to make visible the bonds which unite Christians in universal fellowship."[4]

We must note, however, that *this unity of the Church is primarily interior, invisible, sacramental, and supernatural*, as we said when speaking of the Church as Mystical Body of Christ. United with each other in the Mystical Body, the faithful do not simply tend towards the same end (this bond of union would, by itself, constitute only a "moral body"). Rather, as Pius XII explained in his encyclical on the Mystical Body: "In the Mystical Body, with which we are concerned, there is in addition to this common aspiration another internal principle, really existing and operative both in the whole structure and in each one of its parts, and this principle is of such surpassing excellence that by itself it immeasurably transcends all the bonds of unity by which any physical or moral body is knit together. It is, as we have said above, something not of the natural, but of the supernatural order; indeed, in itself it is infinite and uncreated, namely the divine Spirit, who, in the words of the Angelic Doctor, 'numerically one and the same, fills and unifies the whole Church' [*De veritate*, q. 21, a. 4c]."[5] Vatican II adds: "In order that we may be unceasingly renewed in Him (cf. Eph. 4:23), He has shared with us His Spirit who, existing as one and the same being in the head and in the members, vivifies, unifies, and moves the whole body. This He does in such a way that His work could be compared by the holy Fathers with the function which the soul fulfills in the human body, whose principle of life the soul is" (LG 7h/21-22). "All of you who have been baptized into Christ have clothed yourselves with him. There does not exist among you Jew or Greek, slave or freeman, male or female. All are one in Christ Jesus" (Gal 3:28). "The body is one and has many members, but all the members, many though they are, are one body; and so it is with Christ. It was in one Spirit that all of us, whether Jew or Greek, slave or free, were baptized into one body. All of us have been given to drink of the one Spirit" (1 Cor 12:12-13). The principle of unity in the Church is the Holy Spirit who, "dwelling in those who believe, pervading and ruling over the entire Church, . . . brings about that marvelous communion of the faithful and joins them together so intimately in Christ" (UR 2b/344).

But all this, though true, is not enough: it is also God's will that we be united to Christ within the visible structure of the Church, through the mediation of faith, sacraments, ecclesiastical government, and communion (cf. LG 14b/33). Thus there arises the problem of *visible unity or the unity of the Church.*

External Unity or Unicity of the Church

We must study somewhat more closely the concept of such visible unity, as it runs through the documents of Vatican II. The concept is closely connected with the difficult and much discussed problem of belonging to the Church (who is or is not a "member"? this last term derives from the Pauline image of the body and is conditioned by this image) and to the concept (patristic and recently revived) of "communion." The question was expressly raised and discussed at the Council when the text of *Lumen Gentium*, 14b/33, was being worked out. The position paper that had been presented for discussion at the second session in 1963 (when the present Chapter 2, on the people of God, had not yet been written) read as follows: "Only they are incorporated into the society of the Church in a real (*reapse*) and unqualified (*simpliciter loquendo*) way, who. . . ."[6] The "real" came from Pius XII's encyclical on the Mystical Body and was a key point in the ecclesiological thinking of Peter Tromp S.J., secretary to the Theological Commission of the Council and generally accepted as having written the encyclical. According to this terminology a person either is or is not a member of the Church, either belongs to the Church or does not, either is or is not within the unity of the Church. There are no gradations of more or less, of perfect or imperfect.

One of the first voices to be raised in protest against this simplistic and radical way of resolving the problem came from a united group of 150 Brazilian bishops. Speaking in their name at the thirty-ninth general meeting of the Council (November 2, 1963), Cardinal Camara asked for the omission of the words "in a real and unqualified way" and "only." The reason he gave was that "such terminology is debated among the theologians, and is of little help in solving the problem and presenting the true doctrine."[7] However, no alternative formulation was suggested. On the same day Bishop van Dodewaard spoke in the name of the Dutch bishops and suggested the expression "bond of *perfect unity*," which Pope Paul VI had used some days before (in his discourse of September 29, 1963).[8] On the following day, November 3, at the fortieth general meeting, Cardinal Lercaro suggested the expression "fully and perfectly," on the grounds that the traditional Catholic doctrine is that baptism incorporates man into the Church in an irrevocable way, due to the sacramental character, even if he should fall into schism or heresy.[9] Bishop van der Burgt, speaking in the name of the Indonesian bishops (who were directly influenced by the Dutch theologians) also denounced the "real" as false doctrine (since all the baptized, even non-Catholics, "are incorporated into the Church in a real way") and proposed the phrase "*full* incorporation," which would leave room for a less full or defective, but nonetheless true, union with the Church.[10]

The later (and final) version of the document omitted both the "only" and the "in a real and unqualified way," and adopted the concept of "full incorporation: "They are fully incorporated into the society of the Church . . ." LG 14b/33). The same concept reappears frequently in other documents. The Decree on Ecumenism speaks of the "fullness of unity which Jesus Christ desires" (UR 4a/347), expresses the hope that the ecumenical movement will lead to "full and perfect unity" (UR 5/350), and says that "the ecclesial communities separated from us lack that fullness of unity with us which should flow from baptism" (UR 22c/364). The term "full" also appears linked with "communion." In the Constitution on the Church in the Modern World, the Council says: "Our hearts embrace also those brothers and communities not yet living with us in full communion" and expresses the hope that such communion will grow (GS 92c/306). The Decree on Ecumenism says that "men who believe in Christ and have been properly baptized are brought into a certain, though imperfect, communion with the Catholic Church" (UR 3a/345) and that divisions among Christians prevent the Church from realizing the fullness of Catholicity proper to her "in those of her sons who, though joined to her by baptism, are yet separated from full communion with her" (UR 4j/ 349); it speaks of "the full communion that is desired" between the Churches (UR 14d/358) and says of the Eastern (Uniate) Christians that they "are already living in full communion" with their brethren of the West (UR 17b/360). The Decree on the Ministry and Life of Priests urges priests not to forget "their brothers who do not enjoy full ecclesiastical communion with us" (PO 9f/554).

In the light of Vatican II, then, we may legitimately speak of a certain communion, imperfect union, less full communion, full communion, full incorporation, full unity, less full unity, imperfect unity, full and perfect unity, growing unity ("we hope that it [this unity] will continue to increase until the end of time": UR 4c/348). In his discourse to the Secretariate for Christian Unity on April 28, 1967, Paul VI even speaks of a "basic unity": "a basic unity already exists between all baptized Christians by reason of their faith in Christ and the invocation of the Most Holy Trinity."[11]

This last words of Pope Paul bring us to the delicate problem of the elements or bonds needed for that "fullness of unity which Jesus Christ desires" (UR 4a/347). In the Decree on Ecumenism Vatican II states, with a certain degree of solemnity, the following general principle: "This sacred Synod confirms what previous Councils and Roman Pontiffs have proclaimed: in order to restore communion and unity or preserve them, one must 'impose no burden beyond what is indispensable' (Acts 15:28)" (UR 18/360). Therefore: "unity in essentials" (UR 4g/349).

But what do these essentials include? The Council attempts on various occasions to define them. Thus, in a rather general way, the Decree on Ecumenism states that communion or unity is to be found "in the confession of one faith, in the common celebration of divine worship, and in the fraternal harmony of the family of God" (UR 2d/344). Equally general is the statement of the Decree on the Eastern Catholic Churches, that the "Church, Holy and Catholic, . . . is made up of the faithful who are organically united in the Holy Spirit through the same faith, the same sacraments, and the same government" (OE 2/374). The Decree on Ecumenism also provides something more specific: "Baptism . . . constitutes a sacramental bond of unity linking all who have been reborn by means of it. But baptism, of itself, is only a beginning, a point of departure, for it is wholly directed toward the acquiring of fullness of life in Christ. Baptism is thus oriented toward a complete profession of faith, a complete incorporation into the system of salvation such as Christ Himself willed it to be, and finally, toward a complete participation in Eucharistic communion" (UR 22b/364). However, the most authoritative passage, deliberately drawn up as an answer to our present problem, is to be found in the Dogmatic Constitution on the Church, where the Council intends to speak of those who "are fully incorporated into the society of the Church." For such full incorporation the Council here requires: (1) possession of the Spirit of Christ; (2) acceptance of the entire system of Church organization; (3) acceptance of all the means of salvation; and (4) union with Christ within the visible structure of the Church by the bonds of faith, sacraments, ecclesiastical government, and communion.

If one or more of these elements or bonds linking the baptized person (or group of baptized persons) to the Church are lacking, we have an incomplete form of the Church of Christ and an example of the less full unity or imperfect communion of which we were speaking earlier. If we think of the many elements or bonds involved, it is evident that the degrees of unity may be numerous. For, "the Church recognizes that in many ways she is linked with those who, being baptized, are honored with the name of Christian, though they do not profess the faith in its entirety or do not preserve unity of communion with the successor of Peter" (LG 15a/33-34; the passage goes on to list a number of unifying factors; cf. also UR 3b/345).

In the Decree on Ecumenism the Council refers to a unity that grows: "We hope that it will continue to increase until the end of time" (UR 4c/348). The document on "Catholicity and Apostolicity" which the Joint Working Group (with members from the Catholic Church and the World Council of Churches) produced in 1969, rightly stresses the fact that "the Gospel promises the full achievement of the unity of all in Christ only for the time of his return in glory. Then the universal communion of men will be realized, the final gathering of Israel and the nations (cf. Rom. 11). For, Christ prayed the Father for the unity of all those who should believe in him

(John 17:20 ff.); this unity remains a goal which is never reached on earth, but one towards which we must always be moving, in order that the world might believe that God sent him. The full unity which should unite all men with God in Christ will only be attained at the end. While waiting for this future gift, the Church must become aware of all which is provisional in itself, it must have the courage to acknowledge what is lacking in its catholicity, and make its life and action more and more 'catholic.' "[12]

Unity in Pluralism

Unity, even external unity, is not a synonym for uniformity and does not exclude legitimate diversity. At the present hour of mission and ecumenism this principle is highly important and relevant. The Council admits that in the past the principle "has not always been honored" (UR 16/360) and that its strict observance "is among the prerequisites for any restoration of unity" (*ibid.*).

The fourth Assembly of the World Council of Church at Uppsala (1968) offered some reflections on this point which deserve our special attention: "The quest for catholicity faces us with the question whether we betray God's gift by ignoring the diversities of the Spirit's working. Diversity may be a perversion of catholicity but often it is a genuine expression of the apostolic vocation of the Church. This is illustrated by the New Testament, where through a wide range of doctrinal and liturgical forms, relevant to differing situations, the one unchanging apostolic heritage finds expression. Behind the variety of apostolic activities we discern a double movement: the Church is always 'being called out of the world and being sent into the world' (Lund 1952). This double movement is basic to a dynamic catholicity. Each of the two movements requires different words and actions in different situations, but always the two movements belong together. The constitutive center of this double movement is corporate worship in which Christ himself is the one who both calls and sends. Here we also discern a basis for evaluating the Spirit's gift. A diversity which frustrates the calling and the sending is demonic; the diversities which encourage and advance the double movement, and therefore enhance catholicity, are of different kinds. There are now as in the New Testament rich varieties of charismatic gifts, such as are described in I Cor. 12-14; there are diverse ways of proclaiming the gospel and setting forth its mysteries; there are manifold ways of presenting doctrinal truths and of celebrating sacramental and liturgical events; churches in different areas adopt different patterns of organization. By such diversities, intrinsic to the double movement, the Spirit leads us forward on the way to a fully catholic mission and ministry."[13]

It is worth our while, therefore, to look at the main texts in which Vatican II expounds the principle of variety in unity:

LG 13d/32: "Within the Church particular Churches hold a rightful place. These Churches retain their own traditions without in any way lessening the primacy of the Chair of Peter. This Chair presides over the whole assembly of charity and protects legitimate differences, while at the same time it sees that such differences do not hinder unity but rather contribute toward it."

LG 23e-f/46: "By divine Providence [and not by human stubbornness] it has come about that various churches established in various places by the apostles and their successors have in the course of time coalesced in several groups, organically united, which, preserving the unity of faith and the unique divine constitution of the universal Church, enjoy their own discipline, their own liturgical usage, and their own theological and spiritual heritage. . . . This variety of local churches with one common aspiration is particularly splendid evidence of the catholicity of the undivided Church."

UR 4g/349: "While preserving unity in essentials, let all members of the Church, according to the office entrusted to each, preserve a proper freedom in the various forms of spiritual life and discipline, in the variety of liturgical rites, and even in the theological elaborations of revealed truth. In all things let charity be exercised. If the faithful are true to this course of action, they will be giving ever richer expression to the authentic catholicity of the Church."

UR 16/359-60: "From the earliest times, moreover, the Eastern Churches followed their own disciplines, sanctioned by the holy Fathers, by synods, even ecumenical Councils. Far from being an obstacle to the Church's unity, such diversity of customs and observances only adds to her comeliness, and contributes greatly to carrying out her mission, as has already been recalled. To remove any shadow of doubt, this sacred Synod solemnly declares that the churches of the East, while keeping in mind the necessary unity of the whole Church, have the power to govern themselves according to their own disciplines, since these are better suited to the temperament of their faithful and better adapted to foster the good of souls."

UR 17b/360: "This sacred Synod declares that this entire heritage of spirituality and liturgy, of discipline and theology, in their various traditions, belongs to the full and apostolic character of the Church."

OE 2/374: "This variety [of rites and particular churches] within the Church in no way harms her unity, but rather manifests it."

OE 5/376: "This sacred Synod . . . not only honors this ecclesiastical and spiritual heritage with merited esteem and rightful praise, but also unhesitatingly looks upon it as the heritage of Christ's universal Church. For this reason, it solemnly declares that the churches of the East, as much as those of the West, fully enjoy the right, and are in duty bound, to rule themselves." (This is the only time in the documents that the phrase "solemnly declares" is used.)

GS 92b/306: "Such a mission [of spreading the gospel] requires in the first place that we foster within the Church herself mutual esteem, reverence, and harmony, through the full recognition of lawful diversity. Thus all those who compose the one People of God, both pastors and the general faithful, can engage in dialogue with ever-abounding fruitfulness. For the bonds which unite the faithful are mightier than anything which divides them. Hence, let there be unity in what is necessary, freedom in what is unsettled, and charity in any cases."

These texts of Vatican II are incisive and clear; they call, not for interpretation, but for reading, meditation, and application. In his address at the opening of the third session (1964) Pope Paul VI spoke of the Church's "wondrous ability to unite all men in a bond of brotherhood, to embrace various cultures and languages, distinctive forms of liturgy and spirituality, all kinds of national, social, cultural, and educational differences. She has a marvelous knack of bringing unity out of all this diversity, while preserving every legitimate manifestation of variety."[14] Perhaps the language here smacks of triumphalism and the yearning for an ideal to be achieved rather than a reality that is effectively lived out. At least there is no doubt that Pope Paul was expressing one of the great missionary and ecumenical preoccupations of the Church of Vatican II. Later on, in the text of the Credo of the People of God, Pope Paul inserts the same doctrine: "In the bosom of this Church, the rich variety of liturgical rites and the legitimate diversity of theological and spiritual heritages and special disciplines, far from injuring her unity, make it more manifest."[15]

In his address at Constantinople, on July 25, 1967, Pope Paul said to Patriarch Athenagoras: "In the light of our love for Christ and our fraternal charity, we will become even more aware of the profound identity of our faith, and the points on which we still differ will not keep us from perceiving this profound unity. There too, charity must help us as it helped Hilary and Athanasius to recognize identity of faith, above and beyond differences of vocabulary, at a moment when serious disagreements were dividing the Christian episcopacy. Did not St. Basil himself, in his pastoral charity, defend the genuine faith in the Holy Spirit while avoiding the use of certain words which, correct as they may have been, could have been an occasion of scandal for one part of the Christian people? And did not St. Cyril of Alexandria in 433 agree to give up his very beautiful theology in order to make peace with John of Antioch, once he was sure that aside from different expressions their faith was the same? Is this not an area where the dialogue of charity can extend itself to great advantage through casting aside many obstacles and opening the pathways to full communion of faith in the truth? *To find ourselves again one in diversity and fidelity can only be the work of the Spirit of love.* But if unity of faith is required for full communion, diversity in usage is no obstacle—quite the contrary. Did not St. Irenaeus, 'who was well-named, for he was a peacemaker both in name and in conduct' [Eusebius, *Historia Ecclesiastica*, V, 24, 18], say that difference in custom 'confirms agreement in faith' [*op. cit*, V, 24, 13]? And the great Doctor of the African Church, Augustine, looked upon diversity of usages as one of the reasons for the beauty of the Church of Christ [*Ep.* XIV, 32]."[16]

In the texts listed and quoted above we find the following propositions clearly stated:

1. The visible unity of the Church allows, desires, and even requires pluralism (variety, particularity, diversity). Unity is not uniformity. "Variety within the Church in no way harms her unity, but rather manifests it" (OE 2/374).

2. Catholicity, apostolicity, and the mission of the Church promote pluralism (LG 23e-f/46; UR 4g/349; 16/359-60; 17b/360).

3. The pluralism is manifested in the diversity of rites liturgical pluralism), in the various forms of spiritual life and of disciplines (disciplinary pluralism), and in the theological formulation of revealed truth (theological pluralism).

4. When properly understood, such pluralism or variety (to use the terms the Council uses in the texts cited) is not harm-

ful to the unity of the Church, but is at its service; far from injuring unity, it manifests it; it brings out in a clearer way the catholicity of the Church; it is part of the Church's full catholicity and apostolicity; it is necessary if the Church is to fulfill its mission; it helps in the investigation and presentation of the divine mysteries; far from being an obstacle to Church unity, pluralism increases its beauty. In his discourse at the opening of the second session (1963), Paul VI therefore said that the unity of the Church "allows for a variety of languages, traditional rites and customs, local prerogatives, different schools of spirituality, legitimate institutions, and freedom of choice in the activities of daily life."[17] We are far indeed from the time when Catholics were proud that even the visiting Japanese priest said: "Dominus vobiscum"! Instead we find the Council making its own the words of the *Letter to Diognetus* and saying: "The Christian faithful, gathered together in the Church out of all nations, 'are not marked off from the rest of men by their government, nor by their language, nor by their political institutions.' So they should live for God and Christ by following the honorable customs of their own nation" (AG 15g/603).

This is also the reason why in the formation of future priests there should be "an attempt on the students' part to make contact with the particular way of thinking and acting characteristic of their own people. . . . Let them consider the points of contact between the traditions and religion of their homeland and the Christian religion. . . . All these objectives require that seminarians pursue their priestly studies, as far as possible, while associating and living together with their own people" (AG 16d-e/604-5).

The same principle holds for religious: "Thoroughly enriched with the treasures of mysticism adorning the Church's religious tradition, religious communities should strive to give expression to their treasures and to hand them on in a manner harmonious with the nature and the genius of each nation. Let them reflect attentively on how Christian religious life may be able to assimilate the ascetic and contemplative traditions whose seeds were sometimes already planted by God in ancient cultures prior to the preaching of the gospel" (AG 18b/606-7). The same procedure is also praised in regard to the contemplative life: "All are striving to work out a genuine adaptation to local conditions" (AG 18d/607).

If all that we see and admire in these surprising texts of Vatican II is taken seriously and put into practice, the one and unique Church of Christ will acquire many, varied faces. Apostles and missionaries will no longer seek to bring all peoples into the "Latin Church" (that is, into a Church which represents *one* possible incarnation of the gospel, and that a Western one), but will simply bring these peoples the gospels. It is the gospel that must, as leaven, salt, light, and new life, permeate the peoples of the world, find a new concrete shape in them, and transform them. All then "must give expression to this newness of life in the social and cultural framework of their own homeland, according to their own national traditions. They must be acquainted with this culture. They must heal it and preserve it. They must develop it in accordance with modern conditions, and finally perfect it in Christ. Thus the life of Christ and the life of the Church will no longer be something extraneous to the society in which they live, but will begin to permeate and transform it" (AG 21d/611). It is in this may that "the good news of Christ constantly renews the life and culture of fallen man. It combats and removes the errors and evils resulting from sinful allurements which are a perpetual threat. It never ceases to purify and elevate the morality of peoples. By riches coming from above, it makes fruitful, as it were from within, the spiritual qualities and gifts of every people and of every age. It strengthens, perfects, and restores them in Christ. Thus by the very fulfillment of her own mission the Church stimulates and advances human and civic culture. By her action, even in its liturgical form, she leads men toward interior liberty" (GS 52d/264-65).

Liturgical Pluralism

Liturgical pluralism is specifically sanctioned and even praised in the documents of Vatican II:

UR 4g/349: "The variety of liturgical rites" is perfectly reconcilable with "unity in essentials" and can even help give richer expression to the authentic catholicity and apostolicity of the Church.

UR 15e/359: The Council describes the love which Eastern Christians have for their own liturgy, and ends the section by saying: "All should realize that it is of supreme importance to understand, venerate, preserve, and foster the exceedingly rich liturgical and spiritual heritage of the Eastern churches, in order faithfully to preserve the fullness of Christian tradition, and to bring about reconciliation between Eastern and Western Christians." The primary reason here given is theologically important: "in order faithfully to preserve the fullness of Christian tradition." The Eastern liturgical rites are important by reason of their venerable antiquity; in them is reflected the tradition that derives from the Apostles through the Fathers and is part of the divinely revealed and indivisible patrimony of the universal Church (cf. OE 1/373).

UR 17b/360: The Council repeats that the liturgical heritage of the Eastern Christians belongs to the catholic and apostolic character of the Church.

OE 2/374: The traditions of each particular church or rite are to be preserved whole and entire, since "this variety within the Church in no way harms her unity, but rather manifests it."

OE 6a/376: "All Eastern rite members should know and be convinced that they can and should always preserve their lawful liturgical rites."

SC 4/138: "Finally, in faithful obedience to tradition, this most sacred Council declares that holy Mother Church holds all lawfully acknowledged rites to be of equal authority and dignity; that she wishes to preserve them in the future and to foster them in every way. The Council also desires that, where necessary, the rites be carefully and thoroughly revised in the light of sound tradition, and that they be given new vigor to meet the circumstances and needs of modern times."

We should not think, however, that such liturgical pluralism is valid and desirable only for already existing liturgies. The same catholicity of the Church that required new forms of liturgy and ecclesiastical discipline in the past can require other forms today and in the future. In the Decree on the Missions the Council looks for a liturgy "which harmonizes with the genius of the people" (AG 19c/608). Therefore the Constitution on the Liturgy formally declares: "Even in the liturgy, the Church has no wish to impose a rigid uniformity in matters which do not involve the faith or the good of the whole community. Rather she respects and fosters the spiritual adornments and gifts of the various races and problems. Anything in their way of life that is not indissolubly bound up with superstition and error she studies with sympathy and, if possible, preserves intact. Sometimes in fact she admits such things into the liturgy itself, as long as they harmonize with its true and authentic spirit" (SC 37/151).

This principle is not only immensely valuable to the missionary but also has great ecumenical possibilities. At Paris in 1962 Cardinal Bea had said: "In all these matters, about which there is generally no explicit command by God, Christ has left the Church much more free and, as the history of canon law, liturgy, and forms of devotion shows, the Church has always shown great consideration for the needs of the times, the different customs of people and pastoral requirements."[18]—The Council, in the Decree on Ecumenism, n. 15 (in regard to the Orthodox) and nn. 20-23 (in regard to the Protestants), speaks of all the fine things to be found among non-Catholic Christians. The Orthodox and Protestants would indeed have to become "Catholics" in the best sense of this term, that is, they would have to become integral parts of the one and unique Church of Christ in the unity which the

Savior wants; but this does not mean they would have to become "Latins" or adopt the Latin liturgy in England, Germany, or any other country.

Theological Pluralism

Concerning a possible theological pluralism within the unity which Christ desires for his Church, we must first of all read the conciliar texts themselves. The subject is, after all, a highly important one, and it is therefore worth our while to see clearly the doors which Vatican II opened in this respect. Here are the main passages:

UR 7g/349: "While preserving unity in essentials, let all members of the Church, according to the office entrusted to each, preserve a proper freedom . . . even in the theological elaborations of revealed truth."

UR 17a/360 formally declares the legitimacy of variety in theological formulations of doctrine: "What has already been said about legitimate variety we are pleased to apply to differences in theological expressions of doctrine. In the investigation of revealed truth, East and West have used different methods and approaches in understanding and proclaiming divine things. It is hardly surprising, then, if sometimes one tradition has come nearer than the other to an apt appreciation of certain aspects of a revealed mystery, or has expressed them in a clearer manner. As a result, these various theological formulations are often to be considered as complementary rather than conflicting. With regard to the authentic theological traditions of the Orientals, we must recognize that they are admirably rooted in holy Scripture, fostered and given expression in liturgical life, and nourished by the living tradition of the Apostles and by the writings of the Fathers and spiritual authors of the East; they are directed toward a right ordering of life, indeed, toward a full contemplation of Christion truth."

UR 17b/360: The theological heritage that is specific to the East "belongs to the full catholic and apostolic character of the Church."

GS 62b/268: "Recent studies and findings of science, history, and philosophy raise new questions which influence life and demand new theological investigations." Therefore, "theologians are invited to seek continually for more suitable ways of communicating doctrine to the men of their times. For the deposit of faith or revealed truth are one thing; the manner in which they are formulated without violence to their meaning and significance is another. In pastoral care, appropriate use must be made not only of theological principles, but also of the findings of the secular sciences, especially of psychology and sociology. Thus the faithful can be brought to live the faith in a more thorough and mature way" (62c-d/ 268-69). In relation to this last statement about a purer and more mature life of faith, we should recall that the Council had already noted that "new conditions have their impact on religion" and that "a more critical ability to distinguish religion from a magical view of the world and from the superstitions which still circulate purifies religions and exacts day by day a more personal and explicit adherence to faith" (GS 7c/205). As a remedy against modern atheism it had suggested that the Church should renew and purify itself "by the witness of a living and mature faith, namely, one trained to see difficulties clearly and to master them" (GS 21f/219). In the Decree on Ecumenism, the Council, after saying that the Church has continual need of reform, adds: "If the influence of events or of the times has led to deficiencies in conduct, in Church discipline, or even in the formulation of doctrine (which must be carefully distinguished from the deposit itself of faith), these should be appropriately rectified at the proper moment" (UR 6b/350). This statement evidently supposes that there can be deficiencies in the formulation of doctrine and that these can be corrected.

GS 62i/270: Theologians, therefore, should "through a sharing of resources and points of view . . . try to collaborate with men well versed in the other sciences. Theological in-

quiry should seek a profound understanding of revealed truth
without neglecting close contact with its own times. As a result, it will be able to help those men skilled in various fields
of knowledge to gain a better understanding of the faith" concerning God, man, and the world. The Council recognizes
that "this common effort will very greatly aid in the formation
of priests" and that "our contemporaries" will receive "the
doctrine of the Church . . . in a manner better suited to
them." For all this to become effectively possible and for the
theologian to do his duty in this desirable way, "let it be
recognized that all the faithful, clerical and law, possess a
lawful freedom of inquiry and thought, and the freedom to
express their minds humbly and courageously about those
matters in which they enjoy competence" (GS 62j/270).

GE 11b/650: "It is . . . the responsibility of these [theo-
logical] faculites to explore more profoundly the various areas
of the sacred disciplines so that day by day a deeper understanding of sacred revelation will be developed, the treasure
of Christian wisdom handed down by our ancestors will be
more plainly brought to view, dialogue will be fostered with
our separated brothers and with non-Christians, and solutions
will be found for problems raised by the development of doctrine." Therefore, says the Council in the next paragraph:
"these ecclesiastical faculties should zealously promote the
sacred and related sciences by an opportune revision of their
own bylaws. Adopting also more recent methods and teaching
aids, let them lead their listeners on to more searching in-
quiries."

AG 22b-c/612-13: "Theological investigation must necessarily be stirred up in each major socio-cultural area, as it is
called. In this way, under the light of the tradition of the
universal Church, a fresh scrutiny will be brought to bear on
the deeds and words which God has made known, which have
been consigned to sacred Scripture, and which have been un-
folded by the Church Fathers and the teaching authority of
the Church. Thus it will be more clearly seen in what ways

faith can seek for understanding in the philosophy and wisdom of these peoples. A better view will be gained of how their customs, outlook on life, and social order can be reconciled with the manner of living taught by divine revelation. As a result, avenues will be opened for a more profound adaptation in the whole area of Christian life. Thanks to such a procedure, every appearance of syncretism and of false particularism can be excluded, and Christian life can be accommodated to the genius and dispositions of each culture." The Council then adds that these new particular cultures can then be taken up "into Catholic unity." In 22e/613 the hope is expressed that "Episcopal Conferences within the limits of each major socio-cultural territory [Latin America, for example] will be so united among themselves that they will be able to pursue this program of adaptation with one mind and with a common plan."

GS 44b-c/246: "Thanks to the experience of past ages, the progress of the sciences, and the treasures hidden in the various forms of human culture, the nature of man himself is more clearly revealed and new roads to truth are opened. These benefits profit the Church. For, from the beginning of her history, she has learned to express the message of Christ with the help of the ideas and terminology of various peoples, and has tried to clarify it with the wisdom of philosophers, too. Her purpose has been to adapt the gospel to the grasp of all as well as to the needs of the learned, insofar as such was appropriate. Indeed, this accommodated preaching of the revealed word ought to remain the law of all evangelization. For thus each nation develops the ability to express Christ's message in its own way. At the same time, a living exchange is fostered between the Church and the diverse cultures of people." The Council then admits that to carry on this kind of work the Church needs the help of all, even non-believers, who understand the contemporary mentality; and it adds: "It is the task of the entire People of God, especially pastors and theologians, to hear, distinguish, and interpret the many voices of our age, and to judge them in the light of the divine word. In this way, revealed truth can always be more deeply penetrated, better understood, and set forth to greater advantage" (44d/246). Earlier, in the same document, 4a/201-2, the Council had said: "To carry out such a task, the Church has always had the duty of scrutinizing the signs of the times and of interpreting them in the light of the gospel. Thus, in language intelligible to each generation, she can respond to the perennial questions which men ask about this present life and the life to come, and about the relationship of the one to the other. We must therefore recognize and understand the world in which we live, its expectations, its longings, and its often dramatic characteristics." Further on, in 11a/209: "The People of God believes that it is led by the Spirit of the Lord, who fills the earth. Motivated by this faith, it labors to decipher authentic signs of God's presence and purpose in the happenings, needs, and desires in which this People has a part along with other men of our age." God speaks and manifests his will through the signs of the times. In a way God continues to reveal himself, and theology cannot fail to take account of this important "theological source."

The wealth of conciliar documentation which we have just presented allows us to draw certain conclusions:

1. The Council rejects the idea of a single theology that is ready made, already formulated, definitive, and perennial. It is not enough to repeat what was said and to use the formulations of even the most eminent and distinguished theologians or Doctors of the Church or even of the ordinary and extraordinary Magisterium. The theologian who is satisfied to be a simple repeater or passer-on of traditional theses and doctrines, in their traditional formulation, does not deserve his title or fulfill his duty (cf. GS 44b-d/246; 62b/268).

2. With all desirable clarity the Council affirms that within the unity of the Church a theological pluralism ("different methods and ways of understanding and expressing the divine mysteries") is not only possible but legitimate and necessary

in view of the catholicity and apostolicity proper to the Church (cf. UR 17a-b/360). In his address to the members of the International Theological Commission (1969), Paul VI declared that "We gladly acknowledge development and variety in theological science, that 'pluralism' which aptly describes mankind and its culture in our day."[19]

3. New theological investigations, researches, and formulations are required by the need to understand revelation ever more fully (cf. GE 11b/650), by the recent studies and findings of the sciences, history, and philosophy (cf. GS 62b/268), by a more critical spirit (GS 7c/205); as a remedy against modern atheism (cf. GS 21f/219); by the Church's need of continual renewal and purification (cf. UR 6b/350), by the necessity of grasping revealed deeds and words in the light of the philosophy, wisdom, traditions, usages and customs of the peoples to be evangelized (cf. AG 22b/612; GS 44b/246), and by the signs of the times (cf. GS 4a/201).

4. We must distinguish between revealed truths and the manner in which they are expressed: in the objective truths as such (the "deposit of faith") there can be no error or need of adaptation; but in the manner of expressing them there can be deficiencies (cf. UR 6b/350) and new and more suitable ways of communicating them must be found (cf. GS 62c/268).

5. Theology must make use of "men skilled in various fields of knowledge" (GS 62i/270), even if they be non-believers (GS 44d/246), and of discoveries in the secular sciences (GS 62b/268; cf. OT 20/455).

6. In order that the theologians may carry out their task, they must enjoy proper freedom in research, thought, and expression of ideas (cf. GS 62j/270). The statement of the Synod of Bishops in 1967 declares that "it is the task of theologians to seek an ever more perfect understanding and expression of the revealed mystery, so as to be able to answer, as far as this is possible, the often serious problems which are constantly arising in Christian life. In order to carry out this task in an adequate way, they must be allowed a suitable

freedom in undertaking new researches and perfecting the inherited patrimony of truth."[20] In his just-mentioned address to the International Theological Commission, October 6, 1969, Paul VI said: "We assure you that We have every intention of acknowledging the norms and requirements proper to your disciplines and of protecting the freedom of expression which theological scholarship requires, and the freedom of research which its progress demands."[21]

Unity in Catholicity

When we say that the Church of Christ, as the new People of God, is "catholic," we mean that she must be the sign and instrument of unity, hope, and salvation for all peoples with their immense variety of usages and customs, civilizations and cultures, languages and spiritual gifts, rites and traditions, temporal and spiritual goods, ways of thinking and acting. But, obviously, we are faced with a difficulty here: how can such variety be reconciled with the unity of a People which proclaims itself "one and unique"? Must the people sacrifice their variety or the People its unity? Can so great a variety be possible within a genuine unity? Can unity be preserved amid an authentic respect for variety?

More than once has the Church been accused of being unable to respect the individuality of the peoples she evangelizes. Men even speak of a kind of spiritual colonialism on the part of the Church. This is indeed perhaps the greatest difficulty which missionaries must face. At the Council, which numbered about 800 missionary bishops among its members, the problem arose at a number of points, and the various conciliar documents reveal a pervading preoccupation. It is worth our while, then, to collect and reflect on the main passages:

LG 13b/31: "Since the kingdom of Christ is not of this world (cf. Jn. 18:36), the Church or People of God takes nothing away from the temporal welfare of any people by establishing that kingdom. Rather does she foster and take to herself, insofar as they are good, the ability, resources, and customs of each people. Taking them to herself she purifies, strengthens, and ennobles them." The Dogmatic Constitution teaches, then, that when the Church evangelizes the peoples of the earth she does not lessen them but fosters, makes her own, purifies, strengthens, and elevates their temporal welfare, abilities, resources, and customs, insofar as these are good.

LG 17c/36: "Through her [the Church's] work, whatever good is in the minds and hearts of men, whatever good lies latent in the religious practices and cultures of diverse peoples, is not only saved from destruction but is also healed, ennobled, and perfected unto the glory of God, the confusion of the devil, and the happiness of man." Therefore: everything good in the heart and mind, rites and cultures of men, not only need not disappear but is to be preserved, healed, exalted, and perfected.

GS 42c/241-42: "The Church . . . recognizes that worthy elements are to be found in today's social movements, especially an evolution toward unity, a process of wholesome socialization and of association in civic and economic realms."

GS 42f/242: "This Council . . . looks with great respect upon all the true, good, and just elements found in the very wide variety of institutions which the human race has established for itself and constantly continues to establish." The Church, therefore, accepts as "her task to uncover, cherish, and ennoble all that is true, good, and beautiful in the human community" (GS 76h/289).

SC 37/151: The Church "respects and fosters the spiritual adornments and gifts of the various races and peoples. Anything in their way of life that is not indissolubly bound up with superstition and error she studies with sympathy and, if possible, preserves intact. Sometimes in fact she admits such things into the liturgy itself, as long as they harmonize with its true and authentic spirit."

AG 9c/596: "Whatever good is found to be sown in the hearts and minds of men, or in the rites and cultures peculiar to various peoples, is not lost. More than that, it is healed, ennobled, and perfected for the glory of God, the shame of the demon, and the bliss of men."

AG 18b/606-7: "Religious communities should strive to give expression to these treasures [of mysticism adorning the Church's religious tradition] and to hand them on in a manner harmonious with the nature and the genius of each nation. Let them reflect attentively on how Christian religious life may be able to assimilate the ascetic and contemplative traditions whose seeds were sometimes already planted by God in ancient cultures prior to the preaching of the gospel."

AG 22a/612: "The seed which is the word of God sprouts from the good ground watered by divine dew. From this ground the seed draws nourishing elements which it transforms and assimilates into itself. Finally is bears much fruit. Thus, in imitation of the plan of the Incarnation, young churches, rooted in Christ and built up on the foundation of the apostles, take to themselves in a wonderful exchange all the riches of the nations which were given to Christ as an inheritance (cf. Ps. 2:8). From the customs and traditions of their people, from their wisdom and their learning, from their arts and sciences, these churches borrow all those things which can contribute to the glory of their Creator, the revelation of the Savior's grace, or the proper arrangement of Christian life."

NA 2e/662: "The Catholic Church rejects nothing which is true and holy in these [non-Christian] religions. She looks with sincere respect upon those ways of conduct and of life, those rules and teachings which, though differing in many particulars from what she holds and sets forth, nevertheless often reflect a ray of that Truth which enlightens all men." In the following paragraph the Council exhorts all to "acknowledge, preserve, and promote the spiritual and moral goods found among these men, as well as the values in their society and culture."

In summation, and using only the words and expressions of

the Council itself, we can say that Vatican II assures us of the following: The Church does not destroy or reject, but considers attentively and respectfully, examines in a benevolent spirit, acknowledges, preserves intact, fosters, cultivates, develops, purifies, heals, strengthens, elevates takes into Christian life and even at times into the liturgy, and brings to perfection in Christ—all that is not indissolubly bound up with superstition and error, all that is true, good, just, holy, lovable, and beautiful, whether in the minds and hearts of men and in their spiritual endowment, or in the abilities, resources, temporal and spiritual goods, socio-cultural values, customs, cultures, rites, ascetical and contemplative traditions, arts, teachings, and ways of acting of peoples, nations, and religions. Note well: even religions! For all this ("precious elements of religion and humanity": GS 92e/306) is a preparation for the gospel (cf. LG 16/34-35), a guidance course toward the true God (AG 3a/586), a secret presence of God (AG 9c/596), a hidden seed of the word (AG 11b/598), rays of the truth which enlightens every man (NA 2e/662).

This positive evaluation of pagan religions is very important. In regard to the expression, "hidden seed of the word" (cf. AG 11b/598), we find some reflections of great theological value in an essay of Bishop Elias Zoghby, vicar of the Greek Melkite Catholic Patriarch for Egypt and the Sudan (at the Council he called the attention of the Fathers to various aspects of Eastern theology). After stressing the identity of the Creator Word and the Word made flesh (cf. also GS 38a/235-36; 45b/247), he continues: "The Creator Word has put into every human being a divine seed which the Greek Fathers call the 'seed of the Logos.' Over the centuries the Spirit of God cultivated this seed in souls, preparing them by a 'divine pedagogy' to receive the Word made flesh. In offering Christ to even the most primitive peoples the Church cannot forget that these peoples already have, along with the divine seed, a civilization and traditions that are permeated in varying degrees by the presence of the Word. The Church must try to discover this seed of the Word in such civilizations in order to awaken in these peoples a spontaneous readiness to receive the Word made flesh. The task of the Church is thus not one of replacing the Creator Word by the Redeemer Word but of helping these peoples to recognize the action of the Word in all that is good among them: their worship, their civilization, their aspirations, and of showing Christ to be the Word made flesh, the Word become their Brother. . . . It is this identity of Creator Word and Redeemer Word that makes it possible for the Church of Christ to be universal, that is, to offer the gospel to every man who comes into the world. It is this same identity that also makes it possible for the Church to effect the unity of mankind by offering to men as their common Brother him who has created them all out of nothing. But if the peoples are to recognize in Christ the Word whose seed they carry in themselves, we must present them with the poor Christ of the gospels, the Christ of Bethlehem and Golgotha, and not a Christ whom we have already 'nationalized' and who bears our image and wears our garb, a foreign Christ—be he Greek, Anglo-Saxon, or Latin—whom they cannot assimilate and reshape in their own image and likeness. Christ can effect unity only to the extent that he takes flesh again in each country and each people, so that each man can recognize in him his own Brother, one of his own family and race. Men want a Savior who is 'without a country' and can become their fellow-countryman; a Christ conceived by the Holy Sprit and having no other father than the one Father, so that they can make him their own as 'first-born of all creatures' (Col 1:15). Christ, then, must make his own the various people with what they are and have, for he it is who made them what they are and gave them what they have."[22]

In a note (n. 7) to its Decree on the Missions 3a/586, the Council cites and approves several patristic texts which speak of this ceaseless presence of the Word. St. Irenaeus, for example, in his *Adversus Haereses*, III:18,1, writes: "In the beginning the Word was with God; by him all things were made, and he was always present to the human race"; or again, in IV:6,7: "From the beginning the Son, who is present to the work he has himself made, reveals the Father to all to whom the Father wishes to be reveled, and when and as the Father wishes it." The Constitution on the Church in the Modern World also speaks of the Word, before his Incarnation, being in the world as the true light which enlightens every man (GS 57d/263). In this context we must not forget the grandiose perspective which the Dogmatic Constitution on the Church opens up for us at the beginning of that document, when, after teaching that the Eternal Father did not abandon men, even after they have sinned, but "ceaselessly offered them helps to salvation, in anticipation of Christ the Redeemer," it makes its own the patristic concept of the *universal* Church of which all just men since Adam are a part or, as the holy Fathers used to put it, all who "from Abel the just down to the last of the elect," have been saved, or are now being saved, or are yet to be saved, whether inside or outside the Catholic Church (cf. LG 2b/15-16).

This fundamental principle is the basis for missionary work. "Sent by Christ to reveal and to communicate the love of God to all men and nations, the Church is aware that there still remains a gigantic missionary task for her to accomplish. For the gospel message has not yet been heard, or scarcely so, by two billion human beings. And their number is increasing daily. These are formed into large and distinct groups by permanent cultural ties, by ancient religious traditions, and by firm bonds of social necessity. Some of these men are followers of one of the great religions, others remain strangers to the very notion of God, while still others expressly deny His existence, and sometimes even attack it. *In order to be able to offer all of them the mystery of salvation and the life brought by God, the Church must become part of all these groups for the same motive which led Christ to bind Himself, in virtue of His Incarnation, to the definite social and cultural conditions of those human beings among whom He dwelt"* (AG 10/596-97). We should reread and reflect upon the italicized words, for they provide us with the happy formulation of a great principle which must always be in the forefront of the Church's missionary awareness: As Christ became a Jew, so the Church must become Chinese, African, Latin-American, Brazilian, so that it may be able effectively to offer to all the mystery of salvation and the life brought by God.

To evangelize other peoples does not mean bringing the *Latin* Church (as "Latin" or taking shape at Rome) to other continents. All attempts to latinize Asia or Africa have failed, for such was not the mission Christ gave to his Apostles and through them to the Church. The Western or Latin expression of the Church (in liturgy, theology, and even philosophy) is only one legitimate and possible expression, and it is not necessarily the most perfect expression. But this principle has often been violated in the past and is still violated today. Many men have suffered greatly as a result; their cultural rights were not respected, and the colonialist, imperialist mentality of domination that centuries ago took hold of the nations of Western Europe left its mark on the Church as well. Vatican II attempts to remove this stain from the Church. There is hope now that she who is catholic by right will be catholic in fact as well. In nations or regions that are non-Latin she will have to permit and foster (if the texts we have cited are to be put into practice!) an effort at delatinization, deitalianization, and dewesternization in liturgy, theology, discipline, and pastoral practice. Here new doors and new perspectives will open before us, and we will be able to speak in a proper and legitimate sense of a Brazilian Church, a Latin-American Church, an African Church, etc. To the extent that the Church does not in fact become Brazilian, the Brazilian will not be of the Church. It is not enough to baptize him if we want to make him truly of the Church. Nor is it enough to impose on him a mentality which he cannot in fact accept because he is culturally incapable of such acceptance.

But the catholicity of the Church can be betrayed in many ways. The Joint Working Group's study document on "Catholicity and Apostolicity," to which we have already referred, mentions four ways: "The first lies in succumbing to the temptation of power, whether it be by adopting the ways which belong properly to political power, whether it be by conforming or submitting to the powers of this world in such a way that the Church keeps the poor at a distance and Christian brotherhood is restricted to members of the same race, nation, culture, or class. The second would wish to justify the formation of sects or parties within the Church. The third makes people become proud of their own confession and despise others. The fourth, on the other hand, allowing itself to be seduced by temporal ideologies which assail it, consists in misusing the term 'catholic' and boasting of a tolerance which results finally in the disappearance of Christian identity. The catholicity of the Church cannot disown the Church's bond with Jesus Christ, in whom alone there is salvation for all men (Acts 4:12) and the forms of betrayal which we have mentioned cannot be avoided except by an obedience which is constantly renewed by the Lord, whose love makes his people capable of being open to all human conditions and whose truth enables it to realize its identity and its continuity throughout time, places, and circumstances."[23]

Unity in "Communion"

The Prefatory Note of Explanation on Chapter 3 of the Dogmatic Constitution on the Church says that *"Communion* is an idea which was held in high honor by the ancient Church (as it is even today, especially in the East)" (Abbott 99). In Western ecclesiology, however, the term has only recently come back into use, with its rich contents and perspectives.

In the New Testament the word *communion* (Greek: *koinonia)* occurs 19 times (14 times in the letters of St. Paul) and expresses the relationship that exists among Christians in their common dependence on Christ and the Holy Spirit.

In the Fathers of the Church the word has clearly a relational meaning and refers in general to the relationship of friendship and mutual acceptance that exists within the local churches or with other churches. The sign of this kind of communion was the Eucharist. In the second century, for example, Bishop Polycarp of Smyrna and Pope Anicetus disagreed on the date of Easter, but they did not therefore break off ecclesiastical communion, or, as Eusebius puts it (quoting Irenaeus), "they remained in communion with each other"; that is, Anicetus allowed Polycarp to celebrate the Eucharist in the Church of Rome.[24] Catholics who were travelling through areas under the control of heretics took their own Eucharist with them, and heretics did the same in turn, so as not to enter into communion with each other. When a Christian set out for foreign parts, he took with him a kind of passport supplied by his bishop ("letters of communion" or "letters of recommendation" or "letters of peace"). The bearer of such a passport was received as a brother. The bishops kept a list of the main churches with which they were "in communion"; in that list the Church of Rome was the first to be named, and a church which was "in communion with the Church of Rome" was automatically recognized by the other churches.[25] Admission to the Eucharist ("the sacrament of unity") has therefore been, since earliest times, the expression of "communion" (that is why reception of the Eucharist is even today simply called "Communion") and implies the acknowledgement of the Christian authenticity of the other church or community. Because of the contemporary ecumenical movement we speak a good deal today of "intercommunion," that is, of the admission of Protestants and Orthodox to the Catholic Eucharist (at Medellin, 1968, on the occasion of the Second General Conference of Latin American Bishops) or vice versa. Vatican authorities officially disapprove of such practices. I believe that the main reason for their stance is the ancient and truly traditional practice (an element, it seems, in the Apostolic *paradosis* or tradition) according to which admission to the Eucharist meant the suspension of excommunication and the recognition of the Christian legitimacy and othodoxy of the persons, communities, or churches which were admitted to "communion."

The documents of Vatican II make frequent use of the word "communion" or of such expressions as "hierarchic communion" and "ecclesiastical communion." But they never define the meaning of the term or phrase. Only the already quoted Prefatory Note of Explanation tells us that the word "communion" is understood "not of a certain vague feeling, but of an *organic reality* which demands a juridical form, and is simultaneously animated by charity" (Abbott 99). The Ecumenical Directory *Ad totam ecclesiam* sees in baptism "the basis for communion among all Christians";[26] and the Constitution on the Church teaches that the Eucharist brings us "into communion with Him and with one another" (LG 7c/20). *Koinonia* or "communion" is, in the first place, this interior, invisible, sacramental, and supernatural unity which unites all Christians in a vital way to Christ and, in Christ, to each other. In this sense the Church is "a new brotherly community" established by Christ (GS 32d/231), "a fellowship of life, charity, and truth" (LG 9e/26). This interior, supernatural communion will find its proper external manifestation and thus become "the community of faith, hope, and charity" (LG 8a/22), a community "of faith, liturgy, and love" (AG 19b/608).

In Chapter 4 of the Constitution on the Church Vatican II teaches that there exists in the Church a profound communion among all the baptized: all have in common the same Lord and the same Spirit, all form a single body, all share the same faith and the same baptism, the same grace and the same calling, the same hope and the same love, the same responsibility and the same task (LG 32b-c/58).

But communion is not simply a synonym for unity. There can be unity without communion. Sociology shows that there are various kinds or types of conhesion or unity: family, team, hamlet, school, crowd, municipal council, army. The Church's form of unity is communion. The Council speaks of the "unity of communion" (LG 15a/33), and of fellowship in unity" (UR 2d/344). The Holy Spirit "gives her [the Church] a unity of fellowship and service" (LG 4b/17); he is "the principle of their coming together" (LG 13a/31). We have here a very important but relatively unexplored principle: *the external unity of the Church should be sought and structured in the form of a communion.* If it is, the Church will be the universal congregation of love. "If by the will of Christ some [in the Church] are made teachers, dispensers of mysteries, and shepherds on behalf of others, yet all share *a true equality with regard to the dignity* and to the activity common to all the faithful for the building up of the Body of Christ" (LG 32c/58). Strictly speaking, there are no "superiors" and "inferiors" or "subjects" in the Church. We have to read Mt 23: 8-11 and Lk 22:25-27, and take them seriously. "You are all brothers" (Mt 23:8 JB), brothers in a single great family. In this family there are no special "dignitaries." The Church is and ought to be a brotherhood, a *koinonia*, a communion. It is clear enough, on the other hand, that, although all are brothers and equal in dignity, there must be a variety of *services* or ministries, so that the People of God may grow and all may "freely and in an orderly way" (LG 18a/37) reach the kingdom of God (the brief but rich paragraph 18a should be read attentively.)

The Church is, consequently, a "hierarchic communion." But the word "hierarchic" is an adjective and should not be turned into a noun, which is then treated as co-extensive with the Church. As a brotherhood which is hierarchically organized according to services, the Church lives and has its organization: "He [Christ] continually distributes in His body, that is, in the Church, gifts of ministries through which, by His own power, we serve each other unto salvation so that, carrying out the truth in love, we may in all things grow up into Him who is our head" (LG 7g/21). These services are many and varied, occasional or permanent, deriving from sacraments, callings, or charisms. But "among those various ministries which, as tradition witnesses, were exercised in the Church from the earliest times, the chief place belongs to the office of those who, appointed to the episcopate in a sequence running back to the beginning, are the ones who pass on the apostolic seed. . . . With their helpers, the priests and deacons bishops have therefore taken up the service of the community, presiding in the place of God over the flock whose shepherds they are, as teachers of doctrine, priests of sacred worship, and officers of good order" (LG 20c-d/39-40). However, those who carry out these hierarchical services "were not meant by Christ to shoulder alone the entire saving mission of the Church toward the world. On the contrary, they understand that it is their noble duty so to shepherd the faithful and recognize their services and charismatic gifts that all according to their proper roles may cooperate in this common undertaking with one heart" (LG 30b/57).

In this passage we have, summed up for us in authoritative fashion by the Council, the essential theology of ministry within the "hierarchic communion." We also have enough of the elements that enable us to see *the likenesses and differences between the Church and a democracy.* The theme has been much debated of late. It is clear that in the Church (as in any democracy!) not all are equal in the function or services they provide for the common good. But the diversity here is not a diversity in dignity (since "all share a true equality with regard to . . . dignity": LG 32c/58), but simply a diversity in importance of function. Some services require special competence, authority, or powers, and those who exercise these functions are then called "authorities" (as in any democracy). But the nature and purpose of the authority or power are essentially different in the Church from what they are in a democracy or in any other political order for that matter. Ecclesiastical authority must be seen in the light of the Church's being as mystery or sacrament: the Church is not a society in the ordinary sense (as are democracies and political societies generally), for, precisely as a society, it is the sign and instrument of the glorified Lord and his Spirit, so that through it he may continue his work of saving and sanctifying men and the world. When ecclesiastical authorities act strictly as such, they do it in the place of Christ, they act "in the person of Christ," "in the name of Christ," they are "ministers of Christ," "vicars or legates of Christ." For this reason their authority (which is a "sacred power") is given them by God in a sacramental way. In a democracy things are quite different: those in authority are delegates of the people, they act in the place of the people and in their name, and they receive powers from the people through juridical acts.

It would therefore be illogical, for example, to use the non-democratic nature of the Church as an argument against an active participation of the people in the appointment of candidates to ecclesiastical office. Furthermore, what men find most praiseworthy in democracy—freedom, brotherhood, equality, co-responsibility—are thoroughly at home in the *koinonia*. "Through the loving exercise of authority" God's people will be perfected "in the fraternal harmony of the family of God" (UR 2d/344). The Church is not a democracy; much less is it a monarchy; it is a fellowship in which "all share a true equality with regard to the dignity and to the activity common to all the faithful for the building up of the Body of Christ" (LG 32c/58). This conception must be taken seriously and put into practice.

In drawing up the Constitution on the Church, especially the third chapter on "the hierarchic structure of the Church," the Theological Commission kept constantly in mind the idea that the Church is a "communion." Consequently it stressed the preposition "with" and avoided the preposition "under." Behind each of these two little prepositions there lies a whole conceptual world. It seems that other Commissions, engaged in drawing up other conciliar documents, were not as careful and sensitive. In the Decree on the Missions, for example, we read that the bishops are to exercise their missionary role "with Peter and under Peter." That they should do it "with Peter" is, obviously, an essential and deeply Christian and ecclesial necessity; but that they ought to do it "under Peter" is an idea deriving from an age which is not certainly that of the apostles, and from a mentality which is not necessarily evangelical. The Decree on the Bishops' Pastoral Office uses similar language when it says that "together with the Supreme Pontiff and under his authority, they [the bishops] have been sent to continue throughout the ages the work of Christ, the eternal pastor" (CD 2b/397); or when it says that the bishops share a solicitude for the whole Church "in communion with and under the authority of the Supreme Pontiff" (3a/397).

The expression "under the authority of" and the title "Supreme Pontiff" are not required by the nature of Christianity. The Constitution on the Church is certainly more theologically exact when it teaches that the Catholic Church "is governed by the successor of Peter and by the bishops in union with that successor" (LG 8b/23); or, better still, that the bishops "together with the successor of Peter . . . govern the house of the living God" (LG 18d/38); or that bishops must remain in "hierarchical communion with the head and members of the body [of bishops]" (LG 22a/43); or that "together with its head, the Roman Pontiff, and never without this head, the episcopal order is the subject of supreme and full power over the universal Church" (LG 22c/43); or that the episcopal office can be exercised "only in hierarchical communion with the head and the members of the college" (LG 21d/41). These texts say nothing of "under the authority" or "under Peter"; these latter phrases say something which does not flow necessarily from the nature of the Church as a brotherhood or communion. Even when the Prefatory Note of Explanation asserts that the college of bishops can act only with the consent of the pope, it goes on to explain: "The phrase is 'with the *consent of its head'*; for there should be no thought of a *dependence* on some *outside* person. The word 'consent,' on the contrary, recalls the *communion* existing between head and members" (Abbott 100).[27]

The other intraecclesial relationships are to be seen in the light of these same principles: bishop-laity, bishops-priests, priests-priests, priests-laity. For all, whatever their functions, are always brothers one to another and, as such, are equals. "Christian communion among wayfarers brings us closer to Christ" (LG 50d/82). The essential need will always be to maintain "the bond of unity among themselves and with Peter's successor" (LG 25c/48). This is a simple and brief formula; in it the short word "with" does away with the "under." Communion is the free union of equal brothers, among whom there is neither subjection nor domination. Since the Holy Spirit is "the principle of their coming together" (LG 13a/31) and "brings about the marvelous communion of the faithful" (UR 2b/344), he will assure the necessary ecclesial harmony (cf. LG 22d/44) or "fraternal harmony of the family of God" (UR 2d/344).

In truth, "the heritage of this people [of God] are the dignity and freedom of the sons of God, in whose hearts the Holy Spirit dwells as in His temple. Its law is the new commandment to love as Christ loved us. Its goal is the kingdom of God" (LG 9d/25-26).

This people is "the whole assembly of charity" (LG 13d/ 32).

It is the "Catholic communion" (OE 4c/375).

It is "the sacred mystery of the unity of the Church," and "the highest exemplar and source of this mystery is the unity, in the Trinity of Persons, of one God, the Father and the Son in the Holy Spirit" (UR 2f/344). The Church is "the visible sacrament of this unity" (LG 9f/26): the sign and instrument of intimate union with God and of the unity of all mankind (cf. LG 1b/15). Thus the Church is obedient to God's plan of sanctifying and saving men through communion with one another (cf. LG 9a/25).

Such communion was the object of the Lord's prayer to his Father: "I do not pray for them [the apostles] alone. I pray also for those who will believe in me through their word, that all may be one as you, Father, are in me, and I in you; I pray that they may be [one] in us, that the world may believe that you sent me. I have given them the glory you gave me that they may be one, as we are one—I living in them, you living in me—that their unity may be complete. So shall the world know that you sent me, and that you loved them as you love me" (Jn 17:20-23). Our communion will be the great source of credibility in the eyes of the world. Later on, in his first Letter, the elderly Apostle St. John will write: "What we have seen and heard we proclaim in turn to you so that you may share life with us. This fellowship of ours is with the Father and with his Son, Jesus Christ. Indeed, our purpose in writing you this is that our job may be complete" (1 Jn 1:3-4).

The principle of "unity in communion" also makes possible a better understanding of *the theology of the particular or local church*, a subject on which so much is being said and written today, and with good reason. We no longer think of the universal Church as an immense organization or perfect society with a powerful center upon which all the particular communities or churches converge and upon which they all depend for their life or survival. Today we look upon the universal Church as a great Catholic Communion. That Church is indeed one and unique, but "the one and only Catholic Church" comes into being "in and from [the] individual churches (LG 23a/44). The Mystical Body is "the body of the churches" (LG 23c/45). Each particular church is, in and for itself, a communion in which the ideal of the Church as the Lord intended and established it takes concrete form: in the particular church "the one, holy, catholic, and apostolic Church of Christ is truly present and operative" (CD 11a/403; cf. LG 26a/50; 28c/54). Therefore, "particular

churches are bound to mirror the universal Church as perfectly as possible" (AG 20a/609). The great Catholic Communion (or universal Church) is the harmonious consort of
local communions, and in it the requirements of a unity "in
communion" are obeyed. The necessary but difficult harmony, internal and external, between the local communions
will be the result more of the special action of the Holy Spirit
("principle of their coming together . . . in fellowship": LG
13b/31) than of laws, institutions, and visible persons. St.
Peter (and his successors) is the "visible source and foundation of unity of faith and fellowship" (LG 18c/38): visible
in the sense of being the sign and instrument, or the sacrament, of the invisible but real action of the Holy Spirit.

However (an important point) this is not to say that this
is the Spirit's only or indispensable instrument. For "it is
not only through the sacraments and Church *ministries* that
the same Holy Spirit sanctifies *and leads* the People of God
and enriches it with virtues. Allotting His gifts 'to everyone
according as he will' (1 Cor. 12:11), He distributes special
graces among the faithful of every rank. By these gifts He
makes them *fit and ready to undertake the various tasks or
offices advantageous for the renewal and upbuilding of the
Church*" (LG 12c/30). The important point is this: *we do
not necessarily have to start with the hierarchy in every effort
to renew and build up the Church.* The Church is established
on the "apostles *and prophets*" (Eph 2:20).

We must not neglect this doctrine of Vatican II, a doctrine
that is, any event, both Biblical and patristic. The Council
itself offers us two striking examples of movements of renewal which did not start in the upper echelons of the Church:
the liturgical movement and the ecumenical movement. The
history of the two movements of Church renewal is sufficiently well known, as are the great obstacles which their early
proponents had to overcome on the part of high ecclesiastical
authority, especially at Rome. Today, as the Council tells us,
"zeal for the promotion and restoration of the liturgy is rightly

held to be a sign of the providential disposition of God in our time, *as a movement of the Holy Spirit in His Church*" (SC 43a/153). But this was not what the high authorities said in the days when the movement was beginning to cause unrest in some communities. As for starting the ecumenical movement within the Church, it seems that the Holy Spirit found his first instruments more readily outside the Church than within it: "Among our separated brethren . . . there increases from day to day a movement, fostered by the grace of the Holy Spirit, for the restoration of unity among all Christians. . . . This movement . . . is called ecumenical" (UR 1c/ 342).

These movements provide us with valuable instruction and light on the magisterial action of the Church and its limitations, as well as on the obligations which holders of the magisterial office have of attending to the "sense of the faith" which the baptized have. The Constitution on the Church (12a/29) refers to the unusually strong text (1 Jn 2:20-27) in which the Apostle John speaks of the interior "anointing" which the Christian receives; what is meant is an action of the Holy Spirit who enlightens the soul, teaches it, and guides it in the varying situations of life. The Apostle even says to his readers: "all knowledge is yours" (v. 20), and "you have no need for anyone to teach you" (v. 27). The Lord himself says: "They shall be taught by God" (Jn 6:45); what we have here is the Holy Spirit as the "interior teacher" (cf. PO 11/ 556, note 140). The Council goes on to say (in LG 12a) that "the body of the faithful as a whole, anointed as they are by the Holy One, cannot err in matters of belief." The Council is speaking of a property or special quality proper to the baptized. The manifestation of this quality is called "the sense of the faith." There is no claim that each baptized person is infallible in his act of faith. Rather, when the body of the faithful as a whole, " 'from the bishops down to the last member of the laity,' . . . shows universal agreement in matters of faith and morals," then we have *the infallibility of the*

Church in her act of faith. Notice how the bishops and all the other baptized are here set side by side, on the same level. The Council then says that this sense of the faith is aroused and sustained by the Holy Spirit and that by this sense the People of God "clings without fail to the faith . . . , penetrates it more deeply by accurate insights, and applies it more thoroughly to life" (LG 12b/29-30).

The Council adds, however, that all this activity, though the work of the Holy Spirit, takes place "under the lead" of the Church's teaching authority. This directive role of the hierarchy is certainly important and even indispensable (and is the exclusive and specific action of the hierarchy: cf. DV 10b/117-18), but does not necessarily make the hierarchy a dynamic agent that stimulates and urges to progress. Above all, it must not be exercised only to rein in or even to suppress, as has happened. The hierarchy must not extinguish the Spirit (LG 12d/30). For the "development of tradition," of which the Council speaks in the Constitution on Revelation, *is not the specific, much less the exclusive, work of the magisterium or hierarchy.* On the contrary (the following should be written in extra large letters!), this progress takes place through the contemplation and study of *believers* and through the intimate understanding or vision which the *faithful* have of spiritual things, and *also* through the preaching of the bishops (DV 8b/116). The development of tradition is thus the work of the Church in its entirety, of the whole holy and prophetic people of God and not simply of the Episcopal College or of the successor of Peter and his curia. "Holding fast to this deposit, the entire holy people united with their shepherds remain always steadfast in the teaching of the apostles, in the common life, in the breaking of the bread, and in prayers, so that in holding to, practicing, and professing the heritage of the faith, there results on the part of the bishops *and faithful* a remarkable common effort" (DV 10a/117). In the sense here suggested we can legitimately speak of an authentic, active, and necessary *sharing of the faithful even in the exer-*

cise of the magisterial function ("in holding to, practicing, and professing the heritage of the faith"). It is true that a teaching, once given, does not depend for its validity on the subsequent approval or ratification by the faithful (cf. LG 25d/49); but before they proclaim doctrine, the teachers of the Church, including the successor of Peter, ought to pay attention to the sense of the faith in the faithful and to listen to what the Spirit is saying to the churches and what he is saying in the hearts of men. Genuine communion requires this. The Church is not a monarchy, and the pope is not independent of the sense of the faith which the baptized have.

In addition to the two examples given, it would be quite easy to draw up a list of positions and doctrines which were tenaciously held, protected, and defended by the agents of the Holy See with the approval of the pope or by the pope himself, and which were set aside or tacitly abandoned at the Council and with the Council (that is, when the leaders of the local church actually intervened). One of the moderators at the Council, Cardinal Suenens, recently observed: "Quite an impressive list could be made of theological positions taught in Rome in the recent and more distant past as the only true ones, which were simply done away with by the Council Fathers."[28] We have already seen another striking example when, in Chapter 2, we were studying the question of the identity between the Catholic Church and the Mystical Body; the Council abandoned the position of Pius XII and provided a corrected version.

This fact also throws a new light on the limitations in the teaching authority of the pope and his curia, as well as on the need of active participation by the other members of the Episcopal College in the government of the Church. For the normative truth is that the "bishops, the successors of the apostles, . . . together with the successor of Peter, the Vicar of Christ and the visible head of the whole Church, govern the house of the living God" (LG 18d/38).

Notes for Chapter 5

[1] *A Documentary History of the Faith and Order Movement, 1927-1963*, ed. by Lukas Vischer (St. Louis: Bethany Press, 1963), p. 168.

[2] *The Third World Conference on Faith and Order, Lund 1952*, ed. by Oliver S. Tompkins (London: SCM, 1953), pp. 18, 33-34; also in *A Documentary History*, pp. 87, 103.

[3] *The New Delhi Report: The Third Assembly of the World Council of Churches 1961*, ed. by W. A. Visser 't Hooft (New York: Association Press, 1962), p. 116; also in *A Documentary History*, pp. 144-45.

[4] *The Uppsala Report 1968*, ed. by Norman Goodall (Geneva: World Council of Churches, 1968), p. 17.

[5] Pius XII, *Mystici Corporis*, (June 29, 1943), no. 60, in *Selected Letters*, p. 82.

[6] *Acta Synodalia*, II/1, p. 220.

[7] *Acta Synodalia*, II/1, p. 423.

[8] *Acta Synodalia*, II/1, p. 434.

[9] *Acta Synodalia*, II/2, p. 10.

[10] *Acta Synodalia*, II/2, p. 60. — In *Voi forse sapete: Address to a General Audience*, June 1, 1966, Paul VI asked: "Are all those who have been baptized, even those who are separated from Catholic unity, in the Church? In the true Church? In the one Church?" and his answer was: "Yes!" A little further on he says that they belong "to the Church in at least an initial or partial way" (*TPS*, 11 [1966], 373). On the importance of baptism as the "foundation of communion among all Christians," cf. *Ad totam Ecclesiam: Directory for the Application of the Second Vatican Council Decisions in Ecumenical Matters*, Part 1 (May 14, 1967), in *TPS*, 12 (1967), 253.

[11] Paul VI, *Discourse to the Secretariat for Christian Unity*, April 28, 1967, in *TPS*, 12 (1967), 99.

[12] Study Document Prepared by the Joint Theological Commission on "Catholicity and Apostolicity," in *One in Christ*, 6 (1970), 456.

[13] *The Uppsala Report 1968*, ed. by Norman Goodall (Geneva: World Council of Churches, 1968), p. 15.

[14] Paul VI, *In signo Sanctae Crucis: Address at the Opening of the Third Session of Vatican Council II*, September 14, 1964, in *TPS*, 10 (1964-65), 106-7.

[15] Paul VI, *Solemni hac liturgia: Solemn Profession of Faith at the Closing of Faith*, June 30, 1968, in *TPS*, 13 (1968-69), 280.

[16] Paul VI, *Greetings to Patriarch Athenagoras* (in the Cathedral Church of St. George at Constantinople, July 25, 1967), in *TPS*, 12 (1967), 266.

[17] Paul VI, *Salvete Fratres*, September 29, 1963, in *TPS*, 9 (1963-64), 135.

[18] "The Council and Christian Unity," address at Paris, January 23, 1962, in Augustin Cardinal Bea, *The Unity of Christians*, ed. by Bernard Leeming S.J. (New York: Herder and Herder, 1963), p. 125.

[19] Paul VI, *Gratia Domini Nostri: Address to Members of the International Theological Commission,* October 6, 1969, in *AAS,* 61 (1969), 715-16.

[20] Synod of Bishops, 1967: Report of the Synodal Commission on the Dangers to Faith, in *Osservatore Romano,* October 30-31, 1967.

[21] Paul VI, *Gratia Domini Nostri,* in *AAS,* 61 (1969), 715.

[22] Elias Zoghby, "Unité et divsersité de l'Eglise," in Guilherme Barauna O.F.M. (ed.), *L'Eglise du Vatican II,* 2 (Unam Sanctum 51b; Paris: Editions du Cerf, 1967), pp. 508-9.

[23] *One in Christ,* 6 (1970), 457-58.

[24] Eusebius, *The History of the Church,* V:34, tr. by G. A. Williamson (Baltimore: Penguin Books, 1965), p. 233.

[25] Cf. Ludwig Hertling S.J., *Communio: Church and Papacy in Early Christianity,* tr. by Jared Wicks S.J. (Chicago: Loyola University Press, 1972); Jérôme Hamer O.P., *The Church in a Communion,* tr. by Ronald Matthews (New York: Sheed & Ward, 1964), especially ch. 9.

[26] *TPS,* 12 (1967), 253.

[27] In speaking of Christ establishing the Church, the Decree on Ecumenism asserts, as its basic thesis, that: "In order to establish this holy Church of His everywhere in the world until the end of time, Christ entrusted to the College of the Twelve the task of teaching, ruling, and sanctifying" (UR 2c/344). Then it continues with a second thesis: "Among their number He chose Peter. After Peter's profession of faith, He decreed that on Him He would build His Church; to Peter He promised the keys of the kingdom of heaven (cf. Mt 16:19, in conjunction with Mt 18:18). After Peter's profession of love, Christ entrusted all His sheep to him to be confirmed in faith (cf. Lk 22:32) and shepherded in perfect unity (cf. Jn 21:15-17)" (*ibid.*). When this text was being voted on at the Council, one bishop thought it necessary to distinguish between the office of teaching (given to the college) and the office of governing or ruling. The latter office, this bishop said, was entrusted "to Peter alone and only through Peter to the other apostles" (Modification 19). The Commission replied that such a doctrine would not be consistent with the Constitution on the Church; this answer was then presented to the Fathers and approved. Modification 23 proposed that the text read: "Christ entrusted the task of teaching, ruling, and sanctifying to Peter and, with him and under him, to the other apostles." This formulation, too, was rejected by the Commission with the approval of the Council.

[28] Cardinal Suenens, interview of May 15, 1969, in José de Broucker (ed.), *The Suenens Dossier* (Notre Dame: Fides, 1970), p. 24.

Chapter 6

Papal Primacy and Its Limits

The "*First* Dogmatic Constitution on the Church," solemnly promulgated at Vatican Council I, was to be completed by a "*Second* Dogmatic Constitution on the Church." When, therefore, the Council of Pius IX was interrupted and not reconvened, the necessary second Constitution, so ardently awaited and desired, never appeared. Yet the ecclesiological dogma of Vatican I (primacy and infallibility of the Pope) was partial and incomplete and thus required a complement. Many of the Council Fathers in 1869-1870 were vividly aware of, and denounced in strong terms, what they called the "great gap": the lack of a clear definition of the nature, position, and competence (by divine right) of the bishops in the Church. "We need a treatise on the bishops as successors of the apostles," said Archbishop Melchers of Cologne; "without it the authentic idea of the primacy and its hierarchic place in the Church can neither be understood nor explained." Bishop Haynald reflected: "The doctrine of the Vatican Council on the Church would be imperfect and defective if in speaking of Peter and his successor, the Roman pontiff, the vicar of Christ, nothing were said of the other apostles and their successors, the bishops." Bishop Lyonnet exclaimed: "The hardest thing to take is the silence, so profound as to be inexcusable, on the rights and prerogatives of bishops; the faithful have good reason to ask whether the bishops are not perhaps going to be suppressed." Others of the Council Fathers spoke in similar terms. The Deputation on Faith (as the Council's Theological Commission was called at Vatican I) tried, through its representative, to restore tranquillity by saying: "We shall deal with the bishops in a second Constitution" or "The matter will be taken up in a second Constitution on the Church of Christ."

But the second Constitution never saw the light. In 1871, the great English theologian, Newman, was already prophesying in a letter: "But we must have a little faith. . . . No truth stands by itself—each is kept in order and harmonized by other truths. The dogmas relative to the Holy Trinity and the Incarnation were not struck off all at once—but piecemeal. . . . So will it be now. Future popes will explain and in one sense limit their own power. This would be unlikely, if they merely acted as men, but God will overrule them. Pius has been overruled—I believe he wished a much more stringent dogma than he has got. The new definition needs both correction and complement. . . . Let us have faith and patience. A pope and a new council will be able to guide the ship in a different direction."[1]

In fact, there is no doubt but that Vatican II has completed Vatican I. The Dogmatic Constitution *Lumen Gentium* can be considered to be the promised "Second Constitution on the Church of Christ." Chapter 3 of Vatican II's Constitution is the natural continuation of the dogma proclaimed in Vatican I. After reaffirming the doctrine of Vatican I on the institution, perpetuity, power, and nature of the primacy of the Roman Pontiff, the Constitution on the Church continues: "Continuing in the same task of clarification begun by Vatican

I, this Council has decided to declare and proclaim before all men its teaching concerning bishops, the successors of the apostles, who together with the succesor of Peter, the Vicar of Christ and the visible Head of the whole Church, govern the house of the living God" (LG 18d/38).

As soon as Pope John XXIII had announced his intention of convoking the Twenty-First Ecumenical Council, the great theological journals of Europe began to turn their attention precisely to this subject. It was the great theological theme of the time and of the Council. The exact point at issue was *the harmonization of the relations which exist, can exist, and ought to exist between the primatial power of the pope and the divinely given powers of the bishops.* It was then that the phrase "episcopal collegiality" became widespread. It was evident that something had to be modified in the life of the Church. For this, it was necessary to determine more accurately which elements in the structure of the Church are immutable (of divine origin) and which can be dropped, changed, or replaced.

In order, however, to have a theological panorama of the possible activities of bishops as individuals and as a college, it will repay us first to recall the exact terms of the primatial office held by the successor of Peter, as defined in Vatican I. For the Council of Pius IX will necessarily determine the limits within which the ecclesiological decisions of Vatican II must restrict themselves.

The Primatial Power of Peter's Successor

(1) A genuine primacy of *jurisdiction* and not simply of honor, inspection, direction, or presidency. Vatican I forthrightly declares: "If anyone says that the Roman Pontiff has only the office of inspection or direction, but not the full and supreme power of jurisdiction over the whole Church, not only in matters that pertain to faith and morals, but also in matters that pertain to the discipline and government of the Church throughout the whole world . . . : let him be anath-

ema."[2] The power of jurisdiction includes the ministry of teaching and the legislative, judicial, and coercive powers.

(2) An *ordinary* jurisdictional power, that is, a power connected with the primatial office itself as an essential, constitutive element.[3] It is, therefore, not a power delegated by the Episcopal College or by the whole body of Christ's faithful; it is not just an extraordinary power, depending on some factor outside the person of the pope himself and restricted to certain unusual cases. The Supreme Pontiff can, therefore, intervene jurisdictionally, without anyone's permission, at any moment and in any place.

Later on we shall see that the bishops too have an "ordinary" power. The official and final text of Vatican I is completely silent on how the two jurisdictions, pontifical and episcopal, are to be coordinated when they deal with the same matters. But the record of the debates shows what the majority of the Fathers were thinking and what they did not intend to define. The research of Gustave Thils has thrown light on the matter for us.[4] The term "ordinary" was opposed to the "extraordinary" of Tamburini and Eybel ("extraordinary" in the sense of "not ordinary" and thus in a negative and exclusive sense). By a unanimous vote, in which the minority spoke clearly and vigorously while the majority were serenely confident of the moderation of the Holy See, the Fathers of Vatican I rejected the idea that the Roman Pontiff can intervene in other dioceses "in an ordinary way," that is, in the daily, habitual government of the dioceses. The pope does not have *habitual* ordinary power in the dioceses; such belongs to the local bishops alone. In the discussion (we shall see some texts later on), it was said that the pope cannot intervene in the dioceses "arbitrarily," "in an unreasonable way," "regularly," or "unduly," but only when "salvation" and "unity" are at stake and when "the needs of the Church" and "clear usefulness" require such intervention. This is why the Constitution on the Church, of Vatican II, will say of bishops that "the pastoral office or the habitual and daily care of their sheep is entrusted to them completely" (LG 27b/52).

(3) An *immediate* ordinary judisdictional power.[5] It is "immediate" for two reasons: because it was given to him immediately by Christ, and because he can exercise it over the bishops, priests, and faithful of the whole world, without asking anyone's permission. The canon on jurisdiction, which we have already quoted, continues: "or if anyone says that this power is not ordinary and immediate either over each and every church or over each and every shepherd and faithful member: let him be anathema."

(4) An immediate, ordinary jurisdictional power that is *episcopal*. Vatican I made a point of saying "truly episcopal"; that is, it includes pastoral functions of the same nature as those of the bishops (and is not simply an administrative authority).[6] After listing the functions proper to bishops, the official expositor explained to the Council Fathers: "The episcopal power of each bishop in his own diocese and of the pope in relation to all dioceses is specifically the same. There is this difference that this power exists in an unlimited way in the pope and only in a limited way in the other bishops; that in the pope it is independent, in the other bishops dependent; that it other other bishops it is restricted to the diocese each one rules, while in the pope it suffers no limitation of place but extends to the ends of the earth."[7]

(5) An ordinary, immediate, episcopal, jurisdictional power that is *full*; that is, the Supreme Pontiff has not only the principal part of the supreme power, but the fullness of that power; no ecclesiastical power exists which is not included in the primacy. There was at Vatican I a tendency to make episcopal power act as a limitation on the primacy, so that the latter would have not the fullness but only the principal part of ecclesiastical powers. It was against this tendency that the canon already twice quited adds: "if anyone says that he [the Roman Pontiff] has only a more important part and not the complete fullness of this supreme power . . . :

let him be anathema."[8]

(6) An ordinary, immediate, episcopal, full, jurisdictional power that is *universal*: without limitation as to time, person, place, or subject; a power over all faithful, individually and collectively, over all pastors of whatever rite, in matters of faith and morals, of government, liturgy, and customs. Here again Vatican I was explicit: to the Roman Church "the shepherds of whatever rite and dignity and the faithful, individually and collectively, are bound by a duty of hierarchical subjection and of sincere obedience; and this not only in matters that pertain to faith and morals, but also in matters that pertain to the discipline and government of the Church throughout the world."[9]

(7) An ordinary, immediate, episcopal, full, universal jurisdictional power that is *supreme*: there is no higher authority in the Church, not even an ecumenical Council. Here again the doctrine of Vatican I is categorical: "And because, by the divine right of apostolic primacy, the Roman Pontiff is at the head of the whole Church, we also teach and declare that he is the supreme judge of the faithful; and that one can have recourse to his judgment in all cases pertaining to ecclesiastical jurisdiction. We declare that the judgment of the Apostolic See, whose authority is unsurpassed, is not subject to review by anyone; nor is anyone allowed to pass judgment on its decision. Therefore, those who say that it is permitted to appeal to an ecumenical council from the decisions of the Roman Pontiff (as to an authority superior to the Roman Pontiff) are far from the straight path of truth."[10]

In the face of definitions that are so categorical and decisive, it will seem superfluous to sk whether there is room in the Church for any authority that is not merely delegated or limited to carrying out papal orders and decisions. At the fifty-third general meeting of Vatican I (May 18, 1870), Cardinal Schwarzenberg of Prague related that the impression was abroad in Germany that the Council had been convoked not for the greater good of the Church but for the greater glorification of the Roman Curia.[11] Bishop Vérot, perhaps as joke, even proposed that the Council should also take a vote on the following canon: "If anyone says that the authority of the Roman Pontiff over the Church is so complete that he can dispose of everything as he wishes, let him be anathema."[12]

In an official exposition presented to the whole Council in the name of the Deputation on Faith, Bishop Zinelli referred to these criticisms and declared that the primatial power of the pope is in fact full and supreme "so that it cannot be restricted by any higher human power, but only by natural and divine law."[13] In these words the official expositor granted and indeed proclaimed the possibility of a restriction by natural and divine law. In other words: *the primatial power can be (and is) limited by natural and divine law.* In June, 1871, the Swiss Bishops issued a Joint Pastoral Instruction on the Decrees of the Council, in which they explained: "It in no way depends on the caprice of the pope or upon his good pleasure, to make such and such a doctrine the object of a dogmatic definition: he is tied up and limited to the divine revelation, and to the truths which that revelation contains; he is tied up and limited by the Creeds already in existence, and by the preceding definitions of the Church; he is tied up and limited by the divine law and by the constitution of the Church: lastly, he is tied up and limited by that doctrine, divinely revealed, which affirms that alongside religious society there is civil society; that alongside the ecclesiastical hierarchy there is the power of temporal magistrates, invested in their own domain with a full sovereignty, and to whom we owe in conscience obedience and respect in all things morally permitted, and which belong to the domain of civil society."[14]

Since a limitation on the power of the Roman Pontiff is possible, *it is legitimate to inquire more specifically into these limits.* To this end we shall discuss certain theological principles.

1. *The principle of the ordinary jurisdiction of bishops*

Vatican I itself inserted into the third chapter, which defines the nature and character of the pope's jurisdictional primacy, a special section on epicopal power. The expositor noted that the section was added expressly "to meet the objections, repeated time and again, of those who fear that by asserting the truly episcopal, ordinary, and immediate jurisdiction of the pope over every diocese, we may be denying and doing away with the power of individual bishops." The section itself reads as follows: "This power of the Supreme Pontiff is far from standing in the way of the ordinary and immediate episcopal jurisdiction by which the bishops who, under appointment of the Holy Spirit (*see Acts 20:28*), succeeded in the place of the apostles, feed and rule individually, as true shepherds, the particular flock assigned to them. Rather this latter power is asserted, confirmed, and vindicated by this same supreme and universal shepherd in the words of St. Gregory the Great: 'My honor is the honor of the whole Church. My honor is the solid strength of my brothers. I am truly honored when due honor is paid to each and every one.' "[15]

In this text, and its context, we have several points affirmed:

(1) The bishops possess an ordinary and immediate episcopal power of jurisdiction. The same three adjectives are applied to their power as were applied in the previous paragraph to the primatial power of the pope.

(2) The bishops are "appointed by the Holy Spirit." In the intention of the Council Fathers these words from Scripture affirm the divine institution of the episcopate ("so-that the bishops may be explicitly said to be the successors of the apostles and appointed by the Holy Spirit").

(3) The bishops are the successors of the apostles: at the Council of Trent the Church had declared that the bishops "have succeeded the apostles"[16] and Vatican I repeats the

formula. In his encyclical letter *Satis cognitum*, Leo XIII explains the doctrine thus: "By the fact that the bishops succeed the apostles, they inherit their ordinary power, and thus the episcopal order necessarily belongs to the essential constitution of the Church."[17] In *Mystici corporis* Pius XII says that "the people . . . must venerate them [the bishops] as successors of the Apostles by divine institution."[18]

(4) The bishops are true shepherds: the text mentions only "the particular flock assigned to them" and says nothing of a possible collegial sharing by the bishops on the shepherding of the universal Church.

(5) The bishops feed and rule: the "pastoral" (or "episcopal") power is defined more fully as including the power to sanctify, to teach officially, and to rule (this last involves legislative, judicial, and coercive power).

(6) This power of the bishops must be asserted, confirmed, and vindicated by the pope.

For our purposes here we shall dwell upon two points:

(a) By *divine* institution the bishops have an episcopal, ordinary, and immediate power of jurisdiction over that part of the flock which the pope entrusts to them. However, "full, universal, episcopal, ordinary, and immediate" we may conceive the primatial power of the Supreme Pontiff to be, it is beyond its scope to change what the divine will has made part of the hierarchic structure or constitution of the Church. In other words: *the pope cannot transform the bishops into his functionaries, agents, envoys, officials, vicars or mere executors of his orders and directives.* For, by divine law the bishops are "vicars of Christ, not "vicars of the pope." Vatican I expressly teaches that the episcopal power of the bishops is "ordinary" (that is, not delegated). Leo XIII, in his encyclical *Satis cognitum* (1896), is even more explicit: the bishops "are not to be looked upon as *vicars* of the Roman Pontiffs; because they exercise a power really their own, and are most truly called the *ordinary* pastors of the people over whom they rule."[19] Pius XII, in his encyclical on the Mystical

Body, teaches that each bishop "is also, as far as his own diocese is concerned, a true Pastor who tends and rules in the name of Christ the flock committed to his care."[20] On the other hand, even as "ordinaries," the bishops remain subject to a "higher ordinary": the pope is the "bishop of bishops," and he can increase or lessen the jurisdictional power of the bishops and even, in some cases, for the good of the Church, totally suppress it (but he cannot do this to all the bishops to the point of making them simple delegates or apostolic vicars).

The pope, moreover, is not only the bishop of bishops; he is also the bishop of all the faithful in the entire world. Such a duplication of power should not, however, lead to any confusion about administration. Leo XIII: "The fact that Christians are bound to obey a twofold authority does not beget any confusion in the administration. We are prohibited in the first place by divine wisdom from entertaining any such thought, since this form of government was constituted by the counsel of God Himself. In the second place we must note that the due order of things and their mutual relations are disturbed if there be a twofold magistracy of the same rank set over a people, neither of which is amenable to the other. But the authority of the Roman Pontiff is supreme, universal, independent; that of the bishops limited, and dependent."[21]

In this context we must recall and reflect on a document which, for some reason or other, has not found entrance into our theology textbooks, although it is of great importance for the correct interpretation of the dogma of the pope's primatial power. Immediately after Vatican I, in 1872, chancellor Bismarck drew up a circular-dispatch, intended for the use of the German government, in which he gave tendentious interpretations of the dogma that had just been defined. Bismarck attributes to Vatican I the following doctrines:

(1) The pope can arrogate episcopal prerogatives to himself in each diocese and replace the bishop's power by his own;

(2) Episcopal jurisdiction is absorbed by papal jurisdiction;

(3) The pope no longer exercises, as he has hitherto, only certain well-defined functions which are reserved to him, but has become the depository of episcopal power in its fullness and entirety;

(4) In principle the pope now replaces each individual bishop;

(5) It is for the pope alone to decide whether at any moment he should in practice take the place of the bishops in their dealings with governments;

(6) The bishops are only tools and functionaries of the pope and have no personal responsibility;

(7) In relation to governments the bishops have become simple functionaries of a foreign sovereign and indeed of a sovereign who, in virtue of his infallibility, is absolute, more so than any other monarch in the world.[22]

The Iron Chancellor's dispatch was published in the *Staats-Anzeiger* at the end of 1874. The German episcopate immediately reacted in a document signed during January and February, 1875, by twenty-three bishops: "All these propositions are without foundation and openly contradict both the wording and the meaning of the decisions of the Vatican Council as depeatedly explained by the pope, the bishops, and the representatives of Catholic scholarship." They then explain: "According to the teaching of the Catholic Church the pope is the bishop of Rome, but not bishop of any other city or diocese: not bishop of Cologne, for example, or bishop of Breslau. As bishop of Rome, however, he is also pope, that is, shepherd and supreme head of the whole Church, supreme head of all the bishops and faithful, and his papal power does not come into play only in certain exceptional cases but must be respected and heeded everywhere and always." However, they point out, "the title of absolute monarch cannot rightly be applied to the pope even in purely ecclesiastical affairs, for he is subject to divine law and bound by the dispositions made by Christ for his Church. He cannot change the constitution given the Church by its divine founder, as a secular ruler can change the constitution of the state. The constitution of the Church is based, in all essential points, on a divine ordinance and is not subject to any human will. In virtue of the same divine act of institution by which the papacy came into being, the episcopate, too, exists. It, too, has its rights and duties by reason of God's ordinance, and the pope has neither the power nor the right to change it. It is wholly erroneous then to think that by decisions of the Vatican Council 'papal juris-diction swallows up episcopal jurisdiction'; that the pope 'has in principle taken the place of the individual bishops'; and that the bishops are now 'only tools of the pope and functiona-ries with no personal responsibility.' According to the un-changing doctrine of the Church, bishops are not simply tools of the pope nor papal functionaries without personal responsi-bility, but have, 'under appointment of the Holy Spirit, suc-ceeded in the place of the apostles.' "

In a special letter to the German episcopate (March 4, 1875) Pius IX states his approbation of the document, "for your declaration expounds pure Catholic doctrine and there-fore the doctrine of the Sacred Council and this Holy See, solidly establishing and developing it by sure and irrefutable arguments. A man of good will, therefore, will find absolutely nothing new therein nor anything that could change the existing situation or provide a pretext for bringing pressure on the Church or for hindering the election of a new pope." In his address at the Consistory of March 15, 1875, the Pope again praised the solemnly approved the document of the German bishops: "In your presence and that of the whole Catholic world, we thank with all our hearts each and all of these bishops; we ratify their luminous declarations and pro-testations, so worthy of their courage, office, and religious spirit, and *we confirm them with Our full apostolic authority.*"

Each of the seven propositions of Bismarck must, then, be regarded as false and "in open contradiction" to the decisions of the Council and to Catholic doctrine. If, then, we wish to state the authentic Catholic doctrine, we need only accept as true the contradictory form of each proposition. The result is the following set of statements. (1) The pope *cannot* arrogate to himself in each diocese the rights of bishop and replace the power of the bishops with his own (the limitation here arising from the divine institution of the episcopate; (2) Episcopal jurisdiction *is not* absorbed by papal jurisdiction; (3) The pope *does not*, in virtue of the definitions of the Vatican Council, became the depository of full and entire episcopal power (in such a way as to exclude the power of other bishops); (4) He *does not* in principle replace each individual bishop; (5) He *cannot* at any moment take the place of the bishops in their dealings with governments; (6) The bishops *do not become* tools of the pope; (7) They *are not* functionaries of a foreign sovereign in relation to governments.

(b) The second point we wish to stress in regard to the power of bishops is that divine law imposes on the pope the obligation, not of replacing the episcopate, but of *aiding* it so that it may flourish and be effective. The Church was founded for the salvation of men, not for the glorification of the hierarchy. The sacrament of orders is a grace "freely given" (for the sake of others), not a grace "that makes its possessor holy"; in other words, the person holds his office in order to be a servant and helper, not to be served and flattered. The faithful do not exist for the sake of priests, nor priests for the sake of bishops, nor bishops for the sake of the pope. Rather the pope exists for the sake of the bishops. The fullness of primatial power does not eliminate or weaken the power of bishops, since, as Vatican I teaches, the former is the "principle . . . and . . . foundation" of the latter,[23] and must be used so that "this latter [the ordinary and immediate episcopal jurisdiction] is asserted, confirmed, and vindicated."[24] This is the reason for the divine institution of the primacy. This is why the short section of Vatican I which has been occupying our attention quotes and canonizes the famous words of St. Gregory the Great (here quoted in its original context, only the italicized words being used by Vatican I):

"I do not regard it [my high office] as an honor in which the honor of my brothers is swallowed up. *My honor is the honor of the whole Church. My honor is the solid strength of my brothers. I am truly honored when due honor is paid to each and every one of them.* . . . Away, then, with language that puffs up vanity and wounds fraternal love."[25] This is also why Pius IX closed the Fourth Session of the Council with a solemn declaration: "This supreme authority of the Roman Pontiff does not oppress but helps, does not destroy but builds up, and time and time again confirms the brothers, that is, the bishops, in their dignity, unites them in love, and protects their rights."[26]

2. *The principle of episcopal collegiality*

Bishop D'Avanzo, as official expositor for the Deputation on Faith, explained to the Council that St. Peter had received from Christ the fullness of apostolic power, but that he cannot and may not use other helpers than those given him by Christ, namely, the other apostles, who had received the same pastoral mission. Here is the important text which gives an official explanation of the mind of the Council:

"Well, then, someone may say (indeed, it has been said), is this full and all-embracing power of Peter to have no limitation? Not at all! It has a *twofold limitation*: one active, as it were, and the other passive. The active limitation stems from the fact that Christ gives Peter his power: 'I, Christ, shall give to you . . .'; 'I have prayed for you . . .'; 'Feed my sheep.' Peter has, then, just so much power as Christ has given to him, and this not for the tearing down but for the building up of the Body of Christ. What I am calling the passive limitation likewise originates in Christ and consists of *the other apostles*. Like a wise architect, Christ made Peter the foundation rock on which he would build his Church. But the same Christ appointed other builders, and Peter must make use of them—the other apostles—in building the Church. According to the second text, Peter was made a teacher and was to strengthen others, but these others were to be none other than those whom Christ was giving Peter as brothers in the apostolate: 'Strengthen your brothers,' and whom he had made his own brothers: 'Go to my brothers.' According to the third text, Peter is to feed the lambs; but these lambs are to be born only by the efforts of the sheep whom Christ had won for himself and was entrusting to Peter to be fed. . . . Peter, then, possesses full and supreme power, but *he cannot and may not exercise it* with the help of any other assistants but the apostles and their successors."[27]

This text brings us to the very interesting and important and, of course, highly topical matter of the collegiality of the bishops with whom the pope must work in establishing the Church and saving souls. The expression "collegiality of the bishops" is a recent one (it came into being in the ecclesiological literature produced in France and Belgium), but the idea itself is ancient, dating back even to apostolic times.[28] Even at Vatican I, despite the fact that the problem of the bishops was never formally discussed, the idea of collegiality came up quite often.[29] Some examples:

Cardinal Schwarzenberg of Prague, at the general meeting of May 17, 1870: "It is much more difficult, in fact it is really impossible, to define the primacy in further detail unless we simultaneously define the power of bishops. How can we elaborate a doctrine about the center and apex, the supreme ruler and head, without considering the other agents in the apostolate, who are also members of the sacred hierarchy? *The episcopate is a single organism*; by Christ's institution, not all who compose it are equal, but whatever is established for one part influences the others, whatever is defined about the head affects the members. . . . If Peter is shepherd of the sheep and lambs, the bishops too are shepherds; Peter looses and binds, but so do each of the apostles—is there no connection between Peter and the others? The jurisdiction of the Supreme Pontiff is called ordinary and immediate: how is the ordinary and immediate jurisdiction of the other bishops to be reconciled with the pope's?"[30]

Bishop Papp-Szilágyi offered the following modification: "The bishops, together with the Roman Pontiff and subordinated to him as being the chief shepherd of the whole flock of the Lord, not only rule and govern their own flocks with a power that comes from God, but also bear, with the pope, the burden of care for the whole Church and, with the pope, are *lawgivers and judges for the whole* Church."[31]

Bishop Ginoulhiac, speaking of the pope and bishops: "Together with the pope the bishops live as *one college*, one body; they always and truly form one catholic organism and one undivided episcopate, each having a part of it but responsible for the whole. . . . By this undivided unity of the episcopal college, the unbroken unity of the Church itself is maintained and fostered."[32]

More important is the official declaration of the expositor, Bishop Zinelli: "We willingly grant that in an ecumenical council, that is, *when the bishops are united with their head, they have supreme and full ecclesiastical power over all the faithful*; that is only right when the Church is united with its head. The bishops, then, have genuinely full power when they are gathered together with their head in an ecumenical council (here they represent the whole Church), but *also when they are dispersed*, yet in union with their head (for here they are the Church)."[33]

Later on Pius XII, in his encyclical on the African missions (1957), provided a text that was regarded as basic before Vatican II:

"And so, Venerable Brethren, since you are most intimately associated with Christ and His Vicar upon earth, inspired by a burning charity, be zealous to share that solicitude for all the churches, which lies heavy upon Our shoulders. Urged by the charity of Christ, *may you realize that you are closely bound to Us in the pressing duty of spreading the Gospel and building up the Church throughout the whole world!* May you not cease or falter in your efforts to cultivate widely among clergy

and faithful alike the spirit of prayer and zeal in giving
mutual assistance according to the measure of the charity of
Christ. . . . It is an undoubted fact that it was to Peter alone
and to his successors, the Roman Pontiffs, that Jesus Christ
entrusted the entirety of his flock. . . . But even though each
bishop is pastor of that portion only of the Lord's flock entrusted to him, nevertheless as lawful successors of the Apostles by God's institution and commandment he is also responsible, together with all the other bishops, for the Apostolic
task of the Church according to the words of Christ to the
Apostles: 'As the Father has sent me, I also send you' [Jn
21:16-18]. This mission, or 'sending forth,' embraces 'all
nations . . . even unto the consummation of the world' [Mt
28:19-20] and certainly did not cease with the death of the
Apostles. Nay, it still continues in the bishops who are in
communion with the Vicar of Jesus Christ. For in them, as
being specifically named 'those who are sent,' namely, Apostles of the Lord, the fullness of the apostolic dignity resides,
which as St. Thomas Aquinas testifies, 'is the chief dignity in
the Church' [*In Ep. ad Rom.* cap. 1, lect. 1]."[34]

In all these texts we see a tendency to maintain that the
bishop is not responsible simply for his own diocese. In one
or other way (the precise nature of this "way" was not yet
clear), he is also responsible for the whole Church: "lawgivers
and judges for the whole Church" were the words of a Vatican
Council Father; "when the bishops are united with their head,
they have supreme and full ecclesiastical power over all the
faithful," said the official expositor at the Council: "each
bishop is also responsible, together with all the other bishops,
for the whole Church," was the more recent teaching of Pius
XII. One of the Council Fathers of Vatican II, Archbishop
Guerry, asked in 1963, "What does episcopal collegiality
mean?" He answered: "It means directly *the common re-*
sponsibility which the whole episcopal body, under the pope,
has for the evangelization of the world and the establishment
of the Church throughout the whole world. This collegiality

therefore involves for each bishop, in addition to his role as special shepherd of his particular Church in the diocese which the pope entrusts to him and in which he exercises jurisdiction, a universal responsibility for the apostolic mission of the Church, in union with the episcopal body, under the direction of the pope as head. This shared responsibility even takes priority for each bishop; it is dominant and ought to inspire him in his special mission as head of a diocese. As soon as he becomes a bishop he becomes a member of the episcopal body and thereby shares in the body's all-embracing responsibility."

Archbishop Guerry adds that this exercise of apostolic collegiality is based on divine law and that an ecumenical council (which is of ecclesiastical origin) is only one of the possible ways in which the bishops may exercise a collegial activity: "It is easy to foresee that the variety in types of collegial action will be increased and become ever more specialized. Collective episcopal structures will be elaborated. This is an irreversible movement. Given the evolution of the world, it becomes daily clearer that we need a common outlook, united action, and co-ordination among all who bear responsibility for the pastoral action of the Church in the modern world."[35]

Let us bear in mind one of Archbishop's Guerry's statements: that the bishop, before becoming ordinary of a particular place, is already incorporated into the episcopal college and shares in the comprehensive responsibility of the college; that the bishop is primarily co-responsible for the whole Church and is only secondarily shepherd of a diocese. This is a principle to which appeal is frequently made in current literature on ecclesiology. In summary it may be said that by his consecration each bishop becomes a member of the episcopal college (which is united to Peter) and thereby shares power over the universal Church. The episcopate is collegial by nature: to be consecrated bishop is to be aggregated to the episcopal college (as to be an apostle was to be aggregated to the apostolic college: "[he] was added to the eleven apostles": Acts 1:26).

At the Council of Trent there had already been attempts to treat explicitly of the relations between the papal primacy and episcopal jurisdiction. At that time it was the Spanish bishops, led (on this point) by Archbishop Pedro Guerrero of Granada, who were most keenly aware of the problem. They protested against the continual interventions of the Roman Curia in the administration of dioceses; they thought that the authority of bishops was weakened by benefices reserved to the Holy See and by the numerous privileges granted to the religious orders and to many members of the diocesan clergy; they maintained, therefore, that a true reform of the Church must take the form of strengthening episcopal authority. They considered that they had the necessary theological basis for this in what they called "the divine right of bishops": according to this theory the episcopate is a hierarchic order established immediately by God and not by the pope. It follows from this that each bishop, at his consecration, receives immediately from God not only his power of orders but his power of jurisdiction as well. They concluded that the pastoral authority of bishops is independent, in origin and exercies, of the pope because it comes directly from God, and that the only power the pope has is to assign each bishop the flock over which he is to exercise his pastoral rule.

At the general meeting of September 23, 1562, the Archbishop of Granada asked that the seventh canon on the sacrament of holy orders take this form: "If anyone says that bishops do not *exist by divine right* and that they are not superior to priests . . . : let him be anathema" (the canon in its final form says simply: "If anyone says that bishops are not superior to priests . . ."[36]). Guerrero justified his request with these considerations: "It is appropriate to define this truth, inasmuch as Calvin, Musculus, and others of the innovators challenge it. Bishops were instituted by Christ no less than the pope was; it was not Peter who established the other apostles, but Christ. Consequently, the bishops receive their power not from the successor of Peter but from Christ. This is entirely certain; the heretics deny it; it is right then that it be defined."[37] "The bishop of Segovia, Martín Pérez de Ayala, seconded this view and said that the bishops succeed the apostles as the pope succeeds St. Peter; that if the authority of the bishops is weakened, the authority of the pope suffers as well; that if a divinely instituted hierarchy exists today, then the episcopate must have been instituted by Christ; that episcopal consecration is a sacrament and can have God alone for its source; that an episcopal ordination which conveys no jurisdiction is inconceivable. He concluded that jurisdiction is conferred on each bishop by his consecration and that the pope's function is simply to assign each bishop the field of his pastoral activity.[38] The archbishops of Braga and of Messina and almost all the Spanish theologians thought along the same lines.[39]

The Council of Trent, however, was unwilling to resolve this question. So was Vatican Council I. The expositor at the latter told the assembled Fathers:

"You are aware of how hotly this question was debated at the Council of Trent [Is the jurisdiction of bishops conferred immediately by Christ?]. You are aware that there were forceful and well-known proponents of both answers and that, although according to rule the question could have been given a definitive answer by majority vote, the Supreme Pontiff was unwilling to let the question be settled, since the conflicting views were so irreconcilable. His chief motive in so deciding was that in practice it is a matter of indifference which answer you accept. At the present time it is not possible for either the Deputation on Faith or the Vatican Council to be willing to settle the question without preliminary debate."[40] On another occasion the expositor stated: "The definition of the Supreme Pontiff's complete fullness of supreme power in no way hinders theologians from continuing to hold opinions which have hitherto been freely maintained in the schools on the derivation of episcopal jurisdiction. . . . The question, as we know, was the subject of warm discussion at the Council of Trent, and the Supreme Pontiff at the time was unwilling to have it defined. We in turn certainly do not intend it to be defined by the proposed canon or by the section we have inserted. If we assert that the complete fullness of supreme power resides in the Supreme Pontiff, we are not thereby either maintaining or denying that the power which bishops have is derived immediately from God or from the Supreme Pontiff."[41]

3. *The principle of subsidiarity*

In his encyclical *Quadragesimo anno*, Pius XI formulated the principle of subsidiarity in the following terms: "Just as it is wrong to withdraw from the individual and commit to the community at large what private enterprise and industry can accomplish, so too it is an injustice, a grave evil, and a disturbance of right order for a larger and higher organization to arrogate to itself functions which can be performed efficiently by smaller and lower bodies. . . . Of its very nature the true norm of all social activity should be to help individual members of the social body, but never to destroy or absorb them."[42]

In a consistorial address of February 20, 1946, Pope Pius XII recalled this same principle and added the following remark: "These are surely enlightened words, valid for social life in all its grades *and also for the life of the Church*, without prejudice to its hierarchical structure."[43]

The question of the applicability of the principle of subsidiarity to the Church has been extensively studied by Wilhelm Bertrams S.J., "De principio subsidiaritatis in Iure Canonico," *Periodica*, 46 (1946), 3-65. He concludes: "The principle of subsidiarity can and must be applied in the Church, to the extent that the Church is an authentically human society and carries on its life through organized social activity. The supernatural character of this social activity does not forbid the application of the principle, since, even as supernatural, the activity continues to be genuinely social, and all organized social activity of its nature involves subsidiarity" (pp. 63-64).

Pope John XXIII, in his encyclical *Mater et magistra*, repeated Pius XI's formulation of the principle and added some new elements. As proposed by these various recent popes, the principle in essence affirms the following:

(1) It is not permissible ("it is forbidden," said Pius XI and, after him, John XXIII) to assign to the community what private individuals are capable of doing for themselves.

(2) It is an injustice, a grave evil, and a disturbance of right order to assign or reserve to higher organizations what lower communities are capable of doing for themselves.

(3) Society has the duty of helping its members.

(4) The larger society cannot destroy or absorb the activity of smaller communities or of individuals.

In discussing the principle, the sociologists observe:

(1) The principle is a juridical one, a matter of justice ("it is forbidden," "it is an injustice") and not simply an administrative matter of greater efficiency or utility in social action.

(2) The principle involves a division of competences and a cooperation between the various spheres of social and individual action. The "higher society," therefore, is not limited to merely suppletive action. Pope John, in his encyclical, points out five aspects of the action of those at the top: directing, stimulating, co-ordinating, supplying, and integrating.

(3) The principle of subsidiarity prohibits the larger societies from exercising excessive or abusive power: they are not allowed (in matters of rights) to deprive lesser communities or individuals of what they can do for themselves. The mission of the higher society, after all, is not to destroy or absorb but to foster, stimulate, co-ordinate, and make up for the deficiencies of the action of lesser communities and individuals. The state is for the citizens, not the citizens for the state; as Vatican II puts it: "Man is the source, the center, and the purpose of all socio-economic life" (GS 63a/271), and

"The beginning, the subject, and the goal of all social institutions is and must be the human person" (GS 25a/244).

Pius XI, in *Quadragesimo anno*, drew the following conclusion: "The State should leave to these smaller groups the settlement of business of minor importance. It will then carry out with greater freedom, power, and success the tasks belonging to it, because it alone can effectively accomplish these, directing, watching, stimulating, and restraining, as circumstances suggest or necessity demands. Let those in power, therefore, be convinced that the more faithfully this principle be followed, and a graded hierarchical order exist between the various subsidiary organizations, the more excellent will be both the authority and the efficiency of the social organization as a whole, and the happier and more prosperous the condition of the State."[44] This principle, said Pius XII to the cardinals in 1946, is "valid for social life in all its grades *and also for the life of the Church*, without prejudice to its hierarchical structure," and he continued: "They [the gigantic organisms with no real moral background] evolve of necessity in the direction of an ever greater centralization and more stringent uniformity. As a result their equilibrium, their very cohesion, are maintained solely by force and by dominating material conditions and juridical expediences, events, and institutions."[45]

The fact is, however, that Church order at present is centralized in the extreme. The primatial power of the Roman Pontiff, nonetheless, does not necessitate concentration or centralization of all ecclesiastical power, as codified in the Canon Law Code of 1917. The full, supreme, and universal primacy of episcopal jurisdiction in the Roman Pontiff is a dogma of faith and therefore existed in the Church since the dawn of Christianity (and not simply since 1870). But the centralization of the principal powers in the hands of the man who holds the primatial power is a much later phenomenon. We can infer, then, that the primatial power can very well exist and subsist in a decentralized Church. In other words:

the current centralization of powers is not of divine institution.
It need not be thus. Not all that Canon Law now reserves
to the exclusive competence of the pope (or the Roman curia)
belongs to him by divine law. Many, for example, of the
"quinquennial faculties" need not of their nature or by God's
decree be concentrated on Roman hands; from the dogmatic
standpoint they are not "privileges graciously conceded."
There was a time, after all, and a thoroughly catholic time,
when the bishops did not have to request "special faculties"
in order, for example, to dispense from certain impediments
to matrimony; they simply did the dispensing themselves in
virtue of the ordinary power which they had as bishops, and
not in virtue of a delegated power "graciously granted by
the Holy See." All these matters, then, are a historical development and not part of the gospel; they spring from positive ecclesiastical law ("Church order") and not from divine
law.

The best example for illustrating all that we have been
saying is the Eastern Patriarchate with its extensive ordinary
powers, which existed for a thousand years within the Catholic Church.[46] The existence of the patriarchal function in the
Church is a factual proof that "the full and universal power"
of the Roman Pontiff need not involve a centralization and
uniformity of the universal Church; that, not withstanding the
primatial power, there can exist relatively autonomous ecclesiastical regions, with their own usages, customs, and
liturgical rites; and that there is room in the Church for a
wise pluralism, with diversity in matters not of divine institution, under the immediate and ordinary direction of the
bishops. What existed in the Church for a thousand years
cannot be contrary to the dogma of the primacy.

The papacy was instituted to be the guarantee and basis of
unity ("a perpetual principle of this twofold unity and a
visible foundation."[47]). But the unity need not become uniformity. If all the peoples of all races and cultures are, in
God's plan, to find in the Church their spiritual homeland,

then uniformity, as cultivated in Europe, cannot in the future be continued throughout the entire, now much vaster, world, without "spiritual colonialism" (the phrase Cardinal Lercaro used to the Brazilian bishops at Rome during the first days of the Council). The end of the colonial era, which Pope John XXIII hailed so joyfully in his encyclical *Pacem in terris*, means the liberation and independence of the peoples of Africa and Asia (America had already been westernized). Such independence involves not only political liberty but racial and cultural liberty as well, and the latter must be not only tolerated but respected and fostered by the Church. When St. Gregory the Great sent the monk Augustine to evangelize England, he gave him these wise instructions:

"You are aware, my brother, of the customs of the Roman Church, since you were raised in it. Yet, if you find anything in the Roman or Gaulish or any other church which you think can be more pleasing to you, I would have you carefully preserve it and thus bring with you to the church of the English, which is so new to the faith, the best things to be found in a variety of churches. For we should love what a place offers us more than the place itself. From each church, then, take what is religious and upright and leads to devotion, gather it into a bundle, as it were, and lay it up in the minds of the English so as to form their ways."[48]

At the Synod of Bishops in 1969 there was discussion of the problem of applying the principle of subsidiarity in the Church, and the following statement was approved: "There should be a clearer determination of the competence of bishops as shepherds, in the full sense, of their particular churches: (1) of these bishops regarded individually, in relation to the problems directly confronting them in the pastoral guidance of their particular church; and (2) of the bishops as banded together in synods (in the Eastern Churches) or in episcopal conferences, in relation to the problems which, though requiring adaptation to local conditions, also require uniform solutions for a whole region. Especially within the province of the Supreme Pontiff are matters pertaining to the safe-guarding of unity in faith and communion and matters which are of such a nature as to require, in the judgment of the highest authority, uniform solutions for the whole Church of Christ."[49]

4. *The principle of edification*

At the sixty-seventh general meeting of Vatican I (June 9, 1870), Bishop Landriot asked that the definition of primatial power include a limitation: namely, that the pope does not have the right to act in an arbitrary way and that, therefore, his power is limited by earlier decrees and by the bishops who, like him, receive from Christ an immediate power of jurisdiction. The bishop quoted the words of Pietro Ballerini (1698-1769): "The pope has all power in the Church, but on condition that he use it to build up and not to destroy."[50] These words recall what the Apostle says in 2 Cor 10:8: "If I find I must make a few further claims about the power the Lord has given us for your upbuilding and not for your destruction, this will not embarass me in the least."

The official expositor, Bishop Zinelli, in explaining to the Fathers the meaning of the word "episcopal," made the following concession: "The Supreme Pontiff has indeed the power to perform any properly episcopal act in any diocese whatever. But if he should as it were multiply his presence and should, day after day and without any regard for the local bishop, tear down what the latter has prudently ordained, then he would be using his power to tear down and not to build up. All truly spiritual administration would be subverted. But who could even dream of such an absurd supposition? Let all agree with the doctrine, therefore, and, trusting in the moderation of the Holy See, have no doubt that the latter will use its authority to protect, not to harm, the power of the bishops."[51]

At a later point the same expositor calmed the fears of the opposition concerning possible future abuses of the pope's full, supreme, and universal power, by declaring such objections "empty and vain," since they foolishly suppose that the pope "could annull all the wise and holy canonical sanctions established by the apostles and the Church. But does not the whole of moral theology tell us that the legislator is himself subject *to his own laws*, insofar as they give direction (though not insofar as they are coercive)? Can precepts that are obviously unjust, null, and harmful, require obedience (except for the sake of avoiding scandal?"[52]

In the whole literature on the hierarchy in recent years there has been a salutary stress on the *service* character of ecclesiastical authority, as opposed to the "spirit of domination" that used not infrequently to be evident in the attitude of some holders of hierarchic office. Archbishop Guerry claimed that the "first evangelical value" being reaffirmed at Vatican II was precisely the one of which we are speaking: "Authority looked upon not as domination but as *service*." How often at the general meetings of the Council, he recalls, the Fathers quoted the Savior's words: "The Son of Man . . . has come, not to be served by others, but to serve" (Mt 20: 28).[53] The Message to Humanity recalls the same principle: "The Church too was born not to dominate but to serve" (Abbott, 5). Such was the constant bidding of the Master: Mk 9:33-35 (My 18:1-3; Lk 9:46-48); Mt 20:25-28; Mt. 23: 8-12; Lk 12:41-46; Lk 22:24-30. "Domineering over your faith is not my purpose. I prefer to work with you toward your happiness" (2 Cor 1:24). Here we have the "service" (*diakonia* or *ministerium*) which is a typical and recurring concept in the New Testament writings. Especially pointed are the thoughts which St. Bernard presented to his former pupil, Pope Eugene III. The episcopate, says the Saint, is "service, no domination," and he continues:

"That which he [Peter] had he bequeathed to you, as I have said, namely, 'solicitude for all the churches.' Perhaps dominion also? Listen to him: 'Feed the flock of Christ which is among you, taking care of it, not by constraint, but willing-

ly, according to God: not for filthy lucre's sake, but voluntari-
ly; neither as lording it over the clergy, but being made a
pattern of the flock from the heart' (I Pt 5:2,3). And lest
you should imagine that the Apostle expressed himself in this
fashion more from love of humility than with the intention to
inculcate what he considered to be a true obligation, attend
to what the Lord Himself says in the Gospel: 'The kings of
the gentiles lord it over them; and they that have power over
them are called beneficient.' And immediately He adds: 'But
(be) you not so' (Lk 22: 25-26). From this it is evident that
dominion was interdicted to the apostles of Christ." Later
in the same work we read: "I speak of St. Peter. Now we
nowhere find that Peter ever appeared in public adorned with
silk and jewels, covered with cloth of gold, riding on a white
horse, surrounded by a military escort, and a throng of clamor-
ous attendants. And nevertheless it seemed to him that even
without such aids he could accomplish sufficiently well the
task enjoined him in the words, 'If you love Me, feed My
sheep' (Jn 21: 17). In all that belongs to earthly magnificence, you have succeeded not Peter, but Constantine." Finally, at the end of the whole work: "Remember above all things
that the holy Roman Church, of which God has made you
ruler is the mother, not the *mistress* of the other churches;
and that you are not the lord and master of the bishops, but
one of their number."[54]

The second evangelical value which Archbishop Guerry saw
as reaffirmed by Vatican II was poverty and simplicity. He
comments: "How many ordinary people reproach the Church
for its seeming wealth, the pomp of its ceremonies, its outward show, and the place it seems to give to honors, money,
and class, even in its liturgy!"[55] St. Bernard could well say,
even today: "In all that belongs to earthly magnificence, you
have succeeded not Peter, but Constantine"! Would that this
were no longer true since the Council!

5. *The principle of the Church's proper finality*

The Church is a perfect society, but in the strictly religious and supernatural sphere. It is not a political, scientific, economic, or cultural system; it is simply and solely a *religion*.

In a 1956 address, Pius XII said of the Church: "Her Divine Founder, Jesus Christ, gave her no mandate and established no objective of a cultural nature. The goal which Christ assigns to her is strictly religious; it is, in fact, the very synthesis of all that the idea of a single and absolutely true religion embodies: the Church should lead men to God, in order that they may give themselves wholeheartedly to Him and also find Him in perfect peace. . . . *The Church can never lose sight of this exclusively religious, supernatural end.* All her activities, down to the very last canon of her code can take this direction only—to contribute directly or indirectly to this end."[56]

In an earlier message the same pope had said: "The two powers, the Church and the State, are sovereign. Their nature, and the aims they pursue, define the limits with which they rule *jure proprio*. . . . The Church and the State are independent powers."[57] In purely temporal matters, then, which are entrusted to the care of the State, the Church has no competence. Leo XIII had observed in his encyclical *Satis cognitum*: "Wherefore they who pretend that the Church has any wish to interfere in civil matters, or to infringe upon the rights of the State, know it not, or wickedly calumniate it."[58] Today theologians are unanimous in maintaining that the Church has no "direct power in temporal matters." In fact Pius XI, in *Quadragesimo anno*, even though maintaining the Church's competence in the social question, recognized that "in technical matters . . . she has neither the equipment nor the mission."[59] And Pius XII, in *Summi pontificatus*, declares "in all apostolic sincerity" that "the Church is as far removed as possible from any intention of that kind [namely, of threatening the structure of civil authority and invading its rights];

that she stretches out her motherly arms to men, not asking to have dominion over them but, in every possible way, to be their servant. She does not seek to intrude herself into the position occupied, in a special and perfectly legitimate way, by secular authorities."[60] In this respect, then, there are limits to papal power and episcopal competence.

6. *The principle of catholicity*

Since the Church is meant for all peoples, she must have, and has, the capacity to adapt herself to all races, nationalities, intellectual moulds, practical organizations, political and social regimes, individual temperaments,, milieus and states of life, as long as respect is shown for the goals which God proposes to her and for the indispensable instrumentalities which Christ gives her. Unity does not mean uniformity. The manifold wisdom of God must be manifested in the Church (Eph 3:10). In the Church there is only one Spirit but many gifts, only one word of God but many tongues, only one body but many members. The Church's mission is to bring the gospel of Christ to all, while leaving intact whatever of the true, good, and beautiful is to be found in the various cultures. It is not within the competence even of the full, supreme, and universal power of jurisdiction to do away with the wise elements of each culture that can be rendered Christian. This principle has been clearly affirmed in Vatican II's Constitution on the Sacred Liturgy: "Even in the liturgy, the Church has no wish to impose a rigid uniformity in matters which do not involve the faith or the good of the whole community. Rather she respects and fosters the spiritual adornments and gifts of the various races and peoples. Anything in their way of life that is not indissolubly bound up with superstition and error she studies with sympathy and, if possible, preserves intact. Sometimes in fact she even admits such things into the liturgy itself, as long as they harmonize with its true and authentic spirit" (SC 37/151). And the encyclical *Pacem in terris* reminds us: "Among the essential elements of the common good one must certainly include the various characteristics distinctive of each individual people."[61]

7. *The principles of the natural law*

The fact is obvious enough, but for the sake of completing our picture we recall that the primatial power is also limited by the requirements of natural law. The pope cannot ordain or legislate against the laws of nature. Insofar as these laws are connected with religious and moral life, and in the degree in which the teaching, interpretation, and application of these laws affects morality, the teaching Church can pronounce on them, delimit them, and define them more clearly. In any event it must always respect and obey them. For, declares John XXIII in *Pacem in terris*, "these rights and duties are universal and inviolable, and therefore altogether inalienable."[62] The pope then mentions the natural right to a good name, freedom in investigating the truth, and, within the limits of the moral order and the common good, freedom in manifesting and diffusing one's own thought, the right to cultivate the arts, the right to accurate information on public events, the right to freedom in worshipping God according to the right dictates of one's own conscience and in professing one's religion both privately and publicly, the right to exercise personal initiative, the right to act in collaboration with others on one's own account and at one's own risk, the right to legal protection of one's rights, a protection which must be effective, unbiased, and according to objective norms of justice. As applied to the social life of the Church, the rights listed by John XXIII and repeated by Vatican Council II in its Constitution on the Church in the Modern World would create a number of concrete situations which would have to be handled tactfully and for which ecclesiastical jurisprudence is not yet wholly prepared.

Pius XII refers to one or other such situation, as when he speaks of the right to public opinion. "Public opinion is the mark of every normal society composed of men who, conscious of their personal and social conduct, are intimately concerned with the community to which they belong. . . . When public opinion fails to manifest itself, where it does not exist at all—whatever the reason for its silence or absence—one must see in this lack something vicious, a malady, a disense of social life. . . . To stifle the opinions of citizens, to reduce them forcibly to silence, is, in the eyes of every Christian, an outrage on the *natural rights of man*, a violation of the order of the world as established by God."[63] The pope continued, a bit further on: "We have just recognized public opinion as a natural echo, a more or less spontaneous common resounding of acts and circumstances in the mind and judgment of people who feel they are responsible beings, closely bound to the fate of their community."[64] Later on, finally, the pope says: "Finally we should like to add a word regarding *public opinion within the bosom of the Church* (naturally, with respect to matters left to free discussion). This consideration can surprise only those who do not know the Church or know her only poorly. Because the Church is a living body, *something would be wanting in her life if public opinion were lacking* and the blame for this deficiency would fall back upon the pastors and the faithful."[65]

We might perhaps mention other theological and sociological principles related to the organization and social life of the Church, but the ones we have discussed seem to be the principal ones. They represent neither new doctrine nor personal opinion. Our citations from conciliar and papal texts makes it clear that they express the common teaching of the Church. We are not motivated here by complaints against the pope. As we indicated, we prescind from the currently effective positive determinations of ecclesiastical law, because we are interested in seeing what possibilities exist in the Church for changes in regime and government that might be for the good and salvation of souls. This last, after all, is the main thing, and everything else must serve it. Traditions which are not of divine origin and which do not truly serve the Church's great purpose can and ought to be resolutely discarded. We do not live and work for the sake of such traditions. Or, as Pope John XXIII put it, the Church is not a collection of antiquities.[66] It was with this in mind that Pope John called the Twenty-First Ecumenical Council into existence, in order to achieve an "appropriate adaptation of Church discipline to the needs and conditions of our times"[67] and "for the reorganization of the ecclesiastical organisms."[68]

Notes for Chapter 6

[1] Newman to Miss Mary Holmes, in Wilfrid Ward, *The Life of John Henry Cardinal Newman* (London: Longmans, Green, 1912), II, p. 379. with the addition of the third last and final sentences which are omitted from the text in Ward.

[2] DS, 3064 (D, 1831); *TCT*, no. 211, p. 99.

[3] Cf. DS, 3060 (D, 1827); *TCT*, no. 207, p. 98.

[4] Gustave Thils, *Primauté pontificale et prérogatives épiscopales: "Potestas ordinaria" au Concile du Vatican* (Louvain: E. Warny, 1961).

[5] Cf. DS, 3060 (D, 1827) and DS, 3064 (D, 1821); *TCT*, nos. 207, 211, pp. 98, 99.

[6] DS, 3060 (D, 1827); *TCT*, no. 207, p. 98.

[7] *Coll. Lac.*, 7:351. The same exposition contains the following passage (*ibid.*) defining or describing more clearly the concept of "episcopal power" at Vatican I: "The bishop's function is to feed the flock; no description of episcopal rule is more familiar to the sacred writings, the works of the Fathers, or general Christian usage than the image of the bishop as a shepherd who feeds his flock. A bishop feeds the flock by the exercise of powers given him by sacred orders and of the power of jurisdiction. The exercise of the power of orders is licit only toward his own subjects. The jurisdiction of a bishop therefore extends to all that is required if the faithful are to reach eternal life. The bishop's task, then, is (1) to administer the sacraments; (2) to make laws for the good of the faithful; (3) to see to it, directly or through delegates, that the laws are observed; (4) to visit his diocese; (5) to preach; (6) to pass judgment in disputes; (7) to punish the guilty; etc. These and similar duties are summed up in the term 'to feed.' But the bishop is to do all this only in dependence on the Supreme Pontiff. Such a dependence is, however, simply a limitation on episcopal jurisdiction."

[8] DS, 3064 (D, 1831); *TCT*, no. 211, p. 99.

[9] DS, 3060 (D, 1827); *TCT*, no. 207, p. 98.

[10] DS, 3063 (D, 1830); *TCT*, no. 210, p. 99.

[11] Mansi, 52:92-100.

[12] Mansi, 52:591.

[13] *Coll. Lac.*, 7:357. The text continues: "Empty, then, and vain (forgive me for speaking so strongly!) are the complaints, and hardly to be taken seriously, that if full and supreme power be allowed the pope, he could destroy the episcopate (which, after all, exists in the Church by divine law) and could annul all the wise and holy canonical sanctions established by the Apostles and the Church. But does not the whole of moral theology tell us that the legislator is himself subject *to his own laws,* insofar as they give direction (though not insofar as they are coercive)? Can precepts that are obviously unjust, null, and harmful, require obedience (except for the sake of avoiding scandal)?"

[14] In Cuthbert Butler O.S.B., *The Vatican Council* (London: Longmans, Green, 1930), II, pp. 218-19. Butler notes (*ibid.*) that Pius IX wrote to the Swiss bishops and thanked them for having issued a very pertinent and praiseworthy document.

[15] DS, 3061 (D, 1828); *TCT*, no. 208, p. 98.

[16] DS, 1768 (D, 760); *TCT*, no. 843, p. 331.

[17] *The Great Encyclical Letters of Pope Leo XIII* (New York: Benziger, 1903), p. 382.

[18] *Mystici Corporis*, no. 40, in *Selected Letters*, p. 71.

[19] *The Great Encyclical Letters*, p. 88.

[20] *Mystici Corporis, ibid.*

[21] Leo XIII, *Satis cognitum*, in *The Great Encyclical Letters*, p. 388. During Vatican I the same difficulty was discussed by Bishop Pie in his capacity as official expositor. He defended the compatibility of the two authorities in this way: "When two causes, even if they be all-embracing, are not of the same order but one is subordinated to the other and the two are not mutually causative of each other, then they do not exclude each other nor does confusion arise from their operation. Thus the action of God, when he gives his concursus, neither excludes nor interferes with the action of secondary causes. So too the existence of the pope, as supreme and universal pastor and bishop of the Church, does not prevent an Ordinary being appointed to each local church and acting as its true spouse and bishop" (Mansi 52:33). Cf. Umberto Betti O.F.M., *La Costituzione dommatica "Paster Aeternus" del Concilio Vaticano I* (Rome: Pontificio Ateneo Antonianum, 1961), p. 164.

[22] These propositions are cited in the letter of reply by the German bishops. The letter of the bishops, the letter of Pius IX, and the latter's remarks at the consistory were edited by Olivier Rousseau O.S.B. in *Irénikon*, 29 (1956), 131-50, and now printed (with some omissions) in DS, 3112-17 (the remarks of Pius IX at the consistory are in the introduction to this section of DS). The translation given here follows the fuller text presented by Rousseau.

[23] DS, 3051 (D, 1821); *TCT,* no. 201, p. 95.

[24] DS, 3061 (D, 1828); *TCT,* no. 208, p. 98.

[25] St. Gregory the Great, *Letter to Eulogius, Bishop of Alexandria* (PL, 77:933).

[26] *Coll. Lac.,* 7:497.

[27] *Coll. Lac.,* 7:322-23.

[28] In early 1963, Archbishop Emile Guerry of Cambrai issued a pastoral letter, *Les résultats positifs de la première session du Concile,* reprinted in *Documentation Catholique,* 45 (February 3, 1963) 175-90. He speaks of collegiality as a "great discovery" (175) and explains it thus: "Our Lord called each of the twelve apostles individually. But is was as a body that they received from him their functions and powers. It was as a body that they were sent by their divine Master, invested with the mission of going to teach and baptize all nations. It was as a body that they waited, as the Lord had bidden them, for the coming of the promised Holy Spirit. *Episcopal collegiality is thus written into the very institution of the Church by Jesus Christ himself"* (176). On the collegial action of the Apostles see the richly detailed article of Jean Colson, "Evangélisation et collégialité apostolique," *Nouvelle revue théologique,* 82 (1960), 349-72; cf. also Colson's earlier book, *Les fonctions ecclésiales aux deux premiers siècles* (Paris: Desclée, 1956).

[29] There is an abundant literature on this point. Some examples: Georges Dejaifve S.J., "Conciliarité au Concile du Vatican," *Nouvelle revue théologique,* 82 (1960), 785-802; Giuseppe Colombo, "Il problema dell'Episcopato nella Constituzione 'De ecclesia catholica' del Concilio Vaticano I," *Scuola cattolica,* 89 (1961), 344-72; Jésus Arrieta S.J., "La colegialidad episcopal: Un tema en vistas al proximo Concilio," *Estudios eclesiásticos,* 37 (1962), 295-341 and 38 (1963), 5-56; Plácido Incháurraga, "El primado pontificio y la jurisdiccion episcopal en los Concilios Tridentino, Vaticano I y Vaticano II," *Lumen* (Vitoria) (1963) 3-20; Jean-Paul Torrell O.P., *La théologie de l'épiscopat au premier Concile du Vatican* (Unam Sanctam 37; Paris: Editions du Cerf, 1961).

[30] Mansi, 52:94-95.

[31] Mansi, 52:604.

[32] Mansi, 51:842.

[33] Mansi, 52:1109; *Coll. Lac.,* 7:357-58.

[34] Pius XII, *Fidei donum,* April 21, 1957, in *TPS,* 4 (1957-58), 303-4.

[35] Guerry, *op. cit.* (cf. note 28, above), pp. 176-77, 179.

[36] DS, 1777 (D, 967); *TCT,* no. 850, p. 332.

[37] *Concilium Tridentinum,* ed. by Stephen Ehses, vol. 9, pp. 49-51.

[38] *Concilium Tridentinum,* vol. 9, pp. 137-39.

[39] Cf. Incháurraga, *art. cit.* (note 29, above); J. Pegon S.J., "Episcopat et hiérarchie au Concile de Trente," *Nouvelle revue thèologique,* 82 (1960), 580-88.

[40] *Coll. Lac.,* 7:359.

[41] *Coll. Lac.,* 7:472.

[42] Pius XI, *Quadragesimo anno* (Washington, D.C.: National Catholic Welfare Conference, 1936), p. 22.

[43] Pius XII, *La elevatezza: Address to the College of Cardinals at a Public Consistory,* February 20, 1946, in *Catholic Mind,* 44 (1946), 196.

[44] Pius XI, *Quadragesimo anno,* pp. 26-27.

[45] Pius XII, *loc cit.,* p. 197.

[46] Cf. Wilhelm de Vries S.J., "Papsttum und Patriarchenamt im Osten," *Orientierung,* 27 (1963), 42-45. The author notes (p. 44) that during the first millennium the patriarch's powers were not held as a grant from the pope nor as a privilege from the Holy See, but as ordinary powers.

[47] DS, 3051 (D, 1821); *TCT,* no. 201, p. 95.

[48] St. Gregory the Great, *Letter* 64: *To Augustine, Bishop of the English* (PL, 77:1187).

[49] Synod of Bishops, 1969 (the author's private files).

[50] Mansi, 52:566.

[51] *Coll. Lac.,* 7:353.

[52] *Coll. Lac.,* 7:357.

[53] Guerry, *op. cit.,* p. 181.

[54] St. Bernard, *Treatise on Consideration,* tr. by a Priest of Mount Melleray (Dublin: Browne and Nolan, 1921), Book 2, ch. 6, p. 47; Book 4, ch. 3, pp. 118-19; and Book 4, ch. 7, p. 143.

[55] Guerry, *op. cit.,* p. 181.

[56] Pius XII, *C'est bien volontiers: Address to the International Union of Archaeological Institutes,* March 9, 1956, in *TPS,* 3 (1956), 158-59.

[57] Pius XII, *Vous avez voulu: Message to the International Congress of Historical Sciences,* September 7, 1955, in *TPS,* 2 (1955), 210.

[58] *The Great Encyclical Letters,* p. 371.

[59] Piux XI, *Quadragesimo anno,* p. 14.

[60] Pius XII, *Summi pontificatus,* October 20, 1939, in *Selected Letters,* p. 39.

[61] John XXIII, *Pacem in terris,* April 11, 1963, in *TPS,* 9 (1963-64), 24-25.

[62] *Loc. cit.,* p. 15.

[63] Pius XII, *L'importance de la presse catholique: Allocution to the International Convention of the Catholic Press,* February 18, 1950, in *Catholic Mind,* 48 (1950), 749.

[64] *Loc. cit.,* p. 750.

[65] *Loc. cit.,* p. 753.

[66] John XXIII, *Allocution* of November 7, 1962, in *Osservatore Romano,* November 8, 1962.

[67] John XXIII, Encyclical *Ad Petri cathedram,* June 29, 1959, in *TPS,* 5 (1958-59), 369.

[68] John XXIII, *Letter to Cardinal Alfrink,* May 19, 1960, in *AAS,* 52 (160), 481.

Chapter 7

The Synod of Bishops

In his address at the opening of the last session of the Council, Pope Paul VI announced to the Fathers the coming establishment of an episcopal synod and spoke of it as "this new proposal, full of such splendid possibilities."[1] Later, in his address to the college of cardinals, in which he revealed his decision to convoke the first synod for September 29, 1967, the pope expressed the hope "that this new institution will increase apostolic wisdom and efficacy in the Church."[2] Only the event will show how justified the hopes are which the pope and all of us have for the Synod of Bishops.

The idea of such an episcopal council or synod came into being and matured during the Vatican Council itself, and the final text of the Decree on the Bishops' Pastoral Office in the Church, no. 5/399-400, has a history behind it. The corresponding pre-conciliar text and the position paper of 1963 (debated during the second session) said simply that some bishops from various countries could be designated by the episcopal conferences and appointed by the Holy See as members or consultors of the various sacred congregations within the Roman Curia. In a note, the 1963 paper indicated that such was already a customary procedure in connection with the Congregations. Consequently, nothing really new was intended. The paper was given to the bishops in May, 1963, for study and suggested emendations. Not a few bishops sent in their corrections even before the debates began in the second session. An Italian bishop (Bishop Nicodemo) suggested that the word "members" be dropped since it was enough that the bishops in mind be "consultors." Others, among them a Brazilian bishop (Bishop Joao Batista Przyklenk, M.S.F., of Januária), characterized the proposal in the paper as a "thoroughly inadequate solution," and proposed, instead, a consultative body of bishops, drawn from the whole world, which would meet at Rome at least once each year in order to discuss with the pope and the curia the important problems of the universal Church. The bishops of South Africa, Indonesia, and Holland were of the same mind. The bishops of southern France proposed "delegates of the episcopal college who would direct the Church of God with Peter and under Peter."

Meanwhile John XXIII died. The new Pope, Paul VI, in his well-known address to the Roman Curia, September 21, 1963, supported these ideas with the full weight of his authority: "Should the Ecumenical Council evince a desire of seeing some representatives of the episcopacy, particularly among prelates who direct a diocese, associated in a certain way and for certain questions, in conformity with the Church's doctrine and canon law, with the supreme head of the Church in the study and responsibility of ecclesiastical government, the Curia will surely not oppose it."[3] Some days later, in his address at the opening of the second session of the Council, the new pope said to the Council Fathers: "We have no hesitation in admitting that We await this discussion [of the bishops 'as bishops of God's Church'] with eager anticipation and genuine confidence. The doctrine to which we are referring is that of the episcopate, its functions, and its relations to Peter. Indeed, this doctrine ought to be gone into very thoroughly (while at the same time we hold safe the dogmatic pronouncements of the First Vatican Council concerning the Roman Pontiff). For Us personally it will provide doctrinal and practical standards for the exercise of Our apostolic office. This universal office has been endowed by Christ, as you know, with the fullness and sufficiency of power. Nevertheless, it can marshall to itself added support and assistance from an ever more effectual and responsible collaboration (in ways and means to be determined) of Our beloved and revered brothers in the episcopate."[4]

Then began the great debate on the sacramental character of the episcopacy (that is, on whether the powers of bishops are conferred on them directly by God in a sacramental act and not by the pope in a juridical act), on collegiality (that is, whether, as the Council later put it, the bishops "exercise their own [not a delegated] authority for the good of their own faithful, and indeed of the whole Church" [LG 22d/44], with the body on college of bishops having likewise a supreme and plenary power over the whole Church, a power given them by God and not by the pope), and the concrete way in which the college is to carry out its tasks.

The theological debate took up eight general meetings and brought 123 speakers to the microphones in the Council hall. Once that debate was finished, an important and historic preliminary vote took place on October 30, 1963. The result was that, of 2148 Council Fathers, 1808 approved the principle according to which "the episcopal college succeeds the apostolic college in the task of evangelizing, sanctifying, and governing, and, together with its head, the Roman Pontiff, and never without him, this college of bishops possesses full and supreme power over the whole Church." Moreover, 1717 of 2138 Fathers agreed that this full and supreme power over the whole Church "belongs to the episcopal college by divine right."[5]

There followed the discussion of the pastoral office of bishops (the present decree, *Christus Dominus*). Meanwhile some days earlier, on October 16, while the theological debate was still going on, Bishop Thomas Holland, speaking in the name of all the English bishops, asked that the doctrine of collegiality be immediately put into practice through the creation of a central organism made up of bishops nominated by the various episcopal conferences.[6] This was the first time that the Council Hall heard the proposal to establish what today we call the Synod of Bishops. But during the sixtieth to the sixty-third general meetings, November 5-8, the proposal was repeated seventeen times in varying forms. The series began with an intervention of Cardinal Liénart, who was seconded on the following day by Cardinal Ruffini. Similar proposals came from: Cardinal König, suggesting that once or twice a year the pope summon the presidents of the episcopal conferences and other bishops to discuss subjects of interest to the entire Church; Cardinal Bea, arguing for the necessity of a council to help the pope in governing the Church; Cardinal Alfrink, looking for a central organ which would be the sign of the Church's communion and unity; Cardinal Florit, suggesting a new Central Congregation, made up of residential bishops and possessing powers greater than those of the other Roman congregations, with the purpose of solving problems as the pope judged necessary; Cardinal Barros Camara, speaking here in the name of one hundred and ten Brazilian bishops but making it a point to say that he did not agree with everything that was being said: "I agree only in part").[7] The most incisive, as well as the most typical, intervention on this occasion was that of the elderly Melkite Patriarch, Maximos IV, who sharply criticized the present system of central government in the Church. He suggested that "a limited group of bishops, who would represent their colleagues, should have the concrete task of helping the pope in the general government of the Church; such would be an authentic Sacred College of the universal Church and could be called into session by the pope from time to time, when need required a discussion of general problems affecting the whole Church."[8]

Notable, too, was the address of Cardinal Lercaro, who on this occasion supposedly spoke in the name of the pope. He began by recalling the theological principles which made possible the establishment of a body of representatives of the episcopate for the purpose of studying the more important questions concerning the Church, "even though the final word on them belongs exclusively to the pope." He stated that the question was not strictly within the competence of the Council, since it touched on the rights of the pope; the Council therefore ought to present the pope with a proposal and in it indicate concretely the measure in which the bishops would like to share in the government of the Church.[9] Cardinal Rugambwa spoke on the same day, saying that the matter was so important that it would be better to set up a special conciliar commission with the task of studying the subject and drawing up a special document.[10]

During these days other Council Fathers also spoke: Bishop Gargitter, who strongly opposed the the position paper, argued that even in its central organs the Church should show itself genuinely universal, and suggested the establishment of a council of bishops from around the world; Bishop Simons, who said that the pope should rule the Church in collaboration with the bishops; Bishop Gouyon, who asked for the creation of an apostolic council; Bishop McCann, who urged a consultative episcopal body which would represent the whole college of bishops and meet in Rome at specified times to deliberate with the pope; Bishop M. Browne, who proposed a special council of bishops with legislative power; Bishop A. Ferreira Gomes, who stressed that the episcopal council suggested by the pope would have to be made up of residential bishops; and Bishop Van der Burgt (with thirty Indonesian bishops), who asked for a central organ of government or international episcopal senate, with members nominated by the episcopal conferences.[11]

All these proposals were made before the promulgation of the Dogmatic Constitution on the Church, in which the Council formally taught the sacramental and collegial character of the episcopacy. During the debate to which we have been referring, this doctrine of the Dogmatic Constitution was strongly criticized by Cardinal Ottaviani ("an unacceptable doctrine") and Cardinal Browne ("contradicts the doctrine of Vatican I: on guard!") and by Bishop Castro Meyer (the proposal has no basis in Scripture and does not harmonize with the definition by Vatican I).[12] This opposition accounts for some questionable, confused, and compromising formulations which, as we shall see, became part of the current conception of the Episcopal Synod.

After the debate of 1963, the Theological Commission corrected the text and, in the position paper of 1964 (for the third session), reformulated number 5: Since the pope is in need of ever great help, the Council Fathers wish to see bishops from various nations providing help to the Supreme Shepherd of the Church and, if he be agreeable, meeting as a group or council; such a council could, furthermore, symbolize the sharing of all the bishops in the care of the universal Church. The official expositor (Bishop Gargitter), in presenting the text to the assembled Fathers on November 4, 1964, revealed that there had been pressure to omit the whole section, on the grounds that such a council would represent a restriction or lessening of papal power, but that the Commission had determined to keep the text, since the power of the proposed central council would be no more at odds with the power of the pope than is the power of the episcopal college itself. The expositor observed, however, that such a central council would not be a real representative of the college of bishops but only a small sign of that college's union with the pope. He was admitting that there had been a compromise.

The vote on modification, taken during the 1964 session, produced almost no changes in the text, and, with but very minor emendations, the same text was presented to the

Fathers again in 1965 for a final vote and promulgation. It was in his address at the opening of the final session, on September 14, 1965, that the pope said: "We are happy to announce to you . . . the setting up, in accordance with the wishes of the Council, of an episcopal synod composed of bishops to be chosen for the greater part by the episcopal conferences and approved by Us, which will be convened, according to the needs of the Church, by the Roman Pontiff, for consultation and collaboration when, for the general good of the Church, this will seem opportune to Us. We consider it superfluous to add that this collaboration of the episcopate is meant to be of greatest help to the Holy See and to the whole Church. And in a special way it can be of use to us in the day-to-day work of the Roman Curia."[13]

On the next day the Fathers received the text of the Motu Proprio *Apostolica sollicitudo*, which formally established the Synod of Bishops and was read in the Council hall by Bishop Felici, general secretary of the Council, in the presence of the pope.[14] At the same time, by a new text (the definitive one) of n. 5 of the Decree on the Bishops' Pastoral Office in the Church, the Council put its own seal on the Synod of Bishops. The conciliar document adds: "Since it [the Synod] will be acting in the name of the entire Catholic episcopate, it will at the same time demonstrate that all the bishops in hierarchical communion share in the responsibility for the universal Church" (CD 5/399-400). Without further correction, the paragraph was put to a vote on September 29, 1965, during the 138th general meeting, and was approved with 2171 votes in favor, 8 against, and 3 void.

This sharing of the whole Catholic episcopate in the responsibility for the universal Church receives its concrete, juridical form in the words of the Motu Proprio *Apostolica sollicitudo*: "By its very nature it is the task of the Synod of Bishops to inform and give advice. It may also have deliberative power, when such power is conferred on it by the Sovereign Pontiff, who will in such cases confirm the decisions of the Synod" (Abbott, 721). Therefore: basically ("by its very nature"), the Synod has a purely *consultative* function; if it should have deliberative power, that will only be by a special, unforced grant from the pope.

Here I would like to raise a theological question on the purely academic plane: Would an Episcopal Synod, as conceived and structured in this document of Paul VI, truly be a body that is authentically representative of the episcopal college? In other words: Would the present Synod of Bishops be a genuine post-conciliar exercise of that full and supreme collegial power, the existence of which is taught by the Council in the Dogmatic Constitution on the Church (LG 22c/43)?

I think the answer has to be "No." In its Dogmatic Constitution on the Church Vatican II formally teaches that all the bishops together (the Bishop of Rome is evidently included as the head of the group), in hierarchical communion, make up a college or stable group which exists at all times, although it is not necessarily always in full exercise of its powers. The Council also teaches that this college has supreme and full (lacking nothing) power over the universal Church, a power received from God and not from the pope or from the People of God ("the episcopal college, united with its head, has this power by divine right," said the preliminary formula submitted to a vote on October 30, 1963). The Council teaches, furthermore, that while "faithfully recognizing the primacy and pre-eminence of their head," the bishops "exercise their own authority for the good . . . of the whole Church," and not only of their own dioceses (LG 22d/44). An ecumenical council, the document goes on to say, is only *one* possible (solemn) way of exercising the full and supreme power of the college. There must, therefore, be some *other* concrete, realizable way, non-conciliar or extra-conciliar, of exercising this full and supreme collegial power, "provided that the head of the college calls them [the bishops] to collegiate action, or at least so approves or freely accepts the united action of the dispersed bishops, that it is made a true collegiate act"

(LG 22e/44). In such a case (so different from an ecumenical council), which the Council evidently regards as possible and viable, we would have an authentic exercise "of supreme and full power over the universal Church," which belongs to the college by divine right and not by papal concession or even necessarily by papal convocation.

Such a possible and viable extra-conciliar type of collegial government of the Church is obviously not to be found in the Synod of Bishops as instituted by the Motu Proprio *Apostolica sollicitudo*; for the bishops of such a Synod have a purely consultative role and would have deliberative power only "when such power is conferred on it by the Roman Pontiff."[15] Its members are wholly and unqualifiedly dependent on the pope, "directly and immediately subject to the authority of the Roman Pontiff" (Abbott, 722), since the pope grants them power only in the measure he wishes. Not only this: it is also he who determines the topics for discussion, determines the agenda, and decides on proposals offered by the Synod. In such circumstances the bishops who make up the Synod cannot be regarded as true and accredited representatives of the episcopal college. They are, instead, simply deputized to represented the episcopal conferences in advising the pope and furnishing information on problems and situations in the internal life of the Church (and, even here, only on such points as the pope wishes to raise). Such a system of consultation and information is perfectly possible without bishops (experts would suffice) and without the doctrine of *Lumen Gentium* of the ordinary, supreme, and full power of the college of bishops. There was no need of a Second Vatican Council to achieve such a Synod. In short, the Synod is not, of its nature, a consequence of the Council.

The teaching of Vatican II, which was worked out so painfully, opens up far greater possibilities. God grant that it may not remain a dead letter! In number 4 of the Prefatory Note of Explanation there is no obstacle to a concrete, non-conciliar exercise of supreme collegial power. For the Note only repeats

that the College, though always existing, does not permanently operate through strictly collegiate action or is not always
"in full act"; it operates through collegial actions only at intervals and always with the consent of the pope. However,
"consent" (the word is also used in LG 22) does not mean the
granting of deliberative power!

The Prefatory Note itself explains that "consent of the
pope" means not *dependence* on, but *communion* with the
pope. The essential thing in the Church, after all, is communion, not dependence or subjection. Here is what the Prefatory Note says: "The phrase is *'with the consent of its head'*;
for these should be no thought of a *dependence* on some *outside* person. The word 'consent,' on the contrary, recalls the
communion existing between head and members" (Abbott,
100). The great intention of Vatican II was this: "Continuing
in the same task of clarification begun by Vatican I, this Council has decided to declare and proclaim before all men its
teaching concerning bishops, the successors of the apostles,
who together with the successor of Peter, the Vicar of Christ
and the visible Head of the whole Church, govern the house of
the living God" (LG 18d/38). In *Lumen Gentium* itself the
Council insists on *communion* and not on *dependence*. Thus
the expression "with Peter *and under Peter*" does not occur
in this document and was, indeed, deliberately avoided (although the expression "with the head" implies a real superiority of the head). In speaking of the powers of bishops (LG
21d/41), the Council says that "these, . . . of their very nature,
can be exercised only in hierarchical communion with the head
and the members of the college." Strictly speaking, no more
need be said than this. St. Paul certainly worked "with Peter"
but would not have regarded it as a gain to preach the gospel
"under Peter." However, in the Decree on the Missions,
worked out by another Commission, we read that the bishops
are to preach the gospel "with Peter and under Peter" (AG
38a/624). The Decree on the Bishops' Pastoral Office uses
the same terminology, as when it says that the bishops exer-

cise their solicitude for all the churches "in communion with and under the authority of the Supreme Pontiff" (CD 3a/397) or that "together with the Supreme Pontiff and under his authority, they have been sent to continue throughout the ages the work of Christ, the eternal pastor" (CD 2b/397).

In these critical reflections there is no intention of implying that when he established the present Synod, the pope was acting contrary to the doctrine of Vatican II. After all, the Prefatory Note—though this was rather forcibly added to the Constitution on the Church, without any debate or vote and to the accompaniment of loud muttering in the Council hall— does say that it is for the pope alone, and within his sole discretion, to decide how supreme power in the Church is to be exercised: in a personal way (by the pope alone) or in a collegial way (by the pope together with accredited representatives of the episcopal college). Furthermore, *Lumen Gentium* (22e/44) would, strictly speaking, permit a genuine collegial action without any papal initiative or convocation, since it is enough that the pope "so approves or freely accepts the unified action of the dispersed bishops." I believe, then, that the criticism I have offered is legitimate and constructive. The Motu Proprio *Apostolica sollicitudo* itself says that "this Synod . . . like all human institutions can still be more perfected with the passage of time" (Abbott, 721). Moreover Vatican Council II proclaims: "Let it be recognized that all the faithful, *clerical* and lay, possess a lawful freedom of inquiry and of thought, and the freedom to express their minds humbly and courageously about those matters in which they enjoy competence" (GS 62j/270).

Notes for Chapter 7

[1] Paul VI, *Quarta sessio: Address at the Opening of the Fourth Session of Vatican II,* September 14, 1965, in *Catholic Mind,* 63 (December, 1965), 57.

[2] Paul VI, *Il Cardinale Decano: Address to the College of Cardinals,* December 23, 1966, in *TPS,* 12 (1967), 40.

[3] Paul VI, *Quali siano: Address to the Roman Curia,* September 21, 1965, in *TPS,* 9 (1963-64), 156.

[4] Paul VI, *Salvete Fratres: Address to the Council Fathers at the Opening of the Second Session of Vatican II,* September 29, 1963, in *TPS,* 9 (1963-64), 132-33.

[5] *Acta Synodalia,* II/3, pp. 574 and 670.

[6] *Acta Synodalia,* II/2, pp. 621-22.

[7] *Acta Synodalia,* II/4: Liénart, p. 445; Ruffini, p. 476; König, p. 478; Bea, p. 481; Alfrink, p. 479; Florit, p. 559; Barros Câmara, p. 612.

[8] *Acta Synodalia,* II/4, pp. 517-18.

[9] *Acta Synodalia,* 11/4, pp. 618-21.

[10] *Acta Synodalia,* II/4, pp. 621-23.

[11] *Acta Synodalia,* II/4: Gargitter, p. 453; Simons, p. 499; Gouyon, p. 568; McCann, p. 576; M. Browne, p. 578; Ferreira Gomes, p. 580; van der Burgt, p. 592.

[12] *Acta Synodalia,* II/4: Ottaviani, pp. 624-25; Browne, pp. 626-27; Castro Meyer, pp. 631-33.

[13] Paul VI, *Quarta sessio,* in *Catholic Mind,* 63 (December, 1965), 57.

[14] Paul VI, Motu Proprio, *Apostolica sollicitudo,* September 15, 1965, in Abbott, pp. 720-24.

[15] The reason why I mistrust a synod that is purely consultative in nature may be easier to understand if I give some concrete examples. At Vatican II, we find, there was often no proportion between the number of speakers for and against on a particular question, and the number of those voting for and against. An example: the thirty Fathers who spoke at the Council against Communion under both kinds outnumbered the twenty-nine who spoke in favor of it; yet at the moment of voting (that is, of deliberation and decision) there were only fifty-eight votes against Communion under both kinds, while an absolute and total majority of 2242, who had been silent during the debate voted in favor of it. The same thing happened in regard to the use of the vernacular in the liturgy: if the Fathers had paid greater heed to the number and words of those who spoke in favor of Latin, we would still be using Latin in the Mass today. When the restoration of the diaconate was being discussed, 49 spoke against it and only thirty for it. Examples could be multiplied. If the Council had consisted simply of consultative meetings, without the further enlightment and decisiveness provided by a vote, it would have been difficult to reach new practical conclusions. But in fact the Council made it clear that the theories of the men in the Roman Curia (which were generously

expressed in the seventy position papers prepared for the Council) were not necessarily and automatically reconcilable with the needs of real-life pastoral activity. We know from history that the axiom, "Rome has spoken, the case is closed," can be valid only in really rare and important cases. A wealth of experience in these last years shows that Rome ought normally not speak before receiving the agreement of the local churches. The collegial character of the apostolic college and of the episcopal college which succeeds it seems to require that Rome proceed only in this way. For it is the episcopal college in its entirety that is to "govern the house of the living God" (LG 18d/38). This is the new vision given us by Vatican II.

Chapter 8

The New Theological Portrait
of the Bishop

One of the major focuses of Vatican Council II was undoubtedly the episcopacy. In his address at the opening of
the third session (September 14, 1964), Pope Paul VI noted
that the Council "is . . . particularly concerned to describe the
prerogatives of the bishop and accord them full honor."[1] In
fact, of the 2217 speeches made during the Council 311 were
concerned with the nature and functions of bishops in the
Church.[2] Vatican II explained, went more deeply into, and—
with an eye on the painful impression made on many by the
doctrine of Vatican I on the primacy of the pope[3]—restored
to its proper place the ordinary and immediate pastoral
authority of the bishop in his diocese. Initially, Bishop
Fernando Gomes dos Santos, speaking in the name of sixty
Brazilian bishops (November 6, 1963; sixty-first general
meeting), could denounce the position paper then under discussion, claiming that its bias "makes the bishops simple

218

vicars, not only of the pope, but even of the Roman Congregations, on which the bishops are to depend in the least detail."[4]
But then, with the Council in the hands of the bishops, everything changed. When the historic meeting was at its end,
Pope Paul VI could say to the Italian bishops, on December
6, 1965: "To be a bishop today is a more demanding, difficult,
and perhaps, humanly speaking, more thankless and dangerous task than ever before."[5]

In the light of the conciliar documents, and in the form of
a set of antithetical proposition, I shall try to study this dangerous art of being a bishop today. I shall emphasize the new
orientations given by the Council to the bishop's relations (1)
with Christ, (2) with the episcopal college, (3) with the pope,
(4) with the episcopal conference, (5) with the diocese, (6)
and with his priests, (7) in his office of teaching, (8) sanctifying, (9) and ruling, (10) with an ordinary and immediate
power, (11) in his attitude to the laity, (12) and to the contemporary world.

1. *The bishop must be and act as a living and*
   pre-eminent sign of Christ in His triple
   mission, and not as a simple vicar of the
   pope or as though his authority and power
   were given for his own advantage.

In the new covenant, under which we live, there is only one
Mediator, eternal Priest, and supreme Pontiff, only one great
Prophet, exclusive Teacher, and radiant Light of the world,
only one King, Shepherd, Lord, and Head: Jesus Christ.
"God sent His Son, whom He appointed heir of all things,
that He might be Teacher, King, and Priest of all, the Head
of the new and universal people of the sons of God" (LG 13a/
31. According to a traditional terminology which was systematically adopted in the documents of Vatican II, we can distinguish three essential functions of Christ: teaching (prophet,
teacher, light), sanctifying (priest, mediator, pontiff), and
ruling (shepherd, king, lord, head). All the baptized without

exception share in these three functions of Christ. Therefore, "as members, they share a common dignity from their rebirth in Christ. They have the same filial grace and the same vocation to perfection" (LG 32b/58); "and if by the will of Christ some are made teachers, dispensers of mysteries, and shepherds on behalf of others, yet all share a true equality with regard to the dignity and to the activity common to all the faithful for the building up of the Body of Christ" (LG 32c/58).

This is a fundamental starting-point on which a great deal of stress must be laid, a backdrop that needs constantly to be rediscovered: the Church has no other teachers besides Christ, no other prophets, priests, mediators, pontiffs ("bridge-builders"), shepherds, lords, kings, and heads. Even if the impoverishment and incorrigible limitations of our human vocabulary force us to apply such terms to others than Christ, they are never to be so applied in a strict and univocal sense (that is, applied in the same way that they apply to Christ) but only in an analogous sense, to indicate a sharing. There is a common, equal sharing by all the baptized; at this level, which affects man's being and is permanent and will therefore continue in eternity, all are in fact equal in dignity. There is also a sharing which the Council calls "ministerial" (LG 10b/27); at this level, where the sharing is of its nature transient (that is, it lasts as long as "services" are need and thus will not be found in eternity), there are differences of degree. The episcopacy belongs exclusively to the sphere of ministerial sharing in the function of Christ, and is therefore a transient reality, limited to the time of pilgrimage.

The bishop is the living, sensible, effective, and pre-eminent sign of Christ in the latter's triple function. He is a sign and an instrument: "Living instruments of Christ the eternal priest" (PO 12b/558). The Constitution on the Church teaches that "bishops in an eminent and visible way undertake Christ's own role as Teacher, Shepherd, and High Priest and that they act in His person" (LG 21d/42). Only to the extent that the bishop is indeed a sign of these three functions and is identified with Jesus, will he exercise his specific functions in an authentic and integrated way. All his initiatives in teaching, sanctifying, and guiding (or "governing") must have their origin not in himself, in his personal ideas and ideals, in self-love and self-interest, but in his identification with Christ who is and always remains the sole true teacher, priest, and shepherd. For the sheep of Christ, "although guided by human shepherds, . . . are nevertheless ceaselessly led and nourished by Christ Himself, the Good Shepherd and the Prince of Shepherds, who gave His life for the sheep" (LG 6b/18). For this reason the Constitution on the Church can teach: "In the bishops, therefore, . . . our Lord Jesus Christ, the supreme High Priest, is present in the midst of those who believe" and through them teaches, sanctifies, directs, and guides the People of the New Covenant (LG 21a/40-41). The bishops are "the vicars and ambassadors of Christ" and exercise authority "in Christ's name" (LG 27a/51).

The Council says that bishops act in Christ's place "in an eminent way," for it also says of priests that they act in the person of Christ and represent him: "Priests represent Christ, and are collaborators with the order of bishops in that threefold sacred task which by its very nature bears on the mission of the Church" (AG 39a/626); "in performing sacred functions they [priests] can act as the ministers of Him who in the liturgy continually exercises his priestly office on our behalf by the actions of His Spirit" (PO 5a/541). Priests are "ministers of Christ Jesus among the people" (PO 2e/535); they are "ministers of the Head" so that "they can build up and establish His whole Body which is the Church. . . . They have become living instruments of Christ the eternal priest. . . . Every priest in his own way represents the person of Christ Himself" (PO 12a-b/557-58). "As ministers of sacred realities, especially in the Sacrifice of the Mass, priests represent the person of Christ in a special way" (PO 13d/560). On the concept of the liturgy as the exercise of Christ's priestly function, cf. SC 7d/141.

To bishops, however, a special ministerial sharing ("in an eminent way") in the triple mission of Christ or, as the Council puts it, in "the fullness of the sacrament of orders" (LG 21c/41), is communicated by a sacrament and therefore by God. Before the Council it was customary to distinguish among episcopal functions between the power of orders (that is, of sanctifying) and the power of jurisdiction (that is, of teaching and governing). It was admitted that the power of sanctifying was given the bishop through his episcopal consecration (which many regarded as a true sacrament). But it was commonly held that the power of teaching and ruling (jurisdiction) was conferred upon the bishop directly by the pope. Now the Constitution on the Church teaches that "episcopal consecration, together with the office of sanctifying, also confers the offices of teaching and of governing" (LG 21d/41; cf. CD 3a/397-98).

We must stress the deeper meaning of this important conciliar doctrine. It frees us once and for all from a predominantly juridical conception of the bishop. According to this conception, the bishop was a priest who had received a special jurisdiction from the pope, a head of a diocese, a kind of governor and administrator who, in the measure that he had received jurisdiction, could more or less exercise an immediate and ordinary pastoral function. All the power he had he had by favor of the Holy See, which could also restrict or entirely remove the jurisdiction that had been freely given. In other words, and in practice, this kind of bishop was not a vicar of Christ but a vicar of the pope, who thus seemed to be really the only authentic successor of the Apostles (according to this conception Rome is, even today, "the Apostolic See" as though there were no other) and the only Vicar of Christ, at least as regards the functions of teaching and governing. The new conception of the bishop which Vatican II has given us is predominantly sacramental: the bishop is the recipient of a charism, a power received directly from God; the power must, of course, be exercised within the bonds of hierarchic communion (and is therefore subject to juridical regulation) but it binds him directly to Christ and, as part of the college, to the Apostles, making of him a vicar of Christ and a member of that college which "is the successor to the college of the Apostles in teaching authority and pastoral rule; or, rather, in the episcopal order the apostolic body continues without a break" (LG 22c/43).

The difference between the two conceptions is a deep-going one, and cannot fail to have practical repercussions. The juridical conception of the bishop, reducing him to a kind of papal vicar, seemed to have been definitively sanctioned by the solemn definition of Vatican I on the primatial power. For the latter is truly a full and supreme power of jurisdiction over all the Church, and ordinary power (connected with the primatial office as such), immediate (to be exercised directly over all the bishops and faithful of the whole world), episcopal (including pastoral functions of the same nature as those exercised by bishops), full (there is no ecclesiastical power that is not included in the primacy), universal (without limitation as to time, person, place, or subject-matters; a power that extends to every individual and the whole collectivity of the faithful, the shepherds, and the rites within the Church, in questions of faith, morality, government, liturgy, and customs), and supreme (there is in the Church no higher authority, not even an ecumenical council). In the face of such a categorical and conclusive definition the question arose whether there was any room in the Church for any other authority which was not simply delegated and limited to the carrying out of papal orders and decisions. For this reason, when John XXIII announced his intention to convene a council, everyone hoped that its main focus would be on the episcopacy, so that the definitions of 1870 might find their complement.

As a matter of fact, Vatican II, "continuing in the same task of clarification begun by Vatican I, . . . has decided to declare

and proclaim before all men its teaching concerning bishops"
(LG 18d/38), but not without first reaffirming as a doctrine
"to be firmly believed by all the faithful," what Vatican I
defined on the institution, perpetuity, power, and nature of
the primacy of the Roman Pontiff and on his infallible teaching authority (LG 18c/38). The Council says elsewhere in the
same document that the power of the episcopal college involves no "lessening of his [the pope's] power of primacy over
all, pastor as well as the general faithful" (LG 22b/43). The
same teaching is repeated in the Decree on the Bishops' Pastoral Office, where we find the more explicit statement that
the pope "by divine institution enjoys full, supreme, immediate, and universal authority over the care of souls" and "a
primacy of ordinary power over all the churches" (CD 2a/
397).

But bishops, too, "exercise their own authority for the good
of their own faithful, and indeed of the whole Church" (LG
22d/44). "This power, which they personally exercise in
Christ's name, is proper, ordinary, and immediate. . . . In
virtue of this power, bishops have the sacred right and the
duty before the Lord to make laws for their subjects, to pass
judgment on them, and to moderate everything pertaining to
the ordering of worship and the apostolate" (LG 27a/51-52).

Therefore the following principle is now valid and in effect:
"The pastoral office or the habitual and daily care of their
sheep is entrusted to them [bishops] completely. Nor are they
to be regarded as vicars of the Roman Pontiff, for they exercise an authority which is proper to them and are quite correctly called 'prelates,' heads of the people whom they govern" (LG 27b/52). Despite the strange feudal oath which
they are still obliged to take, the bishops of Vatican II have
ceased to be vassals of a sovereign who was at the same time
successor of St. Peter. The pope is no longer the great feudal
lord but henceforth only the successor of St. Peter; and the
bishops are no longer feudal princes but exclusively the living,
eminent signs of Christ in his threefold mission, and indeed

of a Christ who in his earthly life was characterized by his self-emptying.

2. *The bishop is a member of the episcopal college, with its own power and the duty of solicitude for the well-being of the entire Church, and he cannot limit himself to his own diocese.*

"By virtue of sacramental consecration and hierarchical communion with the head and other members of the college, a bishop becomes a part of the episcopal body" (CD 4a/398-99). Concerning this college or body, the Council makes two basic statements: (1) "The order of bishops is the successor to the college of the apostles in teaching authority and pastoral rule; or, rather, in the episcopal order the apostolic body continues without a break" and (2) "The episcopal order is the subject of supreme and full power over the universal Church" (LG 22c/43).

As a result, by the fact of being a member of the college as such (and not by reason of being a local Ordinary), each bishop necessarily (1) is part of the group of successors to the Apostles, and (2) shares in the proper (nondelegated), supreme, and full power over the Church. For this reason the Constitution on the Church teaches that "the bishops exercise their own authority for the good of their own faithful, and indeed of the whole Church" (LG 22d/44). In the Decree on the Missions the Council declares that "bishops are consecrated not just for some one diocese, but for the salvation of the entire world" (AG 38a/624). It is even permissible to maintain that *a bishop is first of all a member of the college and only secondarily shepherd of a diocese.* His consecration makes him directly part of the college, while his canonical mission or jurisdiction assigns him the concrete field of his habitual, daily pastoral activity (cf. 24b/47). As a member of the college he is obliged to be solicitous for the whole Church (LG 23b/45; CD 3a/397). Though this solicitude "is not exercised by an act of jurisdiction" (LG 23c/45), it is nonetheless an act of the bishops' "own authority," as we may infer from the text already cited, LG 22d/44, that is, it is not a power received from the pope (a delegated power) but is only regulated in its exercise by the successor of St. Peter. According to the Constitution on the Church (23c/45) it is manifested concretely by promoting and safeguarding the unity of faith and the discipline common to the whole Church, by instructing the faithful in love for the whole Mystical Body, by fostering every activity common to the whole Church, and, above all, by taking an interest in the missions, sending out missionaries, providing spiritual and material aid (cf. AG 38g/ 626), and offering brotherly help to other churches (cf. also CD 6c/400).

This is the reason why "bishops should always realize that they are linked one to the other, and should show concern for all the churches. For by divine institution and the require-ment of their apostolic office, each one in concert with his fel-low bishops is responsible for the Church. They should be especially concerned about those parts of the world where the Word of God has not yet been proclaimed or where, chiefly because of the small number of priests, the faithful are in danger of departing from the precepts of the Christian life, and even of losing the faith itself. Let bishops, therefore, make every effort to have the faithful actively support and promote works of evangelization and the apostolate" (CD 6a-b/400). This outlook is required of every bishop; no one is dispensed, and no one can be dispensed. All ought to have a deeply missionary spirituality, an openness to the whole world. Diocesan self-centeredness here receives its death-blow. Even when a diocese has many great internal needs and prob-lems (and what diocese does not?), it must see to it that the missionary orientation remains alive. "The individual bishops, insofar as the discharge of their duty permits, are obliged to enter into a community of effort among themselves and with the successor of Peter" (LG 23d/45). "In his own diocese, with which he comprises a single unit, the bishop stimulates, promotes, and directs the work for the missions. Thus he makes the mission spirit and zeal of the People of God present and, as it were, visible, so that the whole diocese becomes missionary. It will be the bishop's task to raise up from among his own people, especially the sick and those oppressed by hardship, souls who will offer prayers and penance to God with a generous heart for the evangelization of the world" (AG 38b-c/625). "As members of the episcopal college, bishops should always realize that they are linked one to the other" (CD 6a/400), for "from the very first centuries of the Church the bishops who were placed over the individual churches were deeply influenced by the fellowship of fraternal charity and by zeal for the universal mission entrusted to the Apostles. And so they pooled their resources and unified their plans for the common good and for that of the individual churches" (CD 36a/424). The bishop must, then, cultivate within himself "the collegial character and meaning" (LG 22a/42), the "collegial union" (LG 23a/44), the "collegiate sense" (LG 23f/46).

3. *The bishop must carry out his office as part of a living hierarchical communion, and not in a spirit of independence, without any sense of the Church as a whole.*

The primary function of the successor of St. Peter is to be the *visible* foundation and source of unity in faith and fellowship (LG 18c/38) and of unity among the bishops.[6] and the multitude of the faithful (LG 23a/44). Such unity, communion, and union are part of the Church's very life and are produced more directly by the word of God (cf. DV 21/125; PO 4a/538; DH 11g/691), by the Eucharist (cf. LG 3b/16; UR 3a/343; PO 6h/545), and by the Holy Spirit (cf. LG 13a/31; UR 2b/344). The pope is, in truth, only the visible instrument (or sacrament) that has been divinely instituted to safeguard, watch over, defend, and foster the unity of faith and ecclesial communion. To describe the relations of each bishop to the pope and the other bishops, the Constitution on the Church coins the phrase "hierarchical communion" (LG 21d/41; 22a/43). The Prefatory Note of Explanation says that the expression does not denote a vague feeling of companionship or camaraderie, but an objective reality, which therefore demands a juridical form and, at the same time, is animated by charity. Therefore, the Constitution on the Church concludes, "it is the duty of all bishops to promote and to safeguard the unity of faith and the discipline common to the whole Church, [and] to instruct the faithful in love for the whole Mystical Body of Christ" (LG 23c/45). Such is the properly ecclesial outlook, the ancient "thinking with the Church," and it ought to be cultivated with special care by bishops, inasmuch as "the individual bishop . . . is the visible principle and foundation of unity in his particular church, fashioned after the model of the universal Church. In and from such individual churches there comes into being the one and only Catholic Church. For this reason each individual bishop represents his own church, but all of them together in union with the pope represent the entire Church joined in the bond of peace, love, and unity" (LG 23a/44).

The bishops, too, indeed the bishop above all, must be obedient. However, "obedience," in the Church, does not signify primarily a subjection, dependence, or inferiority, but "communal action" or a conscious, free participation in the living hierarchical communion. This concept of obedience is developed by the Council chiefly in the Decree on the Ministry and Life of Priests. "Since priestly ministry [which includes the episcopal ministry] is the ministry of the Church herself, it can be discharged only by hierarchical communion with the whole body" (PO 15c/564). In this communal action the individual's own will is consecrated, in obedience, to the service of God and the brothers, as he accepts and carries out in a spirit of faith what has been ordered or recommended. For "loyalty toward Christ can never be divorced from loyalty toward His Church" (PO 14e/563).

> 4. *The bishop must take part, with a collegi-*
> *ate spirit, in the episcopal conference, and*
> *not give orders like a little all-powerful*
> *pope and sole owner of the diocese.*

The episcopal conference introduces an entirely new factor into the outlook, action, initiatives, and spirituality in the individual bishop in his diocese. After being discussed in detail and ardently desired by the majority at the Council, the episcopal conference was established and given its basic form by the Decree on the Bishops' Pastoral Office (CD 37-38/ 424-26), while detailed regulations were provided in the Motu Proprio *Ecclesiae Sanctae*, n. 41. Here we have a new juridical reality in the Church, one of supreme usefulness and importance; not only should the bishops go along with it but they must (since it was they who approved it at the Council) also understand, defend, and promote it. The episcopal conference was elaborated as the solution to two great problems. On the one hand, there was the need for decentralization; everything had become excessively centralized at Rome, thus hindering the salvation of souls and any immediate pastoral action; the results were an ever more deadly uniformity, a sterile fixism, and a sinful pharisaism, which was the main reason why the Church had retreated into the ghetto out of which we must now emerge, at any cost, if we really want to save men and not institutions. On the other hand, now that the bishop has had his rightful place restored to him and is more aware of his pastoral powers, he must avoid becoming a little all-powerful pope in his own diocese; that would only aggravate the ghetto situation and would alienate from him not only the faithful but religious and priests as well.

The theological basis for the episcopal conference is to be found in two principles taught by the Constitution on the Church. First, as a member of the episcopal college, each bishop has his own authority which is to be exercised "for the good . . . of the whole Church" (LG 22d/44); and this power can be exercised when the bishop is invited to collegial action. Second, as a member of the college, each bishop "is obliged by Christ's decree and command to be solicitous for the whole Church" (LG 23b/45). The episcopal conference, therefore, is not simply an expression of charity or camaraderie but an ontological and juridical requirement of the specifically episcopal status and found its juridical expression in the patriarchate during the first millennium (and still does in the East even today).

On November 13, 1963, Bishop Alfredo Ancel explained at the Council that the basis for territorial collegiality flows from the requirements of the episcopal mission itself. On the one hand, the bishops must have recourse to their brother bishops when they cannot by themselves resolve their own problems. On the other hand, each ought to offer his help to the others, in virtue of the collegiality that binds them together in the episcopate. It is impossible today for a bishop to be self-sufficient in the exercise of his ministry, whereas the episcopal body of a given nation is in a position to develop a much more effective pastoral action. Through his own reflection and effort each bishop will have to acquire a collegial outlook (this implies a form of "interior conversion"). It is no longer possible for each to govern by himself, whereas within a nation or region there exists a common fund of ideas which can be purified, enlightened, and evangelized by collective action. Unfortunately, the bishop has for long been isolated and has grown used to acting by himself (or only with the pope), and when he helps other bishops, he does it more from the impulse of charity than out of collegiality and co-responsibility. Yet it is impossible today to transform a single diocese as though it were an island or a cloister. Interdependence, socialization, and mutual relationships characterize our contemporary world. The current means of communication along with the need and ease of travel constantly break through geographical limits. Therefore the bishop of today has an unqualified need of a sense of collegiality, of communication, of giving and receiving. The bishop as a bishop is essentially a collegial being and he will fulfill the meaning of his episcopacy only in the measure in which he leaves his ivory tower, communicates with others, and gives himself to others. If he is not so minded, he will, in the present state of reality, certainly be less capable of carrying out his mission; this alone, independently of any consideration of age, would be sufficient reason to offer his resignation from office (cf. CD 21/412).

The episcopal conference, then, is based on what the Council called the "collegiate sense," when it said that "the episcopal bodies of today are in a position to render a manifold and fruitful assistance, so that this collegiate sense may be put into practical application" (LG 23f/46). The Decree on the Bishops' Pastoral Office sums it all up when it says: "Nowadays especially, bishops are frequently unable to fulfill their office suitably and fruitfully unless they work more harmoniously and closely every day with other bishops. Episcopal conferences, already established in many nations, have furnished outstanding proofs of a more fruitful apostolate. Therefore, this most sacred Synod considers it supremely opportune everywhere that bishops belonging to the same nation or region form an association and meet together at fixed times. Thus, when the insights of prudence and experience have been shared and views exchanged, there will emerge a holy union of energies in the service of the common good of the churches" (CD 37a/424-25).

We may, in this context, call attention to the pastoral possibilities and avenues opened by the Council but which remain unexplored as yet by any joint pastoral action. The Decree on the Bishops' Pastoral Office remarks that "since pastoral needs increasingly require that some pastoral undertakings be directed and carried forward as joint projects, it is fitting that certain offices be created for the service of all or many dioceses of a determined region or nation. These offices can even be filled by bishops" (CD 42a/427). Here we have a really excellent suggestion from the Council. Each diocesan bishop has his own internal problems which absorb him more or less completely and leave him without the time or energy for accepting new obligations or further responsibilities. As a result certain nation-wide pastoral needs are given insufficient attention and often left unsolved. Take, for example, the broad, urgent, and serious problem of the Umbanda (a form of spiritism) in Brazil; here we have twelve million Brazilians in a state of complete and radical disorientation in the area of doctrine and religion. Yet I see bishops who seem much more preoccupied with the way Communion is distributed than with the thousands of Umbanda enclaves operative in their dioceses. The problem of Umbanda in Brazil (including the whole problem of evangelizing the country's black population which has never been systematically catechized) will be solved at the national level only by an ordinariate for a kind of Umbandist rite.

5. *The bishop must make the one, holy, catholic, and apostolic Church present in his diocese, and not turn the diocese into a mere administrative post of a central organization.*

The Decree on the Bishops' Office gives us a definition of a diocese that contains a whole theology of the local church: "A diocese is that portion of God's people which is entrusted to a bishop to be shepherded by him with the cooperation of the presbytery. Adhering thus to its pastor and gathered together by him in the Holy Spirit through the gospel and the Eucharist, this portion constitutes a particular church in which the one, holy, catholic, and apostolic Church of Christ is truly present and operative" (CD 11a/403).[7]

Gathered in the Holy Spirit: God determined to gather together his scattered children. To this end he sent the Holy Spirit, who "on behalf of the whole Church and each and every one of those who believe, is the principle of their coming together and remaining together in the teaching of the apostles and in fellowship, in the breaking of bread and in prayers" (LG 13a/31). "After being lifted up on the cross and glorified, the Lord Jesus poured forth the Spirit whom He had promised, and through whom He has called and gathered together the people of the New Covenant, who comprise the Church, into a unity of faith, hope, and charity. . . . It is the Holy Spirit, dwelling in those who believe, pervading and ruling over the entire Church, who brings about that marvelous communion of the faithful and joins them together so intimately in Christ that He is the principle of the Church's unity. By distributing various kinds of spiritual gifts and ministries, He enriches the Church of Jesus Christ with different functions 'in order to perfect the saints for a work of ministry, for building up the body of Christ' (Eph. 4:12)" (UR 2a/343-44).

Through the gospel: "The People of God finds its unity first of all through the Word of the living God, which is quite properly sought from the lips of priests. . . . For through the saving word the spark of faith is struck in the hearts of unbelievers, and fed in the hearts of the faithful. By this faith the community of the faithful begins and grows. As the Apostle says: 'Faith depends on hearing and hearing on the word of Christ' (Rom. 10:17)" (PO 4a-b/538-39). In the Decree on the Missions, when describing the establishment of new churches, the Council teaches: "The chief means of this implantation [of the Church] is the preaching of the gospel of Jesus Christ" (AG 6f/591). For "the force and power in the word of God is so great that it remains the support and energy of the Church, the strength of faith for her sons, the food of the soul, the pure and perennial source of spiritual life" (DV 21/125). The Apostles "with a firm faith . . . held that the gospel is indeed the power of God unto salvation for all who believe. Therefore they rejected all 'carnal weapons.' They followed the example of the greatness and respectfulness of Christ. And they preached the word of God in the full confidence that there was resident in this word itself a divine power able to destroy all the forces arrayed against God and to bring men to faith in Christ and to His service" (DH 11h/692).

And the Eucharist: "No Christian community . . . can be built up unless it has its basis and center in the celebration of the most Holy Eucharist. Here, therefore, all education in the spirit of community must originate" PO 6h/545, and cf. note 82). For the Eucharist expresses and brings about the unity of the Church (cf. LG 3b/16; UR 2a/343) and brings it about in a wonderful way (cf. LG 11b/28). It is by the Eucharist that the Church "constantly lives and grows" (LG 26a/50) and "we live the paschal mystery more deeply" (CD 15b/407). It is "the fount and apex of the whole Christian life" (LG 11b/28), the center and summit of Christian community (AG 9b/595), the "center and culmination of the whole life of the Christian community" (CD 30f/418). "The other sacraments, as well as every ministry of the Church and every work of the apostolate, are linked with the Holy Eucharist and are directed toward it. For the most blessed Eucharist contains the Church's entire spiritual wealth, that is, Christ Himself, our Passover and living bread. Through His very flesh, made vital and vitalizing by the Holy Spirit, He offers life to men. They are thereby invited and led to offer themselves, their labors, and all created things together with Him. Hence the Eucharist shows itself to be the source and the apex of the whole work of preaching the gospel" (PO 5c-d/541-42). — The "Church . . . , as the body of the Word Incarnate, is nourished and lives by the word of God and by the Eucharistic Bread" (AG 6f/591-92). "Of all spiritual helps, those acts are outstanding by which the faithful receive nourishment from God's word at the twofold table of Sacred Scripture and the Eucharist" (PO 18a/569-70).

Constitutes a particular church: The Constitution on the Church had already used the expression "particular church" as a name for a diocese (LG 23a-b/44-45). But at an earlier

point the same document had also used the phrase to designate a collection of communities which retain their own traditions; in this sense the phrase is also used by the Decree
on Eastern Catholic Churches, thus identifying it with the
Eastern rites (OE 2/374). By reason of the principle which
we shall be mentioning next, "particular church" is a much
happier designation of a diocese than are some of the others
proposed by various Fathers at the Council: e.g. special
church, episcopal church (which gives the impression that the
diocese is the bishop's personal possession), local church
(which would exclude non-territorial dioceses), portion of the
universal Church (which implies that there are parts or divisions of the Church of Christ).

*In which the one, holy, catholic, and apostolic Church of
Christ is truly present and operative*: Here is a principle that
is rich in consequences for the theology of the diocese. The
Constitution on the Church teaches that particular churches
(i.e., dioceses) are "fashioned after the model of the universal
Church. In and from such individual churches there comes
into being the one and only Catholic Church" (LG 23a/44);
and the Mystical Body is, therefore, also a "body of the
churches" (LG 23c/45). And in the Decree on the Missions
we read: "Particular churches are bound to mirror the universal Church as perfectly as possible" (AG 20a/609). For,
as the Constitution on the Church tells us, "this Church of
Christ is truly present in all legitimate local congregations of
the faithful which, united with their pastors, are themselves
called churches in the New Testament. For in their own
locality these are the new people called by God, in the Holy
Spirit and in much fullness (cf. 1 Th. 1:5). In them the
faithful are gathered by the preaching of the gospel of Christ,
and the mystery of the Lord's Supper is celebrated, 'that by
the flesh and blood of the Lord's body the whole brotherhood
may be joined together.' . . . I these communities, though
frequently small and poor, or living far from any other, Christ
is present. By virtue of Him the one, holy, catholic, and

apostolic Church gathers together" (LG 26a-b/50).

This means, however, as Joseph Ratzinger points out,[8] that the particular church or the diocese is not merely an administrative post of a central organization, but is a living cell in which the whole vital mystery of the one body of the Church is present and operative, and this in such a way that each of these cells may, legitimately and without further qualification, be called "church." Such a cell is, of course, not self-sufficient or autonomous; it is essentially part of a whole and must be open to vital communion with all the other cells. "Each individual bishop represents his own church, but all of them together in union with the pope represent the entire Church joined in the bond of peace, love, and unity" (LG 23a/44). On the other hand, "by governing well their own church as a portion of the universal Church, they themselves [the bishops] are effectively contributing to the welfare of the whole Mystical Body, which is also the body of the churches" (LG 23c/45).

From the principle we are now discussing, the Decree on the Bishops' Pastoral Office draws a further conclusion: "For a diocese to fulfill its purpose, the nature of the Church must be clearly evident to the People of God who belong to that diocese. Likewise, bishops must be able to carry out their pastoral duties effectively among their people" (CD 22a/412). Two principles are here enunciated. One is positive: it must be possible for the nature of the Church to be clearly manifested in the diocese (the diocese cannot, therefore, be very small). The other is negative: the bishop must be able to carry out his charge in an effective way (this is not always possible when the diocese is very large). The Council therefore offers a general norm: "The extent of the diocesan boundaries and the number of its inhabitants should generally be such that, on the one hand, though he may be helped by others, the bishop can exercise his pontifical functions and suitably carry out pastoral visitations, can properly direct and coordinate all the works of the apostolate in his diocese, be especially well acquainted with his priests and with the religious and laity who have some part in diocesan enterprises. On the other hand, an adequate and suitable area should be provided so that bishop and clergy can usefully devote all their energies to the ministry, while the needs of the Church at large are not overlooked" (CD 23d/413).

6. *The bishop must govern the particular church in direct and brotherly collaboration with the presbytery, and not with the outlook of a ruthless administrator or a narrow-minded businessman.*

It is noteworthy that in the very definition of a diocese the Decree on the Bishops' Pastoral Office stresses the cooperation of bishop and presbytery in the pastoral care of the particular church: "A diocese is that portion of God's people which is entrusted to a bishop to be shepherded by him with the cooperation of the presbytery" (CD 11a/403).[9] According to the Constitution on the Church, all the priests form a single priesthood with their bishop (LG 28c/54). The Decree on the Ministery and Life of Priests speaks of priests forming among themselves "an intimate sacramental brotherhood" and being one "presbytery." The Decree on the Bishops at one point says that only the diocesan priests (not religious priests) "form one presbytery and one family, whose father is the bishop" (CD 28a/416-17). Further on, however, it admits that religious priests "in a certain genuine sense . . . must be said to belong to the clergy of the diocese inasmuch as they share in the care of souls and in carrying out works of the apostolate under the authority of the sacred prelates" (CD 34a/420-21).

In its Decree on the Ministry and Life of Priests the Council speaks as follows: "By reason of the gift of the Holy Spirit which is given to priests in sacred ordination, bishops should regard them as necessary helpers and counselors, in the ministry and in the task of teaching, sanctifying, and nourishing the People of God. Already in the ancient days of the Church we find liturgical texts proclaiming this relationship with insistence, as when they solemnly called upon God to pour out upon the candidate for priestly ordination 'the spirit of grace and counsel so that with a pure heart he may help and govern the People [of God],' just as in the desert the spirit of Moses was extended to the minds of seventy prudent men, 'and using them as helpers he easily governed countless multitudes among the people.' Therefore, on account of this communion in the same priesthood and ministry, the bishops should regard priests as his brothers and friends. As far as in him lies, he should have at heart the material and especially the spiritual welfare of his priests. For above all, upon the bishop rests the heavy responsibility for the sanctity of his priests. Hence, he should exercise the greatest care on behalf of the continual formation of his priests. He should gladly listen to them, indeed, consult them, and have discussions with them about those matters which concern the necessities of pastoral work and the welfare of the diocese. In order to put these ideals into effect, a group or senate of priests representing the presbytery should be established. It is to operate in a manner adapted to modern circumstances and needs and have a form and norms to be determined by law. By its counsel, this body will be able to give effective assistance to the bishop in his government of the dioceses" (PO 7a-d/546-48). In the Motu Proprio *Ecclesiae Sanctae*, Pope Paul VI implemented this decision of the Council and ordered that in each diocese "according to the form and manner established by the bishop" a presbyteral council, or senate of priests, should be set up.[10]

In the Constitution on the Church, Vatican II said: "Let the bishop regard his priests, who are his co-workers, as sons and friends, just as Christ called His disciples no longer servants by friends" (LG 28d/54). And in the Decree on Bishops: The bishop "should regard his priests as sons and friends. Thus by his readiness to listen to them and by his trusting familiarity, a bishop can work to promote the whole pastoral work of the entire diocese" (CD 16c/408). Further on, the same Decree insists: "For the sake of greater service to soul, let the bishop engage in discussion with his priests, even collectively, especially about pastoral matters. This he should do not only occasionally but, as far as possible, at fixed intervals" (CD 28b/417).

We are touching here on the heart of the episcopal spirituality and outlook. At the Council, Bishop Pierre M. Théas of Tarbes and Lourdes said (October 13, 1964): "Since we bishops have a clearer grasp of our responsibility as successors to the Apostles, since we have received the fullness of the priesthood, since we belong to the same episcopal college under the authority of the pope, and since we as a body have the task of evangelizing and saving the world, we are well aware that without the cooperation of the priests we are unable to carry out our mission of teaching, sanctification, and pastoral action. Conscious, then, of our weakness and limitations, let us say: 'Do nothing without the priests.' " Either the bishops is a sincere friend and brother of his priests, dialogues with them, even recreates with them, and then all goes well, or the diocese will be in a constant state of tension, bitter criticism, and ill-being. (The bishop will not put a great deal of stress today on being a "father" to his priests. Although the term can be properly understood and is traditional enough, it reminds people of the paternalism that characterized the not too distant past. "The powers of diocesan bishops are personal, like those of a father over his own family, and he is independent of every other ecclesiastical authority except that of the Holy See," said Bishop Geraldo Sigaud at the Council on October 9, 1963![11])

Speaking in the name of sixty Brazilian bishops, Bishop Fernando Gomes dos Santos said (November 6, 1963): "The conception of the bishop as administrator and governor, as a 'lord' . . . set apart from his priests, must be wholly done away with."[12]

The bishop must, then, be watchful over himself and careful about his ways of speaking to his priests, giving them orders, insisting on discipline, and transmitting instructions received from higher authority. Trust our priests- Do not think of them as though they were still seminarians, or as though they were irresponsible. It is precisely the lack of trust in them that leads to their being irresponsible. Paternalist attitudes beget infantile reactions. Yet the Church must never be mistaken for a bunch of children! In speaking of the Church in the modern world, the Council says that "the education of youth from every social background has to be undertaken, so that there can be produced not only men and women of refined talents, but those great-souled persons who are so desperately required by our times" (GS 31a/229). The Council elsewhere expresses the hope that "we are witnesses of a new humanism, one in which man is defined first of all by his responsibility toward his brothers and toward history" (GS 55/261). Seminarians are to learn "to act on their own initiative and energetically" (OT 11c/448).

The Council is not unaware that we are presently in a critical situation and that "not a few can be found who seem inclined to use the name of freedom as the pretext for refusing to submit to authority and for making light of the duty of obedience" (DH 8a/687). But the same document, in attempting to supply a remedy for the evil, does not insist for the thousandth time on the necessity of obedience and submission, but rather on the urgent task of forming men who, in addition to respecting the moral order, "will be lovers of true freedom—men, in other words, who will come to decisions on their own judgment and in the light of truth, govern their activities with a sense of responsibility, and strive after what is true and right, willing always to join with others in cooperative effort" (DH 8b/687).

One point needs to be emphasized: the crisis of obedience has not been and is not a crisis only in those who are "subjects" (a word that is, in any event, an un-Christian one when

applied to the relations between priests and bishop). Those
who demand obedience must also form their conception of
authority in the light of Mt 28:8-11: "You, however, must
not allow yourselves to be called Rabbi, since you have only
one Master, and you are all brothers. You must call no one
on earth your father, since you have only one Father, and
he is in heaven. Nor must you allow yourselves to be called
teachers, for you have only one Teachers, the Christ" (JB).
Or in the light of Lk 22:25-27: "Earthly kings lord it over
their people. Those who exercise authority over them are
called their benefactors. Yet it cannot be that way with you.
Let the greater among you be as the junior, the leader as the
servant. Who, in fact, is the greater—he who reclines at
table or he who serves the meal? Is it not the one who reclines
at table? Yet I am in your midst as the one who serves you."
Is it not time to take these words seriously?

> 7. *The bishop must, first and foremost,
> preach the gospel to the men of his time,
> and not be satisfied to repeat inherited
> formulas and preserve the outward order
> of his diocese.*

The Constitution on the Church teaches that "among the
principle duties of bishops, the preaching of the gospel occu-
pies an eminent place" (LG 25a/47). The Decree on Bishops
repeats the same idea: "eminent among the duties of bishops"
is the task of preaching the gospel of Christ to men (CD
12a/404). The Decree on the Missions expresses it thus: "The
bishop should be first and foremost a herald of the faith, leading new disciples to Christ" (AG 20b/609). It was for this
that he received "the sure gift of truth" (DV 8b/116). It is
for this that he is an authentic teacher of the doctrine of
Christ (cf. LG 20d/40; 25a/47), a "witness to divine and
Catholic truth" (LG 25b/48), a "true and authentic teacher
of the faith" (CD 2b/397). It was for this that he received
by his consecration (therefore by a special sacrament) the

mission of teaching (cf. LG 21d/41). It was for this that in the impressive ceremony of consecration the book of the gospels was placed upon his head. It was to this end, beyond all other purposes, that the Apostles received the promise of the Holy Spirit.

The bishop, then, "must hold fast to the Sacred Scriptures through diligent sacred reading and careful study. . . . This cultivation of Scripture is required lest . . . [he] become 'an empty preacher of the word of God outwardly, who is not a listener to it inwardly' " (DV 25a/137). He must be a specialist and "earn by frequent reading of the divine Scriptures the 'excelling knowledge of Jesus Christ' (Phil. 3:8)" (*ibid.*). The advice given by the Council to priests applies to the bishop as well: "Since they are ministers of God's word, they should every day read and listen to that word which they are required to teach to others. If they are at the same time preoccupied with welcoming this message into their own hearts, they will become ever more perfect disciples of the Lord. For as the Apostle Paul wrote to Timothy: 'Meditate on these things, give yourself entirely to them, that your progress may be manifest to all. Take heed to yourself and to your teaching, be earnest in them. For in so doing you will save both yourself who hear you' (1 Tim. 4:15-16). As priests search for a better way to share with others the fruits of their own contemplation, they will win a deeper understanding of 'the unfathomable riches of Christ' (Eph. 3:8) as well as the manifold wisdom of God. Remembering that it is the Lord who open hearts and that sublime utterance comes not from themselves but from God's power, in the very act of preaching His word they will be united more closely with Christ the Teacher and be led by His Spirit" (PO 13b-c/559-60). The Council also observes that "priestly preaching is often very difficult in the circumstances of the modern world. If it is to influence the mind of the listener more fruitfully, such preaching must not present God's word in a general and abstract fashion only, but it must apply the perennial truth of the gospel to the concrete circumstances of life" (PO 4d/539-40). The charism received through the sacrament does not work automatically. This is why St. Paul recommends to Bishop Timothy: "Devote yourself to the *reading of Scripture*, to preaching and teaching. Do not neglect the gift you received when, as a result of prophecy, the presbyters laid their hands on you. Attend to your duties; let them absorb you" (1 Tim 4:13). Whence the recommendation of the Constitution on the Church: "The Roman Pontiff and the bishops, in view of their office and of the importance of the matter, strive painstakingly and by appropriate means to inquire properly into that revelation and to give apt expression to its contents" (LG 25g/49-50), which they are to communicate in their integrity, preserve whole and intact, and expound faithfully. "The bishops should present Christian doctrine in a manner adapted to the needs of the times, that is to say, in a manner corresponding to the difficulties and problems by which people are most vexatiously burdened and troubled" (CD 13a/405).

This last passage points to one of the most difficult and delicate tasks which pastors face today: to present Christian doctrine (for example, on original sin, the creation of man and woman, the Incarnation, transubstantiation, hell, biblical inspiration and inerrancy, the historicity of the gospels) in terms and concepts that can be objectively understood and accepted by contemporary man who lives in a civilization shaped by technology, the exact sciences, and a developed critical outlook. Pope Paul VI, too, says that he is "fully convinced that bishops and priests cannot worthily carry out their mission of enlightening and saving the modern world if they are not in a position to present, defend, and illuminate the truths of divine faith with ideas and words that are more understandable to minds trained in present-day philosophical and scientific learning."[13]

In the present situation a man can, of course, shut his eyes to the problems being raised (and broadcast by the mass media) and be content to go on repeating traditional formulas which are conditioned in many instances by a culture that no longer exists or else exists only in the minds of some ecclesiastics or the mentality of certain Catholic milieus which are extremely "traditional" but are also quickly vanishing into past history. But if a man acts in this way, he condemns himself to being isolated and unintelligible. Priests involved in the work of communicating Christian doctrine to students or intellectuals are keenly aware of the problem. It takes only a bit of frank discussion to bring it out into the open! The Decree on the Ministry and Life of Priests is forced to admit: "The ministers of the Church and even, at times, the faithful themselves feel like strangers in this world, anxiously looking for appropriate ways and words with which to communicate with it. For the modern obstacles blocking faith, the seeming sterility of their past labors, and also the bitter loneliness they experience can lead them to the danger of becoming depressed in spirit" (PO 22b/574-75).

The Constitution on the Church in the Modern World proclaims, indeed, that "theologians are invited to seek continually for more suitable ways of communicating doctrine to the men of their times" (GS 62c/268). But it is also the case—and I myself am well aware of it—that these same theologians not only do not receive any positive encouragement and help in their difficult task, but even find themselves being constantly, and in a hateful way, watched upon and put under pressure by the very people who ought to be carrying out the mission of speaking out in a clear, intelligible, and acceptable way. It is very easy and quite comforting (you need only be able to read and understand Latin) to repeat the formulas of Trent or earlier Councils. It is not difficult to repeat the old anathemas and to menace people with condemnation: If anyone does not hear and believe, let him be damned. But such cannot be the attitude of a shepherd, of the Good Shepherd.

8. *The bishop must be the high priest of his flock and a sign of the self-emptying of Christ, and not a mere steward of properties or even a prince who seeks a futile glory.*

The bishop is a high priest (cf. LG 21c/41); he is the high priest of his flock and "in a certain sense it is from him that the faithful who are under his care derive and maintain their life in Christ" (SC 41a/152). He possesses "the apex of the sacred ministry" (LG 21c/41), "the fullness of the sacrament of orders" (*ibid.*; cf. also LG 26a/50; 41b/68; CD 15a/4-6). He is " 'the steward of the grace of the supreme priesthood' " (LG 26a/50), the principal steward of the mysteries of God (LG 21c/41; CD 15a/406), moderator, promoter, and guardian of the liturgical life (LG 26c-d/50-51; CD 15a/406), and teacher of perfection (CD 15c/407; cf. LG 41b/68).

In this context the Council refers continually and in the first place to the Eucharist (cf. LG 26c-d/50-51; SC 41b/152). "The other sacraments, as well as every ministry of the Church and every work of the apostolate, are linked with the Holy Eucharist and are directed toward it. . . . Hence the Eucharist shows itself to be the source and the apex of the whole work of preaching the gospel" PO 5c-d/541-42). "As ministers of sacred realities, especially in the Sacrifice of the Mass, priests represent the person of Christ in a special way" (PO 13d/560); "so it is that while priests are uniting themselves with the act of Christ the Priests, they are offering their whole selves every day to God. While being nourished by the Body of Christ, their hearts are sharing in the love of Him who gives Himself as food for His faithful ones" (PO 13f/561). "Pastoral love flows mainly from the Eucharistic Sacrifice, which is therefore the center and root of the whole priestly life" (PO 14d/563). On the other hand, the very holiness of bishops contributes in its turn to the fruitfulness of their ministry: "True, the grace of God can complete the work of salvation even through unworthy ministers. Yet ordinarily God desires to manifest His wonders through those who have been made particularly docile to the impulse and guidance of the Holy Spirit" by union with Christ and holiness of life (PO 12e/559).

It is therefore in the context of the bishop's office of sanctification that the Council reminds bishops: "By the example of their manner of life they must be an influence for good on those over whom they preside" (LG 26d/51); "They . . . can lead the Church to ever-increasing holiness through their own example" (LG 41b/68). "Led, therefore, by the Lord's Spirit, who anointed the Savior and sent Him to preach the gospel to the poor, priests as well as bishops will avoid all those things which can offend the poor in any way. More than the other followers of Christ, priests and bishops should spurn any type of vanity in their affairs. Finally, let them have the kind of dwelling which will appear closed to no one and which no one will fear to visit, even the humblest" (PO 17h/569). "All pastors should remember too that by their daily conduct and concern they are revealing the face of the Church to the world. Men will judge the power and truth of the Christian message thereby" (GS 43h/244). The Decree on Bishops therefore says that "a bishop . . . should arrange his life in such a way as to accommodate it to the needs of the times" (CD 16b/408). But as late as its issue of April 28, 1967, the magazine *Visao* could complain: "There are numerous dioceses in Brazil whose bishops still play the aristocrat: untouchable and cut off from the people, with whom they have scarcely a nodding acquaintance"; and further on, "Many priests and laymen, convinced of the urgent need of renewal, lament that bishops who are turned in upon themselves, set against any dialogue, and, in the last analysis, psychologically immature, still represent a serious obstacle to the dialogue which the Church must carry on with the contemporary world."

At the Second General Conference of the Latin American Bishops (Medellin, 1968), in their document on the "Poverty of the Church," the bishops stated: "We wish our houses and style of life to be modest, our clothing simple, our works and institutions functional, without show or ostentation. We ask priests and faithful to treat us in conformity with our mission as fathers and pastors, for we desire to renounce honorable titles as belonging to another era."[14]

9. *The bishop must fulfill his office as father and pastor in the spirit of service, and not as one who dominates and seeks to be served.*

It is perhaps here that Vatican II will require the most radical change in the mentality and spirituality of bishops. For, according to Vatican II's conception of the hierarchy, the latter's function is essentially ministerial, essentially one of service. The hierarchy exists "for the nurture and constant growth of the People of God" (LG 18a/37). The Council constantly sets before us the example of Christ who came to serve and not to be served: in the likeness of Christ, the Church "is not set up to seek earthly glory, but to proclaim humility and self-sacrifice, even by her own example" (LG 8c/23). Note, too, that in the key passage in which the hierarchical priesthood is compared with the universal priesthood, the former is called "the ministerial . . . priesthood" (LG 10b/27); it exists for the sake of the community and in its functioning (cf. LG 24a/46-47). "That duty, which the Lord committed to the shepherds of His people, is a true service, and in sacred literature is significantly called 'diakonia' or ministry" (LG 24a/47). Bishops undoubtedly have "authority and sacred power," but "this power they use only for the edification of their flock in truth and holiness, remembering that he who is greater should become as the lesser and he who is more distinguished, as the servant" (LG 27a/51). "Since he is sent by the Father to govern His family, a bishop must keep before his eyes the example of the Good Shepherd, who came not to be ministered unto but to minister" (LG

27c/52). A similar thought is voiced in the Decree on the Bishops: "In exercising his office of father and pastor, a bishop should stand in the midst of his people as one who serves" (CD 16a/407). Set in office for the sake of men in their relations with God (CD 15a/406), bishops have but one great mission: to save souls (CD 19a/410). Therefore the supreme norm for them must be the welfare of the Lord's flock (CD 25a/414).

In a discourse to the Italian bishops on December 6, 1965, as the Council was drawing to its close, Pope Paul VI asked: "What is to be the style of such [episcopal] authority? . . . It is clear, for example, that in a former day, especially when pastoral authority was associated with secular authority (the staff and the sword in the same hand!), the characteristics of a bishop were overlordship, external pomp, dignity, at times privilege, arbitrariness, and sumptuousness. In earlier times these traits did not give rise to scandal; the people liked to see in their bishop a figure of greatness, power, pomp, and majesty. Today it is not and cannot be so. Far from admiring, people are disagreeably surprised and scandalized if a bishop is excessively preoccupied with anachronistic marks of his office, and they remind him of the gospel. . . . A sober and dignified outward way of life is possible and required by the office. But let us thank God that we have put aside so many worldly externals!"[15]

The reaffirmation of the "service" character of ecclesiastical authority can, however, have perilous results as well as good ones. Pope Paul VI called our attention to these in an address to the Tribunal of the Sacred Roman Rota on January 28, 1971: "It is true that today some people so stress the character of 'service' of the Church's authority that two dangerous consequences in the constitutional concept of the Church could result. These are: 1. the assigning of priority to the community, thereby ascribing to it effective charismatic power proper to itself; 2. the ignoring of the fact of power in the Church, with a marked discrediting of the canonical functions in the ecclesial society. Thence there is derived the opinion of an indiscriminate liberty, of an autonomous pluralism, while tradition and the normative procedures of the hierarchy is attacked as 'juridicism.' Confronted with these interpretations which are fundamentally at variance with the mind of Christ and of the Church, we would like to repeat once again today that authority, that is, the power of ordering the means suitable for attaining the end of the ecclesial society, is not opposed to the outpouring of the Spirit in the People of God; rather it is the vehicle and guardian thereof."[16]

> 10. *The bishop must be a pastor, with his own ordinary and immediate power, and able to make the decisions which concrete situations require; he must not be a mere executor of universal laws or a subordinate functionary who receives and executes orders issued by a higher authority.*

During the Second Session (1963) of the Council, a number of Fathers objected to the practice of certain faculties, privileges, or indults being "graciously granted" to bishops. It was observed, and with good reason, that such faculties or indults should not be "graciously granted" but should simply be restored, inasmuch as by divine right and in virtue of the sacrament proper to themselves bishops already have all the powers and rights they need for carrying out in an effective and fruitful way their office of pastor, teacher, and priest of souls. For example Cardinal Ritter said during the sixty-second general meeting (November 7, 1963) that if the Council intends to prepare the way for a revision of Canon Law, then the text provided should not speak, as it does, "of faculties, indults, and concessions, but of the restoration of those powers which by divine law belong to bishops and which have been gradually lessened in the course of the centuries."[17] At the previous (sixty-first) meeting Bishop Fernando Gomes

dos Santos, speaking for sixty bishops of Brazil, had asked
for "the explicit acknowledgment that far from having only
those powers expressly allowed them, bishops have all powers
but those which the Supreme Pontiff judges it necessary to
reserve to himself 'because of the very nature of the matter
or because the unity of the Church makes it advisable.' "[18]
The Maronite archbishop of Beirut noted (sixty-second meeting) that "in many questions it is not the little flock but the
pusillanimous pastor that has recourse to the highest authority in even the smallest matters, because he does not know
what he can and cannot do!"[19] Cardinal Alfrink therefore
asserted that the key issue is not special grants but "the
normal exercise of episcopal office, which belongs to the bishops by its nature. No one doubts that the Supreme Pontiff, by
reason of his supreme authority, can reserve to himself what
he thinks right for the good of the Church."[20]

It was against this background of thought that the Decree
on Bishops declared: "As successors of the apostles, bishops
automatically enjoy in the diocese entrusted to them all the
ordinary, proper, and immediate authority required for the
exercise of their pastoral office. But this authority never in
any instance infringes upon the power which the Roman Pontiff has, in virtue of his office, of reserving cases to himself
or to some other authority. Except when it is a question of
matters reserved to the supreme authority of the Church, the
general law of the Church gives each diocesan bishop the
faculty to grant dispensations in particular cases to the faithful over whom he exercises authority according to the norm
of law, provided he judges it helpful for their spiritual welfare" (CD 8/401). Such a special reservation was in fact put
into effect by the *Motu Proprio* on the functions of bishops, of
June 15, 1966.[21]

Elsewhere, as we have seen, the Constitution on the Church
had taught that bishops have "proper, ordinary, and immediate" power (LG 27a/51) and that, by reason of this power,
they have the sacred right and duty before God "to make laws

for their subjects, to pass judgment on them, and to moderate everything pertaining to the ordering of worship and the apostolate" (*ibid.*). "Nor are they to be regarded as vicars of the Roman Pontiff, for they exercise an authority which is proper to them, and are quite correctly called 'prelates,' heads of people whom they govern" (LG 27b/52).

Within his diocese, then, the bishop is and must be, regularly and in the full sense, teacher, priest, and shepherd. There, as vicar of Christ and in the name of Christ, he has the proper (not vicarial), ordinary (not delegated), and immediate (without any intermediary) power that is needed for the exercise of his pastoral office. There he can and must make laws, judge, and see to the ordering of all that has to do with worship and the apostolate. There, in individual cases and for the spiritual good of his faithful, he can and must dispense from the general laws of the Church. Some laws, decisions, and juridical institutions are certainly indispensable. But they exist in order to help men and not simply for the sake of being observed. "The beginning, the subject and the goal of all social institutions is and must be the human person" (GS 25a/224). Here is a principle that is valid for the social life of the Church no less than of civil society. "Hence," says the same Constitution on the Church in the Modern World, "the scoial order and its development must unceasingly work to the benefit of the human person if the disposition of affairs is to be subordinate to the personal realm and not contrariwise, as the Lord indicated when He said that the Sabbath was made for man, and not man for the Sabbath. The social order requires constant improvement. It must be founded on truth, built on justice, and animated by love; in freedom it should grow every day toward a more humane balance. An improvement in attitudes and widespread changes in society will have to take place if these objectives are to be gained" (GS 26c-d/225).

Instead of becoming at every turn the rigid defenders of the law's binding force, bishops should, then, be chiefly the ardent defenders of the dignity and rights of all men and of Christians. The latter, by reason of their education among other things, are often slaves of law (both human and ecclesiastical); they weep and groan under the burden of decisions, prescriptions, laws, and rubrics that were frequently conceived and promulgated with an eye on circumstances and situations that no longer exist. To urge the law upon them ("the law is hard, but it's the law just the same!") and to force their observance of it is often simply to complicate their lives, dishearten them, and crush their spirits. "They bind up heavy loads, hard to carry, to lay on other men's shoulders" (Mt 23:4). The stern guardian of law will always have the juridical apparatus on his side and be defended by the law; he will always be able to show that he is simply following the law. Nonetheless he may well be unfeeling and cruel, a Christian in naught but name, and a pharisee to the fingertips. I am afraid of the bishop who does not recognize the signs of the times; who sees nothing new in the documents of Vatican II; who considers himself to be simply a vicar of the Roman Pontiff; who in every new situation feels he must consult the Nuncio; who has eyes only for Rome; who insists only on the law and has no awareness of the realities of his diocese; who is incapable of being a shepherd and leading his sheep to green pastures; who refuses to descend to human contingencies; who is unable in a positive way to exercise his proper, ordinary, and immediate pastoral power; who is able to dispense from general laws only when these have ceased to be valid and useful. A bishop who is nothing but a vicar of the pope is no longer a Catholic bishop; he ceases to be a pastor.

11. *The bishop must give the laity an active role in the Church's mission and not reserve the latter to himself or to the clergy.*

"In exercising this pastoral care he [the bishop] should preserve for his faithful the share proper to them in Church affairs; he should also recognize their duty and right to collaborate actively in the building up of the Mystical Body of Christ" (CD 16e/409). Bishops, then, "also know that they themselves were not meant by Christ to shoulder alone the entire saving mission of the Church toward the world" (LG 30b/57). It will help us, in reaching a proper understanding of the issue here, to recall the following principles of Vatican II:

1. The laity share in the mission of the whole Christian people in the Church and in the world. "These faithful are by baptism made one body with Christ and established among the People of God. They are in their own way made sharers in the priestly, prophetic, and kingly functions of Christ. They carry out their own part in the mission of the whole Christian people with respect to the Church and the world" (LG 31a/57).

2. Without the active, apostolic presence of the laity the Church could not be the perfect sign of Christ among men: "The Church has not been truly established, and is not yet fully alive, nor is it a perfect sign of Christ among men, unless there exists a laity worthy of the name working along with the hierarchy. For the gospel cannot be deeply imprinted on the talents, life, and work of any people without the active presence of laymen" (AG 21a/610-11).

3. All without exception are called to the apostolate (LG 33a/59; 33c/60; 35e/62; 38/65). "Apostolate" includes every effort to spread the reign of Christ on earth, for the glory of God the Father, by bringing all men to share in redemption and salvation and thereby directing the whole world to Chirst (cf AA 2a/491). "The lay apostolate . . . is a participation in the saving mission of the Church itself" (LG 33b/59). "By its very nature the Christian vocation is also a vocation to the apostolate. . . . The member who fails to make his proper contribution to the development of the Church must be said to be useful neither to the Church nor to himself" (AA 2a/491).

4. The laity receive a deputation to the apostolate from the

Lord himself. "Through their baptism and confirmation, all are commissioned to that apostolate by the Lord Himself" (LG 33b/59). "The laity derive the right and duty with respect to the apostolate from their union with Christ their Head. Incorporated into Christ's Mystical Body through baptism and strengthened by the power of the Holy Spirit through confirmation, they are assigned to the apostolate by the Lord himself" (AA 3a/492).

5. There can be an apostolate that arises from the free initiative of the laity. "In the Church there are many apostolic undertakings which are established by the free choice of the laity and regulated by their prudent judgment. The mission of the Church can be better accomplished in certain circumstances by undertakings of this kind" (AA 24c/513). But the Council adds: "No project, however, may claim the name 'Catholic' unless it has obtained the consent of the lawful Church authority" (*ibid.*). Elsewhere we read that the faithful should "make a clear distinction between what a Christian conscience leads them to do in their own name, whether as individuals or in association, and what they do in the name of the Church and in union with her shepherds" (GS 76a/287).

6. There can also be a group or team apostolate which springs from the spontaneous initiative of the laity (cf. AA 18-19/508-10). "As long as the proper relationship is kept to Church authorities, the laity have the right to found and run such associations and to join those already existing" (AA 19d/510).

7. "It is not only through the sacraments and Church ministries that the same Holy Spirit sanctifies and leads the People of God and enriches it with virtues" (LG 12c/30).[22]

8. "An individual layman, by reason of the knowledge, competence, or outstanding ability which he may enjoy, is permitted and sometimes even obliged to express his opinion on things which concern the good of the Church" (LG 37a/64). "Let it be recognized that all the faithful, clerical and

lay, possess a lawful freedom of inquiry and of thought, and the freedom to express their minds humbly and courageously about those matters in which they enjoy competence" (GS 62j/270).

The duties of bishops:

1. To promote the apostolate of the laity (cf. AA 24a/513). "Let sacred pastors recognize and promote the dignity as well as the responsibility of the layman in the Church. Let them willingly make use of his prudent advice. Let them confidently assign duties to him in the service of the Church, allowing him freedom and room for action. Further, let them encourage the layman so that he may undertake tasks on his own initiative. Attentively in Christ, let them consider with fatherly love the projects, suggestions, and desires proposed by the laity. Furthermore, let pastors respectfully acknowledge that just freedom which belongs to everyone in this earthly city" (LG 37c/64-65). It is interesting to note that the Constitution on the Church twice speaks of bishops as "brothers" of laymen (LG 32e/59; 37a/64).

2. Not to suppress the Spirit's gifts (LG 12d/30; AA 3d/493). For "these charismatic gifts . . . are to be received with thanksgiving and consolation" (LG 12c/30), even with joy (PO 9d/553), and should be diligently promoted (*ibid.*), although they "are not to be rashly sought after, nor are the fruits of apostolic labor to be presumptuously expected from them" (LG 12d/30).

3. To provide the apostolate of the laity with spiritual principles and support (AA 24a/513). "The laity have the right, as do all Christians, to receive in abundance from their sacred pastors the spiritual goods of the Church, especially the assistance of the word of God and the sacraments. Every layman should openly reveal to them his needs and desires with that freedom and confidence which befits a son of God and a brother in Christ" (LG 37a/64).

4. To direct the exercise of this apostolate to the common good of the Church (AA 24a/513). "Various forms of the

apostolate should be encouraged, and in the whole diocese or in given areas of it the coordination and close interconnection of all apostolic works should be fostered under the direction of the bishop. In this way, all undertakings and organizations, whether catechetical, missionary, charitable, social, family, educational, or any other program serving a pastoral goal, will be brought into harmonious action" (CD 17a/409). "In the present circumstances, it is quite necessary that, in the area of lay activity, the united and organized form of the apostolate be strengthened. In fact, only the close pooling of resources is capable of fully achieving all the aims of the modern apostolate and firmly protecting its interests" (AA 18d/509).

5. To attend to the preservation of doctrine and order (AA 24a/513). Even after Vatican II the faith has to be defended. "They [bishops] should also guard that [Christian] doctrine, teaching the faithful to defend and spread it" (CD 13a/405). Thus, "by the apostolate of the word, which is utterly necessary under certain circumstances, lay people announce Christ, explain and spread His teaching according to their situation and ability, and faithfully profess it" (AA 16d/507).

6. "The role of the ecclesiastical hierarchy is to teach and authentically interpret the moral principles to be followed in temporal affairs" (AA 24g/514). This is perhaps the most difficult duty the bishop has at the present time. For, not only contemporary men but the Council as well proclaim the autonomy of the temporal order (cf. GS 36/233-34) and the lack of any direct competence on the part of the Church in these matters (cf. GS 42b/241; 76b-c/287-88), but, at the same time, the need of integrating that same temporal order into the paschal mystery (cf. GS 37-38/234-37), inasmuch as "Christ's redemptive work, while of itself directed toward the salvation of men, involves also the renewal of the whole temporal order" (AA 5a/495). The Council is also aware that the Church does not always have "at hand the solution to particular problems" (GS 33c/232), and, in the same passage

in which it bids the laity to "look for spiritual light and nourishment" from priests, it humbly adds: "Let the layman not imagine that his pastors are such experts, that to every problem which arises, however complicated, they can readily give him a concrete solution, or even that such is their mission" (GS 43e/244).

7. For the sake of the common good of the diocese, bishops can "select and promote in a particular way some of the apostolic associations and projects which have an immediately spiritual purpose, thereby assuming in them a special responsibility" (AA 24e/513). This act on the part of the hierarchy is called, in various Church documents, a mandate. Nonetheless, in giving such a mandate, "the proper nature and individuality of each apostolate must be preserved, and the laity must not be deprived of the possibility of acting on their own accord" (*ibid.*).

12. *The bishop must be open to the signs of the times, and not be a reactionary, locked up in his ghetto.*

The problem most deeply felt by the Second Vatican Council was the problem of the Church's relation to the contemporary world; and the Pastoral Constitution on the Church in the Modern World, as we might expect, gives clearest expression to this concern. It is easy to show that contemporary man, sometimes even contemporary Catholic men (indeed, as high as eighty percent of all Catholics), gives no sign of regarding the Church as necessary, adopts an attitude of indifference to her, sets little store by her decisions, and puts the Church on the same level as other religions. Having cut his ties with the Church, contemporary man began to construct a humanism to his own liking; he seemed to feel at home with it or at least not to feel himself any worse off than in the Church. Meanwhile the Church too, in its prayer life (liturgy), doctrine (dogma), requirements (morality), and discipline (canon law), was gradually adopting definite attitudes, but these were becoming ever more untouchable, beyond discussion, stylized, formalistic, different, esoteric, and unintelligible.

As the Church became ever more committed to this path of action, it also became ever more conscious of its powers and rights, but in an authoritarian, domineering, demanding, and introverted way. It demanded an unqualified and unquestioning acceptance ("with an internal assent," said the theologians), tolerated no criticism of its official documents, even when no definitive pronouncement was involved; sought subjection and obedience without any possibility of dialogue on the matter; condemned books without first speaking to their authors; excommunicated without warning; and put up only very reluctantly with public opinion.

Meanwhile, outside the Church, in the "world," the sense of freedom and autonomy was growing; monarchies were being dismantled and the democracies were taking their place; the universal rights and liberties of man were being proclaimed; a humanism was being shaped that was non-Christian and, frequently, even entirely cut off from God, who, amid the extraordinary advances in science and technology, was becoming a "hypothesis" which could ever more readily be dispensend with. Set in the midst of this "modern world," the Church paid no heed to the signs of the times and found only one path open to it: to become a sect or a ghetto.

Now, and especially at Vatican II, the great pastoral preoccupation made itself felt: How can we emerge from such a situation? After all, the mission of the Church is to save that "world," those men who live in the "modern world"! The Church could not continue to be a sect or a ghetto: isolated, not understood by others, itself not interested in others. In this situation, the absolutely basic rule or norm could only be: If it is to be heard and understood by contemporary man, the Church had to make itself understood and loved. That was the great program set forth by Pope John XXIII in his inspired address at the opening of the Council. The "greatest concern" of this Council, he asserted, is to attempt to explain traditional doctrine, the ancient deposit of faith, "through the methods of research and through the literary forms of modern thought" (Abbott, 713, 715). Therefore, in their Message to Humanity, at the very beginning of the Council, the Fathers declared: "We shall take pains so to present to the men of this age God's truth in its integrity and purity that they may understand it and gladly assent to it. Since we are shepherds . . ." (Abbott, 4).

In speaking of this same problem, the Decree on the Bishops says, in general terms: "Since it is the mission of the Church to converse with the human society in which she lives, bishops especially are called upon to approach men, seeking and fostering dialogue with them. These conversations on salvation ought to be distinguished for clarity of speech as well as for humility and gentleness so that truth may always be joined with charity, and understanding with love. Likewise they should be characterized by due prudence allied, however, with that trustfulness which fosters friendship and thus is naturally disposed to bring about a union of minds" (CD 13b/405). In the Constitution on the Church in the Modern World, the Council says to bishops: "By unremitting study they should fit themselves to do their part in establishing dialogue with the world and with men of all shades of opinion" (GS 43i/245). A little further on, in a section of great importance, after stating that "her [the Church's] purpose has been to adapt the gospel to the grasp of all as well as to the needs of the learned, insofar as such was appropriate. Indeed, this accommodated preaching of the revealed Word ought to remain the law of all evangelization" (GS 44c/246), the Council declares: "It is the task of the entire People of God, especially pastors and theologians, to hear, distinguish, and interpret the many voices of our age, and to judge them in the light of the divine word. In this way, revealed truth can always be more deeply penetrated, better understood, and set forth to greater advantage" (44d/246).

In the same document, the Council says that "theologians are invited to seek continually for more suitable ways of communicating doctrine to the men of their times" (GS 62c/268). This work must be supported, fostered, and given a positive impetus by the bishops, for it is identical with their own primary duty. Otherwise we shall continue not to be understood, and the men of today will go on building a world that is ever more cut off from God, Christ, and the Church. Thus the Church will not in fact be what it claims to be: "a leaven and . . . a kind of soul for human society" (GS 40c/239), "the all-embracing means of salvation" UR 3e/346), "the universal sacrament of salvation" (LG 48b/79; GS 45a/247; AG 1a/584), "an instrument for the redemption of all" (LG 9e/26), "a sign raised above the nations" (SC 2/138; cf. UR 2e/344; AG 36c/623), "a perfect sign of Christ among men" (AG 21a/610), "a sign of God's presence in the world" (AG 15b/602), "a shining beacon of the salvation which comes to us in Christ" (AG 21g/612). The Church will not be able to carry out its proper mission: "By virtue of her mission to shed on the whole world the radiance of the gospel message, and to unify under one Spirit all men of whatever nation, race, or culture, the Church stands forth as a sign of that brotherliness which allows honest dialogue and invigorates it" (GS 92a/305-6). We will continue to be a sect, but not a Church.

The Constitution on the Church makes its own (LG 32e/59) these beautiful sentences of St. Augustine, Bishop of Hippo: "What I am for you terrifies me; what I am with you consoles me. For you I am a bishop; but with you I am a Christian. The former is a title of duty; the latter, one of grace. The former is a danger; the latter, salvation."[23] Today the office of bishop is an especially dangerous one. In an address to the bishops of Italy, April 11, 1970, Pope Paul VI noted "how grave and difficult the bishop's ministry has become" and said that with increasing frequency "bishops in office, and not always those who are infirm or aged, and candidates called to the episcopate, try to decline the office. Today, not only because of its intrinsic demands but also because of extrinsic difficulties the office seems to have become insupportable."[24]

Notes for Chapter 8

[1] Paul VI, *In signo sanctae crucis: Address at the Opening of the Third Session of Vatican II*, September 14, 1964, in *TPS*, 10 (164-65), 111. In his discourse, *Tempus iam advenit*, at the closing of the second session, December 4, 1963, the pope had said: 'The great complex question of the episcopacy, . . . in both logical order and importance, is the primary concern of this Second Vatican Ecumenical Council, a council which, as we shall never forget, is the natural continuation and complement of the First Vatican Council. As a consequence, the aim of our Council is to clarify the divinely instituted nature and function of the episcopacy, not in contrast to, but in confirmation of, the supreme Christ-given prerogatives, which convey all authority necessary for the universal government of the Church, and which are acknowledged as belonging to the Roman Pontiff. The Council's aim is to set forth the position of the episcopacy according to the teaching of our Lord and the authentic tradition of the Church, stating its powers and indicating how they should be used" (*TPS*, 9 [1963-64], 226).

[2] During the debate on what is now Chapter 3 of the Dogmatic Constitution on the Church 123 were made; and 188 were made during the discussion of the Decree on the Bishop's Pastoral Office in the Church.

[3] On this whole question, cf. aboove, Chapter 6, "Papal Primacy and Its Limits."

[4] *Acta Synodalia*, 11/4, pp. 488-91.

[5] Paul VI, *Il concilio é: Address to the Italian Bishops on the Council's Closing*, December 6, 1965, in *AAS*, 58 (1966), 69.

[6] Vatican I teaches that St. Peter was established as a foundation so that "the episcopate might be one and undivided" (DS, 3051 [D, 1821]; *TCT*, no. 201, p. 94).

[7] This definition is due in part to a suggestion made by Bishop Angelo Rossi in the name of 87 Brazilian bishops who during the third session (September 21, 1964) proposed the following definition: "A diocese is that portion of the people of God in which the one, holy, catholic, and apostolic Church is signified and rendered present by the apostolic mission of the bishop, with the help of the prebytery and in communion with the episcopal college and its head."

[8] Joseph Ratzinger, "The Pastoral Implications of Episcopal Collegiality," in *The Church and Mankind* (*Concilium* 1; New York: Paulist Press, 1965), p. 44.

⁹ [On the term "presbytery," cf. Abbott, p. 549, note 105. "Presbytery" in this context is not a section of the church building nor a jurisdiction nor a dwelling, but the body of "presbyters" or priests (as distinct from bishops). — Tr.]

¹⁰ Motu Proprio, *Ecclesiae Sanctae: On Implementing Four Decrees of the Council,* August 6, 1966, in *TPS,* 11 (1966), 383.

¹¹ *Acta Synodalia,* II/2, pp. 366-69.

¹² *Acta Synodalia,* II/4 , p. 489.

¹³ Paul VI, *Siamo particolarmente lieti: Address to Participants in the Symposium on Original Sin,* July 11, 1966, in *TPS,* 11 (1966), 232.

¹⁴ *The Church in the Present-Day Transformation of Latin America in the Light of the Council* (Second General Conference of Latin American Bishops, Bogotá and Medellin, 1968), edited by Louis Michael Colonnese (Bogotá: General Secretariat of CELAM, 1970), volume 2: *Conclusions,* "Poverty of the Church," no. 12, p. 217.

¹⁵ Paul VI, *Il concilio é: Address to the Italian Bishops on the Council's Closing,* December 6, 1965, in *AAS,* 58 (1966), 68-69.

¹⁶ Paul VI, *Come ogni anno: Address to the Judges and Officials of the Tribunal of the Sacred Roman Rota,* January 28, 1971, in *The Teachings of Pope Paul VI: 1971* (Washington, D.C.: United States Catholic Conference, 1972), p. 216.

¹⁷ *Acta Synodalia,* II/4, pp. 556-57.

¹⁸ *Acta Synodalia,* II/4, pp. 488-91.

¹⁹ *Acta Synodalia,* II/4, pp. 595-96.

²⁰ *Acta Synodalia,* II/4, pp. 479-81.

²¹ Motu Proprio, *De episcoporum muneribus,* June 15, 1966, in *Catholic Mind,* 64 (October, 1966), 60-64.

²² Note that elsewhere the Council says the exact opposite: "The Holy Spirit . . . sanctifies the people of God through the ministry and the sacraments" (AA, 3c/492). This is, of course, also true, but there is a new and different emphasis in the Constitution on the Church.

²³ St. Augustine, *Serm.,* 340:1 (PL, 38:1483).

²⁴ Paul VI, *Diamo il benvenuto: Address to the Sixth General Assembly of the Italian Episcopal Conference,* April 11, 1970, in *The Teachings of Pope Paul VI: 1970* (Washington, D.C.: United States Catholic Conference, 1971), pp. 125-26.

Chapter 9

The Theology of the Priesthood

The theology of the laity seems to have put a question mark behind the theology of the priesthood. From Vatican II's abundant instruction on the laity we learn that all the baptized "share a true equality with regard to the dignity and to the activity common to all the faithful for the building up of the Body of Christ" (LG 32c/58); that all share "in the mission of the whole Christian people with respect to the Church and to the world" (LG 31a/57); that all "have an active part to play in the life and activity of the Church" (AA 10a/500); that laymen are now "brothers" to their pastors (LG 32e/59; 37a/64); that all without exception are called upon by the Lord "to expend all their energy for the growth of the Church and its continuous sanctification" (LG 33a/59; cf. AA 2a/491); that all "are commissioned to that apostolate by the Lord Himself" (LG 33b/59); that "upon all the laity . . . rests the noble duty of working to extend the divine plan of salvation ever increasingly to all men of each epoch and in every land" (LG 33d/60); that all the baptized are "made sharers in the priestly, prophetic, and kingly functions of Christ" (LG 31a/57; cf. AA 2b/491; 10a/500); that "the supreme and eternal Priest, Christ Jesus, wills to continue His witness and serve through the laity too" (LG 34a/60), and "gives them a share in His priestly function" (LG 34b/60); that "the great Prophet . . . fulfills His prophetic office . . . not only through the hierarchy who teach in His name and with His authority, but also through the laity" (LG 35a/61) and "for that very purpose He made them His witnesses and gave them understanding of the faith and the grace of speech" (*ibid.*); that the laity too should take an active part in the Eucharistic action and should learn to offer themselves, and this "not only through the hands of the priest" (SC 48/154).

A generous doctrine indeed on the nature of the laity and its place and role in the Church! But it causes many to ask why there are or should continue to be priests (presbyters) in the Church and in what precise way they differ from those who possess the common or universal priesthood. Speaking to the Lenten preachers of Rome on February 25, 1968, Paul VI referred with some bitterness to "the violent waves of questions, doubts, denials, and open-ended new ideas that are crashing against the ministerial priesthood in other countries. . . . Problems are being raised about its true nature and primary function, about its proper place, and about its original, authentic reality. Assailed by these doubts, the priest begins to ask himself questions, and to wonder about his vocation. He begins to question the canonical form of the Catholic priesthood. He fears that he has made a poor choice in his life's work. He no longer sees celibacy as a free offering of sacrifice and love, but as an unnatural burden. Having withdrawn from the world in order to know, evangelize, and serve it better, he now looks back on it, not with apostolic love but with worldly nostalgia. All too easily he can delude himself into believing that he could redeem it better, or at least balance his own inner anxiety, by immersing himself in its temporal and social dimensions."[1]

At the Council itself we had already heard anticipations of such complaints. "In the face of current changes in the world and of the renewal of the Church which the Council is effecting, priests are now asking what the nature of their priesthood is and what the conditions of its exercise," said Bishop Louis Guyot of Coutances at the one hundred and forty-ninth general meeting (October 14, 1965). At the next meeting Cardinal Suenens said: "In today's Church, with its attention to bishops and laity, priests feel neglected by the Council." Two years before, on October 19, 1963, Bishop (now Cardinal) Renard had already been lamenting the lack of conciliar attention to priests; he spoke of the disappointment priests felt when they saw how extensively the Council was discussing bishops and laity, and of how they were asking whether they would have to wait for another Council to speak of their situation.[2] The next year, on October 15, 1964, Cardinal Lefebvre said to the Council Fathers: "Today, when so much is said of the universal priesthood of all the baptized and of the apostolic action of the faithful, many priests are disconcerted. They had become so used to thinking of their priestly action in terms of the action of the laity that they cannot now see clearly the specific character and special efficacy of their priesthood. This is undoubtedly one of the chief reason for their disquiet, for the feeling they have that the action of the laity is superior to their own, and for the less favorable estimate they have of their own priesthood; consequently they are less zealous in discovering, developing, and fostering vocations." The day before, Bishop Fernando Gomes dos Santos, along with one hundred and twelve other bishops, had denounced the position paper under discussion as "a great disappointment" and an "insult to priests" (he was referring to the first draft of the Decree on the Ministry and Life of Priests) and had asked for a richer treatment of the theology of the ministerial priesthood.

Vatican II, in fact, finally provided us with two major texts that contain valuable elements for constructing a theology of the prebyterate: the Constitution on the Church 28/52-55, and the Decree on the Ministry and Life of Priests 2/533-36. The latter (dating from 1965) makes use of the former (1964); on a few points it corrects it (in the sense of furnishing greater precision) and goes beyond it by offering a text that is more systematic, doctrinally richer, and more vigorous and precise in expression. We shall therefore use it as our basic text in this chapter.

It has been traditional in theology (the "tradition" stems from the scholastic era, especially from St. Thomas) to regard the priest as simply the man of sacrifice and to define him in terms of his relationship to the Eucharist.

The sacrament of orders is directed toward the sacrament of the Eucharist, which is, as Dionysius says, 'the sacrament of sacraments.' For like the temple, altar, vessels, and vestments, the ministries related to the Eucharist require a consecration, and this consecration is the sacrament of orders. Distinctions within this sacrament, therefore, are also determined by relation to the Eucharist.[3]

When St. Thomas (and the Scholastics generally, influenced by Ambrosiaster and St. Jerome) spoke of priesthood, he was in fact thinking of presbyteral orders and of the power of offering the Eucharist and consecrating the Body of Christ. Presbyteral priesthood lacked nothing in this regard and was therefore the fullness of priesthood. "The whole fullness of this sacrament is to be found in one order, namely priesthood; the other degrees represent participations in the sacrament."[4] From this point of view St. Thomas sees no essential difference between priest and bishop; the latter is superior only in terms of jurisdictional power, which is conferred on him by a juridical act and not by a sacramental rite. For the same reason episcopal consecration is not viewed as a sacrament (even the Council of Trent shows no intention of teaching the sacramentality of the episcopacy).

This doctrine (which the Council of Trent presupposes[5]) defines the presbyterate in terms of a single function, albeit an important and truly central one. The Commission which worked on the Decree on the Ministry and Life of Priests called such a definition "the scholastic definition of priesthood," and Vatican II abandoned it once and for all. In presenting the proposed Decree in its final form, Bishop François Marty, the official expositor (now archbishop of Paris), strove expressly to make the new position clear:

"The chief and controlling idea in this draft is this: Since priests are, in the sacrament of orders, consecrated by the anointing of the Holy Spirit and made like to Christ the Priests, they are servants of Christ the Head in his Church and deputed to serve the People of God. Therefore in the ministry which they exercise they act in the person of Christ himself, who through them continues to carry out the mission he received from the Father. The Eucharist is consequently the center and source of the priest's whole ministry. But this ministry must be more adequately defined, and that in the light of the apostolic mission on which it depends. If the apostolic ministry itself is viewed in a rounded way and if the doctrine of the New Testament and especially of the Pauline letters is kept in mind, the two ways in which presbyteral priesthood has been explained here at the Council can be readily harmonized. For a genuine apostolate and an authentic adoration of the Father are closely connected, indeed are inseparable one from the other, so that the two aspects must be found in every priest's life. St. Paul himself declares that by preaching the gospel he is adoring God, for by confessing the Lord to the gentiles, he sings praise to the Lord's name (cf. Rom 1:9)."

When modifications of the text were being proposed, a group of Council Fathers attempted to reintroduce the idea that "the essence of presbyteral priesthood is derived from its relationship to the Eucharist" (Modification no. 13), but the Commission simply rejected the proposal and explained its position in a comment on Modification no. 14:

"The majority of the Fathers, as is clear from oral com-

ments made in the Council hall and from written comments
handed in to the Commission, want it shown that the priestly
office of the presbyter derives, as it were, from the episcopal
office and is connected with the latter. Now the functions of
a bishop embrace much more than his Eucharistic function,
although the latter is the crown of his whole work; his total
function is properly to be described as "apostolic," as the
Dogmatic Constitution *Lumen Gentium* (chapter 3) and the
Decree *On the Bishops' Pastoral Office in the Church* make
clear. We must keep these documents in mind, as the Commission constantly did. The priesthood of presbyters must be
seen as being in the same line as the priesthood of bishops,
with the necessary allowances."

This was straightforward language. In his general exposition in connection with these same proposed modifications
Bishop Marty said, in the name of the Commission:

"The Commission cannot agree with the wishes of those
Fathers who think that the position paper should have followed the scholastic definition of priesthood, which is based
on the power to consecrate the Eucharist. According to the
prevailing mind of this Council and the petitions of many
Fathers, the priesthood of phesbyters must rather be connected with the priesthood of bishops, the latter being regarded
as the high point and fullness of priesthood. The priesthood of
presbyters must therefore be looked at, in this draft, as em-
bracing not one function but three, and must be linked with
the Apostles and their mission."

Here we have a clear statement of the will, intention, and
mind of Vatican II when the latter sets out, in the Decree
on the Ministry and Life of Priests, to propose a doctrine on
the nature of presbyteral priesthood. The Council has no desire to play down the central importance of the Eucharist;
in fact, precisely in order to give some satisfaction to those
who in the proposed Modification 13 sought to return to the
scholastical conception, the Council inserted a strong statement: "The ministry of priests is directed toward this work

[of offering the Lord's sacrifice] and is perfected in it" (PO 2f/535). Nonetheless the nature and mission of presbyters must be derived from the nature and emission of bishops; the nature and mission of bishops must be gathered from the nature and mission of the Apostles; the nature and mission of the Apostles must be seen in the light of the nature and mission of Christ. As the Father sanctified and sent Christ, so Christ sanctified and sent the Apostles, and the Apostles in turn sanctified and sent the bishops. *In this consecration and sending of bishops the nature of presbyteral priesthood must be found.* It was this connection which the Council set out to explain in no. 2/533-36 of the Decree on the Ministry and Life of Priests. It does so in seven paragraphs.

1. In paragraph 1 the Council teaches that the anointing and mission of Christ are shared by the whole Church, so that the latter becomes a priestly and apostolic people. "There is no member who does not have a part in the mission of the whole Body." This Christological and ecclesiological vision, which summarizes the doctrine of the Constitution on the Church and the Decree on the Laity, provides a new theological starting-point. It amounts to saying that all members of the people of God "share a true equality with regard to the dignity and to the activity common to all the faithful for the building up of the Body of Christ" (LG 32c/58).

2. In paragraphs 2 and 3 it is said that within this people in which all are priests and apostles ("sent") and in which all are equal in dignity Christ has established a certain number of servants ("ministers") with sacred power to foster unity, offer sacrifice, forgive sins, and exercise the priestly office, publicly and in Christ's name, for the sake of men. The official exposition of the text explains that the expression "perform their priestly office publicly for men in the name of Christ," and especially the word "publicly" (which some Council Fathers thought should be omitted), "is a technical expression, calculated to distinguish the personal, private priesthood common to all the faithful from the priesthood

peculiar to ministers." The Council is, then, giving us here a distinctive element fo the ministerial priesthood (which is different in essence, not in degree only, from the common priesthood: LG 10b/27): the exercise of a *sacred power*, for the sake of men, in a *public way* ("in the name of the whole Church," as the fifth paragraph says) and *in the name of Christ* (or, in the words of paragraph 4: sharing "in the authority by which Christ Himself builds up, sanctifies, and rules His Body"). We should note, however, that the Council speaks, even here, of "ministers" in general and not of presbyters in particular.

The Council evidently considers these elements to be essential for a proper theological understanding of ministry in general and of the presbyter in particular. At the beginning of paragraph 2 it indicates the primary function of all ministry: "to join them [the faithful] together in one body." In other words, the ministry is at the service of Church unity; its purpose is to form and maintain community. Chapter 3 of the Constitution on the Church, which deals with ministry in the Church, begins with a rich doctrinal text (LG 18a/37). The text authoritatively defines the purpose of the ministry generally: "for the nurturing and constant growth of the People of God." It goes on to say that ministers receive a sacred power and are at the service of their brothers "so that all . . . can work toward a common goal freely and in an orderly way, and arrive at salvation." "Freely and in an orderly way": with freedom (here we must take into account the teaching of Vatican II on freedom in general, as explained in the Constitution on the Church in the Modern World (17/ 214-15), and on religious freedom in particular, as explained in the Declaration on Religious Freedom), and in an orderly way or as a community. As the Constitution on the Church had explained a few pages back, it has pleased God to sanctify and save men as a community and not simply as individuals (LG 9a/25). Then, at a later point, when speaking of bishops (LG 20d/40), the same Constitution will say that the latter "have . . . taken up the service of the community, presiding in the place of God over the flock whose shepherds they are." This, then, is the essential task of the priestly ministry in general. All the other functions—teaching, sanctifying, guiding—are to be viewed and understood in the light of this primary purpose. The "service of the community" is not just a function; it is *the* function of those who receive the priestly ministry through the sacrament of holy orders.

The Council then passes from the general to the specific and speaks, first of all, of the Apostles. As the Father had sent Christ, so Christ sends the Apostles. *Their specific mission will be to make always present and operative the mission of Christ the Head.* Christ continues his mission in the Apostles. Here we might turn back to the Constitution on the Church (19/38-39) and to the Decree on the Bishops (2/397), which speak of the consecration and mission of the Twelve, in the light of which we must understand the theology of the episcopacy. "Christ, whom the Father sanctified and sent into the world (Jn. 10:36) has, through His Apostles, made their successors, the bishops, partakers in His consecration and His mission" (LG 28a/52-53). This basic affirmation is now taken up by the Decree on Priests. The bishops are "sharers" (have part in, have in common: a favorite expression of Vatican II) in the consecration (to God) and mission (to men) which received from the Father. (Here we should read LG 20-21/39-42, which contain a wealth of material.) Christ continues to be present and active in the Church. "Although guided by human shepherds, her [the Church's] sheep are nevertheless ceaselessly led and nourished by Christ Himself, the Good Shepherd and the Prince of Shepherds" (LG 6b/18). In all truth, it is Christ himself who continues to guide the visible Church "*through* the Supreme Pontiff and the bishops" (LG 14b/33). The latter are "means" or "instruments" which Christ uses. "Bishops in an eminent and visible way undertake Christ's own role as Teacher, Shepherd, and High Priest, and . . . they act in His person" (LG 21d/42).

The bishop is the living *sign* of Christ. Through him, as through a living instrument (cf. PO 12b/558)—instrument, or sacrament, but nothing more than this[6]—the glorified Lord manifests himself as he sits at God's side. "In the bishops . . . our Lord Jesus Christ, the supreme High Priest, is present in the midst of those who believe" (LG 21a/40).

It is in this same perspective that we must view the presbyter too (we have seen the official exposition of the theological commission saying that "the priesthood of presbyters must be seen as being in the same line as the priesthood of bishops, with the necessary allowances"). Paragraph 3 of PO 12 therefore continues by saying that the ministry proper to bishops has been communicated to presbyters in a limited degree, so that the latter might be "co-workers of the episcopal order in the proper fulfillment of the apostolic mission entrusted to the latter order by Christ."

At this point in the text a significant modification at the last minute had required a vote on the possible change. The earlier text had read: "The bishops have legitimately communicated their ministerial role to presbyters, though in a limited degree." In the voting, eighty-one Fathers expressed the fear that such a formulation could lead to the idea that the presbyteral order had been instituted by the Church and not by the Apostles. The formulation is derived, in fact, from LG 28a/53 (where it is still to be found!). The Commission on PO avoided the difficult historical question and corrected the text (and thus interpreted LG) as follows: "Their [the bishops'] ministerial role has been handed down to priests in a limited degree." This formulation states the fact of the bishops' role being shared, without resolving the historical question (when was the ministerial role of bishops communicated to presbyters? Had this already happened in apostolic time?)! Elsewhere, too, the Theological Commission showed that it was aware of the difficulty, and sought to leave it untouched. In the official exposition of LG 28 (in 1964) we read:

"Whatever be the historical development of presbyters,

deacons, and other ministers and whatever the precise meaning of the terms used to designate them in the New Testament, we are asserting that the divinely instituted ministry is exercised by various orders of persons, who have since early times been called bishops, priests, and deacons." But we must admit that the formulation adopted in LG was not entirely apt and that PO has corrected or improved LG on this point.

If in the light of this doctrine (which sees ministerial priesthood as related to the whole mission of Christ and the Church and not as exhausted by a role in relation to the Eucharist) we ask about the moment in which Church instituted the ministerial priesthood, we think it rather difficult to maintain the doctrine of the Council of Trent which pinpoints the moment rather narrowly. That Council says that Christ at the Last Supper, wishing to leave his Church a visible sacrifice, gave his body and blood to the Apostles, "making them priests of the New Testament *at that time*" (chapter 1); in Canon 2 it sums up with an anthema: "If anyone says that by the words 'Do this in remembrance of me,' Christ did not make the apostles priests. . . ."[7] Vatican II has broadened the vision of Trent and prefers to speak of "ministry" or "ministerial priesthood." Consequently it cannot see in the liturgical action of the Last Supper, extremely important though this is, the *sole* moment of institution of the apostolic ministry and therefore of the presbyterate. The first sentence of paragraph three points to another important moment which may be regarded as the time when the priestly ministry of the New Testament was established. On the other hand, the Council of Trent need not and cannot be understood as speaking in an exclusive way. For, when the Fathers of Trent speak of the institution of the sacrament of penance and of the power given to the Apostles to forgive sins (a power which according to the same Council is an essential part of the priestly power conferred by the sacrament of holy orders[7a]), they refer to another moment and another day.[7b] On this point, therefore, Vatican II does not contradict the Council of Trent but extends it and opens up new vistas for us.

3. In paragraph four a conclusion is drawn which is very important in determining the nature of the presbyterate. Since presbyters are organically linked with the episcopal order (the presbyteralism of St. Jerome is here rejected) and since presbyteral priesthood is in the same line as episcopal priesthood, "the priestly office shares in the authority by which Christ Himself builds up, sanctifies, and rules His Body." This is why ministerial priesthood is communicated by a special sacrament. As the bishops, so the presbyters share in the consecration and mission which Christ received from the Father; they too are anointed by the Holy Spirit, marked with a special character, and "so configured to Christ the Priest that they can act in the person of Christ the Head."

Presbyters, too, therefore, are "living instruments of Christ the eternal Priest" (PO 12b/558). They are "ministers of Christ Jesus" (PO 2e/535); they "represent Christ" (AG 39a/626); they are "ministers of the Head" and "can build up and establish His whole Body which is the Church" (PO 12a/557); "every priest in his own way represents the person of Christ Himself" (PO 12b/558). They serve Christ in his threefold mission: "Priests are promoted to the service of Christ, the Teacher, the Priest, and the King" (PO 1b/533). As bishops receive, through episcopal consecration, the office of sanctifying, teaching, and ruling (cf. LG 21d/41), so presbyters, by their ordination, "are consecrated to preach the gospel, shepherd the faithful, and celebrate divine worship as true priests of the New Testament" (LG 28a/53). In a way which affects them radically (an ontological sharing in three offices of Christ), God equips them for their task by a sacrament; there is no question of a purely juridical adaptation, effected in a juridical act by ecclesiastical authority (that juridical act—the "giving of jurisdiction"—supervenes later on and, although necessary, is not primary). Presbyters, too, sanctify, teach, and rule as ministers of Christ, in Christ's name, in Christ's person.

Presbyters represent the glorified Lord, the Kyrios, the Christ. They do so (we must insist on this point) not only in regard to the Eucharist but in regard to the whole of their presbyteral ministry. On this point too, Vatican II greatly broadens the limited horizons within which the Council of Trent worked. The priest is no longer only the person who presides at the Eucharist in Christ's name; his role as the one who presides in the person of Christ extends to his whole mission and activity. In all that he does as a priest he is and ought to be a sign (a living instrument) of Christ the Head for Christ's Church. *In this his being and action are specifically distinct from the being and action of the layman in the Church.* Here we have the theological image of the presbyter as seen and presented by Vatican II. We have turned from the priest who is characterized only by his power over the Eucharistic Body of Christ to the priest who is characterized by his action in the name of Christ the Head.

This doctrine of the Council is important and central. It constitutes the living center of the spirituality, the greatness, and the excellence of the presbyter.[8] "God, who alone is holy and bestows holiness, willed to raise up for Himself as companions and helpers men who would humbly dedicate themselves to the work of sanctification. Hence, through the ministry of the bishop, God consecrates priests so that they can share by a special title in the priesthood of Christ. Thus, in performing sacred functions they can act as ministers of Him who in the liturgy continually exercises his priestly office on our behalf by the action of His Spirit" (PO 5a/541). In the Constitution on the Liturgy the liturgy is defined as "an exercise of the priestly office of Jesus Christ" (SC 7c/141). The one, eternal Priest is always the principal minister in liturgical actions; it is in order to make his presence perceptible to men that he needs instruments, namely, the ministerial priests (bishops and presbyters) who "are uniting themselves with the act of Christ the Priest" (PO 13f/561). Christ is always present, "so that when a man baptizes it is really Christ Himself who baptizes" (SC 7a/141). Consequently, the presbyter shares in the authority of Christ himself and *not, strictly speaking, in the authority of the bishop*. It is clear that the bishop communicates this authority to the presbyter; but, when the bishops consecrates, he in his turn is only an instrument of Christ. It is Christ who consecrates through the bishop, or, as PO 5a/541 puts it: "Through the ministry of the bishop, God consecrates priests."

Theologically speaking, then, it is inexact to say that the priest is a "minister of the Church." The thirty-fifth modification proposed for the text of *Presbyterorum ordinis* proposed that the expression "minister of the Church" be used. The Commission rejected it, however, and explained that while it is possible to say that the priest acts "in the name of the Church," "priests do not act as ministers of the Church but as ministers of Christ." It is also erroneous (theologically) to say that the priest as such acts "in the name of the bishop" or that he "represents the bishops"; on the other hand, it is exact to say that priests "sanctify and govern under the bishops's authority that part of the Lord's flock entrusted to them" (LG 28c/54). In regard to this last-quoted statement the official exposition indicated that while priests act under the bishop's authority, "they do not, strictly speaking, act in his name." They act always "in the person of Christ," not "in the person of the bishop." It is also inaccurate to say that the priest "depends on the bishop for his power"; it is correct to say that "they are dependent on the bishops *in the exercise* of their power" (LG 28a/53). For, as the two hundred and second modification (from which the formulation derives) explained, "the power comes directly from Christ" and not from the bishop.

The question of the *origin* of priesthood in the presbyter is thus sufficiently answered. Before the Council some theologians had taught that the bishop passes on to the presbyter a part of his (the bishop's) priesthood. The bishop would thus be the source. At the forty-third general meeting (October 4, 1963), a Brazilian bishop, Bishop Carlos Bandeira de Mello of Palmas, had defended this view:

"It is clear from history that, following the example of the Apostles, bishops have in the course of time *gradually* divided their own powers and communicated various of them to presbyters: initially the power to offer the holy Sacrifice; then the power to baptize; in the Eastern Church the power to confirm; at a much later point the power to absolve from sin; in the Letter of St. James the sacrament of last anointing is entrusted to presbyters but it is not clear whether the term "presbyter" has the same reference as it does today; then the power to preach the word of God; and finally the power to rule a part of a diocese, the parish, and to bless marriages. It is evident, then, that the powers which presbyters receive in ordination *originate solely in the ordaining bishop* and not from some higher principle (such as the apostolic succession in the Church) or from some other source. What the presbyter has are elements from the full priesthood of the bishop. Presbyters therefore depend on the bishop not only by reason of jurisdiction but by reason of their very ordination itself. *Bishops can communicate more or less. . . .* I think that this clear doctrine should be explained in the draft [on the Church]. For, unfortunately, there are many priests today who, at least in practice, think otherwise and regard themselves as equal to the bishop in everything but jurisdiction. . . . What a horrible thought!"[9]

In the early drafts of what is now LG 28 it was said that bishops "communicate grace from their paternal fullness of it" (words taken from the Preface of Ordination).[10] But many of the Fathers reacted against this formulation. A new statement was therefore drawn up "in which the *sole source* of presbyteral priesthood is located in the priesthood of Christ" (thus the general exposition read to the Fathers). Therefore, "by the sacrament of orders priests are configured to Christ the Priest so that as ministers of the Head and co-workers of the episcopal order they can build up and establish His whole Body which is the Church" (PO 12a/557). Both presbyters and bishops "share in one and the same priesthood and ministry of Christ" (PO 7a/546).

This whole doctrine will enable us to see more clearly into *the relations between priests and bishops*. When it was thought that priests receive all they have and are from the bishop, there was a good theological foundation for stressing the paternal role of the bishop: he was the father, priests were his sons. But this basis has vanished. The priest is now related directly and immediately to Christ, for "all priests . . . participate in and exercise with the bishop the one priesthood of Christ" (CD 28a/416). However, Vatican II repeats on sixteen occasions that presbyters are "co-workers of the episcopal order." They are not autonomous; their ministry was given to them "in a limited degree" (PO 2c/534). Bishops on the other hand receive the fullness of the sacrament of orders (LG 21c/41) and on this account they act in the place of Christ "in an eminent . . . way" (LG 21d/42). Presbyters "do not possess the highest degree of the priesthood" and therefore "are dependent on the bishops in the exercise of their power" (LG 28a/53). For this relationship of dependence the Council coins the fine expression "hierarchical communion": "The very unity of their [presbyters'] consecration and mission requires their hierarchical communion with the order of bishops" (PO 7a/546).[11] It is in the light of this hierarchical communion that the Council deals with the problem of obedience (cf. PO 15/563-65): obedience should be a conscious, free self-insertion into hierarchical communion and common action (PO 15b-c). It will, therefore, be a "responsible and voluntary . . . obedience" (PO 15e).

If it be true that presbyters came into existence as "co-workers of the episcopal order," then they are also to be regarded as the chief aides and the natural advisers of bishops, and the latter must treat them as "brothers and friends" (PO 7c/547), rather than as "sons and subjects." The Council therefore teaches: "By reason of the gift of the Holy Spirit which is given to priests in sacred ordination, bishops should regard them as necessary helpers and counselors in the ministry and in the task of teaching, sanctifying, and nourishing the People of God" (PO 7a/547). This is also the reason why Vatican II, in defining a diocese, says that it is "entrusted to a bishop to be shepherded by him with the cooperation of the ministry" (CD 11a/403). The same decree therefore urges that the bishops "should regard his priests as sons and friends. Thus by his readiness to listen to them and by his trusting familiarity, a bishop can work to promote the whole pastoral work of the entire diocese" (CD 16c/408).

This kind of brotherly collaboration between a bishop and his priests dates back to the earliest days of the Church. St. Ignatius of Antioch is already familiar with the *presbyterium* or senate of presbyters. Presbyters are, in his phrase, "those who are with him [the bishop]"; they are not simply individual subjects but members of a college of presbyters which, together with the bishop, directs the community. The richest documentation to illustrate the relations between a bishop and his priests is to be found in the letters which St. Cyprian, bishop of Carthage, wrote while hiding during the persecutions of Decius and Valerian. Other bishops are his "colleagues" and priests are his "fellow priests." The address of Letter 41, for example, reads: "Cyprian to Caldonius and Herculanus, his colleagues, and to Rogation and Numidicus, his fellow priests."[12] As a matter of fact, the expressive neologism "fellow priests" (*compresbyteri*) is rather widespread in the ecclesiastical literature of the time. In Letter 14 (250 A.D.), St. Cyprian writes: "I had been hoping to find our clergy all healthy and safe when I wrote. . . . I had every reason to return quickly to you, for I was eager to see you (there is nothing I want more); I was also hoping we might consult together on the needs of Church discipline and, after reviewing the situation, might come to some concrete decisions. But it seemed better that I stay in hiding for the time being. . . .

I now exhort you and bid you . . . take my place in doing whatever administration of the Church requires. . . . I grieve to hear that some among you are unwilling to follow the guidance of the priests and deacons. . . . Our fellow priests, Donatus, Fortunatus, Novatus, and Gordianus, have written to me, but I cannot resolve their problem by myself. I have made it a rule from the beginning of my episcopate not to follow my own uncriticized opinion but to act only after taking your advice and gaining the consent of the people. When God in his goodness restores me to your midst, then, as the consideration we have for each other requires, we shall discuss together what has been done or is to be done."[13] Cyprian's principle, then, is: "Nothing without your advise and the consent of the people"! This was not a simple matter of courtesy among gentlement; the very life of the Church as a communion required that the bishop proceed in this way. In Letter 19 the same idea is made even more explicit: "When God in his mercy reunites us, we shall observe Church discipline in dealing with all the various cases. . . . For moderation, discipline, and the kind of life we all should lead require that the leaders of the Church, together with the clergy and in the presence of all who have kept the faith (and who are to be honored for that faith and for their reverence for God) should be able to regulate all situations after a careful examination in common."[14]

Since all presbyters share in the one priesthood of the glorified Lord and in the same consecration and mission from Christ, there is a new and important basis for determining and directing the relationships of presbyters among themselves. Just as there is an order or college of bishops (a bishop is an essentially "collegial" being, a being who is "in a college"), so there is an order or college of presbyters. This is why the Decree on the Ministry and Life of Priests begins with the words: *Presbyterorum ordinis*, "[The excellence] of the order of priests. . . ." The Decree explains that: "Established in the priestly order by ordination, all priests are united among themselves in an intimate sacramental brotherhood" (8a/549).

The Constitution on the Church had already said: "In virtue of their common sacred ordination and mission, all priests are bound together in an intimate brotherhood" (LG 28e/54).

4. In paragraphs 5 and 6 of PO 2, the Council intends to show that the priest should be both a man of worship or of the Eucharist and a man of evangelization or of God's word. What is being described is not the nature of ministerial priesthood but its content or extension. There were two tendencies at the Council: in the minds of some the priest should be a man of worship, in the minds of others he should be the apostle and evangelizer. In order to break through the impasse the Council takes as its starting point the original Greek text of Rom 15:16, in which, as the official exposition says: "the two ways in which presbyteral priesthood has been explained here at the Council are readily harmonized. For a genuine apostolate and an authentic adoration of the Father are closely connected, indeed are inseparable one from the other, so that the two aspects must be found in every priest's life." Here is how the Council presents its doctrine.

Granting, as has been said, that all priests share in the office of the Apostles, then what the Apostle says of himself holds for them as well: they receive from God (through the sacrament) the grace of being ministers of Christ among the nations and carrying out the sacred service (Greek *hierurgein* = serve as a priest) of preaching the gospel, so that the peoples may become a pleasing sacrifice which the Holy Spirit consecrates. This ministry then embraces two functions:

(a) To preach the word of God. For, "through the apostolic proclamation of the gospel, the People of God is called together and assembled." This important principle is further explained in PO 4a-b/538-39: "The People of God finds its unity first of all through the word of the living God. . . . Since no one can be saved who has not first believed, priests, as co-workers with their bishops, have as their primary duty the proclamation of the gospel of God to all. [N.B. the chief obligation of bishops is to preach the gospel: LG 25a/47; CD 12a/

404].... Thus they establish and build up the People of God. For through the saving word the spark of faith is struck in the hearts of unbelievers, and fed in the hearts of the faithful. By this faith the community of the faithful begins and grows." In note 38 on this passage attention is drawn to the fact that "all that has been said regarding bishops also applies to priests inasmuch as they are cooperators of the bishops." Again, in the Decree on the Missions, we read: "The chief means of this implantation [of the Church] is the preaching of the gospel of Jesus Christ" (AG 6f/591). And since priests share in "the authority by which Christ Himself builds up, sanctifies, and rules His Body" (PO 2d/535), the function of evangelization is *essential* to them. Without it they would not share in the building up (calling together and assembling) of the Church. For the word of God is one of "the most significant elements or endowments which together go to build up ... the Church" (UR 3b/345).

(b) To offer the Eucharistic Sacrifice with the purpose of perfecting the spiritual sacrifice of the faithful and completing it in the sacrifice of Christ. "Through the ministry of priests, the spiritual sacrifice of the faithful is made perfect in union with the sacrifice of Christ, the sole Mediator. Through the hands of priests and in the name of the whole Church, the Lord's sacrifice is offered in the Eucharist in an unbloody and sacramental manner until He Himself returns." Here we have the second *essential* function of the presbyteral priesthood. The text continues in a solemn fashion: "The ministry of priests is directed toward this work [of offering sacrifice] and is perfected in it." The Eucharistic Sacrifice is thus the goal and high point of their ministry. The Constitution on the Liturgy had already said: "The goal of apostolic works is that all who are made sons of God by faith and baptism should come together to praise God in the midst of His Church, to take part in her sacrifice, and to eat the Lord's Supper" (SC 10a/142). For "no Christian community . . . can be built up unless it has its basis and center in the celebration of the most Holy Eucharist" (PO 6h/545). The Eucharist (understood always as the Eucharistic Sacrifice) is "the fount and apex of the whole Christian life" (LG 11b/ 28); it is the "center and summit" of the Christian community (AG 9b/595); it is "the center and culmination of the whole life of the Christian community" (CD 30f/418); by it "the Church constantly lives and grows" (LG 26a/50); by it "the unity of all believers . . . is both expressed and brought about" (LG 3b/16; UR 2a/343). Or, in the expression current today: the Church makes the Eucharist and the Eucharist makes the Church.

I would like to turn aside from my main theme for a moment. What we have just explained provides us with the principal reason why we need priests, *many* priests (at least one for every Christian community). There is new hope in people's voices today as they speak of married deacons and of religious women as parish assistants. For these developments I thank God, but deacons and religious women are not enough. However well organized a community may be, however flourishing it may be from a human and social point of view, if it lacks the Eucharistic Sacrifice, it lacks the fount, the root, the center, the apex of Christian *life*. Nor is it enough to have the Eucharist for adoration and communion; the presence of the sacrifice is indispensable. Without it the faithful cannot transform their spiritual sacrifices (cf. Rom 12:1) into a living sacrifice that is holy and acceptable to God. For in the present economy of salvation and sanctification we have only one means at our disposal for offering to the Father an acceptable spiritual sacrifice: through Christ, with Christ, and in Christ. "For all their [the laity's] works, prayers, and apostolic endeavors, their ordinary married and family life, their daily labor, their mental and physical relaxation, if carried out in the Spirit, and even the hardships of life, if patiently borne— all of these become spiritual sacrifices acceptable to God through Jesus Christ (cf. 1 Pet. 2:5). During the celebration of the Eucharist, these sacrifices are most lovingly offered to the Father along with the Lord's body" (LG 34b/60). This is the law which is operative in the New Testament. I say, then, that every Christian community needs the Eucharistic Sacrifice and has a right to it. "The laity have the *right*, as do all Christians, to receive in abundance from their sacred pastors the spiritual goods of the Church" (LG 37a/64); "such participation [in liturgical celebrations] by the Christian people . . . is their right and duty by reason of their baptism" (SC 14a/144).

Yet in the vast country of Brazil there are very many communities of baptized people which have no priest and therefore no sacrifice. Consequently they are not Christian communities in the proper sense. I myself lived in that situation for many years. I can also vouch for the fact that in these communities there are good and even excellent Christians, fully worthy of being priests; but they are married and do not know Latin! . . . I cannot succeed in grasping the fact that these communities of the baptized—which have a *divine* right to the sacrifice—should be deprived of it for *human* or ecclesiastical reasons. If the law of celibacy is in fact the main reason for the crying lack of priests, then that *law* (I am not speaking of the charism of celibacy) seems to me a serious injustice against the many communities of baptized people which it condemns to live without the presence of the Eucharistic Sacrifice.

As a matter of fact, however, the law of celibacy is only one reason, and not even the main one, for the lack of priests in the marginalized communities of Latin America. In his "Problèmes d'Amérique Latine," *Vie Spirituelle*, 118 (January-June, 1968), 319-343, Joseph Comblin denounced the cultural barrier which exists between the classical-style priest and the people. For the model currently regarded as obligatory for priests supposes an assimilation of the culture of the intellectual class. As a man who is excessively intellectualized, westernized, and turned into a bourgeois, the priest is light-years distant from the intellectual level of the people and no longer accepts the purely "sacral" and "sacralizing" functions which the people expect from him (how terrible the very words sound in a "secularized" and "secularizing" world!). Priest and people belong to two different worlds which do not talk the same language; and the more the priest studies, the broader becomes the gulf between him and the people.

A priest who can identify with the people must be able (1) really to understand the mentality of the illiterate or semi-literate masses and their religious needs; (2) to live permanently among them; (3) to communicate to them an intelligible message; and (4) to be leader of the community. All this will be psychologically difficult, even impossible, for the kind of clergy which we have at present. In consequence, the priest feels himself isolated among his people: and the people feel themselves abandoned by their priests.

The magazine *Pro mundi vita* devoted a whole issue (no. 22 [1968]) to Latin America and its priests, and concluded with strong words to the urgent necessity of diversifying the kinds of priests and of inventing a new canonical form: the "part-time priest" who would give only part of his time to priestly functions, while he continued to exercise his secular profession, somewhat as political, labor, and cultural leaders or, in Brazil, spiritualist and pentecostal leaders divide their time and efforts. The classical-style priest is trained to be liturgist, theologian, ecclesiastical advisers, confessor, director of a community of believers, missionary, preacher, builder, technologist of development, specialist in matters of education, family, etc., etc. Such many-sided and well qualified men will be increasingly difficult to find (even apart from the issue of celibacy), especially in the marginalized regions of Brazil and Latin America.

I attended the First Conference on Pastoral Practice in the Latin American Missions, April 20-27, 1968 (sponsored by the Department of Mission of CELAM, at Melgar, Colombia); about sixty missionaries (fifteen of them bishops) and experts were present.[15] I noticed that one of the greatest worries all these men had was: how to train the priests who will come from the native communities and stay with these communities? Everyone felt the total inadequancy of a mere visit, at long intervals, by a priest from outside, with some communities being left for a year at a time without a priest and without the Eucharistic Sacrifice which is the "basis and center" of the Church community (PO 6h/545). Almost all agreed on one basic point: we need a new kind of priest (a "community-based priest" who, from the sociological viewpoint, is a secular; a "part-time priest"), different from the present classical-style priest, having his roots in the community itself, married or unmarried, leader of that group of people, living with them at the same cultural and social level. The kind of priests we now have would of course continue to exist, but their main function would be to guide and help the local priests and to form, with the bishop, the college of priests.

We have seen that the priest is not only an evangelical but also a man of the Eucharist. Although the nature of the priesthood cannot be derived exclusively from its relationship to the Eucharist, we can maintain, with Vatican II, that "they [priests] exercise this sacred (mediatorial) function of Christ most of all in the Eucharistic liturgy or synaxis. There, acting in the person of Christ, and proclaiming His mystery, they join the offering of the faithful to the sacrifice of their Head" (LG 28a/53). Again: "Priests fulfill their chief duty in the mystery of the Eucharistic Sacrifice" (PO 13e/560); and the ministry of priests "deals principally with the Eucharist" (AG 39a/626).

5. In the seventh and final paragraph of PO 2 the Council wishes to say more explicitly that the true priestly mission of men and the true adoration of the Father are closely, even indissolubly, united in the lives of presbyters. For them, too, the Pauline principle holds true: the preaching of the gospel is a form of worship; it glorifies God (cf. Rom 1:9) and is the exercise of a sacred service (cf. Rom 15:16 in the Greek text).

The ministry and life of the priest can thus have but one finality: "the glory of God the Father as it is to achieved in Christ." God's glory consists in this: that men should, in a free, conscious, and thankful way, accept the work which God has accomplished in Christ. "Hence, whether engaged in prayer and adoration, preaching the word, offering the Eucharistic Sacrifice, ministering the other sacraments, or performing any of the works of the ministry for men, priests are contributing to the extension of God's glory as well as to the development of divine life in men."

We now have before us all the elements which make it possible to describe more exactly the difference (of degree and nature) between the common priesthood and the ministerial priesthood. Vatican II speaks twice of this difference. In the Constitution on the Church (10b/27), it teaches that the ministerial priest has a sacred power (1) to mold and rule the people of God; (2) acting in the person of Christ, to bring about the Eucharistic Sacrifice; (3) to offer it to God in the name of all the people. In the Decree on the Ministry and Life of Priests (2b/534) the Council repeats that, among the faithful, ministerial priests have "the sacred power of their order" (1) to form the community; (2) to offer the sacrifice; (3) to forgive sins; and (4) to exercise the priestly office publicly for men in the name of Christ.

Ministerial priests (bishops and presbyters; deacons, too?) are, then, distinguished by having a sacred power that is received through a special sacrament. Vatican II speaks elsewhere of this "sacred power." At the beginning of Chapter 3 of the Constitution on the Church, it teaches that ministers have been established to feed and foster the growth of the People of God and that they have their sacred power in order to be "servants of their brethren" (LG 18a/37). The same document later says that bishops govern with authority and sacred power and that "this power they use only for the edification of their flock in truth and holiness" (LG 27a/51). In the Decree on Priests the same power is also called a "spiritual power" and is said to be "conferred upon them for the up-building of the Church" (PO 6a/543-44). In LG 24a/47 the Council had called attention to the following principle: "That duty, which the Lord committed to the shepherds of His people, is a true service, and in sacred literature is significantly called 'diakonia' or ministry." Therefore, the "sacred power" which distinguishes priests from the other faithful is defined in terms of its purpose: to build up the flock in truth and holiness. It is not defined in terms of privileges, personal powers for one's private purposes, domination, or monopoly. It is an authority for service, not for domination. Those who possess it have, strictly speaking, only one power and right: to be adequate signs and living instruments of Christ the teacher, priest, and shepherd; to exercise their office publicly for men in the name of Christ. That is the essential definition of ministerial priesthood.

We may at this point also try to describe more exactly the difference (of degree but not of nature) between the ministerial priesthood of bishops and that of simple priests. We have already seen what the two have in common. Both share in one and the same priesthood of Christ and in his consecration and mission. Both are signs, means, and instruments of Christ: they represent Christ the Head, are vicars of Christ, and act with his authority. Both have a sacred power which they exercise publicly in the name of Christ. But when a simple priest is elected bishop, he receives a new consecration in a rite which is a true sacrament (cf. LG 21c/41). The bishop, then, receives, and is, something more. What he receives is "the fullness of the sacrament of orders" (ibid.). Thereby he enters into hierarchical communion, becomes a member of the episcopal college (cf. LG 22a/42), is part of the group which directly succeeds the Apostles (cf. LG 20d/40), and thus shares in full and supreme power over the whole Church (cf. LG 22c/43). All this flows from the sacrament; that is, from God and not from the Church. All this, too, is lacking in simple priests; the latter are, therefore, co-workers of the episcopal college, sharing the episcopal mission in a lesser degree.

At the end of LG 21d/42 a further episcopal function is mentioned: "It devoles on the bishops to admit newly elected members into the episcopal body by means of the sacrament of orders." In an earlier draft it had been said that only bishops can ordain priests. Then, for historical rather than theological reasons, this thesis was abandoned and replaced by another: "Only bishops can, through the sacrament of orders, admit newly elected members into the episcopal body," while the corresponding official exposition indicates that the Council had decided to say nothing on the question of the minister of presbyteral ordination. Then, however, historical diffculties were raised even in regard to the consecration of bishops. (It seems that at Alexandria, before 325 A.D., the college of presbyters chose and consecrated the new patriarch.) For this reason, the expression "Only bishops can . . ." was reduced to a simple statement of fact: "It devolves on the bishops. . . ." Vatican II was unwilling to give a doctrinal solution to the question of the minister of episcopal consecration.

At several points we have seen that rather wide differences exist between the Council of Trent and Vatican II in the doctrine on ministerial priesthood. In an essay on the theology of priesthood from Trent to Vatican II,[16] Henri Denis analyzes the differences: (1) point of departure: celebration of the Eucharist (Trent) vs mission of the Church (Vatican II); (2) institution of presbyterate: the Supper (T) vs the establishment of the apostolate as a totality (V); (3) specific element in priesthood: power over the Eucharistic Body of Christ (T) vs action in the name of Christ the Head (V); (4) understanding of content of priestly ministry: cultic priest (T) vs apostolic minister (V); (5) theocentrism of the ministry, and way of understanding the priest's presence in the world: a theocentrism of worship (T) vs a theocentrism of the priest's whole life and ministry. There can be no doubt that the new climate at Vatican II had an influence on the doctrinal position the Council took. There was no longer, as at Trent, a preoccupation with "defending" the sacramental nature of orders and with the challenges of Luther. Instead there was a greater sensitivity to the common priesthood of all the baptized and a great desire for a less juridical kind of theology. At Trent priority went to the dogmatic intention of protecting Catholic doctrine against the exaggarted innovations of the Reformers. At Vatican II priority went to the more pastoral preoccupation with encouraging today's priests for a difficult and very delicate and complex mission in a world in which they feel increasingly like strangers, "anxiously looking for appropriate ways and words with which to communicate with it. For the modern obstacles blocking faith, the seemingly sterility of their past labors, and also the bitter loneliness they experience can lead them to the danger of becoming depressed in Spirit" (PO 22b/574-75); a world which "though entangled indeed in many sins . . . is also endowed with great talents" and in which the Holy Spirit is "impelling the Church to new avenues of approach" (PO 22c/575).

In Trent we have primarily a theology of priesthood (Trent uses the word constantly, as did St. Thomas before it) as specifically correlated with sacrifice; in Vatican II we have a theology of the presbyter in relation to the whole mission of the Church (though presbyters are, of course, "'true priests of the New Testament": LG 28a/53). What Trent taught concerning the sacrament of holy orders is undoubtedly the authentic (and in that sense definitive) expression of Catholic faith. But that does not imply that Trent said everything there was to be said about the matter; in this sense the documents of Trent are not definitive. Vatican II is not opposed to Trent but completes it and introduces broader perspectives. The mistake of the post-Tridentine period was to take a partial doctrine as exclusive. Insufficient heed was given to the historical and doctrinal context in which Trent occurred, and to the basic intention of that Council, which was to counteract Protestant errors. This anti-heretical outlook was absent from Vatican II, and this Council was therefore able to be more free in its positive exposition of doctrine, in response both to the inherent exigencies of the revealed datum and to the pastoral needs of the day. Vatican's expressly ecumenical stance of sincere dialogue with Protestants (not of polemics against them) had a positive influence on its theology. Here, as in so many other areas, the Council did not scruple to accept without reserve certain Biblical and patristic doctrines on which Protestants had been insisting, even if in an exclusive way, such as the common priesthood of the faithful, the cultic value of the preaching of God's word, the real efficacy of the word of God and of preaching, etc. Undoubtedly, there is an essential continuity between the teaching of Trent and of Vatican II: both teach that priestly ordination is a true sacrament which confers a special grace and imprints a character. Yet we cannot but notice the ease with which Vatican II passes over some Tridentine positions which had seemed definitive.

In all this we have an example and a precious lesson for the future. Our attitude to the teaching authority of the Church, even when it takes its supreme form in an ecumenical council, cannot and ought not always be one of pure and simple acceptance, repetition, and fixation upon what it has said. There must always be left open the possibility of amplification and homogeneous development. Councils have not decided every matter definitively, nor have they always decided in the best possible way. Theology, therefore, cannot be limited to being a passive, subservient repeater of dogmas formulated in the past. That would be barren fixism. We shall always be urged by the Spirit to seek and find new paths (cf. PO 22c/575). That is what life requires—and the Church and its teaching are life. Vatican II provides proofs of this which will be classical models for the future.

There is, then, no serious cause for pessimism concerning the theology of the priesthood—at least not in Vatican II. There is good reason for the priest's existence and continued activity within the priestly and apostolic people of God. He is even indispensable to it, and the need is to find ways and means of increasing his number and of developing new concrete existential forms of priesthood (the lack of the latter being the real root of the present crisis). For, without him and, therefore, without the Eucharistic Sacrifice, there can be no authentic Christian communities. The mystery of Christ is present and operative only through the ministerial priesthood. The priest, the man chosen by God,[17] is the visible sign, the means and living instrument, of Christ the eternal Priest amid the community of believers. Through the special sacrament he receives, the priest is ontologically qualified to build, sanctify, and rule the Church in the name and person of Christ and with his authority. As possessor of a genuine sacred power that is to be exercised publicly for men in the name of Christ, the priest can present himself to the people as the authentic representative or vicar of Christ, in whose name and with whose authority he preaches, sanctifies, and directs. He can also present himself to God in the name of the whole people in order to gather up and perfect their desires, prayers, sacrifices, works, plans, joys, weaknesses, and whole lives in the one sacrifice of the eternal Priest and thus to offer everything to the Father with, through, and in Christ. Only thus shall we be accepted by the Father.

Notes for Chapter 9

[1] Paul VI, *Questa udienza: To the Pastors and Lenten Preachers of Rome,* February 26, 1968, in *TPS,* 13 (168-69), 115.

[2] *Acta Synodalia,* II/2, pp. 418-19.

[3] St. Thomas, *Summa theologiae, Supplementum,* q. 37, a. 2.

[4] *Op. cit.,* q. 37, a. 1, ad 2.

[5] DS, 1739-41 (D, 938) and 1752 (D, 948); *TCT,* nos. 747 and 757, pp. 291-92 and 295.

[6] Vatican II has a preference for the word "instrument": the humanity of Christ was the instrument of our salvation (SC 5a/139); the Church is the instrument of intimate union with God (LG 1b/15); the people of God is the instrument of redemption for all (LG 9e/26); the Sacred Scriptures are an instrument in the hand of God for achieving unity in the Church (UR 21d/363); and priests should be living in-

struments of Christ, the eternal Priest (PO 12b/558), instruments useful for the service of all God's people (PO, 12f/559).

[7] DS, 1740 (D, 938) and 1752 (D, 948); *TCT, nos.* 747 and 757, pp. 291-92 and 295.

[7a] Cf. DS, 1764 (D, 957) and 1771 (D, 961).

[7b] Cf. DS, 1670 (D, 894) and 1703 (D, 913).

[8] Vatican II invites us to speak, in literature on the priestly vocation, of the "excellence of the priestly vocation" (OT, 2e/440), "the excellence . . . of the priesthood" (PO, 11b/556), and the "excellence of the priestly ministry" in which "weighty responsibilities are mixed with profound joys" (PO, 11f/557).

[9] *Acta Synodalia,* II/2, p. 117.

[10] *Acta Synodalia,* II/1, p. 234.

[11] The same expression had already been used in LG, 21d/41, to describe the relationship of bishops and pope.

[12] St. Cyprian, Ep. 41, in *S. T. C. Cypriani opera omnia* 2, ed. Wm. Hartel (CSEL 3/2; Vienna, 1871), p. 587.

[13] Ep. 14, Hartel, pp. 509-13.

[14] Ep. 19, Hartel, pp. 525-26.

[15] Cf. *La postoral en las misiones de America Latina: Documento final del primo encuentro continental de misiones en America Latina,* Melgar, Colombia, April 21-27, 1968 (Bogotá: Departmento de misiones de CELAM, 1968).

[16] Henri Denis, "La théologie du presbytérat de Trente à Vatican II," in *Les prêtres: Formation, ministère, et vie* (Unam sanctum 68; Paris: Editions du Cerf, 1968), pp. 193-232.

[17] "Divinely chosen," says the Council (CT, 2d/440). The same passage adds that divine providence gives these men the necessary fitness and the helps of grace and entrusts them to the existing lawful ministers of the Church so that the latter may call them and "exercise the further commission of consecrating such men with the seal of the Holy Spirit to the worship of God and the service of the Church." Therefore, before being called by the bishop, they are already chosen by God and readied for the service of priestly ministry. The Decree on Priests speaks of those whom the Lord "calls," but goes on to say: "This voice of the Lord in summons, however, is never to be looked for as something which will be heard by the ears of future priests in any extraordinary manner. It is rather to be detected and weighed in the signs by which the will of God is customarily made known to prudent Christians. These indications should be carefully noted by priests" (PO 11e/556). In note 140 on this passage the Council quotes an allocution of Paul VI, May 5, 1965, in which the pope says: "The voice of God that calls is expressed in two different ways, wondrous and converging: the one interior, that of grace, that of the Holy Spirit, the expressible way of that interior charm exercised by the silent and powerful voice of the Lord in the unsearchable depths of the human soul; the other exterior, human, perceivable, social, juridical, concrete" —that of the bishop.

Chapter 10

The Nature of Religious Life

The question of the nature of religious life is the subject of a great deal of discussion today in Europe and the Americas. These discussions have almost immediate practical influence, not always of the most positive kind. It is said, at times, that Vatican II is vague and undecided on the matter. Perhaps the remarks that follow, which are mainly historical and informational in character, can help resolve some doubts and give new heart to some people in their vocations.

In 1963, during the second session of the Council, the Fathers received a new text on the Church; it included a chapter (the fourth) on the call to sanctity, and this chapter contained five numbers on religious life.[1] The text concentrated heavily on affirming the universal vocation of all the baptized to sanctity and perfection; as a result it tended to play down the absolute value of religious life as a special way of achieving Christian santity in the Church. The following of the evangelical counsels was presented as but one means of attaining to the perfection of charity. The text said nothing of the divine origin of religious life and even implied the contrary when it asserted that the Church knows of only two states that are of divine institution: the lay and the clerical. In a note attached to what was then number 33 (now 44), which spoke of the importance of the states of perfection, the sign-value of the religious state was stressed as being the primary value.[2] On October 18, 1963 (even before the debate on chapter 4 began, on October 25), Bishop A. Tabera Araoz of Albacete, Spain, sharply criticized the thrust of the next and said: "The draft . . . exhibits such a mentality and outlook on religious life and uses such expressions that one might be easily led to think . . . it accepts the doctrine or view of those who praise the excellence of our common Christian state and make it the equal of the state of perfection. These people maintain that sanctity is one and the same for each and every state of life in the Church, any difference being accidental and minimal. Or they maintain that the state of perfection differs from ordinary Christian life only in the use of certain secondary means (the 'evangelical counsels'), which are neither entirely necessary nor always apt for attaining the one sanctity set before all. Or they maintain that these counsels, proper to the state of perfection, are to be regarded simply as means and even, so to speak, as negative tools, intended for overcoming the obstacles to perfection but not as positive elements of sanctity or supernatural perfection; at most, they would say, the counsels are simultaneously means and effects, or, to put it differently, a form of exercise of a sanctity common to all. From the principles invoked, the equating of the two states logically follows; or rather, there follows the downgrading of religious life at which the Reformers aimed."[3]

Others among the Council Fathers, however, defended the position paper of 1962. Bishop A. M. Charue of Namur, who spoke on October 25, 1963, expressed the mentality and outlook for a good number of the Fathers and theologians. Bishop Charue was himself a member, and vice-president, of the Theological Commission which had drawn up the next. In his address Charue insisted on the doctrine that by the Church's essential constitutive structure and by divine institution the members of the Church are divided into only two categories: laity and clergy, whereas the division into religious and non-religious is of purely ecclesiastical origin. "The organization of religious as a sub-group is not part of the Church's essential structure. They are an institution *in* the Church, not an institution *of* the Church."[4] In Charue's view, the chief value of the religious state as such is to be found in the Spiritual influence and stimulus given to others for a holier life; in other words, Charue was stressing the relational or *sign* value of religious life and not the intrinsic value it has of itself.[5]

At the same meeting (October 25, 1963), Cardinal Silva Henriquez, of Chile, speaking in the name of fifty Latin American bishops, defended the scheme and instisted on the *sign* aspect of religious life: "The life of the counsels will thus be more clearly seen to be a charism for bearing eschatological witness on behalf of the Christian community." On October 31, Bishop Leiprecht of Rottenburg likewise emphasized the sign value: "The ecclesiological reason for the existence of the religious state is its function of bearing witness to the kingdom of God and to the new life in Christ."[6]

There was, however, a rather strong opposition to this somewhat minimalist conception of religious life. Bishop R. L. Guilly of Georgetown, for example, called attention to the danger involved in laying excessive emphasis on the sign aspect. Religious life, he said, is indeed a sign, but it is more than a sign: "A reality does not have value because it is a sign; it is a sign because it has value." This principle will reappear in various other addresses to the Council. It is not correct to say, Bishop Guilly continued, that the chief purpose of religious life is to be a sign and witness, for it has a value *in itself*: "The primary value of religious life lies in the fact that by a gift of undivided love to Christ and God, it binds its members more closely to Christ and God, binds them more closely to his Body which is the Church, and makes them share more fully in the redemptive work which is being divinely continued in and for the Church."[7]

Father John Baptist Janssens, then general of the Society of Jesus, focused on the same principle in a document signed by thirteen archbishops, thirty-five bishops, and seven superiors general of religious orders. "The religious state indeed has the value of sign and witness, but this is not its main value. For the religious state does not have value because it is a sign; it is a sign because it has value, both sanctifying and redemptive." The superior general of the Jesuits also objected to the tendency to maintain that there is only one sanctity in the Church:

"The emphatic assertion that all Christians are called to a single sanctity needs further clarification. There is indeed only one Christian sanctity, which consists in sharing the one life of Christ. This does not mean, however, that all the faithful, taken either individually or according to states, are called to the same kind of sharing in the life of Christ. Each person is called to holiness in the Church according to the measure of Christ's gift to him. The religious state as a state leads its members to a specifically new and more perfect holiness, which flows from the full and effective observance of the evangelical counsels. This doctrine, based on the words of Christ and the Apostles, is clearly taught by the millennial tradition of the Church, by the unanimous consent of learned theologians, and by the supreme teaching authority in the Church. It is not right, therefore, to imply that the difference in states (as far as holiness and effective sanctification are concerned) rests solely on the different means used. The theological basis of the authentic doctrine I am propounding is the fact that members of religious orders are called to cleave to God and Christ with undivided love and to dedicate themselves wholly to him in the Church. We may indeed grant that all Christians ought to practice poverty, chastity, and obedience. There remains, however, the total and unconditional gift of self, confirmed by vow, to Christ in his Church, a self-gift made in order to advance to a more stable and closer union with the poor, virginal, and obedient Christ, and in order to involve men more fully in the work of the Redeemer who willed to redeem and sanctify us by his poverty, virginity, and obedience even to the cross. This consecration of self to Christ in the Church is also for the sake of the Church, so that in and for her what is still wanting in Christ's sufferings may be made up."[8]

On November 8, 1963 a *Commission of Council Fathers from Religious Orders* was established; its function was to pull together the various efforts at revising what was then Chapter 4 and at producing a new chapter on religious. The chairman of the commission was Bishop Perantoni, former minister general of the Franciscans, its secretary Bishop Compagnone. The chief result of the group's work was a document submitted to the Theological Commission (which had the responsibility of drawing up conciliar texts) on December 20, 1963, It was signed by sixteen cardinals, two patriarchs, nine-two archbishops, four hundred and thirty-seven bishops, ten prelates *nullius* [without jurisdiction], eight abbots *nullius*, thirty-two prefects apostolic, and eighty-two superiors general — a total of six hundred and seventy-eight Council Fathers. This document ("Recommendations to the Conciliar Commission on Doctrine") had a decisive influence on the later and final version of the present Chapter 6, "Religious," of the Constitution on the Church. Its content:

1. The discussion of the universal call to sanctity should be put in the chapter on the people of God.

2. Affirm the oneness of all essential sanctity as consisting in an ontological and moral union with Christ, but affirm just as strongly that this sanctity, as realized in individuals, has various modes and degrees according to the vocation of each person, according to the measure in which Christ gives his grace, and according to the personal cooperation of the individual with that grace.

3. Speak more fully and clearly of the specific call to perfection and holiness which bishops and priests receive and distinguish it from the call given to the laity; speak, too, of the perfection proper to married life.

4. Reaffirm clearly the doctrine solemnly put forth by the Council of Trent on the superiority of the celibate state over the married state.[9]

5. There should be a separate chapter on religious: (a) because religious have, in fact, a special place in the structure of the Church; (b) because they have a specific role in the Church; and (c) in order that there may be space to explain all aspects of the ecclesial presence of those who follow the evangelical counsels.

6. Among the points to be explained in such a chapter, the following should be included:

(a) an express affirmation of the divine origin of the evangelical counsels;

(b) a clear statement that the effective and total practice of the counsels, as confirmed by perpetual vows, implies and requires the exercise, heroic at times, of many virtues not required in other forms of Christian life or simply by the *spirit* of the counsels. Moreover, such an effective and total practice of the counsels does not mean simply the exercise of special means of sanctification. On the contrary, it supposes and requires an undivided love of God, a love which, therefore, is different from a divided love. It should be stated, then, that such a practice of the counsels constitutes, *of itself*, a more perfect state of the following of Christ and of closer conformity to him;

(c) The ecclesiological value of the religious state is not adequately described if we look only to the external apostolate of religious. For, the chief value of religious life consists in this, that by their total surrender to Christ in the Church, religious are more closely associated with the work of the Redeemer who by his poverty, virginity, and obedience even to the cross willed to redeem and sanctify men. It is on account of this holocaust, which embraces a person's whole life, that the spiritual treasure of the Church is increase and its apostolate is enriched and made fruitful;

(d) The ecclesiological value of the religious state would, therefore, be diminished if we were to say that this state "has chiefly the value of a sign," as the exposition maintained. It cannot, of course, be denied that the religious state does also have the value of sign and witness; but this value is in no way the main value, much less the sole value. The religious state does not have value because it is a sign; it is a sign because it has value for santification and redemption;

(e) The Church is enriched in many ways by the spirit and purpose proper to each religious institute. It will therefore be greatly beneficial to the Church to preserve this multiplicity.

7. The chapter of religious should be drawn up by a Joint Commission composed of members of the Theological Commission and of the Commission for Religious.

The desired Joint Commission for drawing up a new text was in fact established on January 24, 1964. Its chairman was Cardinal Browne; its members were the Council Fathers Charue, Seper, Gut, Burler, Fernández (from the Theological Commission) and Compagnone, Sipovic, Stein, Kleiner and Sépinski (from the Commission on Religious), as well as the theological experts Abellán, Benjamin of the Most Holy Trinity, Boyer, Gambari, Gagnebet, Labourdette, Lio, Philippon, K. Rahner, Tascon, Thils, and Verardo. This Joint Commission met eleven times.

The new text was presented to the Council on September 30, 1964 by Abbot (later Cardinal) Gut as official expositor in the name of the Theological Commission. This exposition (previously discussed in and approved by the Commission) contains some important statements. It sees the difference between religious and other baptized Christians in this way: "Other Christians, with a view to the sanctity intended for all, receive not only the precepts but also the counsels *as counsels*; for religious, however, these same counsels, once confirmed by vows under the authority of the Church, become precepts and religious obligations." It is for this reason that those in the Church who profess the evangelical counsels receive a new state in the Church. The expositor then continues: "It is in this perspective that the whole matter of religious is viewed: whether there is question of the profession of the counsels in the Church (n. 43), or of the nature and importance of the religious state (n. 44), or of its relationship to Church authority (n. 45), or of the esteem which all should have for the consecrated life in the Church (n. 46)."

In the new draft, which became the final text approved by the Council, we find almost all the elements desired or asked for by the document of the six hundred and seventy-eight Fathers (only the first and fourth wishes were not respected). The attentive reader can easily turn them up. I would note only that at the beginning of Chapter 5 the Council affirms the holiness of the Church (union with Christ), the vocation of all to holiness and the manifold forms this holiness takes, and the fact that this holiness "shines out in the practice of the counsels customarily called 'evangelical'" (LG 39b/66). Shortly afterwards it is again said that "in the various types and duties of life, one and the same holiness is cultivated by all" (LG 41a/67); the Council then goes on to speak specifically of the holiness of bishops, priests, deacons, and married people (41b-g/68-69). In the following number (LG 42e/71) there is a further allusion to religious: "The holiness of the Church is also fostered in a special way by the observance of the manifold counsels proposed in the gospel by our Lord to His disciples," and special mention is made of virginity or celibacy as chosen for "God alone"; it is said that "Mother Church rejoices at finding within her bosom men and women who more closely follow and more clearly demonstrate the Savior's self-giving" (LG 42g/72). These various remarks are followed by the detailed treatment of religious in Chapter 6. The official exposition states that, in order to meet the wishes of the six hundred and seventy-eight Fathers, Chapter 6 begins with an affirmation of the divine origin of the evangelical counsels (LG 43a/73); the exposition then, however, directs the attention of theologians to n. 44.

We are told that the text was formulated "so that the nature of the religious state with respect both to God and to consecration by vow might be brought out." Then, after referring the Fathers to some addresses by Council Fathers (which we shall consider just below), the exposition continues: "It is, then, clear that the religious state is distinguished, primarily and properly, from that of the other faithful by the fact that religious oblige themselves by vow to observe certain evangelical counsels which make them men and women wholly dedicated to God." The exposition then quotes St. Thomas: "If a person dedicates his whole life to God by vow, he enters, without any qualification, into the condition or state of perfection." All this explains why the Council begins its description of the nature of religious life as it does: "The faithful of Christ can bind themselves to the three previously mentioned counsels either by vows, or by other sacred bonds which are like vows in their purpose. Through such a bond a person is totally dedicated to God by an act of supreme love, and is committed to the honor and service of God under a new and special title" (LG 44a/74). It is in the bond and the total loving dedication it involves that Vatican II sees the essence of religious life.

To help us understand this key text, the exposition refers us to an address by Aniceto Fernández, O.P., master general of the Dominicans and a member of the Joint Commission. The latter first quotes St. Thomas: "Religious, in the strict and unqualified sense, are those who give themselves wholly to the service of God, making of themselves a holocaust as it were."[10] Fernández maintains, therefore: "This is the essence of religious life: total consecration to the service of God. To achieve this consecration is the purpose and reason for the three vows by which the religious, exercising the virtue of religion, offers himself and all he is and has to God—soul, body, outward things. In this total consecration the whole essence of religious life resides; it is expressed by the vows which are acts of that virtue of religion which commands the acts of the other moral virtues and is itself commanded by charity, the perfection of which is the goal of this state of life."[11]

The exposition also refers us to an address of Bishop Paul Philippe O.P., at that time secretary of the Congregation for Religious. Philippe called attention to the fact that the religious *state* "is ordered *exclusively* to the perfection of charity, that, to union with God and the service of the neighbor for the sake of God, whereas other states of life among the faithful involve or allow goals, functions, and obligations of the temporal order." He concluded: "It ought therefore be more explicitly said that men established in the state of perfection by religious vows are consecrated to God so as to be separated from the world and wholly dedicated to the service of God."[12]

The exposition refers, finally, to the address of Roland Huot, superior general of the Sulpicians, in which we read: "The counsels of poverty, chastity, and obedience should be proposed and explained in the way that religious and the Church understand and practice them; that is, not only as means of sanctification which all can use, but rather as essential elements which are found in the special form of the life of perfection in the Church."[13]

What these three speakers and the conciliar text are saying is also the doctrine of Pope Paul VI, propounded earlier in 1964 (the Council refers to it in note 210 on LG 43c/74): "We think it necessary to call attention once again to the inestimable value of the religious life and its vital task. This state in life, distinctively characterized by the profession of the evangelical vows, is a perfect way of life according to the teaching and example of Jesus Christ. For it seeks to ensure continued growth in charity until perfection is reached. Other

states in life have different aims, different values, and different duties which are, however, legitimate in themselves."[14]

The Council thus teaches, to begin with, that the essence
of religious life (that is, that which distinguishes it from other
states of Christian life) consists in the total self-gift or consecration or dedication to God who is loved beyond all else;
that by this consecration the Christian is in a new and special
way ordered to the service and honor of God; and that this
total consecration or self-gift is expressed in vows by which
the baptized person *obliges* himself to the evangelical counsels
of poverty, chastity, and obedience. The Constitution on the
Church then goes on to say that by baptism the believer has
already died to sin and been consecrated to God. This baptismal consecration is the background against which, and
the basis upon which, the Christian who enters religious life
will make the total, undivided, and exclusive dedication of
himself to God. The religious state seeks to bring the baptismal consecration to its perfection. In his new state the
Christian will "derive more abundant fruit from this baptismal
grace," since he will be enabled, "by the profession of the
evangelical counsels in the Church, to free himself from those
obstacles which might draw him away from the fervor of charity and the perfection of divine worship. Thus he is more
intimately consecrated to divine service" (LG 44b/74). In
a note (n. 213), the Council again refers us to the discourse of
Paul VI on May 23, 1964, in which the pope had said: "The
profession of the evangelical vows in connected with the consecration proper to baptism. It is, as it were, an act of personal consecration which completes the former. The individual dedicates himself wholly to God, making his entire life
an act of service to Him alone."[15]

In the Decree on the Appropriate Renewal of Religious Life,
the Council teaches the same doctrine in a more straightforward and clearer way. After reminding religious that by
professing the evangelical counsels they have renounced the
world in order to live for God alone and to dedicate their

whole lives to his service, the Council says that "they have handed over their entire lives to God's service in an act of special consecration which is deeply rooted in their baptismal consecration and which provides an ampler manifestation of it" (PC 5a/470).

In another context the Council teaches that "baptism, of itself, is only a beginning, a point of departure, for it is wholly directed toward the acquiring of fullness of life in Christ" (UR 22b/364), and that "in the consecration of baptism" we have "received the sign and the gift of so lofty a vocation and a grace that even despite human weakness" we "can and must pursue perfection" (PO 12a/557-58). This is to say that baptism is only a great beginning and should stimulate us to a life of perfection. Religious life aims at fostering or facilitating the fuller realization of the many virtualities baptism bestows upon us. If it be true that religious life is the most perfect expression of baptismal grace (cf. PC 5a/470), then it seems to follow that a deepening of the theology of baptism can lead to a better theology of religious life. Such a deeper theological penetration of religious life on the basis of baptism is a desideratum.

In order simply to indicate some lines of thought, it will be be useful to draw up here a list of the effects of baptism as indicated in the conciliar documents. The following picture emerges:

1. By baptism we are consecrated to God (LG 44b/74; PO 12a/557); we are consecrated as a spiritual house (LG 10a/27) and to form a kingly priesthood and holy people of God (AA 3a/492); by it we become really holy (LG 40b/67).

2. By baptism we are plunged into the paschal mystery of Christ (SC 6/140); we share the life of Christ and have been made like him and been raised up with him, until we reign together with him (LG 7f/21); we are truly incorporated into the crucified and glorified Christ (UR 22a/363); we have died to sin (LG 44b/74), been begotten to a new life (AG 15a/601), and become new creatures (GE 2a/640).

3. By baptism we are reborn as sons of God (LG 11a/28); we truly become sons of God and sharers in the divine nature (LG 40b/67); we are reborn to a sharing of the divine life (UR 22a/362); we receive the spirit of adoption as sons (SC 6/140); we are called, and truly are, children of God (GE 2a/640), so that we may endlessly share in a divine life beyond corruption (GS 18d/215), in an intimate and vital union with God (GS 19b/216), and to communion with God and a share in his happiness (GS 21c/218).

4. By baptism we are made like Christ (LG 7f/21) and share in his priestly, prophetic, and kingly functions (LG 31a/57; AA 2b/491).

5. By baptism we share in the anointing of the Spirit with which Christ himself was anointed (PA 2a/533); we are endowed with understanding of the faith (LG 35a/61) and are anointed by the Holy Spirit (LG 12a/29).

6. By baptism we are incorporated into Christ's Mystical Body (AA 3a/492); we are incorporated into Christ (LG 31a/57; UR 22a/362; AG 7b/593; 15h/603); we are established among the people of God (LG 31a/57) and made members of the Church (LG 11a/28; AG 6f/591).

7. By baptism we are ontologically fitted to offer acceptable spiritual sacrifices (LG 10a/27; PA 2a/533); we are consecrated to the exercise of the cult of the Christian religion (LG 11a/28); we become true adorers of the Father (SC 6/140).

8. By baptism we are obliged to profess before men the faith we have received from God (LG 11a/28); we are oriented toward a complete profession of faith (UR 22b/364).

9. By baptism we are enabled to proclaim the great deeds of him who called us from darkness into his wonderful light (LG 10a/27; PO 2a/533-34), that we may bear witness to Christ (AA 3a/492); we are commissioned to the apostolate (LG 33b/59), made witnesses to Christ (LG 35a/61), and endowed with the grace of speech (*ibid.*); we share in the mission of the whole Christian people with respect to the Church and

the world (LG 31a/57; PO 2a/534; AA 2b/491).

All this should contribute to a fuller and more perfect realization of the religious life.

After describing the theocentric, and primary, aspect of religious life (LG 44a-b/74), the Council moves on to the ecclesiological or apostolic aspect (LG 44c/74, etc.). Here again the exposition indicates that the passage is due to the intervention of the six hundred and seventy-eight Fathers who asked that the document speak of the sanctifying and redemptive value of religious life. That is, just as Christ sanctifies and redeems men through his poverty, his virginity, and his obedience even to the acceptance of the cross, so also religious life, as such, intrinsically possesses a sanctifying and redemptive value for the Church and mankind. Earlier (LG 42e/72), the Council had already stated that virginity "for God alone" is a "unique fountain of spiritual fertility in the world." In our present passage (LG 44c/74-75), the Council again teaches that "by the charity to which they lead, the evangelical counsels join their followers to the Church and her mystery in a special way." Further on, we come upon the definitive statement of the place of religious life in the Church: "Thus, although the religious state constituted by the profession of the evangelical counsels does not belong to the hierarchical structure of the Church, nevertheless it belongs inseparably to her life and holiness" (LG 44f/75). "Belongs inseparably"! The exposition explains: "This is, as it were, an inference from the nature and importance of the religious state; for the latter belongs to the Church's life in the Spirit and to her holiness. Thus it is true that religious life is not part of the Church's hierarchic structure (cf. LG 43d/74); nonetheless it does form part of the Church's pneumatic and charismatic structure." The exposition then refers us to the address, which we have already cited, of Bishop Paul Philippe, in which we read "It must be recognized that the religious state is an essential part of *the Church's very life*, and is a factor in her holiness, so that the Church can never be

without the state of those who profess the evangelical counsels."[16] Priests should member that all religious, both men
and women . . . have a distinguished place indeed in the
house of the Lord" (PO 6f/545).

Finally, the Council speaks of the eschatological aspect of
religious life, that is, its value as a sign. On this point the exposition states: "The religious state also [therefore, not exclusively, as in the earlier draft of the document] has the
nature, importance, and value of a sign and witness: an
eschatological sign of the earthly life of Christ, a sign of the
quest for the kingdom of God even in the present life through
the imitation of Christ's virtues and by the power of the Holy
Spirit." Here again we find an echo of the document signed by
the six hundred and seventy-eight Father, who did not deny
the sign value but insisted that this value is secondary or
consequent: religious life is a sign because it has an intrinsic
value for sanctification and redemption.

Notes for Chapter 10

[1] Text of draft in *Acta Synodalia*, II/1, pp. 270-74 (nos. 31-35).
[2] *Acta Synodalia*, II/1, p. 281.
[3] *Acta Synodalia*, II/3, pp. 74 and 77, note 17.
[4] *Acta Synodalia*, II/3, pp. 382-84; quotation, p. 283.
[5] *Acta Synodalia*, II/3, p. 370.
[6] *Acta Synodalia*, II/4, p. 42.
[7] *Acta Synodalia*, II/4, p. 196.
[8] *Acta Synodalia*, II/4, pp. 227, 226.
[9] DS, 1810 (D, 980); *TCT*, no. 866, p. 338.
[10] St. Thomas Aquinas, *De perfectione vitae spiritualis*, ch. 15, in
Opuscula theologica, 2 (Turin: Marietti, 1954), no. 651, p. 134.
[11] *Acta Synodalia*, II/4, p. 176. The sentence of St. Thomas is from
Summa theologiae, 2-2, q. 186, a. 1.
[12] *Acta Synodalia*, II/4, p. 300.
[13] *Acta Synodalia*, II/4, p. 225.
[14] Paul VI, *Magno gaudio affecti: Address to Members of the General
Chapters of Several Religious Orders and Congregations*, May 23, 1964,
in *TPS*, 9 (1963-64), 398.
[15] *Ibid.*
[16] *Acta Synodalia*, II/4, p. 300.

Chapter 11

The Layman and the Salvific Mission of the Church

1. *The "Layman" in the Church*

If we are to grasp the full range and richness of what Vatican II has to say about the layman in the Church, we must do more than read and reflect on Chapter 4 of the Constitution on the Church, the chapter dedicated specifically to the laity. Chapter 1, on the mystery of the Church, chapter 2 on the people of God generally, and chapter 5 on the universal call to sanctity in the Church, all provide further elements of doctrine and open surprisingly rich spiritual perspectives to laymen. For, the term "layman," as understood in chapter 4 of *Lumen Gentium*, is a further specification of a wider and more general term: "Christian," "believer," "member of the people of God." Before someone is looked upon as either layman or deacon or priest or bishop or even pope, he should be considered first of all as a Christian or member of

God's people. These terms express the basic condition, the primal state, the common element, the most important aspect, indeed the very reason why there exists a divine plan for the human creature. It is in this common foundation on which all else rests, that the greatness, dignity, and newness brought by Christ properly reside. Without it we would be nothing, whether we happened to be pope, bishop, priest, deacon, or layman. "The chosen people of God is one: 'one Lord, one faith, one baptism' (Eph 4:5). As members, they share a common dignity from their rebirth in Christ. They have the same filial grace and the same vocation to perfection. They possess in common one salvation, one hope, and one undivided charity. Hence, there is in Christ and in the Church no inequality on the basis of race or nationality, social condition or sex, because 'there is neither Jew nor Greek; there is neither slave nor freeman; there is neither male nor female. For you are all "one" in Christ Jesus' (Gal. 3:28, Greek text; cf. Col 3:11). If therefore everyone in the Church does not proceed by the same path, nevertheless all are called to sanctity and have received an equal privilege of faith through the justice of God (cf. 2 Pet 1:1). And if by the will of Christ some are made teachers, dispensers of mysteries, and shepherds on behalf of others, yet all share a true equality with regard to the dignity and to the activity common to all the faithful for the building up of the Body of Christ" (LG 32b-c/58).

It is very important to grasp this basic point if we are to be able to see the Church and its varied membership as Vatican II does. This basic fact about the Church explains why the chapter on the hierarchy comes only in third place; it is also why those who make up the hierarchy (pope, bishops, priests, deacons) are deliberately and consistently presented as "servants of the people of God," nothing more. They are not the owners of the Church, the diocese, the parish, the community; they are not masters to be served and florified. The frequency and insistency with which the Constitution on the Church uses the words "service," "ministry," "diakonia" in speaking of the action of members of the hierarchy, indicates that the Council is here attempting to correct an outlook which is not quite evangelical but to which we had nonetheless become accustomed due to an unfortunate tradition dating back for centuries. The "prince," in the Church, with his tiaras and robes and rings and palaces and other adornments certainly did not originate with Christ or the first Apostle. We have been used to thinking of the Church as a pyramid: at the top, the pope, bishops, and priests, who preside, teach, sanctify, and govern, possessed of authority and power; at the base, the Christian people, passive recipients who seem to occupy a clearly inferior and secondary place.

There was a great deal of lively reaction to this kind of triumphalist clericalism as early as the first session of the Council (1962). In a memorable address of December 1, 1962 (thirty-first general meeting), Bishop Emile-Joseph de Smedt of Bruges made this incisive observation: "We must bear in mind that hierarchic power is a transitory thing, limited to this time of pilgrimage. In the life to come, our final state, such power will have no place, for the elect will have reached perfect unity in Christ. The people of God abides forever, the ministry of the hierarchy passes away. We must be careful not to fall into a 'hierarchism' when we speak of the Church; we must avoid every appearance of clericalism or bishopolatry or papolatry. The important thing is the people of God" (*Acta Synodalia*, I/4, p. 143). To this people of God, spouse of the Word, temple of the Holy Spirit must be rendered humble service by the hierarchy, so that it may grow and reach the mature age and full stature of Christ.

Such, then, is the general perspective within which we must view the position of the believer or Christian as "layman" in the Church; such is also the perspective within which we must think of the position of believer or Christian when he becomes "hierarch" in the Church. Both must be seen against the same background in which full equality exists between them. Both groups—"laymen" and "hierarchs"—are equally "believers," equally "Christians," equally members of God's people, temples of the Spirit, configured to Christ, and living with, through, and in him. Only after this common foundation has been laid do differences begin: "For the nurturing and constant growth of the people of God, Christ the Lord instituted in His Church a variety of ministries, which work for the good of the whole body. For those ministers who are endowed with sacred power are servants of their brethren, so that all who are of the people of God, and therefore enjoy a true Christian dignity, can work toward a common goal freely and in an orderly way, and arrive at salvation" (LG 18a/37). However, as the Council observes at the beginning of chapter 4 (on the laity) of the same document, those in a hierarchical role "also know that they themselves were not meant by Christ to shoulder alone the entire saving mission of the Church toward the world" (LG 30b/57). It is precisely here that the specific action of the Christian believer, as "layman" in the Church, begins. Let us then consider first of all the typological definition of the layman (consider, that is, what is typical or specific to the layman insofar as he is engaged in the saving mission of the Church); then we can pass on to the various competences he can or ought to have or receive in the apostolate.

2. Typological Definition of the "Layman"

The Constitution on the Church three points which characterize the Christian as "layman" in the Church:

(1) *Generic positive element* (not something exclusively proper to laymen, but which laymen must never forget does apply always and integrally to them as well as to others): "Everything which has been said so far concerning the people of God applies equally to the laity, religious, and clergy" (LG 30a/56). In this context we must lay stress, in the teaching of theology, on sanctifying and elevating grace (or on our elevation to the supernatural state, on man's adoptive but very real sonship in relation to God, and on the sanctification

of man), on the Mystical Body of Christ (or on our ontological insertion into Christ, our "Christification"), on the effects of the sacraments (or on the transformation effected in us by reception of the means of sanctification which Christ has instituted), and on the action of the Holy Spirit in the Church and in each of its members. The Council sums up the doctrine thus: "These faithful [specifically meant are the laity] are by baptism made one body with Christ and are established among the people of God. They are in their own way made sharers in the priestly, prophetic, and kingly functions of Christ. They carry out their own part in the mission of the whole Christian people with respect to the Church and the world" (LG 31a/57). This generic description offers an extraordinary rich content for a right understanding of the layman: it puts an end to the purely negative and passive conception of the layman, unequivocally rejects clericalism (the conception of the Church as domain of the clergy and the world as domain of the laity), gives the layman an active role in the Church, and makes him a sharer in the three powers (of sanctifying, teaching, and ruling) or total mission of the Church.

(2) *Negative element*: the layman does not receive the sacrament of orders (that is, is not a member of the hierarchy, which, according to chapter three of the Constitution on the Church, is made up of bishops, priests, and deacons), nor does he oblige himself to the evangelical counsels of consecrated chastity, poverty, and obedience (that is, he is not in the religious state which is approved by the Church and of which chapter six of the Constitution on the Church speaks at length). The Christian "layman" is thus distinguished from the Christian "cleric" and the Christian "religious" or "religious cleric."

(3) *Specific and functional element*: after stating the two elements already mentioned and after declaring that the layman is characterized by his "secular quality," the Council continues: "The laity, by their very vocation, seek the king-

dom of God by engaging in temporal affairs and by ordering them according to the plan of God. They live in the world, that is, in each and in all of the secular professions and occupations. They live in the ordinary circumstances of family and social life, from which the very web of their existence is woven. They are called there by God so that by exercising their proper function and being led by the spirit of the gospel they can work for the sanctification of the world from within, in the manner of leaven. In this way they can make Christ known to others, especially by the testimony of a life resplendent in faith, hope, and charity. The layman is closely involved in temporal affairs of every sort. It is therefore his special task to illumine and organize these affairs in such a way that they may always start out, develop, and persist according to Christ's mind, to the praise of the Creator and Redeemer" (LG 31c-d/57-58).

In this basic passage on the laity the Council twice says that we are dealing with a vocation, with men who are called by God. Therefore, to be a layman in the Church, in the sense that the Council understands the term "layman," implies a special call from God; it is a divine vocation to a special task. The layman is to "seek the kingdom of God by engaging in temporal affairs and by ordering them according to the plan of God." Among the various kinds of lay apostolate—sanctification, evangelization, and Christian involvement—the Council singles out the apostolate of involvement as the specific one to which God calls laymen. This is the layman's special vocation in the Church. It is not enough for the layman, then, to exercise his secular functions on a simply ethical and naturalistic basis; it is not enough for him simply to act correctly in his daily life; he may not limit himself to being a good secular man alongside other good secular men. Rather, he has the duty (the divine call!) to "seek the kingdom of God by engaging in temporal affairs and by ordering them according to the plan of God." If he does not live this calling, he empties his life of specifically Christian meaning. For, as one incorporated into Christ by baptism, the layman shares the priestly, prophetic, and royal functions of Christ and, as such, lives among temporal realities as a leaven in the mass, as the salt of the earth, as a light for the world. The Constitution on the Church says, therefore, that all, "whoever they are, . . . are called upon, as living members, to expend all their energy for the growth of the Church and its continuous sanctification" (LG 33a/59).

The text at this point continues: "The lay apostolate, however, is a participation in the saving mission of the Church itself. Through their baptism and confirmation, all are commissioned to that apostolate by the Lord Himself" (LG 33b/ 59). (This statement appeared in the text only after some discussion at the Council.) By baptism and confirmation all are (or ought to be) apostles; all share in the mission of the Church. And this mission consists essentially in spreading the kingdom of Christ throughout the world and bringing all men to share in the redemption so that they may, in turn, order the whole world to Christ and impregnate the temporal order with the spirit of the gospel. Each and every effort directed to that end is, in the proper sense of the word, an "apostolate" (cf. AA 2a/491).

Let us turn now to the various facets which this apostolate has inasmuch as laymen share in the priestly, prophetic, and royal offices of Jesus Christ.

3. The Priestly People of God and Its Apostolate of Sanctification

By their rebirth and their anointing with the Holy Spirit the baptized are "consecrated into a spiritual house and a holy priesthood" (LG 10a/27). Speaking directly of the laity, at a later point in the same document, the Council says that the eternal high priest, in uniting the laity in an intimate way with his own life and mission, grants them a share in his priestly function of spiritual worship, so that God may be glorified and men be saved (cf. LG 34b/60). Never has any document issued by the teaching authority in the Church spoken so explicitly and positively of this common priesthood (cf. LG 10 and 34). We need have no scruple about speaking of the "priestly people" (cf. LG 10a/26-27) or the "priestly community" (LG 11a/27-28). The document also speaks at generous length of the properly priestly action of the laity:

—offering spiritual sacrifices through all the works befitting the Christian man (LG 10a/27);

—proclaiming the power of Him who has called them from darkness into his light (*ibid.*);

—persevering in prayer and praising God together (*ibid.*);

—offering themselves as a living sacrifice, holy and pleasing to God (*ibid.*);

—taking part in the offering of the Eucharist (SC 10a/142; 11/143; 48/154);

—receiving the sacraments (LG 10/26-27 and, more explicitly 11/27-29), praying, giving thanks, witnessing by a holy life, practicing self-denial and active charity (LG 10b/27).

In another passage the Council opens up a broad and promising vista: "The laity, dedicated to Christ and anointed by the Holy Spirit, are marvelously called and equipped to produce in themselves ever more abundant fruits of the Spirit. For all their works, prayers, and apostolic endeavors, their ordinary married and family life, their daily labor, their mental and physical relaxation, if carried out in the Spirit, and even the hardships of life, if patiently borne—all of these become spiritual sacrifices acceptable to God through Jesus Christ (cf. 1 Pet 2:5). During the celebration of the Eucharist, these sacrifices are most lovingly offered to the Father along with the Lord's body. Thus, as worshippers whose every deed is holy, the laity consecrate the world itself to God" (LG 34b/60).

The Council thus presents us with a moving, holy, and deeply Christian picture of the layman's life, and one to which we must habituate ourselves much more than we have. It is a picture that ought to be the constant backdrop of our daily life, inspiring us to enter with ever growing awareness into the wonderful priestly community which the people of God is. Of that community the layman is a part: the layman aware of his dignity, sharing in the Mass by putting on the celebrant's paten his own works, undertakings, plans, and desires, his married and family life, his rest and recreation, his joys and troubles, all of them transformed into spiritual offerings, all of them united to the divine victim, all of them presented to God "through Him and with Him and in Him," so that God may receive all honor and glory. Such is, in essence, our living, conscious sharing in the priesthood of Christ.

The priestly people of God, after all, is and should be, above and before all else, a holy people. The Constitution on the Church devotes a whole chapter (the fifth) to "the call of the whole Church to holiness." It repeatedly insists on this vocation in expressions that admit of no exceptions: "In the Church, everyone belonging to the hierarchy, or being cared for by it, is called to holiness, according to the saying of the Apostle: 'For this is the will of God, your sanctification' (1 Th 4:3; cf. Eph 1:4)" (LG 39a/66); "The Lord Jesus, the divine Teacher and Model of all perfection, preached holiness of life to each and every one of His disciples, regardless of their situation" (LG 40a/66); "All the faithful of Christ of whatever rank or status are called to the fullness of the Christian life and to the perfection of charity" (LG 40c/67); "All of Christ's followers, therefore, are invited and bound to pursue holiness and the perfect fulfillment of their proper state" (LG 42h/72). "For He [the Lord Jesus] sent the Holy Spirit upon all men that He might inspire them from within to Love God with their whole heart and their whole soul, with all their mind and all their strength (cf. Mk 12:30) and that they might love one another as Christ loved them (cf. Jn 13:34; 15:12)" (LG 40a/66-67). Since all have truly become the children of God and sharers in his divine nature and since all have been rendered truly holy, they must preserve and bring to perfection in their lives the holiness they have received; they ought to live as holy people whom God has chosen for himself; they ought to put on the sentiments of compassion, generosity, humility, mildness, and patient endurance, and to produce in themselves the fruits of the Spirit. These fruits of the Spirit are: 'love, joy, peace, patient endurance, kindness, generosity, faith, mildness, and chastity" (Gal 5:22).

Only in these conditions will the layman be able effectively to carry on his apostolate. For the effectiveness of any apostolate depends on union with Christ "who is the light of the world, from whom we go forth, through whom we live, and toward whom our journey leads us" (LG 3b/16). Either we carry on our apostolate in union with Christ or we accomplish nothing: "Live on in me as I do in you. . . . He who lives in me and I in him, will produce abundantly, for apart from me you can do nothing" (Jn 15:4-5).

This apostolate of sanctification is, for the layman, a more individual and familial affair. The Constitution on the Church says, when speaking of the sacrament of matrimony, that Christian spouses, in virtue of this sacrament, "help each other to attain to holiness in their married life and by the rearing and education of their children" (LG 11d/29). The Council here speaks of the family as a kind of "domestic Church," in which "parents should, by their word and example, be the first preachers of the faith to their children" (LG 11e/29). The same subject comes up later on in the document: "Married couples and Christian parents should follow their own proper path to holiness by faithful love, sustaining one another in grace throughout the entire length of their lives. They should imbue their offspring, lovingly welcomed from God, with Christian truths and evangelical virtues. For thus they can offer all men an example of unwearying and generous love, builds up the brotherhood of charity, and stand as witnesses to and cooperators in the fruitfulness of Holy Mother Church. By such lives, they signify and share in that very love with which Christ loved His Bride and because of which He delivered Himself up on her behalf" (LG 41g/69).

In speaking of that apostolate of sanctification which the laity are to exercise in a direct way, we cannot forget the decision of the Constitution of the Liturgy, that some sacramentals may be administered even by lay people (SC 79/163). This important conciliar resolution has not been implemented as yet by the post-conciliar liturgical council. But I do not think the day far off when the father or mother of the family may exercise the priesthood they have in Christ by officially and solemnly blessing the food before meals, the labor before the harvest, the tools of their work, their home and children, etc.

4. *The Prophetic People of God or the Apostolate of Evangelization*

According to the Constitution on the Church the laity also share in the prophetic office of Christ (cf. LG 12/29-30; 31/57-58; 35/61-62). In the new covenant we have but one eternal high priest, one bridge-builder and mediator, namely, Christ who is a priest forever and in whose priestly function all the baptized share, though in various manners and degrees. So too we have but one prophet and teacher, namely, Christ, who is the light of the world and in whose prophetic mission all the baptized share, though in various manners and degrees. "Christ, the great Prophet, who proclaimed the kingdom of His Father by the testimony of His life and the power of His words, fulfills His prophetic office until His full glory is revealed. He does this not only through the hierarchy who teach in His name and with His authority, but also through the laity. For that very purpose He made them His witnesses and gave them understanding of the faith and the grace of speech cf. Acts 2:17-18; Apoc. 19:10), so that the power of the gospel might shine forth in their daily social and family life" (LG 35a/61).

Here, once again, is a basic conciliar text. At the very beginning of this fourth chapter the Constitution on the Church has already said: "Pastors also know that they themselves were not meant by Christ to shoulder alone the entire saving mission of the Church toward the world" and that they ought to "recognize their [the laity's] services and charismatic gifts that all according to their proper roles may cooperate in this common undertaking with one heart" (LG 30b/57). The Council speaks again, and rather emphatically, in LG 37/64-65, of the need that pastors should recognize the responsibility of the laity in the Church. Here, however, in LG 35, the Council declares in so many words that Christ continues to carry on his prophetic mission "not only through the hierarchy . . . but also through the laity." Furthermore, "He made them His witnesses and gave them understanding of the faith and the grace of speech, so that the power of the gospel might shine forth in their daily social and family life."

He made them His witnesses. Not only the hierarchy, then, but laymen as well are witnesses to Christ and are intended by Him to have this purpose and function. The Constitution frequently insists on this point. Some examples:

—"Everywhere on earth they must bear witness to Christ and give an answer to those who seek an account of that hope of eternal life which is in them" (LG 10a/27).

—They should offer the witness of a holy life (LG 10b/27).

—By their baptism they are obliged to "confess before men the faith which they have received from God through the Church" (LG 11a/28).

—Through confirmation they are especially enriched with the power of the Holy Spirit and thus "are more strictly obliged to spread and defend the Faith both by word and by need as true witnesses of Christ" (*ibid.*).

—They manifest Christ to others, "especially by the testimony of a life resplendent in faith, hope, and charity" (LG 31d/58).

—"Every layman . . . is at the same time a witness and a living instrument of the mission of the Church herself" (LG

33b/60).

—The laity "show themselves to be children of the promise, if, strong in faith and in hope, they make the most of the present time, and with patience await the glory that is to come. Let them not, then, hide this hope in the depths of their hearts, but even in the framework of secular life let them express it by a continual turning toward God and by wrestling 'against the world-rulers of this darkness, against the spiritual forces of wickedness' (Eph 6:12)" (LG 35b/61).

—Let them "steadfastly join to their profession of faith a life springing from faith. This evangelization, that is, this announcing of Christ by a living testimony as well as by the spoken word, takes on a specific quality and a special force in that it is carried out in the ordinary surroundings of the world" (LG 35c/61).

Above all, let us say it again, it is in married and family life that laymen carry on this kind of apostolate. "Where Christianity pervades a whole way of life and ever increasingly transforms it, there will exist both the practice and an excellent school of the lay apostolate. In such a home, husband and wife find their proper vocation in being witness to one another and to their children of faith in Christ and love for Him. The Christian family loudly proclaims both the present virtues of the kingdom of God and the hope of a blessed life to come. Thus by its example and its witness it accuses the world of sin and enlightens those who seek the truth" (LG 35d/61-62).

We must also remark how in all these texts the Council stresses the theological virtues of faith, hope, and charity. Above all, it stresses hope, a neglected but basic virtue. The contemporary world, so much in the grip of anxiety, fear, and desperation, has a very great need of hope. This is why, today especially, the laity must be living witnesses of Christian hope "and give an answer to those who seek an account of that hope of eternal life which is in them" (LG 10a/27). They must not hide that hope within themselves but express it in the structures of secular life" (LG 35b/61), so that, especially in the Christian family, they will loudly proclaim "the hope of a blessed life to come" (LG 35d/61). Then others—the despairing, those tormented by anxiety—will feel drawn to the same blessed life of faith, hope, and love. That is a real apostolate. The laity who exercise it will indeed be a light for the world, salt for the earth.

He gave them understanding of the faith. The "he" here is Christ who gives laymen a "sense of the faith" so that they may better share in his prophetic mission. Back in chapter 2 on the Constitution on the Church, in a similar context (the shaaring of the people of God generally in the prophetic mission of Christ), the Council had given a brief explanation of the understanding of faith which the Christian people possesses. "Anointed as they are by the Holy One (cf. Jn 2:20, 27)," the baptized have a supernatural sense of the faith, that is, a special ability by reason of which the people as a whole cannot be deceived in the act of faith but receive God's word, cling to it without fail, penetrate more deeply into it, and apply it to their lives (LG 12a-b/29-30). In these paragraphs the Council teaches that the sense of faith "is aroused and sustained by the Spirit of truth" and that this sense produces its wonderful effects "under the lead of a sacred teaching authority to which it [the people] loyally defers" (LG 12b).

As the Council understands it, this sense of faith in Christians (and therefore in laymen too) is not simply the act of faith in God's word as guarded and infallibly taught by the teaching authority in the Church. Rather, in all, " 'from the bishops down to the last member of the laity' " (LG 12a; the Council is here quoting some words of St. Augustine), the sense of faith is aroused and sustained by the Holy Spirit and not by the teaching activity of the Church's teaching authority. By this same divine action each individual receives God's word, clings to it without fail, penetrates more deeply into it, and applies it to his life. In all this the teaching activity of the Church plays a merely directive or orientational role ("under the lead of a sacred teaching authority"). The

Constitution on the Church supposes a doctrine similar to this when it says that the Apostles, in preaching the gospel everywhere, were "accepted by their hearers under the influence of the Holy Spirit" and in this way gathered together the universal Church (LG 19b/39).

He gave them the grace of speech. He did so with the intention of making them better sharers in his own prophetic function. In this context (LG 35a/61), the Council does not explain what it means by "the grace of speech." But the fact that "the grace of speech" is closely linked with "the understanding of the faith" is an implicit reference back to LG 12c/30 where, after speaking of the "sense of faith," the Council goes on to expound a doctrine concerning the charisms or gifts which the Holy Spirit bestows on the Christian people. The text is clear enough: "It is not only through the sacraments and Church ministries that the same Holy Spirit sanctifies and leads the people of God and enriches it with virtues. Allotting His gifts 'to everyone according as he will' (1 Cor. 12:11), He distributes special graces among the faithful of every rank. By these gifts He makes them fit and ready to undertake the various tasks or offices advantageous for the renewal and upbuilding of the Church, according to the words of the Apostle: 'The manifestation is given to everyone for profit' (1 Cor 12:7)."

Note here that the Council distinguishes between the action of the Holy Spirit that is exercised through the sacraments and ministries and the action of the Holy Spirit that is exercised through the charisms; the Council is saying, in other words, that there can be a divine action which is not bound up with the sacraments and ministries. The Holy Spirit is not inseparably bound up with a certain circle of persons. When we speak of charisms, however, we often succumb to the temptation to think only of extraordinary and astounding gifts, such as the gift of tongues, the gift of healing, the gifts of miracles, etc. St. Paul knew these very spectacular gifts but he also speaks of the gift of explaining the highest religious truths as well as of presenting the most elementary teaching on Christ (the charism or grace of speech). He speaks, too, of the charisms of faith, preaching, exhortation, consolation, service, discernment of spirits, helping the needy, the administration and direction of churches, etc. (cf. Rom 12 and 1 Cor 12). For St. Paul, the Church is not simply a well organized administrative entity. It is rather above all a living complex of gifts, charisms, and services. The Spirit is given to all the baptized; to each and all he distributes his gifts and charisms, "that differ according to the favor bestowed on each of us" (Rom 12:6). The Constitution on the Church goes on to say: "These charismatic gifts, whether they be the most outstanding or the more simple and widely diffused, are to be received with thanksgiving and consolation, for they are exceedingly suitable and useful for the needs of the Church. Still, extradorinary gifts are not to be rashly sought after, nor are the fruits of apostolic labor to be presumptuously expected from them. In any case, judgment as to their genuineness and proper use belongs to those who preside over the Church, and to whose special competence it belongs, not indeed to extinguish the Spirit, but to test all things and to hold fast to that which is good (cf. 1 Th. 5:12, 19-21)" (LG 12c-d/30). Later on, the Constitution reminds pastors of their duty of recognizing the charismatic gifts of the laity (LG 30b/57). The Council also bids priests to "acknowledge with joy, and foster with diligence the various humble and exalted charisms of the laity" (PO 9d/553).

The "grace of speech," then, is given the laity by Christ so that they may more readily share in his prophetic mission and so that the power of the gospel may shine forth more perfectly in their daily social and family life (LG 35a/61). The grace is a special gift of the Holy Spirit and shall not be lacking in anyone who sincerely dedicates himself to the apostolate of evangelization. For, very often, the simple apostolate of witnessing is not enough. In speaking of the effects of confirmation, the Council teaches that the faithful "are endowed by the Holy Spirit with special strength. Hence they are more strictly obliged to spread and defend the faith both by word and by deed as true witnesses of Christ" (LG 11a/28). Again, in speaking of the missionary nature of the Church, the same Constitution declares that "the obligation of spreading the faith is imposed on every disciple of Christ, according to his ability" (LG 17c/36). Similarly, when speaking directly of the layman's sharing in the prophetic function of Christ, the Council expressly mentions the "evangelization . . . of Christ . . . by the spoken word" (LG 35c/61), and ends this latter section with the opportune, and even necessary, admonition: "Therefore, let the laity strive skillfully to acquire a more profound grasp of revealed truth, and insistently beg of God the gift of wisdom" (LG 35c/62). In this way it can be said of each lay person, as the evangelist said it of John the Baptist: he came "only to testify to the light, for he himself was not the light" (Jn 1:8).

5. *The Royal People of God and Its Apostolate of Involvement*

Christ is our eternal priest, sole mediator, and supreme pontiff; in him all the baptized have been incorporated and have thus become the priestly people of God. Christ is our great prophet, exclusive teacher, and radiant light of the world; in him all the baptized have been incorporated and have thus become the prophetic people of God. Christ is our king, shepherd, lord, and head; in him we have been incorporated and have become the royal people of God. "It was for this reason that God sent His Son, whom He appointed heir of all things (cf. Heb 1:2), that He might be Teacher, King, and Priest of all, Head of the new and universal people of the sons of God" (LG 13a/30-31). The Constitution on the Church expressly affirms that by reason of their baptism the faithful also share in the kingly function of Christ (LG 31a/57) and dedicates the whole of no. 36/62-64 to this subject. After recalling that "to Him all things are made subject until He subjects Himself and all created things to the Father, that God may be all in all," the Council declares that the divine King "has communicated this power of subjection to His disciples" (LG 36a/62). His disciples must, first of all, overcome the reign of sin in themselves through self-denial and a holy life. Thus they will achieve the necessary inner freedom and self-mastery. Such spiritual liberty, which includes the power to overcome oneself, is basic if we are to exercise our sharing in the kingly mission of Christ.

But the Lord wishes "to spread His kingdom by means of the laity also, a kingdom of truth and life, a kingdom of holiness and grace, a kingdom of justice, love and peace. In this kingdom, creation itself will be delivered out of its slavery to corruption and into the freedom of the glory of the sons of God (cf. Rom 8:21)" (LG 36b/62). Such cooperation in the king's service, however, supposes a Christian conception of life and the world, as well as a profound understanding of creation, its value and eternal destiny. Therefore the Council adds: "The faithful . . . must learn the deepest meaning and the value of all creation, and how to relate it to the praise of God" (LG 36c/62). Once they have absorbed this Christian conception of the world, the laity will be able to undertake the apostolate most proper to them: that of animation or inspiration, that is, the effort to imbue with the Christian spirit the mentality and customs, the laws and institutions of society or the community. This is the apostolate of restoring the temporal order to Christ.

The temporal order includes the good things of life, family, culture, the economy, the arts and professions, national politics and international relations, and the development and progress of these (cf. AA 7b/497). All these things have more than a simply subsidiary value in relation to the ultimate purpose of man; they also have their own specific value, their autonomy and natural finality, their own laws, and their importance in the service of man. To the extent, therefore, that these things do help man, God wants to raise them to the supernatural order, in Christ Jesus, "so that primacy may be his in everything" (Col 1:18). In striving to accomplish this elevation, we must recognize that the temporal order has been seriously distorted by man. Many people make an idol of the temporal order and thus become its slaves instead of its masters. This is what an apostolate of restoration of the temporal order (what is called today an apostolate of "animation") is required. "It is his [the layman's] special task to illumine and organize these [temporal] affairs in such a way that they may always start out, develop, and persist according to Christ's mind, to the praise of the Creator and Redeemer" (LG 31d/58). "In this way [by relating all to the praise of God] the world is permeated by the spirit of Christ and more effectively achieves its purpose in justice, charity, and peace. The laity have the principal role in the universal fulfillment of this purpose. Therefore, by their competence in secular fields and by their personal activity, elevated from within by the grace of Christ, let them labor vigorously so that by human labor, technical skill, and civic culture created goods may be perfected for the benefit of every last man, according to the design of the Creator and the light of His Word" (LG 36c-d/62-63). Laymen are to bring healing to the institutions and conditions of the world, so that all things may be done in justice and favor the practice of virtue. Thus they will harmonize human works and culture with moral values, "better prepare the field of the world for the seed of the word of God" and "open wider the Church's doors, through which the message of peace can enter the world" (LG 36e/63).

The Council notes, however, that even while laymen "distinguish carefully between those rights and duties which are theirs as members of the Church, and those which they have as members of human society," they must bear in mind "that in every temporal affair they must be guided by a Christian conscience. For even in secular affairs there is no human activity which can be withdrawn from God's dominion" (LG 36f/63).

According to the knowledge, competence, and ability of each one, the layman has the right and even, at times, the duty "to express his opinion on things which concern the good of the Church" (LG 37a/64). He is to do this "in truth, in courage, and in prudence" (*ibid.*). (The word "courage" was expressly kept in the text despite the objections of some bishops.) In this same number of the Constitution on the Church, the Fathers address the following serious recommendation to those in authority in the Church: "Let sacred pastors recognize and promote the dignity as well as the responsibility of the layman in the Church. Let them willingly make use of his prudent advice. Let them confidently assign duties to him in the service of the Church, allowing him freedom and room for action. Further, let them encourage the layman so that he may undertake tasks on his own initiative. Attentively in Christ, let them consider with fatherly love the projects, suggestions, and desires proposed by the laity. Furthermore, let pastors respectfully acknowledge that just freedom which belongs to everyone in this earthly city" (LG 37c/64-65). In another document, the Council urges priests to "sincerely acknowledge and promote the dignity of the laity and the role which is proper to them in the mission of the Church. They should scrupulously honor that just freedom which is due to everyone in this earthly city. They should listen to the laity willingly, consider their wishes in a fraternal spirit, and recognize their experience and competence in the different areas of human activity, so that together with them they may be able to read the signs of the times. . . . Priests should also confidently entrust to the laity duties in the service of the Church, allowing them freedom and room for action. In fact, on suitable occasions, they should invite them to undertake works on their own initiative" (PO 9c-d/552-53).

The Council ends its important no. 37 of the Constitution on the Church with the following words: "A great many benefits are to be hoped for from this familiar dialogue between the laity and their pastors: in the laity, a strengthened sense of personal responsibility, a renewed enthusiasm, a more ready application of their talents to the projects of their pastors. The latter, for their part, aided by the experience of the laity, can more clearly and more suitably come to decisions regarding spiritual and temporal matters. In this way, the whole Church, strengthened by each one of its members, can more effectively fulfill its mission for the life of the world" (LG 37d/65).

The same document expressly describes the apostolate of animation in the last paragraph of Chapter 4: "Each individual layman must stand before the world as a witness to the resurrection and life of the Lord Jesus and as a sign that God lives. As a body and individually, the laity must do their part to nourish the world with spiritual fruits (cf. Gal 5:22), and to spread abroad in it that spirit by which are animated those poor, meek, and peacemaking men whom the Lord in the gospel calls blessed (cf. Mt 5:3-9). In a word, 'what the soul is to the body, let Christians be to the world'" (LG 38/65).

Chapter 12

The Ecclesial Community
after Death

1. *The Church beyond the Grave*

All those who in the Church are vitally united to Christ and
his Spirit are united by the same bonds to each other and
form a *koinonia* or communion of saints. Strictly speaking,
sinners (that is, those who do not live in Christ and do not
possess his Spirit) are not his disciples, even though they are
affiliated with the Church. (The Constitution on the Church
teaches that the sinner "remains indeed in the bosom of the
Church, but, as it were, only in a 'bodily' manner and not
in his heart'": LG 14b/33.). Consequently, when Vatican
II deals with the eschatological character of the pilgrim
Church and with its union with the heavenly Church (in
chapter 7 of the Constitution on the Church), it divides the
disciples of Christ into three categories: "Some of His disciples are exiles on earth. Some have finished with this life and

are being purified. Others are in glory, beholding 'clearly God Himself one and triune, as He is' " (LG 49a/80).

Those who will "go to hell" are not truly disciples of Christ, and there is, therefore, no special category for them. When modifications of the text were being suggested, one Council Father asked for a clearer statement of fact that some people are indeed condemned to hell (Modification no. 40): "One Father wishes the introduction of a statement to the effect that there are in fact some who are reprobate (lest damnation remain a simple, unrealized possibility)." The Theological Commission replied that the proposed statement did not belong in LG 49 and that LG 48, in speaking of hell, cites texts of Christ "in which the Lord speaks of the damned as of a future fact."

The Council teaches, then, that all in the above-mentioned three categories form a unity or, as LG 50a/81 puts it, "the whole Mystical Body of Jesus Christ" (the Council avoids the expression "communion of saints"). "For all who belong to Christ, having His Spirit, form one Church and cleave together in Him" (LG 49b/81). *Death, therefore, does not mean an interruption of ecclesial communion.* "The exchanging of spiritual goods" (LG 49b/81) or the "vital fellowship" (LG 51a/83) is not only not broken; it is even strengthened. For, the Council argues, "by reason of the fact that those in heaven are more closely united with Christ, they establish the whole Church more firmly in holiness, lend nobility to the worship which the Church offers on earth to God, and in many ways contribute to its greater upbuilding" (LG 49c/81).

In this doctrinal context some Fathers suggested (in Modification no. 35) that something be said clearly about the calling up of spirits or spiritualism; they were afraid that the doctrine about our exchange of spiritual goods with the deceased could be the occasion for interpretations of a spiritualist kind. The Council therefore added note 228, in which it refers to various earlier documents of the Holy See "against any evoking of the spirits" (which, the Commission declares, has nothing to do with the "supernatural communion of the saints". The Commission then went on to point out what it is that is wrong in spiritualism: "The act of evocation which claims to give rise to a perceptible exchange, by human means, with spirits or separated souls, with the purpose of receiving messages or other kinds of help." As the description shows, the essential thing in a communication of the spiritualist kind is the claim "to give rise, by human means, to a perceptible exchange" with spirits or separated souls. Communications which do not arise by human means (for example, spontaneous apparitions) or which are not perceptible (for example, the invocation of saints or souls) are not spiritualist in character. Vatican II refers to earlier documents of the Holy See (Pope Alexander IV spoke on the subject as early as September 27, 1258), chiefly to the statement of August 4, 1856, and the reply of April 24, 1917. The former document repeated the prohibition against "calling up the souls of the dead and receiving their replies"[1] (this was at the period when Allan Kardec and his followers at Paris were systematically practicing the evocation of spirits[2]). In the reply of 1917, the Holy Office says that it is wrong "to attend spiritualist seances or manifestations (whether or not a medium or hypnotism be used), however good and pious such meetings may seem, and to question souls or spirits, or to listen to their answers, or even just to look on while protesting overtly or covertly that one wants nothing to do with evil spirits."[3]

Our relations with those who still require purification after their earthly life is over (who are still being purified after death": LG 51a/83-84) must be seen in the light of Vatican II's doctrine on the fact that death does not interrupt ecclesial communion and that the exchange of spiritual goods is even intensified. The Church, says the Council has always "cultivated with great piety the memory of the dead, and it cites the well-known text from Maccabees: "It is 'a holy and wholesome thought to pray for the dead that they may be loosed from sins' (2 Mach 12:46)" (LG 50a/81).

In an earlier draft the text went on to say that, as the inscriptions in the Roman Catacombs and the Church's prayers for the dead show, she also trusts in the prayers of the dead for us. This passage was removed; and when suggestions were being made, one Father (Modification no. 44) asked that it be restored. The Commission refused, "lest the text seem to resolve a disputed question."

In *Lumen Gentium* 51a/83-84 the Council again refers to "this vital fellowship with our brethren . . . who are still being purified after death" and renews the decrees of the Councils of Florence and Trent. In its Decree for the Greeks, the Council of Florence (1439 A.D.) speaks of the dead who require purification and can be helped by the prayers of their brothers on earth, that is, by Masses, prayers, alms, and other acts of piety.[4]

More important is Vatican II's reaffirmation of the doctrinal and pastoral decisions of the Council of Trent. Vatican II refers to the Tridentine Decree on Purgatory and to Canon 30 of the Tridentine Decree on Justification. The latter (from the year 1567) condemns anyone who says that "after receiving the grace of justification, the guilt of any repentant sinner is remitted in such a way that no debt of temporal punishment remains to be paid, either in this life or in purgatory, before the gate to the kingdom of heaven can be opened."[5] The Decree on Purgatory (1563 A.D.) refers to Canon 30 on justification, and to the doctrine that the Mass can be offered "for those who have died in Christ and are not yet wholly cleansed,"[6] and "commands the bishops to be diligently on guard that the true doctrine on purgatory . . . be preached everywhere, and that Christians be instructed in it, believe in it, and adhere to it. But let the more difficult and subtle controversies, which neither edify nor generally cause any increase of piety, be omitted from the ordinary sermons to the poorly instructed. Likewise, they should not permit anything that is uncertain or anything that appears to be false to be treated in popular or learned publications. And they should forbid as scandalous and injurious to the faithful whatever is characterized by a kind of curiosity and superstition, or is prompted by motives of dishonorable gain. . . ."[7] The Council of Trent, was evidently, rather moderate and reserved in its anti-Protestant position in favor of purgatory. In its pastoral practice, however, though not in its official doctrine, the post-Tridentine Church took much less reserved positions, and a large number of pastors disobeyed the wise pastoral norms of the Council of Trent.

2. Our Communion with the Saints

By "saints" we mean those who, canonized or not, are in heavenly glory, "beholding 'clearly God Himself triune and one, as He is' " (LG 49a/80). Or, as it was explained by Pope Benedict XII in 1336 ("We, with our apostolic authority, make the following definition"): "those souls which need no purification or have been purified "see the divine essence with an intuitive and even face-to-face vision, without the interposition of any creature in the function of the object seen; rather, the divine essence immediately manifests itself to them plainly, clearly, openly. . . . Those who see the divine essence in this way take great joy from it, and . . . because of this vision and enjoyment the souls of those who have already died are truly blessed and possess life and eternal rest."[8]

Other descriptions of the "saints":

—those who are "finanlly . . . caught up in peace and utter happiness in that fatherland radiant with the splendor of the Lord" (GS 93b/307);

—those who are "joined to Him in an endless sharing of a divine life beyond all corruption" and "have found true life with God" (GS 18d/215);

—those who realize their "call to communion with God" (GS 19a/215) and "to share in His happiness" (GS 21c/218);

—those who "communicate in life and glory with Himself" (AG 2b/585);

—those who live in "a personal relationship with Him in Christ" (AG 13b/600);

—those who "inherit the kingdom prepared for you [them] from the creation of the world" (Mt 25:34) and enter into "eternal life" (Mt 25:46);

—those who already have "the glory to be revealed in us" (Rom 8:18);

—those who are with Christ (cf. Phil 1:23);

—those who possess the "imperishable inheritance, incapable of fading or defilement, which is kept in heaven for you [them]" (1 Pet 1:4);

— those who know from experience what it means to be a child of God and to be like God (cf. 1 Jn 3:2).

If we are to grasp the doctrine on Vatican II on our relations with the saints, we must turn to the Constitution on the Church, no. 49, in which the Council offers us a short but accurate theological explanation of *the action of the heavenly saints in our favor.* This action can only be parallel to the intercessory activity of the glorified Christ (cf. Heb 7:24-25), which is the *prolongation of His salvific activity on earth.* So with the saints: "Their good works accompany them" (Rev 14:13). In heaven now "they show forth the merits which they won on earth through the one Mediator between God and man, Christ Jesus (cf. 1 Tim. 2:5). There they served God in all things and filled up in their flesh whatever was lacking of the sufferings of Christ on behalf of His body which is the Church." Now, "received into their heavenly home and . . . present to the Lord (cf. 2 Cor 5:8), through Him and with Him and in Him, they do not cease to intercede with the Father for us." The Council concludes: "Thus by their brotherly interest our weakness is very greatly strengthened" (LG 49c/81).

Earlier, in the Constitution on the Liturgy, the Council had taught that "raised up to perfection by the manifold grace of God, and already in possession of eternal salvation, they [the saints] sing God's perfect praise in heaven and offer prayers for us. By celebrating the passage of these saints from earth to heaven the Church proclaims the paschal mystery as achieved in the saints who have suffered and been glorified with Christ; she proposes them to the faithful as examples who draw all to the Father through Christ, and through their merits [acquired on earth] she pleads for God's favors" (SC 104/168).

In the chapter on our Lady, especially in nos. 61-62, the Council describes in greater detail the intercessory activity of heaven. In this context, too, Vatican II is careful to connect the present mediatorial action of heaven with the earlier earthly life. Thus, during her life on earth Mary "cooperated . . . in the Savior's work of restoring supernatural life to souls" (LG 61/91). The Council continues: "This maternity of Mary in the order of grace began with the consent which she gave in faith at the Annunciation and which she sustained without wavering beneath the cross. This maternity will last without interruption until the eternal fulfillment of all the elect. For, taken up to heaven, she did not lay aside this saving role, but by her manifold acts of intercession continues to win for us gifts of eternal salvation. By her maternal charity Mary cares for the brethren of her Son who still journey on earth surrounded by dangers and difficulties, until they are led to their happy fatherland" (LG 62a-b/91).

In these considerations we have, evidently, the main justification for our confidence in the heavenly saints, the basis for our devotion to them, and the foundation of the traditional veneration of the saints. "It is supremely fitting, therefore, that we love these friends and fellow heirs of Jesus Christ, who are also our brothers and extraordinary benefactors, that we render due thanks to God for them and 'suppliantly invoke them and have recourse to their prayers, their power and help in obtaining benefits from God through His Son, Jesus Christ, our Lord, who is our sole Redeemer and Savior' " (LG 50e/83). But the Council is careful to add an explanation: "For by its very nature every genuine testimony of

ECCLESIAL COMMUNITY AFTER DEATH

love which we show to those in heaven tends toward and terminates in Christ, who is the 'crown of all saints.' Through Him it tends toward and terminates in God, who is wonderful in His saints and is magnified in them" (*ibid.*).

The Council's care *not to dissociate the saints from Christ and Christ from God* frequently reappears in other documents and contexts. This fact does not represent a simple concern with answering an often voiced objection of Protestants; it is due primarily to the desire to correct a distortion and contradiction in some popular piety. For in the latter the saint sometimes becomes an autonomous figure, cut off from the mystery of Christ. When the saint is thus absolutized, he becomes an idol, and the veneration paid him becomes idolatry. What the Council teaches us in the chapter on our Lady is in principle valid for the saints and their relation to Christ as well. The point is important enough to merit special attention here.

Let us read, first, the carefully worded text of the Council: "We have but one Mediator, as we know from the words of the Apostle: 'For there is but one God, and one Mediator between God and men, himself man, Christ Jesus, who gave himself a ransom for all' (1 Tim 2:5-6). The maternal duty of Mary toward men in no way obscures or diminishes this unique mediation of Christ, but rather shows its power. For all the saving influences of the Blessed Virgin on men originate, not from some inner necessity, but from the divine pleasure. They flow forth from the superabundance of the merits of Christ, rest on His mediation, depend entirely on it, and draw all their power from it. In no way do they impede the immediate union of the faithful with Christ. Rather, they foster this union" (LG 60/90-91).

Here we are in the presence, once again, of the principle of mediation and representation in God's plan which is the basis of our whole doctrine on the Church. Theoretically speaking, there could have been many possible ways of determining how man was to be related to God. We can say with the Council that the dispensation or situation which is actually our originates "not from some inner necessity, but from the divine pleasure." The Lord decided that this is how it is to be. This positive will of God is known to us only by revelation. God could, then, have given us his gifts directly, without any mediation and even without any petition or intercession. But in fact, as revelation tells us, God makes the gift of his blessings dependent onp rayer, intercession, mediation, and representation. "Ask and you will receive" (Mt 7:7-16; Lk 11:1-13; Jn 16:23-24; and many other texts). If a person does not ask, he will not receive. We must even ask persistently (Lk 11:5-8). God wants secondary causes to come into play; in the order of grace, he looks for at least this minimal initiative on our part.

The Apostle's words on the one mediator should, moreover, be read in their context. In the immediately preceding verses, St. Paul urges "that petitions, prayers, intercessions, and thanksgivings be offered for all men. . . . Prayer of this kind is good, and God our savior is pleased with it" (1 Tim 2:1,3). He goes on to argue that God is one, and his will to save embraces all men; therefore we should not imagine that any people is saved by its own "gods." As there is only one God, so there is only one Mediator between God and men: the man Jesus Christ, and not many mediators, with a different one for each people. It is with this in mind, and against this background, that the Apostle insists on the oneness of the Mediator. He is not implying at all that there is not or cannot be any cooperation by men in the mediatorial work of Christ; on the contrary, he straightway speaks of himself as chosen to be this truth's "herald and apostle . . . , the teacher of the nations in the true faith" (1 Tim 2:7).

It is clear that this "subordinate role" (LG 62d/92) of the saints' mediation must always be so understood as not to "take away from nor add anything to the dignity and efficacy of Christ the one Mediator" (LG 62b/92). The Council illustrates its meaning by two comparisons: "Just as the priesthood of Christ is shared in various ways both by sacred ministers and by the faithful, and as the one goodness of God is in reality communicated diversely to His creatures, so also the unique mediation of the Redeemer does not exclude but rather gives rise among creatures to a manifold cooperation which is but a sharing in this unique source" (LG 62c/92).

We are interested in the saints not only because they intercede for us and are our benefactors, but also because they are *examples for us to follow.* "When we look at the lives of those who have faithfully followed Christ, we are inspired with a new reason for seeking the city which is to come (Heb 13:14; 11:10). At the same time we are shown a most safe path by which, among the vicissitudes of this world and in keeping with the state in life and condition proper to each of us, we will be able to arrive at perfect union with Christ, that is, holiness" (LG 50c/82). Here Vatican II refers us to Heb 13:7; Sir 44-50; Heb 11:3-40, and a passage from Pius XII's encyclical *Mediator Dei.*

Heb 13:7: "Remember your leaders who spoke the word of God to you; consider how their lives ended, and imitate their faith." Sir 44-50 is a lengthy panegyric to those who had gone before. In Heb 11:3-40 the Apostle describes the heroes of earlier times, down to the coming of Christ, who believed without seeing and who died as believers without having received the promises, since "without us they [the ancestors] were not to be made perfect." In *Mediator Dei* Pius XII writes: "In the virtues of the saints the virtue of Jesus Christ is variously reflected, and we must imitate them as they imitated Christ. In some we see apostolic zeal, in others an heroic fortitude that shrank not from the shedding of their blood; in some we see constant watchfulness in expectation of the Redeemer, in others a virginal purity of soul and the gracious modesty of Christian humility; and in all we see a burning love of God and their neighbor. All these gems of holiness are set before our eyes by the liturgy that we may gaze upon them with profit to our souls and that 'rejoicing in their merits we may be set on fire by their example' (Roman Missal, Third Collect for Feast of Several Martyrs outside Paschal Time). Thus we must observe 'innocence in simplicity, harmony in charity, modesty in humility, diligence in administration, vigilance in helping those who labor, mercy in assisting the poor, constancy in defending the truth, and strictness in self-discipline; so that in all good works we may follow their example. These are the footsteps which the saints, on the way back to their heavenly country, have left behind them, so that following in their path we may share their joys' (St. Bede the Venerable, *Homily* 70: *Feast of All Saints*). And in order that our senses also may be stimulated to salutary purpose the Church desires images of the saints to be exposed in our churches, always to the end that 'we may imitate the virtue of those whose images we revere' (Roman Missal, Collect in Mass of St. John of Damascus)."⁹

The lives of the saints thus have for us a genuine *apologetic value*. "In the lives of those who shared in our humanity and yet were transformed into especially successful images of Christ (cf. 2 Cor 3:18), God vividly manifests to men His presence and His face. He speaks to us in them, and gives us a sign of His kingdom, to which we are powerfully drawn, surrounded as we are by so many witnesses (cf. Heb 12:1), and having such an argument for the truth of the gospel" (LG 50c/82). This was one of the arguments for the credibility of the Church to which Vatican I (here cited by Vatican II) called our attention: "The Church itself, because of . . . its exalted sanctity, and its inexhaustible fruitfulness in all that is good, . . . is a great and perpetual motive of credibility and an irrefutable proof of its own divine mission."¹⁰

It is by contemplating the lives of those who have now reached true life with God that we can better understand the meaning of our own existence. For such men and women have become what we hope to be. As the Council puts it in an eloquent passage on the Blessed Virgin Mary: "In her the Church . . . joyfully contemplates, as in a faultless model, that which she herself wholly desires and hopes to be" (SC 103/ 168). For, "in the most holy Virgin the Church has already reached . . . perfection" (LG 65a/93). The same can, in substance, be said of the saints. Our life, activity, suffering, and death acquire their meaning and become transparent only in the light of divine revelation concerning our full vocation and final destiny. The eschatological hope which shines forth so splendidly in the saints encourages, strengthens, and guides us. Without God and his revelation the riddles of life and death, of sin and suffering, would remain unsolved. For, when left to his own resources, man is a mystery and insoluble problem to himself. "When God is forgotten, the creature itself grows unintelligible"; "without the Creator the creature would disappear" (GS 36e/234). The saints, therefore, are the living example of what God wants to make for us. In them we contemplate the fulfillment of God's plan for men.

3. *Our Veneration of the Saints*

In the light of what we have been saying, we will not be surprised by the Council's statement in the Constitution on the Church concerning the veneration of the saints: "This most sacred Synod accepts with great devotion the venerable faith of our ancestors regarding this vital fellowship with our brethren who are in heavenly glory or who are still being purified after death. It proposes again the decrees of the Second Council of Nicea, the Council of Florence, and the Council of Trent" (LG 51a/83-84).

At the Second Council of Nicea (787 A.D.) the Church took a strong stand against the iconoclasts; we shall see the text when we come to speak of images. The Council of Florence (1439 A.D.) dealt with purgatory; we have already seen the passage in question. Vatican II refers us to three documents of the Council of Trent, one on the saints and two on purgatory (these last have already been cited). On the invocation of the saints Trent says: "The holy council orders all bishops and others who have the official charge of teaching to instruct the faithful diligently, in accordance with the practice of the Catholic and apostolic Church from the early years of the Christian religion, and in accordance with the common teaching of the holy Fathers and the decrees of the sacred councils. First of all they should instruct the faithful carefully concerning the intercession and the invocation of the saints, the honor due to their relics, and the lawful use of images—teaching the faithful that the saints, reigning together with Christ, pray to God for men; it is a good and useful thing to invoke the saints humbly and to have recourse to their prayers and to their efficacious help to obtain favors from God through his Son Jesus Christ our Lord who alone is our redeemer and savior. Moreover, they should teach the faithful that only men of irreligious mentality deny that the saints enjoying eternal happiness in heaven are to be invoked, or claim either that the saints do not pray for men or else that calling upon them to pray for us even as individuals is idolatry or is opposed to the word of God or is prejudicial to the honor of the one Mediator of God and men, Jesus Christ (see 1 Tim 2:5); or say that it is foolish to make supplication by word or by thought to those who are reigning in heaven."[11]

The text of the Constitution on the Church continues: "At the same time, as part of its own pastoral solicitude, this Synod urges all concerned to work hard to prevent or correct any abuses, excesses, or defects which may have crept in here and there, and to restore all things to a more ample praise of Christ and of God. Let the faithful be taught, therefore, that the authentic cult of the saints consists not so much in the multiplying of external acts, but rather in the intensity of our active love. By such love, for our own greater good and that of the Church, we seek from the saints the 'example of their way of life, fellowship in their communion, and aid by their intercession.' At the same time, let the people be instructed that our communion with those in heaven, provided that it is understood in the more adequate light of faith, in no way weakens, but conversely, more thoroughly enriches the supreme worship we give to God the Father, through Christ, in the Spirit" (LG 51a-b/84).

The Council here implies that "abuses, excesses, and defects" do exist and should be prevented or corrected. Anyone acquainted with popular piety will have no difficulty in honestly admitting that abuses and excesses indeed exist and that in some places they are even frequent and widespread. It would be very easy to give a list of examples (at least for Brazil): practices that are frivolous and extravagant, or at times even grotesque and brutal; prayers that are absurd and ridiculous and, frequently, even irreverent, erroneous, and heretical.[12] The Second General Conference of Latin American Bishops, at Medellin in 1968, took up the subject in its document on "Pastoral Care of the Masses." The bishops state that "the expression of popular religiosity is the fruit of an evangelization carried on since the time of the conquest, and has its special characteristics. It is a religion of vows and promises, of processions and pilgrimages, and numberless devotions; it is based on the reception of the sacraments, particularly baptism and the Eucharist. First Communion is a ceremony having greater social significance than influence in the exercise of the authentic Christian life."[13] But the bishops also note that: "In our evaluation of popular religion, we may not take as our frame of reference the westernized cultural interpretation of the middle and upper classes; rather we must judge its meaning in the context of the sub-cultures of the rural and marginal urban groups."[14] Therefore, they urge "that serious and systematic studies be made concerning popular religious sense and its manifestations, either by Catholic universities or by other centers of socio-religious research."[15] In their document on catechesis, the bishops say: "Popular religiosity, despite an observable increase in the process of secularization, continues to be a valid element in Latin America. It cannot be overlooked, because in the lives of our people, especially the common people, it plays an important, serious, and authentic role. This popular religious sense may be used as the occasion or point of departure for the proclamation of the Faith. The times call for a revision and scientific study of popular religion in order to purify it from those elements that threaten its authenticity, being careful not to destroy but rather to enhance its positive values."[16]

Consequently (the point seems especially important at the present moment), real abuses in devotion to the saints should not drive us to the extreme of trying to put an end to the devotion as such. Vatican II accepts such devotion as a permanent part of Church life: "The saints have been traditionally honored in the Church" (SC 111a/170). In the chapter on our Lady in the Constitution on the Church the Council even seems to speak in a more solemn tone when it says: "This most holy Synod deliberately teaches this Catholic doctrine [on devotion to Mary]. At the same time, it admonishes all the sons of the Church that the cult, especially the liturgical cult, of the Blessed Virgin, be generously fostered. It charges that practices and exercises of devotion toward her be treasured as recommended by the teaching authority of the Church in the course of centuries, and that those decrees issued in earlier times regarding the veneration of images of Christ, the Blessed Virgin, and the saints, be religiously observed" (LG 67a/94-95). Here, again, the Council refers us to the decrees of the Second Council of Nicea (787 A.D.) and the Council of Trent (1563 A.D.).

The veneration of images is a subject that requires careful handling. The principle, which Vatican II has several times reaffirmed, is quite clear: "The practice of placing sacred images in churches so that they may be venerated by the faithful is to be firmly maintained" (SC 125/175). The Eighth Ecumenical Council (the Fourth Council of Constantinope, 869-70 A.D.) compared the image of Christ to the book of the gospels; as we are saved by what is written in that book, so all of us, literate or illiterate, draw profit from what is imaged. For "the realities which the written word contains, are also proclaimed and brought home to us by the writing which is the colors."[17] The Seventh Ecumenical Council (the Second Council of Nicea, 787 A.D., twice cited by Vatican II) had already condemned the opponents of sacred images and had defined ("with complete certainly and careful diligence") that "as the image of the priceless and life-giving cross is exposed, so too venerable and holy images—in paint, mosaic, or other suitable material—are to be exposed in God's holy churches, on sacred vessels and vestments, on walls and plaques, in our homes and on our streets: the images, that is, of our Lord God and Savior Jesus Christ, of our Lady, the spotless Mother of God, of the venerable angels, and of all the saints." The reason the Council gives for such a practice: "The more often these visual images are seen, the more readily are those who see them stirred to remember and yearn for the originals."[18] Finally, the Council of Trent, in its Twenty-Fifth Session (1563), authoritatively repeats the same instruction: "Further, the images of Christ, of the Virgin Mother of God, and of other saints are to be kept with honor in places of worship especially, and to them due honor and veneration is to be paid."[19]

The Church does not, however defend every kind of veneration paid to images. She is not satisfied simply to decorate a holy place with images. The Council of Trent spoke expressly of "the lawful use of images." This supposes, of course, that there can be an unlawful and reprehensible use of them. We should not think here only of the superstitious and fetishistic abuse of images of the saints, which is so obvious among the Umbanda and Quimbanda in Brazil. We should also recall how in our churches certain images are venerated to the point that they seem to become idols and fetishes. There we see the devotee, hand outstretched and clutching the statue, staying sometimes for long moments in this position, as if in hope that some mysterious healing and life-giving fluid might flow from the image and pass through his hand and arm into his body and very soul.

"The holy council [of Trent] orders all bishops and others

who have the official charge of teaching to instruct the faithful diligently . . . concerning the intercession and the invocation of the saints, the honor due to their relics, and the lawful use of images."[20] Then, in speaking directly of the veneration of images the Council noted that due veneration could be undermined in two ways: "because it is believed that there is any divinity or power intrinsic to them [the images] for which they are reverenced" (thus fetishism is condemned) or "because it is from them that something is sought, [or] a blind trust is . . . attached to images as it once was by the Gentiles who placed their hope in idols."[21] This text is fundamental to a correct Catholic understanding of the true meaning of image veneration: images are to be honored "because the honor which is shown to them is referred to the prototypes which they represent. Thus it follows that through these images which we kiss and before which we kneel and uncover our heads, we are adoring Christ and venerating the saints whose likenesses these images bear."[22] The Council is therefore careful to add: "If historical and other narratives of the Holy Scriptures are sometimes portrayed and pictured for the benefit of an unlettered group, let the people be taught that although the Divinity is represented in figures, this is not because it is such as can be seen by bodily eyes or portrayed in color or form. . . ."[23]

After saying that the practice of exhibiting sacred images for the veneration of the faithful in churches is to be retained, Vatican II adds: "Nevertheless, their number should be moderate and their relative location should reflect right order. Otherwise they may create confusion among the Christian people and promote a faulty sense of devotion" (SC 125/ 175). Just before this, the Council urged that bishops "carefully exclude from the house of God and from other sacred places those works of artists which are repugnant to faith, morals, and Christian piety, and which offend true religious sense either by their distortion of forms or by lack of artistic worth, by mediocrity, or by pretense" (SC 124b/175).

It is chiefly, however, in the liturgy that our union with the heavenly Church is best realized. For it is in the liturgy that the power of the Holy Spirit acts in us through the sacramental signs. In the liturgy, too, we join together in joyfully singing the praise of the divine Majesty. "Then all those from every tribe and tongue and people and nation (cf. Apoc. 5:9), who have been redeemed by the blood of Christ and gathered together into one Church, with one song of praise magnify the one and triune God" (LG 50f/83). The celebration of the Eucharistic Sacrifice is the greatest means for thus uniting ourselves with the worship of the heavenly Church, "as we join with and venerate the memory first of all of the glorious ever-Virgin Mary, of Blessed Joseph, and the blessed apostles and martyrs, and of all the saints" (ibid.). It will be useful to recall here the words of the Council of Trent: "Although it is the custom of the Church occasionally to celebrate some Masses in honor and in memory of the saints, the Church teaches that the sacrifice is offered not to the saints, but to God alone who has given them their crown. Therefore, 'the priest does not say: "I offer this sacrifice to you, Peter and Paul' "; but giving thanks to God for the victories of the saints, the priest implores their help that they may pray for us in heaven, while we remember them on earth."[24]

Thus we venerate the saints in the very act by which we adore God, and not separately, as though they were God's competitors. We turn to the saints in order that, united with them and in their company, we may praise the Lord and thank him for the wonders he has worked in his saints. The new Preface of All Saints and Patron Saints echoes all the ideas we have been discussing: "You [O Lord] are glorified amid the assembly of the saints, and in crowning their merits are crowning the gifts you have given them. You afford us in their lives good example, a place in their fellowship, help through their intercession. Surrounded with such a cloud of witnesses, we can run our appointed course with patience and receive with them the unfading crown of glory, through Jesus

Christ of Lord."[25]

"In the earthly liturgy, by way of foretaste, we share in that heavenly liturgy which is celebrated in the holy city of Jerusalem toward which we journey as pilgrims, and in which Christ is sitting at the right hand of God, a minister of the sanctuary and of the true tabernacle (cf. Rev 21:2; Col 3:1; Heb 8:2); we sing a hymn to the Lord's glory with all the warriors of the heavenly army; venerating the memory of the saints, we hope for some part and fellowship with them; we eagerly await the Savior, our Lord Jesus Christ, until He, our life, shall appear and we too shall appear with Him in glory" (SC 8/141-42). And "when Christ shall appear and the glorious resurrection of the dead takes place, the splendor of God will brighten the heavenly city and the Lamb will be the lamp thereof (cf. Rev 21:24). Then in the supreme happiness of charity the whole Church of the saints will adore God and 'the Lamb who was slain' (Rev 5:12), proclaiming with one voice: 'To him who sits upon the throne, and to the Lamb, blessing and honor and glory and dominion, forever and ever' (Rev 5:13-14)" (LG 51c/84-85).

Then the Church will be gloriously fulfilled. "Then, as may be read in the holy Fathers, all just men from the time of Adam, 'from Abel, the just one, to the last of the elect,' will be gathered together with the Father in the universal Church" (LG 2b/15-16).

Notes for Chapter 12

[1] Letter of Holy Office to Bishops, on abuse of magnetism, August 4, 1856, in DS, 2825 (D, 1654).
[2] [On Kardec, cf. B. Kloppenburg, in *New Catholic Encyclopedia*, 8:132. — Tr.]
[3] Reply of Holy Office on Spiritualism, April 24, 1917, in DS, 3642 (D, 2182).
[4] DS, 1304 (D, 693); *TCT*, no. 889, p. 351.
[5] DS, 1580 (D, 840), *TCT*, no. 604, p. 246.

[6] DS, 1743 (D, 940); *TCT*, no. 749, pp. 292-93. Cf. DS, 1753 (D, 950); *TCT*, no. 758, p. 295.

[7] DS, 1820 (D, 983); *TCT*, no. 890, p. 352.

[8] DS, 1000 (D, 530); *TCT*, no. 886, p. 350.

[9] Pius XII, *Mediator Dei*, no. 179, in *Selected Letters*, pp. 235-36.

[10] DS, 3013-14 (D, 1794); *TCT*, no. 68, p. 30.

[11] DS, 1821 (D, 984); *TCT*, no. 522, pp. 214-15.

[12] Cf. B. Kloppenburg, "Nossas superstiçoes," *Revista Eclesiástica Brasileira*, 18 (1958), 699-723.

[13] *The Church in the Present-Day Transformation of Latin America in the Light of the Council* (cf. above, Introduction, note 1), volume 2: *Conclusions*, Document 6: "Pastoral Care of the Masses," no. 2, p. 121.

[14] *Op. cit.*, no. 4, p. 122.

[15] *Op. cit.*, no. 10, p. 125.

[16] *Op. cit.*, Document 8: "Catechesis," no. 2, p. 139.

[17] DS, 654 (D, 337).

[18] DS, 600-1 (D, 302).

[19] DS, 1823 (D, 986); *TCT*, no. 524, p. 215.

[20] DS, 1821 (D, 984); *TCT*, no. 522, pp. 214-14.

[21] DS, 1823 (D, 986); *TCT*, no. 524, pp. 215-16.

[22] *Ibid.*

[23] DS, 1830 (D, 988); *TCT*, no. 526, p. 216.

[24] DS, 1744 (D, 941); *TCT*, no. 750, p. 293. Cf. Canon 5: DS, 1755 (D, 952); *TCT*, no. 760, p. 295.

[25] *The English-Latin Sacramentary for the United States of America* (New York: Cath. Bk. Publishing Co., 1966), Appendix IV, pp. 708-711, 718.

Appendix

Opening to Ecumenism

The ecclesiology of Vatican II is ecumenical; that is, in substance and expression it arises within the contemporary historical context in which Christian, separated from each other, are seeking a visible unity in Christ. This ecumenical aspect was not overlooked when we were studying the nature of the Church (Chapter 2) and its unity (Chapter 5). But because of its great importance at the present time it deserves some special attention.

"Moved by a desire for the restoration of unity among all the followers of Christ" (UR 1d/342), Vatican II gave us the Decree on Ecumenism. "Promoting the restoration of unity among all Christians is one of the chief concerns of the Second Ecumenical Synod of the Vatican" (UR 1a/341). Even in the first laconic report in which *Osservatore Romano* revealed Pope John XXIII's intention of convoking an ecumenical council, it was said: "As for the celebration of the Ecumenical Council, in the Holy Father's view, it is meant not only for the edification of the Christian people; it is also an invitation to the communities of our separated brethren to seek that unity which many souls yearn all over the world."[1]

After being elected on October 28, 1958, Pope John XXIII spoke as follows in his first radio message, at a time when he was not yet thinking of convoking a council: "We embrace the whole Church, Western and Eastern, with warm fatherly love. We open Our loving heart and extend Our outstretched arms to all who are separated from this Apostolic See. . . . We long for their return to the house of the common Father and repeat the words of the Divine Redeemer: 'Holy Father, keep in your name those whom you have given me, that they may be one even as we are' (Jn 17:11). For then 'there shall be one fold and one shepherd' (Jn 10:16). We pray that they might all return freely and gladly. . . . They will not find it a strange house, but one that is truly their own, a house which has from time immemorial been enlightened by the teachings and adorned by the virtues of their forefathers."[2]

Pope John XXIII died on June 3, 1963, before the second session of the Council. His successor, Pope Paul VI, in the homily he spoke at his coronation, made his own the ecumenical hopes of John XXIII: "To those who are not Catholics but are united to us by the powerful ties of faith and love for the Lord Jesus and are marked with the seal of the one and only baptism—*unus Dominus, una fides, unum baptisma* (Eph 4:5: 'One Lord, one faith, one baptism')—We address ourselves with respect augmented by an immense desire. This desire, the same that has long stirred many of them—to hasten the blessed day that will see, after centuries of distressing separation, the perfect realization of Christ's insistent prayer on the eve of his death: *ut sint unum!* (Jn 17:11), that they may be one! In this regard we embrace the heritage of our unforgettable predecessor, Pope John XXIII. Moved by the Holy Spirit, he brought into being in this domain great hopes which we consider it a duty and an honor not to disappoint. No more than he, certainly, do we nourish illusions concerning the vastness of the problem to be solved and the seriousness of the obstacle to be overcome. But faithful to the great Apostle whose name we have taken, *veritatem faciens in caritate* (Eph 4:5: 'doing the truth in charity'), and supported solely by the weapons of truth and charity, we intend to pursue the dialogue that has been begun and to advance to the utmost the works already undertaken."[3] It was with the same intention and in the same spirit that Vatican II offered us its Decree on Ecumenism.

The doctrine and norms contained in Vatican II for our attitude and action in ecumenical affairs can be summed up in the following points:

1. The current ecumenical movement among Christians came into existence by the action of the Holy Spirit and is not a whimsical utopian dream. The Council says that "among our separated brethren also there increases from day to day a movement, fostered by the grace of the Holy Spirit, for the restoration of unity among all Christians" (UR 1c/342). Again it declares: "Today, in many parts of the world, under the inspiring grace of the Holy Spirit, multiple efforts are being expended through prayer, word, and action to attain that fullness of unity which Jesus Christ desires" (UR 4a/347). The context for these initiatives and for the activities Christians are undertaking in order to obtain the visible unity of all who call themselves Christ's followers is the "ecumenical movement" (cf. UR 4b/347). The latter is one of the authentic "signs of the times" (UR 4a/347), by which we are to discern the will of the Lord of history (cf. GS 11a/209).

2. Catholics have a duty to take part in this movement. The Council "exhorts all the Catholic faithful to recognize the signs of the times and to participate skillfully in the work of ecumenism" (UR 4a/347). It is "gratifying to note that participation by the Catholic faithful in ecumenical work is growing daily" (UR 4k/349). This "concern for restoring unity pertains to the whole Church, faithful and clergy alike" (UR 5/350). The Council expects, then, that "the initiatives of the sons of the Catholic Church" will be "joined with those

of the separated brethren" (UR 24b/365).[4] It "commends this work to bishops everywhere in the world for their skillful promotion and prudent guidance" (UR 4k/350). The Ecumenical Directory adds: "To fulfill her ecumenical responsibility, the Church must have at her disposal an adequate number of experts in ecumenical matters—clergy and religious, laymen and laywomen. They are needed everywhere, even in regions where Catholics form the greater part of the population."[5]

3. Our ecumenical action must be fully and sincerely Catholic (to use the words of the Council itself: UR 24a/365). The Council explains itself: this action must be "loyal to the truth we have received from the Apostles and the Fathers, and in harmony with the Faith which the Catholic Church has always professed, and at the same time tending toward that fullness with which our Lord wants His body to be endowed in the course of time" (UR 24a/365). For, in fact, "nothing is so foreign to the spirit of ecumenism as a false conciliatory approach which harms the purity of Catholic doctrine and obscures its assured genuine meaning" (UR 11a/354). This is why the Decree on Ecumenism begins with a firm and clear doctrinal account of the unity and unicity of the Church (UR 2/343-44).

Subsequently it maintains that within the one and only Church of Christ Christians have unfortunately committed the sin of separation and brought about developments "for which, at times, men of both sides were to blame" (UR 3a/345). It declares: "Our separated brethren, whether considered as individuals or as communities and churches, are not blessed with that unity which Jesus Christ wished to bestow on all those whom He has regenerated and vivified into one body and newness of life—that unity which the Holy Scriptures and the revered tradition of the Church proclaim. For it is through Christ's Catholic Church alone, which is the all-embracing means of salvation, that the fullness of the means of salvation can be obtained. It was to the apostolic college alone, of which Peter is the head, that we believe our Lord entrusted all the blessings of the New Covenant, in order to establish on earth the one Body of Christ into which all those should be fully incorporated who already belong in any way to God's people" (UR 3e/346). Here we have a clear formulation of a well-known Catholic tenet.

Our attitude to the other articles of our Faith must be the same. "It is . . . essential that doctrine be clearly presented in its entirety" (UR 11a/354). *Only in this way shall we avoid the real danger of doctrinal indifferentism* which regards as equally valid all views of the mystery of Christ and the Church. Pope Paul VI was not referring to an imaginary danger when he wrote: "The desire to come together as brothers must not lead to a watering down or whittling away of truth. Our dialogue must not weaken our attachment to our Faith. Our apostolate must not make vague compromises concerning the principles which regulate and govern the profession of the Christian Faith both in theory and in practice. An immoderate desire to make peace and sink differences at all costs (irenicism and syncretism) is ultimately nothing more than skepticism about the power and content of the word of God, which we desire to preach."[6] The Council foresees that Catholic disposed to take part in ecumenical dialogue may be tempted to "superficiality or imprudent zeal" (UT 24a/365). These are real dangers and we must be aware of them, for only on this condition can we open ourselves fully to the ecumenical spirit.

4. Ecclesial elements exist among non-Catholic Christians. The doctrine expressed in this proposition is of basic importance for ecumenism. It is also, however, to some extent a novel doctrine for Catholics of post-Tridentine and anti-Protestant mentality. We were raised to think that non-Catholic communities ("schismatics" and "heretics") simply were not part of the Church of Christ. We claimed that only the Catholic Church is the true Church of Christ and his Mystical Body, that all others, consequently, are "false" and

not the Church of Christ, and that the adherents of these
other churches are not members of the Mystical Body of
Christ. Such was the doctrine taught by Pius XI in *Mortalium
animos* (1928: on true religious unity) and by Pius XII in
Mystici Corporis (1943: on the Mystical Body) and *Humani
generis* (1950: on dangerous philosophical and theological
errors). However, the Second Vatican Council changed this
outlook and judgment in its Dogmatic Constitution on the
Church (LG 8b/23) and especially in its Decree on Ecumenism (UR 3b-d/345-46). In these documents the Council
uses the concept of "ecclesial elements," which refers to values
or "endowments which together go to build up and give life
to the Church herself" (UR 3b/345). These elements are,
then, constitutive of the Church. It is worth noting that the
World Council of Churches uses the same terminology in its
documents; it says that Christ decided upon a certain number
of visible and invisible "ecclesial elements" which, taken together, constitute or "build" his Church.

According to the Lord's will, then, the Church exists fully
only when all the ecclesial elements which he has determined
are actually present. The Council maintains that this state
of affairs is realized in the Catholic Church, for it claims that
the Church of Christ "subsists in the Catholic Church" (LG
8b/23). The Council also recognizes quite frankly, however
(and this is what is new in the ecumenical attitude of Vatican
II) that "outside of her [the Catholic Church's] visible structure" (*ibid.*) or "outside the visible boundaries of the Catholic Church" (UR 3b/345) ecclesial elements also exist. The
number of such elements is smaller or greater according to
the condition and doctrine of each church or ecclesial community. *In these communities, too, therefore, the Church
of Christ exists, although in an incomplete or imperfect way.*
Recognition of this fact obliges us to a radical revision of the
way in which we speak ow non-Catholic Christians. Earlier
we simply said: They depart from Jesus and are not the
Church of Christ. Now we must say: They walk with Jesus

and are the Church of Christ, even if in an incomplete way.
Thus, in its Decree on the Missions, the Council says of new
Christians: "They should rightly consider that the [non-
Catholic] brethren who believe in Christ are Christ's disciples,
reborn in baptism, sharers with the people of God in very
many riches" (AG 15e/602). "It follows that these separated
churches and communities, though we believe they suffer from
defects already mentioned, have by no means been deprived
of significance and importance in the mystery of salvation.
For the Spirit of Christ has not refrained from using them as
means of salvation" (UR 3d/346). In the immediately preceding paragraph this latter document had said that "many
of the sacred actions of the Christian religion" are carried out
in these other communities and that "undoubtedly, in ways
that vary according to the condition of each church or community, these actions can truly engender a life of grace, and
can be rightly described as capable of providing access to the
community of salvation" (UR 3c/346).

5. Catholics should rejoice when they discover ecclesial
elements in other churches. This is a matter of mentality
rather than of doctrine. But it is an important matter and
requires that we undergo a change of heart. "Catholics must
joyfully acknowledge and esteem the truly Christian endowments from our common heritage which are to be found among
our separated brethren" (UR 4h/349). It is a good and salutary thing, after all, to recognize the riches and virtues of
Christ in the lives of others; God is always sublime and wonderful in his works. Not infrequently non-Catholic Christians
can even "contribute to our own edification" (UR 4i/349);
they can be living examples of Christian life.

From the Orthodox, for example, we can learn love of the
liturgy (UR 15a/348), devotion to our Lady and the saints
(15b), and a rich monastic tradition (15d). Therefore, "all
should realize that it is of supreme importance to understand,
venerate, preserve, and foster the exceedingly rich liturgical
and spiritual heritage of the Eastern churches, in order faith-

fully to preserve the fullness of Christian tradition, and to bring about reconciliation between Eastern and Western Christian" (15e). Moreover, "with regard to the authentic theological traditions of the Orientals, we must recognize that they are admirably rooted in Holy Scripture, fostered and given expression in liturgical life, and nourished by the living tradition of the Apostles and the writings of the Fathers and spiritual authors of the East; they are directed toward a right ordering of life, indeed, toward a full contemplation of the Christian truth" (UR 17a/360). This is the reason why, "to the pastors and faithful of the Catholic Church, it [the Council] recommends close relationships with those [Orthodox Christians] no longer living in the East but far from their homeland, so that friendly collaboration with them may increase in a spirit of love, without quarrelsome rivalry" (UR 18/361).

In regard to Protestants, the Council calls our attention to the "love, veneration, and near cult of the Sacred Scriptures" which "lead our brethren to a constant and expert study of the sacred text" (UR 21a/362). "Calling upon the Holy Spirit, they seek in these Sacred Scriptures God as He speaks to them in Christ, the One whom the prophets foretold, God's Word made flesh for us. In the Scriptures they contemplate the life of Christ, as well as the teachings and actions of the Divine Master on behalf of men's salvation, in particular the mysteries of His death and resurrection" (21b). "The Christian way of life of these brethren is nourished by faith in Christ. It is strengthened by the grace of baptism and the hearing of God's word. This way of life expresses itself in private prayer, in meditation on the Bible, in Christian family life, and in services of worship offered by communities assembled to Praise God" (23a/364). They have "a lively sense of justice and a true neighborly charity. This active faith has produced many organizations for the relief of spiritual and bodily distress, the education of youth, the advancement of humane social conditions, and the promotion of peace throughout the world" (23b).

6. We should acquire a better knowledge of the mentality of non-Catholic Christians. Under number 5 we have already noted that such knowledge can greatly enrich our own doctrine and Christian life. But the Council also expressly says: "We must come to understand the outlook of our separated brethren. Study is absolutely required for this, and should be pursued with fidelity to truth and in a spirit of good will. When they are properly prepared for this study, Catholics need to acquire a more adequate understanding of the distinctive doctrines of our separated brethren, as well as of their own history, spiritual and liturgical life, their religious psychology and cultural background. Of great value for this purpose are meetings between the two sides, especially for the discussion of theological problems, which each can deal with the other on an equal footing. Such meetings require that those who take part in them under authoritative guidance be truly competent. From dialogue of this sort will emerge still more clearly what the true posture of the Catholic Church is. In this way, too, we will better understand the attitude of our separated brethren and more aptly present our own belief" (UR 9/353).

As an example of how such meetings and joint research can lead to rather concrete results, cf. the Anglican-Roman Catholic Declaration on the Eucharist, issued in May, 1967, at Milwaukee, by a joint Anglican-Catholic Commission during its fourth working meeting. The statement begins: "Since the time of the Reformation, the doctrine of Eucharistic Sacrifice has been considered a major obstacle to the reconciliation of the Anglican Communion and the Roman Catholic Church. It is the conviction of our commission that this is no longer true. We have made a careful study of the documents of the Second Vatican Council, the Lambeth Conference Report of 1958, the 1949 statement of faith and order of the Protestant Episcopal Church in the U.S., and other statements of the contemporary position of both our churches. From these statements it is clear to us that the findings of modern Biblical, theological and liturgical studies have transcended many of the polemical formulations of an earlier period. We believe that it is of utmost importance for the clergy and laity of our two churches to acknowledge their substantial identity in this area of Eucharistic doctrine and to build upon it as they go forward in dialogue. Whatever doctrinal disagreements may remain between our churches, the understanding of the sacrificial nature (of the Eucharist) is not among them."[7]

A joint Lutheran-Catholic commission reached a similar agreement. After two years of study and discussion the members found themselves at one on the following points: (1) Christ is present in the Eucharist as the Crucified One who died for our sins and rose for our jusification; (2) the celebration of the Eucharist is a sacrifice of praise and personal self-oblation; (3) the sacrifice of the Cross cannot be repeated; (4) the Catholic practice of offering Christ in the Mass is an acceptable explanation of the gift offered by the Eucharistic assembly by the power of the Hoy Spirit, for, apart from Christ, we can offer to God neither gifts nor adoration; (5) the presence of the sacrifice of the Cross is effective for the forgiveness of sins and the life of the world. Protestants and Catholics agreed that Christ is present in the Lord's Supper as true God and true man, whole and entire, with his body and blood, under the signs of bread and wine. As for the *how* of the presence, the Lutherans could not wholly accept the doctrine of transubstantiation, not on the grounds that it is a wrong kind of explanation, but on the grounds that it is insufficient and open to theological misunderstanding.[8]

In a report of March 11, 1970, on the activities and hopes of the Secretariat for Christian Unity, Cardinal Jan Willebrands said: "It is evident that the dialogue between the churches cannot go on indefinitely. We may hope that theological dialogue and practical cooperation will, with the help of God's grace and by the power of the Holy Spirit, bring us sooner or later to agreement on the essential truths of faith and on the practical consequences of those truths. The time required to reach such an agreement could be from five to ten years, depending on the varied relations now existing between the Catholic Church and the non-Catholic churches or ecclesial communities." The cardinal, in this report, quoted an official statement of the International Catholic-Anglican Commission: "No member [of the Commission] has the least doubt that the ultimate goal of our work is the achievement of full organic unity between the two communions."

7. Special care must be given to the manner and method of formulating our Faith. The Council says: "The method and order in which Catholic belief is expressed should in no way become an obstacle to dialogue with our brethren" (UR 11a/354). Moreover, "Catholic belief needs to be explained more profoundly and precisely, in ways and in terminology which our separated brethren too can readily understand" (UR 11b/354).

The suggestions of dialogue which were issued by the Secretariat for Christian Unity in 1970 remarks, in this context, that "the same words may signify quite different realities in one church and in another, while different words may express the same reality. Since it is a question of establishing real and complete communication, of eliminating the risk of misunderstandings and of not traveling unawares along parallel ways, it is absolutely necessary that the dialogue participants— even though they be formed by the spirit of the Scriptures and express themselves in a language inspired by the Scriptures— should submit the language they use to a critical, hermeneutic study."[9] The same documents notes: "By language is meant not just just vocabulary, but above all mentality, the heritage of a culture, philosophical tools, traditions, and style of life."[10]

The Ecumenical Directory (Part 2, 1970) offers some more concrete suggestions: "Students should learn to distinguish between revealed truths, which all require the same assent of faith, and theological doctrines. Hence they should be taught taught to distinguish between 'this deposit of faith, or truths, or truth which are contained in our time-honored teaching' and the way in which they are enunciated; between the truth to be enunciated and the various ways of perceiving and more clearly illustrating it; between apostolic tradition and merely ecclesiastical traditions. From the time of their philosophical training, students should be prepared to recognize that there is a legitimate diversity in the manner of expressing things in theology also, because of the diversity of methods or ways by which theologians understand and express Divine Revelation. Thus these various theological formulations are often complementary rather than conflicting."[11]

This last statement brings us back once again to the Council's Decree on Ecumenism, which speaks of legitimate diversity in the theological formulation of doctrine and says: "In the investigation of revealed truth, East and West have used different methods and approaches in understanding and proclaiming divine things. It is hardly surprising, then, if sometimes one tradition has come nearer than the other to an apt appreciation of certain aspects of a revealed mystery, or has expressed them in a clearer manner. As a result, these various theological formulations are often to be considered as complementary rather than conflicting" (UR 17a/360). The Secretariat's set of "Reflections" therefore says: "Each partner should seek to expound the doctrine of his own community in a constructive manner, putting aside the tendency to define by opposition, which generally results in certain positions becoming overstressed or unduly hardened. This is a purifying process; the warping from which our respective theologies suffer can only be corrected at this price."[12] The Council had already stressed the same point: "It is highly important that future bishops and priests should have mastered a theology carefully worked out in this [ecumenical] way and not polemically, especially in what concerns the relations of the separated brethren with the Catholic Church" (UR 10b/353).

8. The principle of the hierarchy of truths in Catholic

teaching. Here we find one of Vatican II's boldest positions. The text we are going to quote was not in the position paper discussed at the Council in 1963. It was proposed during the preliminary voting in which modifications of the text were offered.[13] The proposal was accepted by the Commission and approved by the Council on November 11, 1964 (one hundred and twentieth general meeting) by a vote of 2021 to 85. The text read as follows: "Catholic theologians engaged in ecumenical dialogue, while standing fast by the teaching of the Church and searching together with the separated brethren into the divine mysteries, should act with love for truth, with charity, and with humility. When comparing doctrines, they should remember that in Catholic teaching there exists an order or 'hierarchy' of truths, since they vary in their relationship to the foundations of the Christian Faith" (UR 11c/354).

We should think, therefore, rather of the quality or importance of the various revealed truths than of a quantitative mass of truths. On this point the Ecumenical Directory observes: We should always preserve the sense of an order based on degree, or of a 'hierarchy,' in the truths of Catholic doctrine which, although they all demand a due assent of faith, do not all occupy the same principal or central place in the mystery revealed in Jesus Christ, since they vary in their relationship to the foundation of the Christian Faith."[14] The Secretariat for Christian Unity adds, in its "Reflections": "Neither in the life nor in the teaching of the Church is everything presented at the same level. Certainly all revealed truths demand the same acceptance of faith, but according to the greater or lesser proximity that they have to the basis of the revealed mystery, they are variously placed with regard to ane another, and have varying connections among themselves. For example, the dogma of Mary's Immaculate Conception, which may not be isolated from what the Council of Ephesus declared about Mary, the Mother of God, presupposes, before it can be properly grasped in a true life of faith, the dogma of grace to which it is linked and which, in its turn, necessarily rests upon the redemptive Incarnation of the Word."[15]

9. The ecumenical action of Catholics must begin at home. The Constitution on the Church speaks as follows: in order to foster unity among Christians, "Mother Church . . . exhorts her sons to purify and renew themselves so that the sign of Christ may shine more brightly over the face of the Church" (LG 15b/34). Not infrequently the life and behavior of us Christians and of us Catholics in particular (including the clergy) is not the luminous sign of the risen Christ that it should be, but a negative sign. The Council openly admits that among the causes of atheism is "a critical reaction against religious beliefs, and in some places against the Christian religion in particular. Hence believers can have more than a little to do with the birth of atheism. To the extent that they neglect their own training in the Faith, or teach erroneous doctrine, or are deficient in their religious, moral, or social life, they must be said to conceal rather than reveal the authentic face of God and religion" (GS 19g/217).

Similarly, the imperfectly Christian or even completely un-Christian life and attitudes of many Catholics are often the source of disillusionment for their brothers in the Faith and lead to divisions. These Catholics are guilty of the sin of scandal. Pope John XXIII was well aware that the reunion of Christians was impossible without an inner renewal of the Catholic Church. Two years before the Council, the man behind the Council said: "The first and immediate objective of the Council is to show the world the Church of God in its perennial vigor of life and truth, with its legislation brought into harmony with contemporary situations so as to be always more responsive to its divine mission and ready for the needs of today and tomorrow. Then, if the separated brothers, who are still divided among themselves, wish to reduce to practice the common desire for unity, we will be able to say to them with lively sentiments: 'Here is your house! Here is the house of all who raise the standard of Christ!' "[16] Two years later, on March 8, 1962, still before the Council, the same pope expressed his anxious hope that he would see the day when, the Council over, he could say to the separated brothers: "Our intention of restoring our house and adapting it to the new conditions of the world, has been carried out in fidelity to the Lord's will. Here it is, our house and the ancient house in which our fathers and yours lived together! Come! Come!"[17]

The Decree on Ecumenism likewise recognizes: "Church renewal therefore has notable ecumenical importance" (UR 6c/351). For this reason the Council asks Catholics "to make an honest and careful appraisal of whatever needs to be renewed and achieved in the Catholic household itself, in order that its life may bear witness more loyally and luminously to the teachings and ordinances which have been handed down from Christ through the Apostles" (UR 4e/348). If the Catholic Church is thus able to renew itself and cleave more closely to the will of Christ; if the Orthodox make a similar examination of conscience and the same sincere effort at renewal and identification with Christ; if Protestants likewise seek greater closeness to the Lord—then, when the churches have completed this courageous act of repentance, Christians will no longer be separated brothers. All will in fact be brothers in Christ. What is needed of all the churches is that they "examine their own faithfulness to Christ's will for the Church and, wherever necessary, undertake with vigor the task of renewal and reform" (UR 4b/347). We shall foster and practice Christian unity in the exact measure that we try to live a life that is more fully in accord with the gospel (cf. UR 7c/351).

10. Dialogue is the indispensable instrument in the encounter of the churches. Dialogue is one of the signs of the times. Modern man seeks dialogue as a privileged means of reestablishing or developing understanding, esteem, respect, and love among groups and individuals. Dialogue is a necessity in a world that is become daily more diversified. Dialogue was officially introduced into the Catholic Church by Pope

Paul VI in his encyclical on the Church (1964): "Speaking generally of the dialogue which the Church of today must take up with a great renewal of fervor, we would say that it must be readily conducted with all men of good will, both inside and outside the Church."[18] In its Constitution on the Church in the Modern World, Vatican II declared: "For our part, the desire for such dialogue, which can lead to truth through love alone, excludes no one. . . . We include those who cultivate beautiful qualities of the human spirit, but do not yet acknowledge the Source of these qualities. We include those who oppress the Church and harass her in manifold ways" (GS 92f/306-7).

"Dialogue" means any form of encounter and communication between individuals, groups, or communities, with the intention of achieving a better understanding of the truth or improving human relationships, and in an atmosphere of sincerity, respect for persons, and mutual trust.[19] Dialogue exists, therefore, when the participants are open and responsive, when they seek to understand and be understood, when they ask questions and are willing to answer questions, when they express their own views and listen to the views of others concerning a situation, an investigation, or an action. Mutuality and genuine interest are thus the essential elements of dialogue.[20]

Dialogue is, however, not an end inn itself. Its goal depends on the participants. For ecumenical dialogue the Secretariat for Christian Unity lists four objectives.[21] (1) By means of dialogue Christians are to move together towards a deeper sharing in the reality of the mystery of Christ and his Church. In this way they will bring to light the convergence that exists between their different ways of looking at the revealed mystery and of translating it into thought, life, and witness. (2) By means of dialogue Christians should learn to give a united witness to the mission which Jesus Christ entrusted to his Church, so that all Christians may, "before the whole world . . . profess their faith in God, one and three, in the incarnate

Son of God, our Redeemer and Lord" (UR 12a/354), and that the world may believe. (3) Inasmuch as the world puts the same questions to all the churches and ecclesial communions today, the churches should listen to and understand these questions with the help of dialogue. In sensitive receptivity to the action of the Spirit they should work together towards the answer which the Lord expects of them. In this way they will be at the service of the world, especially where the gospel has not yet been preached (cf. AG 15e-f/602-3; 29e/620). (4) Many Christian communities are faced with similar internal problems. Each community can formulate these problems from different standpoints; such problems, for example, as may arise concerning the laity, the ministry, catechesis, the Christian family, etc. Is the Holy Spirit not calling upon us to examine these problems together?

It is clear, then, as the same document points out, that ecumenical dialogue is not limited to being purely academic or conceptual. Rather, by promoting a fuller communion between the Christian communities, a common service of the gospel, and a closer collaboration in thought and action, the dialogue contributes to a transformation of the mentality, behavior, and daily life of these communities. Thus it paves the way for their unity in the profession of faith, within one visible Church. "The result will be that, little by little, as the obstacles to perfect ecclesiastical communion are overcome, all Christians will be gathered, in a common celebration of the Eucharist, into that unity of the one and only Church which Christ bestowed on His Church from the beginning. This unity, we believe, dwells in the Catholic Church as something she can never lose, and we hope that it will continue to increase until the end of time" (UR 4c/348).

11. Our "spiritual ecumenism." "There can be no ecumenism worthy of the name without a change of heart" (UR 7a/351). "This change of heart and holiness of life, along with public and private prayer for the unity of Christians, should be regarded as the soul of the whole ecumenical movement,

and can rightly be called 'spiritual ecumenism' " (UR 8a/352). For, "this Synod declares its realization that the holy task of reconciling all Christians in the unity of the one and only Church of Christ transcends human energies and abilities. It therefore places its hope entirely in the prayer of Christ for the Church, in the love of the Father for us, and in the power of the Holy Spirit" (UR 24b/365-66). We noted, in the first of our points in this chapter, that the ecumenical movement of our day came into existence among Christians through the action of the Holy Spirit. The Holy Spirit is the soul of the Church and the source of her unity. If unity does not exist, it is because the Holy Spirit is not given his due place. Man's worst sin is to try to substitute his own action for that of the Holy Spirit. Here again, and above all here, we must never forget that the Church is by nature a mystery. We are not of ourselves the Church; rather, Christ and his Spirit make us be the Church. We are only the sacrament, that is, the sign and instrument, of Christ. Christ is always the principal agent of all ecclesial actions. We must let him act freely through us as docile instruments. That is why the Council prays that we may "go forward without obstructing the ways of divine Providence and without prejudging the future inspiration of the Holy Spirit" (UR 24b/365).

Notes for Appendix

[1] *Osservatore Romano,* January 26-27, 1959. The report refers to an address of the pope to the College of Cardinals at the Benedictine Monastery adjoining St. Paul outside the Walls, January 25, 1959. Text of address in *AAS,* 51 (1959), 65-69; reprinted in *Acta Ante-Praeparatoria,* vol. 1, p. 6.

[2] John XXIII, *Hac trepida hora: First Public Radio-Address,* October 29, 1958, in *TPS,* 5 (1958-59), 136.

[3] Paul VI, *Ea quae: Homily at His Coronation,* June 30, 1963, in *TPS,* 9 (1963-64), 9.

[4] How things have changed in the Church since the 1928 encyclical of Pius XI, *Mortalium animos!* In this document ecumenists are called

"pan-Christians" and Catholics are strictly forbidden to take part in the movement: "Certainly such movements as these cannot gain the approval of Catholics" (*Mortalium animos: The Promotion of True Religious Unity*, January 6, 1928 [Washington, D.C.: National Catholic Welfare Conference, 1928], p. 2).

⁵ *TPS*, 15 (1970-71), 79.

⁶ Paul VI, *Ecclesiam suam*, in *TPS*, 10 (1964-65), 282-83.

⁷ *Documents on Anglican/Roman Catholic Relations*, compiled by the Bishops' Committee on Ecumenical and Interreligious Affairs in cooperation with the Joint Commission on Ecumenical Relations (Washington, D.C.: United States Catholic Conference, 1972), p. 3.

⁸ Cf. *Lutherans and Catholics in Dialogue* 3: *The Eucharist as Sacrifice* (Washington, D.C.: United States Catholic Conference; New York: U.S.A. National Committee of the Lutheran World Federation, 1967).

⁹ Secretariat for Promoting Christian Unity, *Reflections and Suggestions on Ecumenical Dialogue*, September 18, 1970, in *TPS*, 15 (1970-71), 425-26.

¹⁰ *Ibid.*

¹¹ *Ad totam Ecclesiam: Directory on the Application of the Second Vatican Council Decisions in Ecumenical Matters*, Part 2: May 16, 1970, in *TPS*, 15 (1970-71), 179.

¹² *Reflections and Suggestions on Ecumenical Dialogue*, p. 427.

¹³ The Council Father who made the proposal backed it up and improved it in his explanation: "It seems of greatest importance for the ecumenical dialogue that both the truths on which Christians agree and those on which they disagree be weighed rather than counted. It is undoubtedly true that to all revealed truths the same assent of divine faith is to be given. Nonetheless the importance and 'weight' of each truth differ in proportion to its connection with the history of salvation and the mystery of Christ." It is not known which Father made the proposal. However, on November 25, 1963, Archbishop André Pangrazio of Gorizia, Italy, made a notable statement at the Council, and said among other things: "If the unity that already exists between Christians as well as the diversity that still persists are to be correctly judged, I think it very important to be aware of the hierarchy within the revealed truths which express the mystery of Christ and the hierarchy, too, within the constitutive elements of the Church. All revealed truths are to be given the same assent of divine faith, and all the constitutive elements of the Church are to be retained with the same fidelity. Nonetheless not all the truths and elements have the same importance. Some truths concern the *goal*: for example, the mysteries of the Most Holy Trinity, the Incarnation of the Word, our Redeemer, God's gracious love for sinful mankind, and eternal life in the kingdom of God. Other truths concern the *means* of salvation: for example, the truths concerning the sacraments as being seven in number, the hierarchic structure of the Church, apostolic succession, the

primacy of the Roman Pontiff. These latter truths deal with the means given the Church by Christ for its earthly pilgrimage; when the latter is finished, the truths cease to operate. Now, in point of fact, the doctrinal *diversity* among Christians does not affect so much the primary truths concerning the end as it does those truths which concern the means to the end and which are subordinate in importance to the primary truths. The *unity* which exists between Christians consists on the contrary in a common faith in and profession of the truths concerning the goal. If the document we are discussing were to make explicit use of this hierarchic distinction among truths and elements, it would make clearer the unity that already exists among all Christians, and Christians would be seen to form a family that is united by the adherence to the primary truths of the Christian religion."

[14] *Ad totam Ecclesiam*, Part 2, in *TPS*, 15 (1970-71), 177.

[15] *Reflections and Suggestions on Ecumenical Dialogue*, p. 425.

[16] John XXIII, *Conclusosi felicement: Address to the General Council of Italian Action*, February 14, 1960, in *Osservatore Romano*, February 15-16, 1960; reprinted in *Acta Ante-Praeparatoria*, vol. 1, p. 74.

[17] Private files of the author.

[18] Paul VI, *Ecclesiam suam*, August 6, 1964, n. 93, in *TPS*, 10 (1964-65), 284.

[19] This is the description given by the Secretariat for Non-Believers, "Catholic Guidelines for Dialogue," in *TPS*, 13 (1968-69), 367.

[20] *Reflections and Suggestions on Ecumenical Dialogue*, by the Secretariat for Christian Unity, thus complements the description of dialogue given above in the text. — In *Nous sommes heureux: Address to a Symposium on Dialogue in the Church*, March 20, 1971, Paul VI lists some hindrances to dialogue: inertia; individualistic failure to collaborate; the deliberate isolation of groups which claim self-sufficiency and the ability to find the Church in their own way, against the whole tradition of the Scriptures and the Fathers; bitter criticism and some forms of disloyalty; a negative style of protest; deaf opposition within the Church; a frightening violence that does not spring from the spirit of Christ and seems drunk with the prospect of immediate success (*AAS*, 63 [1971], 289).

[21] *Reflections and Suggestions on Ecumenical Dialogue*, pp. 421-22.
    A List of Important Documents on Ecumenical Relations
(1) Secretariat for Christian Unity:
    (a) *Ad totam Ecclesiam: Directory for the Application of the Second Vatican Council Decisions in Ecumenical Matters.* Two parts:

    Part I, issued May 14, 1967; translation in *TPS*, 12 (1967), 25-63, and in *One in Christ*, 3 (1967), 326-343. This first part deals with the establishment of ecumenical commissions, the question of the validity of baptism, "spiritual ecumenism" in the Catholic Church, and spiritual exchanges with the separated brethren (joint prayer, sharing of spiritual activity and resources [*communicatio in sacris*]).

Part II, issued April 16, 1970; translation in TPS, 15 (1970-71), 172-85, and in *One in Christ*, 7 (1971), 76-93. This part provides norms for training in ecumenism at higher institutions of learning (general principles and means of such formation; the ecumenical dimension in religious and theological training; specific norms for ecumenical formation; cooperation with the separated brothers).

(b) *Reflections and Suggestions on Ecumenical Dialogue,* issued September 18, 1970; translation in *TPS,* 15 (1970-1971), 420-31, and in *One in Christ,* 7 (1971), 93-111. The document "does not have strict juridical authority." It addresses itself to the nature and purpose of ecumenical dialogue, its basis, conditions, method, themes, and form. The third part of Pope Paul VI's Encyclical Letter *Ecclesiam Suam,* August 6, 1964, deals with ecumenical dialogue and must be considered a fundamental document on the subject; translation in *TPS,* 10 (1964-1965), 275-292.

(c) On intercommunion, the document issued on January 7, 1970 (*TPS,* 15 (1970-1971), 59-63) reports the norms of Vatican II and of the Ecumenical Directory on the sharing of spiritual activity and resources, and forbids intercommunion. On the same matter, cf. the earlier statement of October 6, 1969, in *TPS,* 13 (1968-1969), 326-28.

(2) Joint Working Group, with members from the Roman Catholic Church and the World Council of Churches. (On the origin and activities of this group, cf. Lukas Vischer, "The Activities of the Joint Working Group between the Roman Catholic Church and the World Council of Churches, 1965-1969," *Ecumenical Review,* 22 (1970), 36-69.)

(a) The origin of the group: cf. *Relationships between the World Council of Churches and the Roman Catholic Church*: Statement adopted by the Central Committee at Enugu, Nigeria, January 12-21, 1965, in *Ecumenical Review,* 17 (1965), 171-73. Cf. also Cardinal Bea's address at Geneva, February 18, 1965, in *One in Christ,* 1 (1965), 202-206.

(b) First Report of the Joint Working Group, February 16, 1966, dealing with basic questions, areas of cooperation, and some particular matters (Bible, Easter, Liturgy), in *Ecumenical Review,* 18 (1966), 243-252, and in *One in Christ,* 2 (1966), 173-85.

(c) Second Report, August, 1967, dealing with the faith and work of the Churches, unity and tension, laity and unity, service to humanity, and some particular problems (study of proselytism, mixed marriages, national and local councils), in *Ecumenical Review,* 19 (1967), 461-473.

(d) Study Document on *Catholicity and Apostolicity,* 1969, in *One in Christ,* 6 (1970), 452-482. The document, in addition to the main text, has seven appendices: "Apostle" in the New Testament; Identity, Change and Norm; Ministry and Episcopate; The Sacramental Aspect of Apostolicity; Conciliarity and Primacy; Unity and Plurality; The Local Church and the Universal Church.

(e) Study document on *Common Witness and Proselytism,* produced by a Joint Theological Commission for the Joint Working Group; the commission met at Arnoldshain, Germany, in 1968, and at Zagorsk, U.S.S.R., in 1969. Document, dating from May, 1970, in *Ecumenical Review,* 23 (1971), 9-20.

(3) World Council of Churches:

(a) Report of the Central Committee to the Third Assembly of the World Council of Churches: *Christian Witness, Proselytism, and Religious Liberty in the Setting of the World Council of Churches,* in *Evanston to New Delhi 1954-1961* (Geneva: World Council of Churches, 1961), pp. 239-245.

(b) Section Reports at the Fourth World Conference on Faith and Order (Montreal, 1963) on: The Church in the Purpose of God; Scripture, Tradition, and Traditions; The Redemptive Work of Christ and the Ministry of His Church; Worship and the Oneness of Christ's Church; "All in Each Place": The Process of Growing Together; in *The Fourth World Conference on Faith and Order: The Report from Montreal 1963,* ed. by P. C. Rodger and L. Vischer (London: SCM, 1964), pp. 41-90.

(c) Central Committee of the World Council of Churches apropos of Vatican II (meeting of February 8-17, 1966); cf. *Ecumenical Review,* 18 (1966), 255-261.

(d) Message of the World Conference on Church and Society, 1966, in *World Conference on Church and Society: Christians in the Technical and Social Revolution of Our Time,* ed. by M. M. Thomas and Paul Abrecht (Geneva: World Council of Churches, 1967), pp. 48-51; also in *Ecumenical Review,* 19 (1967), 59-61.

(e) Section Reports at the Fourth General Assembly of the World Council of Churches (Uppsala, July, 1968) on: The Holy Spirit and the Catholicity of the Church; Renewal and Mission; World Economic and Social Development; Towards Justice and Peace in International Affairs; Worship; Towards New Styles of Living; in *The Uppsala Report, 1968,* ed. by Norman Goodall (Geneva: World Council of Churches, 1968), pp. 7-97.

(4) Dialogue with the Orthodox Churches:

(a) Meeting of Paul VI and Athenagoras I, Jerusalem, January 1964.

(b) Third Pan-Orthodox Conference, Rhodes, November 1964:

Message of Paul VI;
Reply of the Conference;
Conclusions of the Conference.

(c) Dialogue of Charity between Rome and Orthodoxy, February 25, 1965:
Letter of Athenagoras I to Paul VI;
Address of Metropolitan Meliton;
Allocution of Paul VI.

(d) Absolution from censures and excommunications between Rome and Constantinople, December 7, 1965:
Joint Declaration (*TPS*, 11 (1966), 67-69; *One in Christ*, 2 (1966), 167-169);
Apostolic Letter, *Ambulate in dilectione* (On the duties of charity to the Church of Constantinople);
Tomos of Athenagoras I.

(e) Ecumenical meeting of Paul VI and Athenagoras I in Turkey, July 25, 1967:
documents (all of Pope Paul) in *TPS*, 12 (1967), 265-274;
One in Christ, 3 (1967), 467-471.

(f) Joint Declaration of Paul VI and Athenagoras, October 26, 1967;
Address of Pope Paul to Athenagoras, *TPS*, 12 (1967) 342-46.

(5) Dialogue with the Anglican Communion:

(a) Meeting of Rome and Canterbury, March 23, 1966: address of Archbishop Ramsey; reply of Pope Paul; Joint Declaration, in *One in Christ*, 2 (1966), 273-278.

(b) Anglican-Roman Catholic Declaration on the Eucharist, Milwaukee, May 1967, in *Documents on Anglican-Catholic Relations* (Washington, D.C.: United States Catholic Conference, 1972), pp. 3-5.

(c) Communique of the Anglican-Roman Catholic Preparatory Commission (2nd meeting, August 30—September 4, 167), in *One in Christ*, 3 (1967), 513-515.

(d) Communique of the Joint International Commission of the Roman Catholic Church and the Anglican Communion (1st meeting, January 9-15, 1970), in *One in Christ*, 6 (1970), 228-230.

(e) Anglican-Roman Catholic International Commission, Agreed Statement on Eucharistic Doctrine, September 7, 1971 (the "Windsor Statement"), in *Documents*. . . . (This first collection of *Documents* contains various other reports and some addresses of Cardinal Bea, Cardinal Willebrands, and Pope Paul. *Documents on Anglican-Roman Catholic Relations, II* (Washington, D.C.: United States Catholic Conference, 1973), contains a series of comments on the Windsor Statement by various bodies, as well as an extended commentary on the documents by a Roman Catholic theologian.)

(6) *Dialogue with the Lutheran Churches*:
Roman Catholic Church and the Lutheran World Federation: cf. *Lutherans and Catholics in Dialogue* (Washington, D.C.: United States Catholic Conference; New York: U.S.A. National Committee World Federation), I: *The Status of the Nicene Creed as Dogma of the Church* (1965); II: *One Baptism for the Remission of Sins* (1966); III: *The Eucharist as Sacrifice* (1967); IV: *Eucharist and Ministry* (1970).

(7) Secretariat for Non-Christian-Religions:
Principles for Dialogue with Non-Christian Religions, Chapter 3 of *On the Encounter of Religions,* published by the Secretariat for Non-Christian Religions, June 1967.

(8) Secretariat for Non-Believers:
  (a) *Guidelines for Dialogue with Non-Believers,* August 28, 1968, in *TPS,* 13 (1968-1969), 364-376.
  (b) Theses for Dialogue between Christians and Marxists; document signed by Cardinal König, President of the Secretariat for Non-Believers, April, 1968.
  (c) The Study of Atheism, July 10, 1970.